S0-AFY-162

Best
WORDS,
Best
ORDER

ALSO BY STEPHEN DOBYNS

POETRY

Common Carnage (1996)
Velocities: New and Selected Poems 1966 – 1992 (1994)
Body Traffic (1990)
Cemetery Nights (1987)
Black Dog, Red Dog (1984)
The Balthus Poems (1982)
Heat Death (1980)
Griffon (1976)
Concurring Beasts (1972)

FICTION

Saratoga Fleshpot (1995)
Saratoga Backtalk (1994)
The Wrestler's Cruel Study (1993)
Saratoga Haunting (1993)
After Shocks/Near Escapes (1991)
Saratoga Hexameter (1990)
The House on Alexandrine (1990)
The Two Deaths of Señora Puccini (1988)
Saratoga Bestiary (1988)
A Boat Off the Coast (1987)
Saratoga Snapper (1986)
Cold Dog Soup (1985)
Saratoga Headhunter (1985)
Dancer with One Leg (1983)
Saratoga Swimmer (1981)
Saratoga Longshot (1976)
A Man of Little Evils (1973)

Best
WORDS,
Best
ORDER

Essays on Poetry

STEPHEN DOBYNS

BEST WORDS, BEST ORDER (SECOND EDITION)
Copyright © Stephen Dobyns, 1996, 2003.

All rights reserved. No part of this book may be used or reproduced in any manner whatsoever without written permission except in the case of brief quotations embodied in critical articles or reviews.

First published in hardcover in 1996 by St. Martin's Griffin
First St. Martin's Griffin paperback edition: 1997
PALGRAVE MACMILLAN™ second edition: April 2003
175 Fifth Avenue, New York, N.Y. 10010 and
Houndmills, Basingstoke, Hampshire, England RG21 6XS.
Companies and representatives throughout the world.

PALGRAVE MACMILLAN is the global academic imprint of the Palgrave Macmillan division of St. Martin's Press, LLC and of Palgrave Macmillan Ltd. Macmillan® is a registered trademark in the United States, United Kingdom and other countries. Palgrave is a registered trademark in the European Union and other countries.

ISBN 1-4039-6147-6

Library of Congress Cataloguing-in-Publication Data available from the Library of Congress.

A catalogue record for this book is available from the British Library.

PALGRAVE MACMILLAN second edition: April 2003

Book design by planettheo.com

10 9 8 7 6 5 4 3 2 1

Printed in the United States of America.

PERMISSIONS

Charles Baudelaire's *Selected Writings on Art and Artists* tranlation by P. E. Chaver. John Johnson Limited, Penguin Group. Reprinted by Permission.

"On the Willow Branch," from *Armored Hearts* by David Bottoms. Copyright © 1995 by David Bottoms. Reprinted by permission of Copper Canyon Press, P. O. Box 271, Port Townsend, WA 98368.

Selections from Chekhov's letters, from *Anton Chekhov's Short Stories: A Norton Critical Edition*. Ralph E. Matlow, editor and translator. Copyright © 1979 by W. W. Norton & Company, Inc. Reprinted by permission of W. W. Norton & Company, Inc.

Robert Creeley. *Collected Poems of Robert Creeley, 1945-1975*. "I Know A Man." Copyright © 1983. The Regents of the University of California. Reprinted by permission.

"Flirt" from *The Island Itself* by Roger Fanning. Copyright © 1991 by Roger Fanning. Used by permission of Viking Penguin, a division of Penguin Books USA, Inc.

"Signs" by Jean Follain, © 1960 by Éditions Gallimard, as translated by W. S. Merwin in *The Transparence of the World.* © 1968 by W. S. Merwin. Reprinted by permission.

"Hawk's Shadow," from *The Triumph of Achilles* by Louise Glück. Copyright © 1985 by Louise Glück. First published by The Ecco Press in 1985. Reprinted by permission.

Nikolai Gumilev, *On Russian Poetry*, edited and translated by David Lapeza, © Ardis, 1977. Reprinted by permission.

"Heroic Simile," from *Praise* by Robert Hass. Copyright © 1974, 1975, 1976, 1977, 1978, 1979 by Robert Haas. First published by The Ecco Press in 1979. Reprinted by permission.

"Absences," from *New and Selected Poems* by Donald Justice. Copyright © 1995 by Donald Justice. Reprinted by permission of Alfred A. Knopf, Inc.

Simon Karlinsky, *Anton Chekhov's Life and Thought: Selected Letters and Commentary*. The University of Chicago Press.

"The Sculpture" and "An Obsolescent and His Deity (Polyptych)" from *Poems: 1963-1988*, by Bill Knott, copyright © 1989. Reprinted by permission of the University of Pittsburgh Press.

"High Windows" from *Collected Poems* by Philip Larkin. Copyright © 1988, 1989 by The Estate of Philip Larkin. Reprinted by permission of Farrar, Straus & Giroux, Inc.

"The Explosion," "Reference Back," "High Windows," by Philip Larkin from *Collected Poems* by Philip Larkin. United Kingdom reprinted by permission of Faber and Faber Limited.

"Coming," "At Grass," and "I Remember, I Remember" by Philip Larkin, reprinted from *The Less Deceived* by permission of The Marvell Press, England and Australia.

"A Little Tooth" by Thomas Lux. Reprinted by permission of Thomas Lux.

Osip Mandelstam, *Mandelstam: Critical Prose and Letters*, translation by Jane Gary Harris and Constance Link © Ardis, 1979. Reprinted by permission.

Osip Mandelstam, *Mandelstam: Critical Prose and Letters*, reprinted by permission of The Harvill Press, London. U.K. rights only.

"[The Stalin Epigram] Our lives no longer feel ground under them" by Osip Mandelstam as translated by Clarence Brown and W. S. Merwin in *Osip Mandelstam: Selected Poems*. English translation ©1973 by Clarence Brown and W. S. Merwin. Reprinted by permission.

Mandelstam, Osip translated by Robert Tracy; "Notre Dame" from *Stone* by Osip Mandelstam. Copyright © 1981 PUP. Reprinted by permission.

Heather McHugh "I Knew I'd Sing" from *To the Quick* copyright © 1987 by Heather McHugh, Wesleyan University Press reprinted by permission of University Press of New England.

"When You Go Away" from *The Lice*. Copyright © 1967 by W. S. Merwin. Reprinted by permission.

Fifteen translated maxims, aphorisms and metaphors to be used as examples of metaphors from *Asian Figures*. Translation © 1973 by W. S. Merwin. Reprinted by permission.

"A Nest of Hooks" by Lon Otto from *A Nest of Hooks* published by the University of Iowa Press. Copyright 1978 by University of Iowa Press. Reprinted by permission.

"In a Station of the Metro" by Ezra Pound, from *Personae*. Copyright © 1926 by Ezra Pound. Reprinted by permission of New Directions Publishing Corporation. United Kingdom by permission of Faber and Faber Limited.

From *Letters on Cezanne*, by Rainer Maria Rilke, edited by Clara Rilke. Copyright 1952 Insel Verlag, Frankfurt, translation by Joel Agee copyright 1985 Fromm International Publishing Corporation. Reprinted by permission of Fromm International Publishing Corp.

Reprinted by permission of North Point Press, a division of Farrar, Straus & Giroux, Inc.: "From a Childhood" from *The Book of Images* by Rainer Maria Rilke. Translation copyright © 1991 by Edward Snow. "The Panther" from *New Poems [1907]* by Rainer Maria Rilke. Translation copyright © 1984 by Edward Snow. "Archaic Torso of Apollo," "Falconry," and "The Temptation" from *New Poems [1908]: The Other Part* by Rainer Maria Rilke. Translation copyright © 1987 by Edward Snow.

From *Letters of Rainer Maria Rilke: 1892-1910* by Jane Bannard Greene and M. D. Herter Norton. Copyright 1945 by W. W. Norton & Company, Inc. Renewed © 1972 by M. D. Herter Norton. Reprinted by permission of W. W. Norton & Company, Inc.

"Motionless Swaying," from *Gestures* by Yannis Ritsos. Tranlation copyright © Nikos Stangos, 1971. Reprinted by permission of John Johnson Limited.

"Association," "The Day of a Sick Man," and "Approximately," from *Selected Poems* by Yannis Ritsos. Translation copyright © Nikos Stangos, 1974. Reprinted by permission of John Johnson Limited.

Ritsos, Yannis translated by Edmind Keeley: "Triplet," "Point," and "Marking" from *Parentheses 1950-1961;* "The Meaning of Simplicity," "Maybe, Someday," and "Miniature" from *Parentheses 1946-1947;* "From Poseidon" from *Repetitions 1963-1965;* "The More

Sufficient" from *The Distant,* "Penelope's Despair," copyright © 1991 E. Keeley. Reprinted by permission of Princeton University Press.

Yannis Ritsos: "Necessary Explanation" copyright © 1989 by BOA Editions, Ltd. Reprinted from *Yannis Ritsos: Selected Poems 1938-1988,* with the permission of BOA Editions, Ltd., 92 Park Ave., Brockport, NY 14420.

"Midnight Stroll" by Yannis Ritsos from *Scripture of the Blind,* translated by Kimon Friar and Kostos Myrsiades, 1979. Ohio State University Press. Reprinted by permission.

"When I Was Conceived," by Michael Ryan from *In Winter,* Holt, Reinhart & Winston, 1981. Used by permission of the authors. University of California Irvine.

"Drawn to Perspective," by Charles Simic. Reprinted by permission of George Braziller, Inc.

"B. C." Copyright © 1977 by William Stafford, from *Stories That Could Be True* (Harper & Row, 1977). Reprinted by permission of the Estate of William Stafford.

"Face to Face," by Tomas Transtomer, translated by Robin Fulton, from *Tomas Transtomer, Selected Poems: 1954-1986* edited by Robert Haas. Copyright © 1987 by Robert Haas. First published by The Ecco Press in 1987. Reprinted by permission.

"Amaryllis," reprinted from *The Lotus Flowers* by Ellen Bryant Voigt, with the permission of W. W. Norton & Company, Inc. Copyright © 1987 by Ellen Bryant Voigt. Originally appeared in *The New Virginia Review.*

"Petition to the Terms," and "A Fishing Song" from *This Journey* by James Wright. Copyright © 1977, 1978, 1979, 1980, 1981, 1982 by Anne Wright, executor of the estate of James Wright. Reprinted by permission of Random House, Inc.

James Wright. "Outside Fargo, North Dakota" from *Collected Poems* by James Wright, Wesleyan University Press reprinted by permission of University Press of New England.

"Leda and the Swan" by W. B. Yeats. Reprinted by permission of A. P. Watt Ltd. Reprinted by permission.

Permissions for the second edition, chapters 14 through 16:

Charles Baudelaire, "For Her Who is Too Gay" from *The Flowers of Evil & Paris Spleen,* translated by William H. Crosby. Copyright © 1991 by William H. Crosby. Reprinted with the permission of BOA Editions, Ltd.

Charles Baudelaire, "To the Reader" from *The Flowers of Evil.* Reproduced by permission of W. W. Norton.

"Shoelace," from *Homesick* by Roger Fanning, copyright © 2002 by Roger Fanning. Used by permission of Viking Penguin, a division of Penguin Putnam Inc.

"The Woman Who Sew Livery" by W. S. Merwin © 1968 by W. S. Merwin, reprinted with the permission of The Wylie Agency.

"The Dog Has Run Off Again," from *West Wind: Poems and Prose* by Mary Oliver. Copyright © 1997 by Mary Oliver. Reprinted by permission of Houghton Mifflin Company. All rights reserved.

"First Elegy" from *Duino Elegies* by Ranier Maria Rilke, translated by Edward Snow. Translation copyright © 2000 by Edward Snow. Reprinted by permission of North Point Press, a division of Farrar, Straus and Giroux, LLC.

"The Crazy" from *Late into the Night: The Last Poems of Yannis Ritsos,* translated by Martin McKinsey, FIELD translation Series #21, Oberlin, OH, Oberlin College Press, copyright 1995. Reprinted by permission of Oberlin College Press.

To the memory of Ellis Settle, 1924–1993

CONTENTS

PREFACE

HOW DOES A WORK OF LITERATURE ORIGINATE? Some argue it is determined entirely by factors outside the writer, others that it is controlled by the writer's intention. And think of the multitudes of positions in between.

Extreme literary theorists argue that the writer's experience, education, culture, sexual, racial and political prejudices and psychology control not only the writing but the ideas and motivation: all of which make the writer little more than a puppet. But there are many writers who believe that the work is equally determined. For instance, those who argue "First word, best word" believe that the work comes from someplace else—from the unconscious, from the muse, from the ether.

Between these extremes are writers who have a passion for revision, who believe in authorial intention but also believe their work is influenced by their culture, education, experience, prejudices and so on. Additionally, language is reductive. The artist has a star in his or her brain, and language is the doodle that attempts to bring that star to life. Language is an approximation, but by using discursive and nondiscursive language, the poet tries to create or re-create an event and to make the reader experience this event. This is the sort of writer I aspire to be, and I trace my lineage back to the preface to the second edition of the *Lyrical Ballads*, where Wordsworth wrote that poetry "is carried alive into the heart by passion."[1] And that reminds me of the remark by Kafka that I love and constantly misquote: Literature must be an axe to smash the frozen sea of the heart.

This reveals my prejudices: a work of literature is something made by a writer that is meant to move the heart of a reader.

Added to this is a remark of William Carlos Williams: "If it ain't a pleasure, it ain't a poem." While this oversimplifies, it *is* a beginning. It also suggests that writing is a craft and a craft can be learned. Not everyone can learn it, but if one has imagination, a certain intelligence, the ability to make metaphor, a passion for language, for the world, for communication, as well as a passion for the medium, then usually there is a chance of learning the craft. After 30 years of teaching creative writing, I still believe that.

But these first pages are about aesthetics: What position does one write from, what guides one's aesthetic choices? The former I have explained. The latter is more difficult.

We have at the end of the century several hundred ideas about how poetry and fiction should be written. This is a blessing and a curse. There are many who will say "If it is not written in such and such a way, then it is not a poem." Yet if one traces English prosody back to Chaucer or French poetry back to the first alexandrines, one sees that every generation has made alterations— some big, some little—and that prosody has never remained constant for long. We see many examples of poets of my generation being reviewed by older poets, or poets of a younger generation being reviewed by my generation, and the reviewers say: "This is not done. Not only is it bad, it is stupid." In the same way did Sainte-Beuve dismiss the poems of Baudelaire. These complaints consist of territorial disputes and have little to do with aesthetics.

I believe that a poem is an emotional-intellectual-physical construct that is meant to touch the heart of the reader, that it is meant to be reexperienced by the reader. I believe that a poem is a window that hangs between two or more human beings who otherwise live in darkened rooms. I also believe that a poem is a noise and that noise is shaped. A poem is not natural speech; it is artificial speech. I believe that whether one is a formal poet or a free verse poet, one is always involved with the relation between stressed and unstressed syllables. And I believe that a poem doesn't try to present reality but presents a metaphor that represents some aspect of the writer's relation to the world: a metaphor that can be potentially reexperienced and become meaningful to the reader. In the next several hundred pages I will expand upon these ideas and ideally they will grow more precise.

The following essays began as craft lectures mostly given in the MFA program at Warren Wilson College in Asheville, North Carolina. All, by this time, have been given at half a dozen places and all have been revised, seemingly endlessly. The oldest—the one on metaphor—dates from the summer of 1979 at the MFA program at Goddard College in Plainfield, Vermont. The most recent—on tone—dates from the fall of 1993, when I gave it as a lecture at Syracuse University. In revising the essays again for inclusion in this book, I have tried to link them into an aesthetic and an analysis of how poetry works.

I am neither a theorist nor an academic, for which I am grateful, but the ideas here are the sum of more than 35 years of study and they lie beneath my poetry and fiction. To believe in authorial intention, to be a humanist, to believe in communication, to believe that literature can be an extension of moral experience, to believe in the apprehension of beauty, to believe that literature enriches my life, to value much that our imperfect culture has produced—these form my delight. The chasm between the beliefs of many critics and many writers seems ever deeper. It was incredible to me recently at Syracuse University to hear a Marxist critic call creativity "reactionary."

For a writer, a critic is often someone peering through a restaurant window, trying to guess what the food tastes like. For a critic, a writer is often a childlike creature blindly making human-oid figures in the mud. These disagreements are a pity because they add more divisions to a divisive world. One doesn't mind disagreement but one balks at dismissal. Yet as aesthetics and morality become increasingly entwined, it is hard not to alter those ideas that one believes true and right and not be heretical to one's own beliefs.

I see the following essays as being written for writers, for students of writing and for readers looking for a greater appreciation of writing. Four deal with specific writers: Rainer Maria Rilke, Osip Mandelstam, Anton Chekhov and Yannis Ritsos. I admire other writers as much and perhaps there are writers who have influenced me more, but these four combine for me what it is to be a writer: a mixture of the life and the work, the craft and the imagination, the responsibility and freedom.

No writer changed as much as Rilke, no one worked harder to change his work, to make it larger and more dangerous, to be always at the very edge of his ability. Perhaps no writer has been as morally centered as Mandelstam, and his sense of how he had to live and write led directly to his death. No writer has had such a sense of personal freedom as Chekhov, and nothing within him interfered with his writing: not fears, ambitions or vanities. Perhaps no writer has had as great a sense of the mystery that surrounds us as Yannis Ritsos, and he wrote nearly 100 books of poetry testifying to the existence of that mystery.

My task as a writer is to strive to determine what it is to be a human being and what is one's relation and responsibility to other human beings. These chapters form part of that task, while the last chapter, "Communication," written to explicate one of my own poems for a book of such essays, *Singular Voices*, edited by Stephen Berg, attempts to show what I try to do in my own work.

1 | Deceptions

ON THE DESK WHERE I WRITE, I keep a nineteenth-century clay statue about a foot tall from Santiago, Chile. It shows a dwarf dressed in a jester's costume hunched over and laughing. It's not a pretty laugh. The dwarf's knees are bent, his arms are clasped behind his back, his ugly face is thrust forward. It is the donkey's bray, the horse laugh of mockery. I keep it on my desk to remind me that I am practicing a deception, not only to the world but to myself.

In my poetry, I believe I try to describe the world. No matter how fabulous or extravagant the poem, one of its intentions is to chart the world in which it is written. It comes into existence when emotion suddenly links with image, idea and language, and what is constructed is a metaphor that stands for some aspect of my relation to my fellow creatures and the world around me. It is a verbal box that conveys feeling.

In my novels, whether mystery novels or serious fiction, I try to create alternative worlds. They may resemble this world, but each creates a world that is someplace else. This is partly the nature of the novel. One of the subjects of a novel is the society in which it was written. As the Irish short-story writer Frank O'Connor once wrote, any novel posits an ideal society and then creates its own society, which, as it were, is set alongside the ideal. The novel's commentary on society lies within the difference between the posited ideal and the society presented in the novel.1 This is part of the power of Kafka's novels: that discrepancy between an ideal society and the society found in *The Trial* or *The Castle*. But to some degree this is true of any novel, even a mystery novel.

So in my poetry I believe I deal with the existing world and in my novels with alternative worlds. If I feel badly about the world, dislike its people, feel pessimistic about its future, then I can't write poetry. Fiction I can write at any time, because it is not connected to my immediate feelings about the world. I don't need to love human beings in order to write it.

One writes a poem when one is so taken up by an emotional concept that one is unable to remain silent. This is something Philip Larkin describes in a short essay called "The Pleasure Principle," but it is also reminiscent of the prescription that William Wordsworth laid down in his preface to the second edition of *The Lyrical Ballads*. It is the standard Romantic formula for how a poem gets written. One writes when one is unable to remain silent, and what one does is to make a small machine out of words that re-creates the same feeling in another human being, any time, any place—meaning that without the reader, there can be no poem.

It can even be argued that it is the reader who makes the poem, because if the ideal reader cannot re-create the emotion out of the poet's words, then no poem exists. Likewise, the reader has to be able to make the emotion his or her own. It is not enough for the reader to understand, to be a witness to somebody else's experience. So it can be said that the poem is not about the writer but the reader, and that without this link to the reader the poem is only a jumble of words.

A novel handles this differently. It is roomier. It contains lots of time. Stories are told, people go on journeys. I write a novel when an incident comes together with a character and language to make a narrative. A novel creates an alternative world; a poem creates a metaphor for an aspect of the existing world. The world within the novel may also be metaphor—as in Camus's *The Plague*—but it is still a complete world. Neither poem nor novel can exist without the reader, but in the novel the reader is more distant. A poem invites the reader into its room; with the novel the reader walks around the fence surrounding the house. With a poem one often creates a single experience, with the novel a body of experience. With a poem the connection with the reader is more physical: Because of the noise of the poem, its rhythms and music, because of the intensity of its emotion, the connection with the reader can feel more intimate.

But if I feel hostile toward the world and dislike its people, I can't write poetry—there is nothing I wish to say to that reader on the other side of the page except Go Away. For me, writing a poem is to engage with the world; writing a novel is to escape from its immediacy. W. H. Auden claimed that people write novels because they have no lives of their own. Novelists, of course, deny this. While I deny it as well, I also feel that when I am writing a novel, I am stepping out of my life to enter another, while in poetry I am intensifying my life.

I would find it impossible to write without a conception of the reader, that impossibly ideal figure who holds the other end of the string. He or she is the person I am talking to. The writing of both fiction and poetry entails the accumulation of verbal information intended to create an emotional experience meant to affect the reader. Not only is language information, but so is tone, rhythm, syntax, line length—all elements of writing. And what the writer does with these elements is not simply to tell a story or present an emotional concept, he or she makes the reader want to know, makes him or her want to find out what happens next. From the very first sentence, from even the title, the writer is concerned with engaging and controlling the reader's interest.

The writer has his or her original intuition, which may come in a rush, but then it must be sorted out. In fact, one of the reasons for writing is to discover the nature of the intuition. But once the writer begins to make that intuition meaningful to a reader, then he or she begins to engage in reason and calculation. The process of writing and revising is the process by which the writer becomes conscious of his or her intuition. The writer also calculates the effect of the words on the reader—what piece of information should be placed first, what second and third? Certainly it was calculation that led Kafka to begin "The Metamorphosis" with the sentence "Gregor Samsa awoke one morning from uneasy dreams to find himself transformed in his bed into a gigantic insect." Mr. Kafka must have laughed and slapped his knee. He knew that after reading that sentence, it would be impossible for the reader not to read a second and a third.

The British mystery writer Margery Allingham once described the writing of her first novel. She was an adolescent and both of her parents were writers. Suddenly the housekeeper dashed into her room. "Your mother's upstairs writing lies in one room!" shouted the housekeeper. "Your father's upstairs writing lies in another, and now you're writing lies as well. I won't have it!" Whereupon the housekeeper tore up the manuscript.

There has always been the sense that a fiction, a novel, is no more than a pack of lies. This is why many people prefer to read biography or history. They would prefer to read about Madonna than Anna Karenina. Madonna is real, Anna Karenina is not. Simplistically, this is also why Plato refused poets entry to the Republic: Their stories were too removed from life. The counter-argument runs that the novel tries to distill the very essence of life, even that art creates life.

Even so, when I write a novel, part of me knows that I am engaged in a deception. Not that I am lying or the novel is a lie, but that I am creating a fictional world that I want the reader to believe in. I am creating a verbal illusion. At the same time I like to see how much I can get away with. But I also have to deliver. If I promise an amazing experience, I have to provide that experience. The first sentence of Kafka's "The Metamorphosis" isn't a trick; it is entirely in keeping with the nature of the story. A writer makes the reader want to believe, makes the reader want to know what comes next. But if the writer betrays that promise, then he or she has failed. After all, he or she is an entertainer. No matter how seriously I take my poetry and fiction, I know that I am descended from the court jester.

This returns me to my Chilean dwarf and his mocking laugh. One of the reasons I keep him on my desk is to remind me of my connection to the reader, to remind me of the theater, that I am creating an illusion and that illusion is a deception.

That is a lesser reason for the dwarf. A greater reason is to remind me that I am lying to myself. The dwarf's mocking laughter is aimed at me. How foolish, he says. How ridiculous.

When I first began to write, I was concerned with being clear and logical and learning to move the pieces around. I am still concerned with such things but more recently I have come to understand that my greatest enemy is self-deception; that is, that I lie to myself about what I am writing. A writer is always engaged in making choices based on some idea of cause and effect. What interferes with this, as much as any lack of skill, is self-deception, that we lie to ourselves about what works and what doesn't work, what is necessary or unnecessary.

When I write, I have certain desires. I want the piece to work and I want it to be finished. Beyond that, I may want it to reflect credit on me, to make me liked or respected, to bring me financial reward. My self-deceptions fall into two categories— how I deal with the work and how I deal with myself in relation to the work: that is, matters within the work and matters outside it. At some level a piece of writing must be written only for its own sake. It tries to encapsulate an emotional experience. To be successful it must separate itself from the life of the writer. If I want the work to reflect credit on me or make me respected, then I am engaged in self-deception. The deception is that the work can remain tied to the writer, even that it expresses him or her. The finished piece of writing belongs to the reader, not the writer. If the work is successful, the writer has to become invisible.

It is even a deception to tie the writing to financial reward. One lessens a novel or poem by writing first of all for publication. If something works and is interesting, then it will be published. But to write while imagining a future for what one is writing means that some aesthetic choices will be governed by reasons outside the work. It may lead to making conservative choices for fear of offending a future editor; and it will make one think in terms of scenes and lines, of small effects rather than the whole effect. For not only does the piece of writing have to transcend the writer, it must also transcend itself. It must amount to more than the sum of its parts. That is a difference between art and journalism. A writer can keep this from happening by not trying to guide what he or she is writing toward a specific future, for instance, the achieving of fame and fortune.

An interviewer once asked John LeCarré why he continued to write. He was rich, famous and in good health, so why didn't he retire and enjoy life? LeCarré said, "When the writing is going well, the money doesn't matter; and when it's going badly, the money doesn't help." That is the answer of someone who puts the writing over the publishing.

That I may want a book to make me rich and famous is a self-deception that stands outside the work. Others are less obvious. For instance, it is a self-deception to think that the reader doesn't matter. It is a self-deception not to believe, as Coleridge said, that poetry is the best words in the best order. The same is true of good fiction. All aesthetic theories become self-deception if they are embraced too tightly. No theory can be more important than the work itself.

The more difficult forms of self-deception exist inside the work. What do you think the work is about? Why do you think it is funny, sad or true? Why do you feel you have said too little, too much or just enough?

The Polish poet Zbigniew Herbert once said in an interview: "To extract meaning is our primary task." But it isn't enough to extract meaning, the writer must communicate it. The self-deception affects what one thinks constitutes meaning, how one extracts it and how one communicates it. What is it to be meaningful? Is it meaningful only to me? Why should anyone else care about it? As human beings we not only have a need to extract meaning, we also have a need to be right. This need to have a corner on truth is a powerful source of self-deception.

A common self-deception for beginning writers has to do with clarity. Because the writer has the clearest idea of what is being written, he or she often falls into the error of thinking it is equally clear to a reader. This is never true. The writer knows all the referents and connections; the reader doesn't. It is extremely hard for the writer to read his or her work from the point of view of the reader: to read dumb, as it were. Yet if the writer can't do this, there is little hope of success. In such a reading, the writer must give up all theories and be a complete pragmatist. He or she must ask constantly: What am I trying to do? He or she must measure the words against intention and demand how each word, sentence or image contributes to the whole.

Another self-deception caused by the writer's superior knowledge of the work is the failure to guard against alternative meanings. The writer often knows so well what he or she is trying to say that he or she assumes that the words convey it. But words are ambiguous and have multiple meanings. Too often the writer is reading something in his or her brain, rather than something on the page. I remember a student poem that described some soldiers being sent off to war. It was the last night of basic training and the soldiers sat on their cots sharing a couple of cigarettes, handing them back and forth. The writer used the line, "We passed our butts from mouth to mouth." So clearly did the writer hold his intended meaning in his mind that he failed to read what he had written.

Another form of self-deception comes from being mistaken as to what is necessary to the work. When has one said too much or too little? Any piece of writing has an ideal number of words. To go over or under even by one word is to diminish the success of the finished piece. This is hard to calculate, but it means strictly defining what the piece is about and what one is trying to do. If the writer says too little, it is often because he or she is being too reticent or feels the point is already clear. If too much is said, it is because he or she feels the point is obscure, or because the writer is too much in love with the language, or is self-indulgent or simply uncertain. It is a common mistake in a first novel for writers to pack in all sorts of extraneous but fascinating detail because they feel that their main story is not sufficiently interesting.

About ten years ago I went through my second published novel, *Saratoga Longshot*, editing it for a paperback edition. Ten years and ten other books followed the original writing. I was amazed at the material I had included because I thought it necessary—extraneous detail, unnecessary explanations and motivation. Without rewriting, I cut 10 percent, and if I had chosen to rewrite, I could have shortened the book by 15 percent. It was a depressing discovery. I had not hurried over that book. I had spent a year on it, saw it through four drafts, and it was as good as I could have made it at the time. Yet I had constantly over-explained myself, used two details where one would do and failed to define each part by the needs of the whole. It was full of self-deception.

It was then that I began to keep my Chilean dwarf on the desk where I work. Liar, it says. You haven't done enough, it says.

But there is a third issue symbolized by the dwarf. The jester laughs at the king, yet the jester himself has nothing. The dwarf reminds me of that mixture of gall and humility that one must have in order to write. You see, self-deception is also necessary. It is one of the writer's basic tools. He or she must have the self-confidence, the gall, to break the silence, to feel that what is being said is worth hearing. This is why it is easier for the young to write. They don't worry that what they say may be unimportant. It is also why so many British poets were outsiders who lacked a traditional education and didn't go to Oxford or Cambridge where they would have been told that being a poet was a very serious affair and much too serious for the likes of them. Nobody told John Keats he couldn't be a poet and so his gall remained intact.

Graduate writing students tend to write far more cautiously than undergraduates. In those few years the graduate writing students have assumed the burden of history. Dante, Shakespeare and Milton sit on their shoulders. They are more concerned with what they can't do than with what they can. They are afraid of appearing inadequate so they constantly censor themselves or push their work into obscurity where their intentions can't be seen.

The function of gall is to allow the original intuition to express itself without being interfered with by the conscious mind. In Freudian terms, it allows the unconscious to express itself without interference from the superego. Hesitancy is the surest destroyer of talent. One cannot be timorous and reticent; one must be original and loud. New metaphors, new rhythms, new expressions of emotion can only spring from unhindered gall. Nothing should interfere with that intuition—not the fear of appearing stupid, nor of offending somebody, nor jeopardizing publication, nor being trivial. The intuition must be as unhindered as a karate chop.

But once the intuition, in all its rawness, is sprawled on the page, then it must be turned into a poem or piece of fiction. This is where the humility comes in. In order to make the piece successful, the writer must place his or her needs and wishes after the needs of what is being written. He or she must determine what the intuition is saying and guide it in that direction. Ideally, the writer moves from total intuition to total consciousness, from the completely subjective to the completely objective. After the original intuition, the writer doesn't make the piece so much as allow it to come into being. The poet Osip Mandelstam talked about the revision process as being like the process of memory: that a glimpse of the whole piece comes in a flash and the writer spends months and years trying to remember it exactly.

But to do this, the writer must set aside the ego. He or she must listen to the work and not to the self. He or she must be careful not to censor or limit the work for reasons that stand outside the work. A work of art is the expression of the artist's whole self, not just of the improved self. The two are very different. A poem or work of fiction doesn't have enough room for both the writer's ego and the reader. The finished work, after all, belongs to the reader. It is where the reader finds his or her own life reflected. After the original intuition, the writer's role is to make sure that happens.

A work of art gives testimony as to what it is to be a human being. It bears witness, it extracts meaning. A work of art is also the clearest nonphysical way that emotion is communicated from one human being to another. The emotion isn't referred to; it is re-created. The emotion shows us that out most private feelings are in fact shared feelings. And this offers us some relief from our existential isolation.

When I first began writing, I felt I had to do little more than to learn my craft to be successful. What I have been describing was for me a rude discovery—that even though I was learning, I was also lying to myself about what I had learned, that throughout the whole revision process I was lying about what worked and what didn't. I will always lie to myself—that is the nature of the beast—but I don't want to forget I am doing it. Maybe I can catch a few lies and make the work better. So I let this little statue face me as I work—hunched over, eyes squinched shut, mouth open in a bray of mockery.

2 | Metaphor and the Authenticating Act of Memory

THERE IS AN OLD CONUNDRUM THAT ASKS, Is a bathtub a bathtub on Mars? Implied by this is the idea that something is defined by its function. Consequently, if you rocket a bathtub to Mars where it cannot be used, it will cease to be a bathtub.

Art, too, can be defined by its function: that is, a work of art, such as a poem, seeks to communicate with a reader. If that communication does not take place, then the work of art has failed, although that failure may be the fault of the reader and not of the work of art.

This has not been a particularly popular idea in poetics. Many of the French Symbolist poets felt that a poem was like a bright light. It wasn't required for a reader to understand or not understand. In that poetry dealt with the inexpressible, communication was hardly relevant. All that was needed was for the reader to be within range of the poem to feel its beneficial effects. These ideas influenced Eliot, Pound, Stevens and other Modernists with the result that their sense of a reader was often high-handed. If they thought of the reader at all, it was to say he or she was lucky to be there. The poet doesn't speak to the reader; rather, the reader overhears the poet.

Against this idea is Samuel Johnson, who wrote, "By the common sense of readers uncorrupted with literary prejudices, after all the refinements of subtlety and the dogmatism of learning, must be finally decided all claim to poetic honors."[1]

For Dr. Johnson, the ideal reader is not simply a bystander but the final judge, and part of the judgment derives from how well the poem communicates. In a modified version, this idea influenced W. B. Yeats and William Carlos Williams. Indeed, Yeats would study the poems of Mallarmé, trying to determine the exact line between communication and obscurity, thinking that to cross it, as he felt Mallarmé had often done, would destroy the poem.

These two extremes are found in all poetry as well as in contemporary American poetry. For the purpose of this essay, I would like to offer a definition that is an extension of Dr. Johnson's: that is, the most successful poem is an expression of formally heightened emotion that seeks to establish an intimate relationship with the reader in part by making the reader a participant in the creative process; and further, if the poem doesn't seek to establish this relationship or doesn't succeed in establishing it or is incapable of establishing it, then the poem fails and, at best, the reader becomes an interested bystander.

By "formally heightened" I only wish to indicate a close relationship between content and form without attempting to define it. By "successful" I wish to refer back to the judgment "of readers uncorrupted with literary prejudices."

Furthermore, this definition deals only with the poem's responsibility. The reader, too, has a responsibility to read aggressively, to ask questions and require answers, to be active rather than passive.

What I want to discuss here are ways in which the poem's relationship with the reader may be strengthened. One way is through the use of metaphor, in which I include simile, analogy and allegory. Generally, they are forms of comparison that exist to heighten the object of the comparison. Another way is through the authenticating act of memory, which means that the reader must be able to recognize and respond to the world of the poem, either through imagination or personal experience, which further requires a certain clarity as to the physical, emotional and intellectual contexts to be found within the poem.

Gertrude Stein once wrote about the difficulty of writing in a period of late language, by which she meant a period in which people are so used to the meanings of words that they tend to take them for granted, seeing them as no more than signs. She argued that when the language was younger it was possible for a writer to say "Oh Moon, I am lonely," and still have the language communicate intense loneliness. But in a period of late language the reader's linguistic sophistication stops the emotion and he or she takes the word "lonely" only as a sign indicative of the speaker's emotional state and doesn't let it communicate any feeling of loneliness. Instead of creating a sense of emotion on the page, the words refer to an emotional state existing off the page. As a result, the reader doesn't become a participant, if only because such a simple expression of loneliness isn't enough to jar him or her into empathy.

The more sophisticated we get about language, the less we are moved by its simple expression. Because of this, poets constantly seek ways to make emotion fresh. One of the obvious functions of metaphor is to heighten emotion. In a poem to be discussed later, W. S. Merwin replaces the statement "I am lonely" with "When you leave, the wind clicks around to the north." Another metaphor for aloneness is:

> Unless she is the one
> sail on to death
> like an empty ship.

That metaphor, along with others I will use, comes from W. S. Merwin's *Asian Figures*, which is a collection of translated folk sayings and aphorisms from half a dozen Asian countries.

A metaphor can exist to heighten just a small part of the poem or it can be the entire poem. To be successful, however, the metaphor must be functional rather than decorative, meaning it has to further the general intent of the poem and it must be necessary to the reader's understanding and involvement in the poem. Any decorative use of metaphor is basically rhetorical; the author is trying to convince the reader by what amounts to technical effects rather than by content.

A metaphor consists of the object half and the image half. The image half is most successful when it is open-ended or when the mind cannot fully encompass it: that is, when it creates the impression that it could give additional meaning each time the reader returns to it. Compare, for example, the stale metaphor "as quiet as a mouse" with:

Quiet
like a house where the witch
has just stopped dancing.

When it is open-ended, the image works like a symbol, which in its simplest form is something that represents more than its literal meaning. The witch's dance is not described and, while we may have some idea of it, we cannot encompass it, nor what the house is like without it, except that it is wonderfully quiet. In a similar way, the symbol of the cross can be to some degree understood but it cannot be encompassed, while the meaning of a stop sign, like the quietness of a mouse, can be.

This difference is partly the difference between sign and symbol, and clearly the image of a mouse to represent quiet approaches being a sign. So it would seem that the image half of the metaphor has the greatest possibility of touching the reader the more closely it works as a symbol. This is what Yeats wrote in his essay, "The Symbolism of Poetry": ". . . metaphors are not profound enough to be moving when they are not symbols, and when they are symbols they are the most perfect of all, because the most subtle . . ."[2]

The open-ended quality of the image half of the metaphor allows it to become to some degree mysterious. The more we think about the potentially frightening qualities of the witch's dance, think what makes the house so silent when the dance is over and of the fear implied by that silence, then the more we draw understanding from the entire metaphor.

In the witch metaphor, the object is obviously the word "quiet," but in other metaphors, the object can be a situation. This is true in the two Asian figures:

> Talk about tomorrow
> the rats will laugh

> Spits straight up
> learns something

Both aphorisms tell us something about ignorance, and so we could say that ignorance is the implied object. Since the object half of the metaphor attempts to provide a context for the image, the object itself should be easily discoverable. When someone accuses a poem of being vague, this often means that the object of a metaphor is unclear or that the relationship between object and image is imprecise. Vagueness is withheld information, and usually no amount of thought will supply what is missing or, if it does supply the information, the struggle to supply it is irrelevant to the poem and does not heighten the metaphor, which means we should have had the information in the first place. Consider the Asian figure: "Full of danger / as an egg pyramid."

If the word "danger" were removed and the reader were forced to guess at it, nothing would be gained by that guessing. The purpose of the metaphor is to heighten our sense of the object. If we don't know the object, that heightening cannot occur.

A mystery is potentially capable of being understood. What is mysterious lends itself to the search for understanding, but what is vague leads to confusion. Many weak poems substitute vagueness for mystery. They withhold information as to the object of the metaphor and offer only image or what appears to be image, which gives the poem an aura of mystery and meaning. But image without object is nonfunctional, since its contemplation won't increase our understanding. It is not the contemplation of image that leads to understanding; rather, it is thinking about the relationship between the object and the image. This is very important. Image without object is evocative but it is a dead end. The image has no function without the object, while the purpose of metaphor is to draw attention to the relationship between its parts.

This is not to suggest that the object must be always stated, but even if the image stands by itself, let's say to create a mood, we have some sense of an object, even if it is only the slightest inference.

Many of the Imagist poets felt that the image had a value entirely by itself. What they called image was similar to what an earlier generation called symbol. Both groups tended to feel that the mere presence of image or symbol energized the poem, but by putting little value on the audience, they ignored the need of communication. Even a symbol must give a sense of what it symbolizes. The Imagists often erased the comparative role of the image, but it is that comparison that makes the image important. We go to art partly to learn about the world. In a metaphor, that world is represented by the object, while the comparison with the image gives us a new sense of that world. To remove the object, destroy the comparison and present only the image is to reduce the reader's interest and limit communication.

This criticism of Imagist poems is also made by Graham Hough in "Reflections on a Literary Revolution." Hough writes: "In all of them we find a host of examples where immediate communication between poet and reader fails on two planes; both on the plane of reference, all that is ordinarily called 'the sense' of the poem; and on the plane of feeling, the emotional attitude toward the situation presented. Whatever tradition Imagist poetry may have recalled to us, the most important tradition of all, that of a natural community of understanding between poet and reader, has been lost."[3]

Examples of metaphors with clear objects and open-ended images are these Asian figures:

The mouth is
one gate of hell

Neglect is a dog
in a dead man's house

Stepping on a long thorn
to me the sight of her hair

Every metaphor is based on withheld information that the comparison given by the metaphor tries to uncover. Implied in each metaphor is the question of how the image is like the object. In the act of answering this question the reader becomes a participant by authenticating the comparison from his or her own memory and/or imagination.

Simply stated, every metaphor is a riddle, since, if the object is clear, the reader always asks how is A like B. That kind of asking and answering is almost unconscious because the brain, when presented with a question, automatically attempts to solve it. Only when the brain tells itself to stop does the questioning process come to a halt. If I ask myself what is the square root of 85, I am aware of my brain beginning to question and then stopping itself because I can't solve such a problem in my head. But that beginning to question is automatic.

The question implied by the metaphor makes the reader define the relationship between the object and image, and this (1) forces the reader to participate actively in the poem and (2) gives the reader knowledge about something unknown or only partly known by making it analogous to something he or she can imagine. And this act of imagining increases the reader's participation by forcing him or her to draw on memory to authenticate the metaphor.

When I give the simile "A liar is like an egg in midair," I am trying to particularize your sense of a liar by saying how fragile and short-lived the lie is. When you hear the simile, your mind automatically asks the questions of how and why. In order to answer these questions, your mind draws on its knowledge of eggs, and, equally important, it imagines a temporal context. The egg in midair exists in one moment of time. In order to understand the simile, you have to imagine a past and future.

Take another simile from *Asian Figures*: Silent / like the thief the dog bit." Again, the action exists in one point of time, and you have to invent a temporal context: a narrative with a past and future. What I find amazing is the speed at which the mind arrives at the information. Were I to write down how a liar is like an egg in midair, it could take pages, but I wouldn't say anything that I hadn't already realized in a split second. We tend to take this process for granted, but if it weren't for our ability to compare one thing to another, then to draw seemingly spontaneous knowledge from the comparison, poetry would be impossible.

The speed of this process also gives the metaphor the advantage of surprise, as can be seen in these Asian figures:

The hissing starts
in the free seats

Close to death
see how tender
the grass is

Who looks at a mirror
to see a mirror

Life
candle flame
wind coming

In each case, the speed of our understanding is so rapid that we seem to take ourselves by surprise, and the presence of this surprise helps to convince us, sometimes falsely, of the accuracy of the metaphor. The surprise almost functions as a rhetorical device, since our sense of surprise can distract us and cause us to overlook the logic of the metaphor.

For a metaphor to be successful, it must be logical; it has to conform to our knowledge of the known world. I expect we can accept this without further inquiry. But logic by itself isn't enough; the metaphor must also be precise. To say "Ask the mouth, it says food" is certainly logical, but it doesn't have the precision of "Ask the mouth, it says cake." The former says what we already know, what we can encompass, but the latter says something about self-indulgence and how the body doesn't necessarily know or care what is good for it. Now, in a sense, we know this, too, but it is as if we weren't really aware that we knew it until the memory surprised us with it.

Another Asian figure: "Where there's no tiger / the hares swagger." If "swagger" is replaced by "call attention to themselves," the metaphor is diluted by being nonvisual. It makes sense but it is uninteresting. The memory is more actively engaged by verbs that engage the senses. This act of engaging is how the memory authenticates metaphor, and this authenticating act of the memory is how the conscious mind is given information that already seems to exist in the unconscious.

What I call the unconscious may be no more than memory: that the best metaphors are those complex enough to need validating by dredging up information we forgot we had. On the other hand, we can take Freud's definitions of the conscious and unconscious to explain this process, while accepting the possibility that his definitions are themselves metaphors for something we still don't understand. Generally, I would say that the best metaphors are those that engage the unconscious mind, that part of the mind that contains psychic material of which the ego is unaware.

The more the metaphor involves the entire mind, the greater its chance of success. The figure "When he draws a tiger it's a dog" startles us with a new sense of the ineffectual. Yet to verify it, there is a split second when I ask myself how it means. It is that act of questioning that seems to submit the conscious to the unconscious mind. Recent right brain–left brain studies have suggested other interpretations for this process. The non-discursive material of the metaphor is first understood by the nonanalytical right brain. Then comes a moment of communication between the two halves of the brain as the left asks for meaning and the right provides it. It is this that gives the sense that the authenticating response is not simultaneous, that one part of the brain understands before the other.

Look at these figures:

Needle thief
dreams of spears

Talk of tomorrow
the rats will laugh

Start to speak
lips feel the cold autumn wind

Here it seems that one part of the mind understands before the other. One can see this as right brain–left brain or, perhaps, the unconscious and conscious. In any case, it seems that I understand before I know why I understand. The effect is to surprise me with myself. I suddenly come face to face with myself and my view of the world. And that face-to-face quality occurs during the moment when part of me is struck by the precision of the metaphor and another part is still trying to understand. I expect this happens with most good metaphors: There is a moment of combined knowing and not-knowing where we confront ourselves. Think again about the figures: "Ask the mouth, it says cake" or "The hissing starts / in the free seats" or "Spits straight up / learns something." First comes a moment of recognition and ignorance, then a moment of asking how and why, then the ignorance resolves itself into knowledge. But that recognition, which is also knowledge, seems there from the first.

Much information comes to us accumulatively, arriving word by word, number by number. We build verbal structures of argument and persuasion. This is how the left brain works. But information also comes through nonverbal perceptions. If I ask myself what would happen if terrorists blew up the UN, I respond with an immediate nonverbal perception, which ranges from a sense of the explosion's effect on New York City, to how it would influence world politics. Right brain–left brain studies indicate that the two halves of the brain have entirely different ways of taking in information and that the most effective way is to have both halves working together. This is how metaphor functions. In the first moments after this nonverbal perception, we experience a period of confusion while the mind seems to question itself, and right away we are surprised by a large body of information.

A nonverbal perception of this nature is very convincing, which is not to say it is true. The perception seems to come from outside, almost like a vision, an exterior voice telling us something important. And this has the peculiar side effect of momentarily taking us out of our isolation and joining us to some larger idea of the world. I expect this sense of the perception being an exterior voice is caused somewhat by the fact that the conscious mind or left side of the brain (I am not using those terms synonymously) is endlessly verbal. As a result, a nonverbal perception appears to come from outside. Certainly this is how it seems in the writing of poetry, where in a moment of nonverbal perception I suddenly "see" how the poem is going to work itself out. It also helps to explain a theory we find in Plato's dialogue "Ion," where Socrates argues that the poem does not originate with the poet, but rather the poet is the medium through which the poem passes from a higher sphere to the world.

It is the ability of metaphor to elicit large, nonverbal perceptions that is one of the great strengths of poetry and what can make a poem convincing. W. B. Yeats loved to entwine the nonverbal perception created by the metaphor with the intellectual argument of the poem. He would so carefully link argument and metaphor at the conclusion of a poem that the nonverbal perception completely absorbs the verbal argument. This is the strategy he uses to close "The Second Coming," "Among School Children" and "Sailing to Byzantium," where he seems to leave his argument and turns to a metaphor that illustrates his conclusion. What helps to convince us of these endings is not necessarily their intrinsic truth but the manner of their presenting: that is, by forcing us to experience the nonverbal perception that confronts us with a moment of combined knowing and ignorance, and that, through questioning, we resolve into knowledge.

Theodore Roethke suggested people dislike poetry because it asks questions of their lives. But what it may really do is present them with metaphors that make them ask certain questions of themselves. Consider these figures: "If you're going to be a dog be a rich man's dog," "Waiting till he's falling then push," "If it's dirty work borrow the tools." The questioning process by which the reader submits to the metaphor makes him or her vulnerable to its suggestion, while the cynicism of these particular figures can force the reader to examine the way he or she perceives the world.

I said originally that a poem seeks to establish an intimate relationship with the reader. I want to expand this to say that a poem seeks to establish this relationship in order to force the reader to become increasingly aware of his or her relationship with the self by making the reader become aware of how he or she sees the world.

Another aspect of this process is the way a metaphor can surprise us with a piece of information that it feels we know but didn't realize we knew until the metaphor revealed it to us. If we see this in terms of right brain–left brain, then the fact that the right brain understands the question before the left brain makes it seem that this information already resided within us. The left brain verbalizes its perceptions which makes it seem to move more slowly than the right brain. Also, the immense speed of nonverbal perception can create the illusion that we already possessed the knowledge. Or again this can be seen in terms of the conscious and unconscious. Does the information already exist in the unconscious or does it only appear that way because the unconscious answered the question first?

We think of the unconscious as having a sort of pragmatic honesty. It is incompletely civilized. So when we are presented with a politically incorrect Asian figure like "Wait till he's falling then push," we are also presented with the inhibitions and rationalizations of the more politically correct conscious mind. I expect the ability to lie is an ability of the conscious and we lie just as much to protect ourselves from ourselves as to protect ourselves from other people. But the unconscious seems unable to lie. It may misinterpret, but it doesn't intentionally deceive. It takes in information and interprets it according to the knowledge it has. In this sense it seems honest.

It would appear then that the successful metaphor confronts one part of the mind with another—either right brain–left brain or unconscious and conscious—and this results in a heightening of the reader's relationship with himself or herself. Consequently, the degree to which we call a metaphor precise is perhaps the degree to which the metaphor is authenticated in this confrontation between two parts of the mind. Further, it is the function of metaphor to create this confrontation.

I want to look at three poems to see how metaphor works more exactly. All are examples of simple metaphor, and understanding comes from working out the almost linear accumulation of image.

The first is Tomas Tranströmer's "Face to Face"; the translation is by Robin Fulton.

> In February living stood still.
> The birds flew unwillingly and the mind
> chafed against the landscape as a boat
> chafes against the bridge it lies moored to.

The trees stood with their backs turned toward me.
The deep snow was measured with dead straws.
The footprints grew old out on the crust.
Under a tarpaulin language pined.

One day something came forward to the window.
Dropping my work I looked up.
The colors flared. Everything turned around.
The earth and I sprang towards each other.[4]

Here we have a clear example of the relationship between the object and image. The first line immediately states the object—living in February, which in this case would be in the author's homeland of Sweden—while the verb-adverb construction "stood still" is also a metaphoric usage. The object is then heightened by two examples—the birds flying unwillingly and the mind chafing against the landscape. These are basically realistic but also contain metaphor. Do the birds really fly unwillingly, or does it only seem that way? The second example is further heightened by the simile of the boat chafing against the bridge.

The first stanza is a fairly straightforward description. The second stanza, however, describes a metaphoric reality. The link between the two is the simile concluding the first stanza: that the mind in winter chafes against the winter landscape as a boat chafes against a bridge to which it is tied. But looking more closely at lines 2, 3 and 4, we see that each contains a greater degree of metaphor until it is only a small step to line 5, which is pure metaphor. Without that gradual increase of metaphor, the second stanza might seem an exaggerated description: that is, hyperbole.

In the second stanza, the four images have an accumulative strength. They are strange, cannot be encompassed and each, by being an example of immobility, refers back to the "stood still" in line 1. Along with immobility, we have the sense of life withheld; and by line 8, where language is said to pine, we see what is also being talked about is the writer's relationship to his work.

Additionally, the phrase "under the tarpaulin" returns us to the boat moored to the bridge and perhaps we think of a boat covered by a tarpaulin and put up for the winter.

The third stanza seems to return to an objective reality, but the nature of the "something" in line 9 is kept from us. What we find in the stanza is the presence of movement and color where none existed before. By answering the question as to what caused the movement and color, we learn the nature of that "something."

Our understanding of the poem comes from considering the relationship between the first and second stanzas, while in the third stanza a metaphoric and objective reality are joined together and confused. One could preface each of the lines in the second stanza with the phrase "it was as if," but that cannot be done so easily in the third stanza. It is by heightening objective reality to a point of transcendence that Tranströmer is able to communicate the poem's closing sense of wonder and joy.

The second poem is W. S. Merwin's "When You Go Away," which was dedicated to his wife, Dido.

> When you go away the wind clicks around to the north
> The painters work all day but at sundown the paint falls
> Showing the black walls
> The clock goes back to striking the same hour
> That has no place in the years
>
> And at night wrapped in the bed of ashes
> In one breath I wake
> It is the time when the beards of the dead get their growth
> I remember that I am falling
> That I am the reason
> And that my words are the garment of what I shall never be
> Like the tucked sleeve of a one-armed boy[5]

This is a highly metaphoric poem, but when we break it down we find a direct and uncomplicated subject: that is, when you leave it is my fault because I am fallible and because my words don't express an actual reality but an idealized and yearned-for reality that I will never be able to achieve. Merwin presents this subject with two clear statements of an objective reality—when you go away, in the first stanza, and at night I wake and remember that I am the reason, in the second—and eight images. Six of the images use the title as their object. Another—the eighth line about the beards of the dead—has as its object the time at which the speaker wakes at night, while the last image uses "I am the reason" and "my words" as its object.

The three images of stanza 1 represent loneliness and desolation. Obviously they are more than this, but they work by taking those feelings and heightening them. The fourth and seventh images—the bed of ashes and falling—are variations on the first two, while the last image—"the tucked sleeve of a one-armed boy"—presents the conflict between the two realities: the idealized and actual.

The subject of the poem is simple. If we don't recognize it from our lives, we can imagine it. But with this accumulation of image, Merwin is able to take a relatively common feeling and make it fresh again, make us experience it as if for the first time. The strategy of the poem is like the strategy of metaphor itself. We are presented with an object and a series of images that heighten that object, and we come to understand the poem by thinking about the relationship between object and image.

The third poem to be considered is "Signs" by the French poet Jean Follain. The translation is by Merwin.

> Sometimes when a customer in a shadowy restaurant
> is shelling an almond
> a hand comes to rest on his narrow shoulder
> he hesitates to finish his glass
> the forest in the distance is resting under its snow
> the sturdy waitress has turned pale
> he will have to let the winter night fall

has she not often seen
on the last page
of a book of modest learning
the word end printed
in ornate capitals?[6]

We work out this poem by asking the significance of the hand in the third line. The answer that allows the poem to unfold most simply is to say that the hand is the hand of death. Once we understand that, the poem becomes quite direct. A man in a restaurant has a sense of his approaching death, and a waitress, watching him, sees him experiencing this awareness and she, or the narrator, relates this to seeing the word "end" or "*fin*" on the last page of a book.

What I also like about the poem and what helps make it mysterious is that along with the concluding metaphor, which strikes us directly, are indirect and hidden metaphors, which communicate almost subliminally. The best way to disclose these hidden metaphors is to question the word choices.

For instance, why make the nut an "almond" and why a "narrow" shoulder? This questions leads us to realize that the shapes are similar, which leads us to see that as the man is so much greater than the almond he is touching, so is death so much greater than the man who is being touched. Then Follain presents the reader with another image: the snow resting upon the trees. Thinking about it, we can see that many trees, like pine trees, have that same almond shape, and further, as the touch of snow is cold upon the living tree, so is the touch of death cold upon the shoulder of the living man.

Then with the phrase "he will have to let the winter night fall," we see that is how he will have to let his own life fall, which is also how he is letting the almond shells fall, while buried within the phrase is the simile that where he is in his life is like the winter night. When we reread the poem, a word like "shadowy" in the first line takes on further meaning not only by foreshadowing the forest but also by describing a place between light and dark, life and death.

The poem is two scenes about the apprehension of death that are woven together by those mysterious lines about the forest and letting night fall. Both lines modify the first scene, but by separating them with the waitress and her sudden understanding, they also modify the second scene. This allows the metaphors to do extra work. For example, just as the forest is reposing under the white snow, so is the customer under the regard of the pale-faced waitress. Also, in the same way that he must put down his glass, so he will have to let the winter night fall.

I admire how Follain lets these images shift in the poem. In the end, he further heightens our sense of life and death with the simile that compares them to a book of modest learning and the ornate capitals. Even the word "modest" becomes a small joke about the man, while the visual image of the black letters of the word "*fin*" surrounded by the white of the page again evokes the black trees surrounded by snow. What should be clear is that Follain would not be able to let his images do such an immense range of work if the objects of his metaphors—if the context and situation of the poem—were not ascertainable.

But metaphors form only part of a poem. We must also see how the metaphors relate to the poem as a whole. Ideally, a poem takes hold of the reader and forces him or her to respond to it with the emotions. The poem is where the reader sees himself or herself afresh, briefly freed from the trappings of the world. But for this to occur, the reader must be able to find a way into the poem as a participant. Metaphor, through its question-asking process, is one way to do this. But it is also necessary for the reader to authenticate the event of the poem with the memory; he or she must engage in an act of recognition.

This recognition can be divided into intellectual, physical and emotional. When I say $5 \times 5 = 25$, we engage in an act of intellectual recognition. When I describe the smell of rotting apples, the recognition is physical. When I talk of the difficulty of love, the recognition is emotional.

It is rarely so simple. Any recognition may be made up of all three parts, although one may predominate. But the degree to which the reader becomes a participant in the poem is the degree to which he or she is involved in these acts of recognition. What we also notice about these types of recognition is that they engage different parts of ourselves. Physical recognition involves the five senses. Intellectual recognition primarily involves the conscious mind (or, if you prefer, the left brain), while emotional recognition involves the unconscious (or perhaps the right brain). And the more the entire entity of the reader is involved in the recognition process, the more the reader will be involved in the poem.

For this act of recognition to take place, the intellectual, physical and emotional contexts of the poem must be discoverable. Look at the poem "I Knew I'd Sing" by Heather McHugh.

> A few sashay, a few finagle.
> Some make whoopee, some
> make good. But most make
> diddly-squat. I tell you this
>
> is what I love about
> America—the words it puts
> in my mouth, the mouth where once
> my mother rubbed
>
> a word away with soap. The word
> was *cunt*. She stuck that bar
> of family-size in there
> until there was no hole to speak of,
>
> so she hoped. But still
> I'm full of it—the cunt,
> the prick, short u, short i,
> the words that stood

for her and him. I loved the thing
they must have done, the love they must
have made, to make
an example of me. After my lunch of Ivory I said

vagina for a day or two, but knew
from that day forth which word
struck home like sex itself. I knew
when I was big I'd sing

a song in praise of cunt—I'd want
to keep my word, the one with teeth in it.
Forevermore (and even after I was raised) I swore

nothing—but nothing—would be beneath me.[7]

The first six and a half lines give an intellectual context: Language is being discussed. The next six lines give a physical context: a bar of soap shoved into the mouth. The emotional context exists in the sentence "I loved the thing they must have done, the love they must have made, to make an example of me." There is also an emotional resonance to the word "must" that suggests sadness: as if proof of love must always be sought, as if love were a chimera that one doesn't really believe in. Yet even if love exists, it is fleeting, and if it is fleeting, then can it be said to exist?

The last eight and a half lines combine the intellectual, physical and emotional, joining them and shifting from one to another with puns and verbal sleight of hand. The "song of praise" celebrates the intellectual, physical and emotional. Those contexts are also joined in the verbal play that concludes the poem: "I swore nothing—but nothing—would be beneath me."

If the intellectual, physical and/or emotional contexts were obscured, then the reader would be led to ask questions in order to make them clear. The reader needs the physical grounding of the poem supplied by the bar of soap. It is by clearly presenting these three types of contexts that McHugh is able to engage in the complicated word play that concludes the poem.

Obscurity must be a tool. It works to force the reader to ask questions that will direct him or her to an understanding of the poem. Any question that does not increase our understanding detracts from it. It hurts to be obscure about the intellectual, physical and/or emotional contexts of the poem in the same way that it hurts to be obscure about the object of the metaphor. It is useless to make the reader ask questions about the nature of the context because it is not by thinking about the context that we understand the poem; rather, it is by thinking about the relationship between the three types of context and the events of the poem that understanding is reached.

Often, when one or more of these contexts is unclear, a poem will be criticized as being too private, which usually means that the writer is withholding too much information. The result is the reader isn't able to examine the relationship between one or more of the three contexts and the narrative, which limits his or her access to the poem. Also there must be a balance between these three types of context, even though one may predominate. But if one is exaggerated to the detriment of the whole, then the poem breaks down. For instance, when the intellectual context is exaggerated, the poem tends to become emotionally barren; and when the emotional is exaggerated, the poem becomes sentimental. The overly discursive, the decorative and the sentimental all attempt to function independently of the whole and to affect the argument of the poem in a way that is basically rhetorical.

I now want to look at two poems as examples of balance among intellectual, physical and emotional contexts. The first is "A Little Tooth" by Thomas Lux.

> Your baby grows a tooth, then two,
> and four, and five, then she wants some meat
> directly from the bone. It's all

over: she'll learn some words, she'll fall
in love with cretins, dolts, a sweet
talker on his way to jail. And you,

your wife, get old, flyblown, and rue
nothing. You did, you loved, your feet
are sore. It's dusk. Your daughter's tall.[8]

Generally, the first stanza presents the physical context, the second stanza presents the intellectual and the third the emotional context, but by using the surprises created by the enjambed lines Lux is able to mix and emphasize different aspects of these contexts. For instance, the two words concluding line 3 seem to present a physical context, but the word after the break changes it to an intellectual context ("It's all / over."). The last two words of line 4 seem to present a physical context, but the first two words of line 5 changes it to an emotional context ("she'll fall / in love . . ."). The last two words of line 7 seem to suggest an emotional context, but the word after the line break changes the emotion and brings in an element of the intellectual: the fact that one has no regrets.

The line breaks in lines 2, 5, and 8 also create surprises, especially "sweet / talker on his way to jail." At least six of the line breaks work to startle our expectations and to expand and/or confuse one of the three types of context, with the result that the last line, which would seem to present only a physical context, presents all three. The word "sore" is made to suggest more than pain. "It's dusk" also suggests the end of life. "Your daughter's tall" suggests that she is a complete human being, that she is successful, even that she has taken the place of the parent.

The poem ends up as a statement about complexity and how events turn out in ways that astonish us yet may be pleasing. The surprises in seven of the nine line breaks work as little metaphors for those ways that astonish us. And perhaps the poem is also surprising in its formality: iambic tetrameter tercets with an

ABC-CBA-ABC rhyme scheme. One of the poem's subjects is how events can seem to go out of control, yet at the end we see that events have not gone out of control: It is just that events have turned out differently than we anticipated. The poem's closure and the closure of its rhyme scheme demonstrate order being brought out of apparent disorder. And one of the ways that Lux creates apparent disorder is to blur the distinctions between the physical, intellectual and emotional contexts.

Here is a poem by James Wright.

OUTSIDE FARGO, NORTH DAKOTA

Along the sprawled body of the derailed Great Northern
     freight car,
I strike a match slowly and lift it slowly.
No wind.

Beyond town, three heavy white horses
Wade all the way to their shoulders
In a silo's shadow.

Suddenly the freight car lurches.
The door slams back, a man with a flashlight
Calls me good evening.
I nod as I write good evening, lonely
And sick for home.[9]

At first it seems that the poem is simply a clear physical description followed by a clear emotional description with little or no intellectual context. But then we see intellectual context appear in that odd line, "I nod as I write good evening," which makes us realize that the whole experience may be a memory that the narrator is recalling as he writes the poem. We also see intellectual context, although emblematically, in the line, "I strike a match slowly and lift it slowly," which can symbolize understanding or intellectual perception, like a light bulb over a cartoon character's head.

Here again the emotional context, is stated clearly at the end, but looking at the physical context, we see it contains buried metaphors concerning the emotional state of the narrator. We realize that the narrator in his loneliness and isolation is like the sprawled body of a freight car and, second, that the three white horses wading into the shadow are an image of companionship and love in the face of the unknown, creating an emblem of what the narrator yearns for.

What Wright is trying to do is make the last phrase "lonely / And sick for home" jolt the reader into recognition, but for it to work he has to build a foundation that will justify that phrase, yet keep the reader from anticipating it. The reader proceeds through the poem trying to determine the reason for the description. Then, with that last phrase, all becomes clear. At that point, however, the reader goes back into the poem and it is by considering the relationship among the three types of context and how they relate to the narrative that he or she comes to understand what Wright is doing.

The French poet Mallarmé said that to name is to destroy and to suggest is to create. I would agree even though I have spent some pages arguing that the poet should name clearly, meaning the reader must have sufficient information. Suggestion won't work until the reader has enough information to brood about. The poem works when the reader can contemplate the relationship between its parts. Ideally, the more he or she thinks about that relationship, the more it ramifies and the more the poem gives back. But the reader can't engage in the act of contemplation if necessary information is withheld or if he or she keeps interrupting that act with questions about information he or she should already know.

3 | Writing the Reader's Life

A PIECE OF WRITING IS A BODY OF information governed by a purpose, and that purpose, determines how the information is ordered. Actually, two purposes govern any piece of writing: the purpose of the particular category of writing (menus, traffic tickets, poems) and the purpose of the particular example of writing. The purpose of the particular category of writing is determined by its function, which, in art, may be no more than to give pleasure, which further means that it must be communicated to an audience. That function also governs the individual example of writing.

Function directs purpose. A specific poem, for instance, may try to make the reader see the world in a new way. It may try to engage the reader's emotions. It may try to amuse or frighten or teach or do all the above. These are aspects of a specific poem's purpose. At the same time, a certain tension exists between the form as it is defined at any moment within the culture and the individual example of the form. A reader is always reading a poem through his or her opinions about poetry as well as through every poem he or she has ever read, and the writer is writing the poem through his or her opinions and through every poem ever read. We call a work original when it surprises these opinions and expands our preconceptions of the limits of the form.

Purpose is predominantly communicated through structure. It is through structure that a piece of writing releases its information to the reader. Most simply, structure is strategy imposed upon time. The fact that the piece of writing has a purpose makes it necessary that it have a structure, which means, in turn, that it must have a beginning, middle and end. But the writer can have no real sense of the beginning, middle and end until he or she has a sense of the work's purpose. Even the most original and avant-garde work can be seen to have a beginning, middle and end, although perhaps only after some time has passed and the work has been subjected to strict analysis. Otherwise, the piece of writing will be no more than a fragment, which doesn't mean it is worthless. Consider Coleridge's "Kubla Khan."

Structure is two things at once. It is the order in which information is released, and it is also information itself. This double function of structure becomes most important in the arts where the structure of a poem or story or novel can carry nearly as much information as the actual content. We can further define structure as the formal elements of language, texture, pacing and tone imposed upon the informal elements of action, emotion, setting and idea. In this definition, form becomes an element of structure so that structure is both the order and the manner in which the information is released. This information is composed of those elements that the writer feels important and that are intended to affect the reader, and clearly they are chosen from a much larger body of information. Consequently, we can further define structure as the selection and organization of significant moments of time. The decision as to what is significant is one of the functions of talent, which Chekhov once defined as the ability to distinguish between the essential and inessential.[1]

Aristotle described plot as the most important principle governing a work of art.[2] No matter how brilliant the writer's idea or how strong the emotion, if the plot or structure is weak, everything else fails. Structure then is not only what allows the work to be complete in itself but also what enables the work to be communicated and become a source of pleasure.

A work of art has certain requirements that make it a work of art and not something else, such as a restaurant menu or instructions on how to operate a car. A work of art must engage the intellect. It must engage the emotions. It must engage the imagination. It must function as metaphor. It must contain within it some definition of beauty. Why it must be these things is perhaps another matter, but it must be these things to the writer and it must be these things to the reader. Consequently, the structure, too, must engage the intellect and emotions and imagination. It, too, must be beautiful and function as metaphor. The structure of Pope's "Rape of the Lock" is, among other things, a metaphor of Pope's perception of the world: a world that is orderly and rational. The structure of Apollinaire's "Zone" is a metaphor of Apollinaire's perception of the world: a world that is disorderly and surprising.

Structure cannot be accidental. Even if structure is determined by chance methods, the use of chance constitutes a chosen method. Additionally, structure not only conveys information but it is also a thing in itself, beautiful, metaphoric and so on, although divorced from its content it is nothing. Information without structure is cacophony. Structure without information is a theoretical abstraction. We can speak of certain traditional forms, such as the sonnet form, but that form is only a part of the structure of a particular sonnet. But the fact that structure itself may be informative and beautiful allows us to have many novels or stories or poems on similar subjects. We have an unlimited number of ways to present a limited amount of information.

It would seem that the world itself has no structure other than what is given to it by the passage of time, while entropy, gravity, the alternation of light and dark and the cycles of reproduction become elements of its form. Human beings require structures, looking for them either in the master plan of some deity or imposing them to protect life and to protect and increase property. Consequently, the creation and imposition of structure is done both to protect against and in defiance of the apparent anarchy of what exists. The imposition of structure makes human beings feel they have some sort of control over the anarchy. A government is an imposed structure, as are the Ten Commandments and the Bill of Rights. One of the functions of these structures is to give us the apparent ability to divide actions and events into right and wrong, good and bad.

Structure in a piece of writing allows us to divide actions not into good and bad—that may come afterward—but into probable and improbable. A main requirement of a piece of writing is probability. A story must be probable. Even if it is fantastic or surreal or a fairy tale, it must be probable within its governing situation. The world itself need not be probable. That is one of the things we find most frightening about it. In the world, the hero may be struck by lightning as he is getting ready for battle. In a story, that lightning, if it is to exist, must be explained. One of the functions of the gods in *The Iliad* is to make lightning bolts probable.

We read a work presuming that nothing is accidental, all is purposeful, whether consciously or unconsciously, and so we move through a story or poem by asking questions of it—why this, why that? By coming up with answers, we separate the possible from the probable and follow the trail of probable. We try to do that in the world, as well, but the world is not governed by any such rules of probability, or rather there are far more things affecting events than we can possibly see, and the result is a sense of randomness. One of the ways that fiction and poetry work is by making the reader anticipate what is going to happen next and, further, by making the reader want to know what is going to happen. Always balanced against the reader's anticipation is possible frustration, the fear that the whole thing is going to fall apart.

But the reader is going to anticipate and want to know what is going to happen only if he or she trusts that the events stretching ahead are in some way probable within the whole, that they are not gratuitous nor arbitrary nor merely possible. This suggests something about art: that we require of it certain conditions that we don't find in life, that is, that it be probable. The ending of a story may be tragic or comic or surreal or trivial, it may surprise and shock, but it must also be probable and, ideally, inevitable. That is one of the paradoxes of writing, that the conclusion of a given piece must appear both inevitable and surprising. This inevitability is something we find particularly satisfying. It suggests the world has an intrinsic structure, which in fact it may not have. Virtue is rewarded; the guilty are punished; love prevails.

A poem or piece of fiction exercises the imagination like little else. Not only do we imagine the scene we are reading, but we also imagine what might happen next and then measure what is happening against what we imagined was going to happen. Also, if the work has engaged us, we have a series of desires and fears about what may lie ahead: desires and fears that may actually become painful. Furthermore, as we read, we are measuring what we are reading against all we have ever read. Whenever we read a poem we are also, at some level, holding that poem against every other poem we have ever read. We don't necessarily judge the new poem against the others, although we may, but we are using our previous reading to help us anticipate what might happen next in the poem presently at hand. Whatever we read is always filtered through what we have ever read; in the same way it is filtered through where we are in history, filtered through our culture and psychology, our various ideologies, our precarious card house of opinions. Ideally, the writer knows this and makes use of it. Structure is not only a matter of knowing what word to put down next, but also knowing how the reader will respond to that word, knowing how you want the reader to respond and why.

Any work is tied to the writer's life even if it isn't specifically autobiographical. Structure always reflects the writer's view of the world and is tied to the writer's psychology. Whenever we write, we describe ourselves. The writer is not presenting us with reality. That has been a critical fallacy that has moved in and out of popularity since Plato: that art attempts to imitate reality. Rather the writer gives us a metaphor for his or her own emotional/psychological/ intellectual/physical relationship with what he or she imagines reality to be, a metaphor that we value in part because either it is similar to our own relationship with reality (or what we imagine reality to be) or simply because it wakens us to our relationship with reality.

Reality itself is a hidden thing. The word forms a paradox because it stands for a great mystery. We are born into this mystery. Then two things happen: we gather information about it and we grow used to it. Both are necessary. But because we grow used to the mystery, we feel that our information about it must be correct. This is not necessarily true. The function of our information (apart from its possible validity) is to make us feel comfortable in the world around us: that medium in which our time is spent. In fact, the world continues to be as much a mystery as it was at the beginning, but now as adults we have formed opinions and grown used to it, meaning we have worked to diminish its oddness, its menace and its surprise.

Neurosis, according to Freud, allows us to believe the lies we make about the world in order to reduce its threat and be able to function within it. Neurosis shields us from the fact of our mortality. We constantly speculate about reality, but we are unable to see it accurately because of (1) our conditioning (social, cultural, class and family background), (2) our psychology, (3) our limited perspective in space and time, (4) the questionable trustworthiness of our senses (is the blue that I see the same blue that you see?), (5) the degree of our intelligence and imagination, (6) our emotional engagement, (7) our dependence on language, which is reductionist and inexact, and so on. But despite our ignorance, we do know a few things, and that little knowledge is supported by endless opinions.

Perhaps we would not care so much if we didn't know that reality can hurt us. In fact, it will someday kill us. And so we gather information about it. This is one of the reasons we read fiction and poetry. It gives us information about our lives. We read in part to see ourselves. We read to see what our future will be. We read to see that our most private joys and fears are in fact shared within the human community. And we read to have our opinions about the world challenged or even strengthened. Our question is what is it to be a human being, what is it to be me. At some level the subject of any story or poem is always the reader, and the writer who ignores this does so at his or her peril. No matter how caught up we are in the story of *Lord Jim*, the novel is finally a metaphor of how human beings behave in this world. We read it to learn about ourselves.

We read to learn about our lives and be distracted from our fate. And the more the writer engages our attention and makes us want to read, the more we are distracted. Clearly, some writing offers more distraction than information, but we value the information more than the distraction, and if we sufficiently value the information, then we call the writing literature. Dostoevsky's *Crime and Punishment* and Raymond Chandler's *The Big Sleep* are both mysteries, but we value Dostoevsky more because (1) he gives us more information about the world, (2) his novel is not limited by its conception, which, in the Chandler novel is simply the problem of who killed whom, and (3) he creates a metaphor that tells us something about our own lives.

All fiction and poetry begin in metaphor. We sometimes forget this in fiction because the narrative, during the act of reading, tends to overshadow the metaphor, but the work still began as metaphor and if it remains important to us, it remains important as metaphor. Joyce's *Ulysses* began as a metaphor that stood for the author's relationship with some aspect of reality, a subjective reality. The same is true of Conrad's *Lord Jim* or Yeats's "The Second Coming" or Chekhov's "The Duel" and so on.

The act of inspiration is, I think, the sudden apprehension or grasping of metaphor. When we understand a metaphor, that understanding comes all in a flash. At one moment the mind is blank—it is merely questioning—and in the next there is knowledge. Look at these metaphors or aphorisms from W. S. Merwin's *Asian Figures*:

Thief
plans even his naps

Quiet as
a crane watching
a hole over water

Tree grows the way they want it to
that's the one they cut first

Don't curse your wife
at bedtime[3]

The move from ignorance to knowledge in these examples seems spontaneous. Actually what we do is imagine a past and future, and this provides a context in which to understand the single moment presented by the metaphorical aspect of the aphorism. A metaphor has an image (or an analog) and an object. Inspiration is the act of hitting upon something that will function as the image for a particular object. The act of writing most usually begins with this discovery. Even if what is discovered is no more than a sound or picture or word, the writer's attentiveness to it is caused by the fact that he or she sees it potentially functioning as metaphor.

We write in part to discover why we are writing. The work begins in the intuition, and, by writing and learning about what we have written, we carry that intuition toward consciousness.

A major idea of the Romantics was that the writer surrenders himself or herself to the writing process. The work must emerge from the whole of the writer's personality (possibly even from the outside), not just from the ego. The writer cannot force the work into existence. The writer must submit himself or herself to the metaphor in order to discover its meaning, not seek to dominate it. These ideas continue among us. But where they split into different theories is in the amount of conscious control that the writer asserts in the revision process.

On one side, it is felt that the writer should take no control, that to tamper with the intuition is to diminish it. "First word, best word," Allen Ginsberg has said. On the other side is the belief that the intuition provides only so much raw material, which the revision process shapes, much as a sculptor shapes his stone. Baudelaire mocked those writers who "make a parade of negligence, aiming at a masterpiece with their eyes shut, full of confidence in disorder, and expecting letters thrown up at the ceiling to fall down again as a poem on the floor."[4] He also wrote,

"Everything that is beautiful and noble is the product of reason and calculation."[5] Poetry has swung back and forth between these two positions since before Homer.

Personally, I feel that structure isn't intuited so much as chosen. That original inspiration gives us metaphor and may prioritize a series of images, but it doesn't show how to arrange the words. It simply gives information. The work can be structured only when the writer has a degree of understanding about his or her meaning and purpose, and that may require a lot of writing and revision. The writing itself is a process of discovery, the discovery of the meaning of the metaphor. But eventually the writer decides what he or she is about and at that time the work evolves into its final form.

In praising Edgar Allen Poe's control of the short story, Baudelaire wrote, "If the first sentence is not written with the preparation of the final impression in view, the work is a failure from the start. In the whole composition, not a single word must be allowed to slip in that is not loaded with intention, that does not tend, directly or indirectly, to complete the premeditated design."[6]

What Baudelaire was praising was structure. He was saying that each poem, story or novel has an optimum number of words, an optimum number of pieces of information, that their order must be determined by the writer's intention, and to go over or under even by one word weakens the whole. In fact, he argued that anything that does not contribute to the whole detracts from the whole. "There are no minutiae in matters of art," he wrote.[7]

It is often a weakness of beginning writers to see structure in terms of chronology: First this happened, then this. But the selection and organization of significant moments of time in no way requires one to be chronological. The first sentence has to be written, as Baudelaire points out, with the final impression in view. "Everything for the final impact!" he quoted Poe as saying.[8] Chekhov encouraged writers to take the story they had written, throw away the first half and start in the middle. He was urging writers to start with action, not background. But Chekhov's dictum had purpose other than just starting with something important. His purpose was to start with something that would actively engage the interest of the reader.

Interest is partly created by making the reader ask questions, by creating tension. Chekhov argued that if a pistol is introduced at the beginning of a story, it must be fired by the end of the story. The introduction of that pistol creates tension in the form of suspense. Reading is done partly with our memories: We know that pistols get fired and people get killed. Inevitably, the presence of the pistol affects our expectations.

Structure is nothing without creating in the reader a desire to know what is going to happen. Once that desire is created, then the reader's attention is driven forward by means of pacing, which is accomplished by creating patterns of tension and rest, by making the reader anticipate, then sometimes frustrating and sometimes rewarding that anticipation. The energy in a work—meaning whatever keeps us reading—comes in part from (1) the balance between what we know and what we don't know and (2) how well the writer has made us want to know. A failure in much writing, especially poetry, is that the writer has not created sufficient tension, has not done enough to make us want to know. If the writer takes the reader's interest for granted, then he or she will fail.

So far I have lumped fiction and poetry together, but here we come to a division. Fiction requires narrative: events moving from one moment in time to one or more other moments of time. It may even be a prerequisite of fiction that it have narrative. We go to fiction for the story and the writer creates the tension to make us read by creating suspense, by making us want to know what is going to happen. Once the suspense is created, the writer controls our attention by varying the mix of primary and secondary information. Primary information is "Bob shot Alice." Secondary information is "It was a sunny morning in the second week of June." Secondary information is completely necessary. It gives the setting, controls our sense of space and time, develops the characters and may present Idea, but it also stands in the way of what we want to know most: Is Bob going to get away with shooting Alice? This is a difficult balance. If there is too much secondary information, then we don't care what Bob did. If there is too little, then the situation is not plausible and we don't believe in Bob and Alice. Obviously other things also affect tension in fiction, but primarily it works by the writer making us want to know and then creating suspense by delaying our access to primary information.

In much poetry what is important is the lyric moment, a sort of fervent crescendo when the emotional world of the writer joins with the emotional world of the reader. The primary function of narrative in poetry is to set up these moments. We are more interested in these moments than we are in the story. Also, in a poem, there is not the same mix of primary and secondary information. And clearly, a poem need not have any narrative at all, or perhaps only the smallest degree of narrative, since an element of narrative exists whenever we have two moments of time. This diminishment or absence of narrative limits the role of suspense in poetry. Of course, some suspense may occur within whatever narrative exists and suspense may also be created by other means. When Philip Larkin titles his poem "The Explosion," he is creating suspense. But in poetry, what the writer uses most often to create tension is surprise. In fiction, because of its use of narrative, the main element of tension is suspense and the secondary element is surprise. In poetry, however, suspense tends to be secondary to surprise.

Both suspense and surprise affect our anticipation, and again I want to stress that we read on four levels of time. We read in the present, word by word. We read in the future, anticipating what will happen next. We read in the past, remembering at any moment what has already happened. And we read in the more distant past, through our knowledge and the books we have already read. But it is our anticipation and curiosity that keep us reading. Without that, we stop. The writer seeks to control the degree of our anticipation and curiosity through suspense and surprise. Both deal with the future. Suspense is a state of mental uncertainty. It means wanting some specific thing to happen or not happen. Surprise is the sudden occurrence of an unanticipated event that creates tension partly by shaking our faith in our anticipation and producing uncertainty. All good metaphor incorporates surprise. Here are three more of Merwin's *Asian Figures*.

> Sudden
> like a spear from a window
>
> His hundred days of sermons
> all gone in one fart
>
> Full of danger
> as an egg pyramid[9]

Our understanding in each case is sudden and unexpected. A good poem constantly uses surprise. Even originality is a form of surprise. A poem works by setting up various patterns that heighten the reader's anticipation. Rhyme and meter are the most obvious examples but there are also repeated words, half rhymes, alliteration and other more complicated patterns. Once a pattern has been established, then any variation creates surprise, while any unexpected rhyme or half rhyme or any aural echo can also become a surprise. And clearly, line breaks can create surprise, as well. Look at Philip Larkin's poem "The Explosion."

> On the day of the explosion
> Shadows pointed towards the pithead:
> In the sun the slagheap slept.
>
> Down the lane came men in pitboots
> Coughing oath-edged talk and pipe smoke,
> Shouldering off the freshened silence.

One chased after rabbits; lost them;
Came back with a nest of lark's eggs;
Showed them; lodged them in the grasses.

So they passed in beards and moleskins,
Fathers, brothers, nicknames, laughter,
Through the tall gates standing open.

At noon, there came a tremor; cows
Stopped chewing for a second; sun
Scarfed as in a heat-haze, dimmed.

The dead go on before us, they
Are sitting in God's house in comfort,
We shall see them face to face—

Plain as lettering in the chapels
It was said, and for a second
Wives saw men of the explosion

Larger than in life they managed—
Gold as on a coin, or walking
Somehow from the sun towards them,

One showing the eggs unbroken.[10]

Although there is suspense in the fact that we suspect an explosion is going to occur, Larkin greatly diminishes the actual explosion, reducing it to a tremor that makes the cows stop chewing for a second. What we have instead is the great surprise of the eggs: eggs that are transformed from a piece of secondary information to the primary metaphor of the poem, a metaphor that tells us something about the immortality of the soul.

Larkin surrounds this surprise with other surprises. For instance, the poem is written in trochaic tetrameter, and the use of the same meter as Longfellow's "Hiawatha" is itself a surprise. Through the first four stanzas the meter is regular and each line is end-stopped. In the fifth stanza, the stanza of the explosion, Larkin completely overthrows the meter and enjambs the lines, making a small metaphor for the explosion itself. The next stanza, from the prayerbook, also comes as a surprise, and again the meter is thrown over and the first line is enjambed. The first line of the seventh stanza reasserts the meter. The next line breaks it and the third line reasserts it. The first two lines of the last full stanza reassert the meter and then Larkin breaks it again in the last two lines, a metrical surprise to go with the surprise of the eggs, while the presence of the one line by itself also forms a surprise.

There are additional surprises. For instance, Larkin uses a series of spondees or double stresses in the first half of the poem: pithead, slagheap, pitboots, oath-edged, pipe-smoke, larks' eggs, moleskins, nicknames, tall gates, heat-haze. They are not placed in any particular pattern, yet after a bit we come to expect them, while their irregular appearance creates a surprise. He also uses alliteration to make small aural surprises, as in his use of the s'es and p's in the first two stanzas. Although there is no regular rhyme, there is a lot of irregular rhyme, such as coughing/shouldering, lost them/showed them/lodged them, brothers/laughter/tremor, standing/chewing. Each of these rhymes creates a small surprise. Some of this is simple texturing, but much of it directs our attention or underscores particularly important parts of the poem.

In terms of the arrangement of information, the first stanza establishes the context and the second stanza begins the action. We are given two different times: the time of the explosion and the time in church. In the first, there is a sort of stationary camera. Then the camera disappears in the prayer and reappears at the end. There are two kinds of language: that of the poem and that of the prayer. There are two realities: the events around the explosion and the vision of the women in the chapels. The shifts in time, language and levels of reality all create surprises, that is, they are unexpected. We have not anticipated them. These surprises leave us uncertain as to what lies ahead and set us up for the main surprise, which is the reappearance of the eggs.

These surprises build tension. Tension is also affected by line breaks. An enjambed line creates tension and an end-stopped line relaxes tension. Sentence length and syntax affect tension. Rhythm affects tension. Tone and pacing affect tension. Tension can also be increased and relaxed by moving back and forth between obscurity and clarity. The poet uses tension to drive the reader through the poem, to make the reader want to read and anticipate what is going to happen. Consequently, tension becomes a key element of structure, since if the poet has not made the reader want to read, the rest doesn't matter. Tension is the fuel that propels the reader through the landscape that the writer has created.

Fiction does it a little differently. First of all, far greater importance is given to narrative, character and conflict. Frank O'Connor once wrote: "There are three necessary elements to a story— exposition, development, and drama. Exposition we may illustrate as 'John Fortescue was a solicitor in the little town of X'; development as 'One day Mrs. Fortescue told him she was about to leave him for another man'; and drama as 'You will do nothing of the kind,' he said."[11]

In this definition suspense becomes part of drama: What will happen next? Exposition, development and drama form part of plot, which Aristotle called "the first principle, and, as it were, the soul of a tragedy."[12] Plot is the ordering of information, the arrangement of incidents within the narrative to create a pattern of causality. A *Handbook to Literature* defines it as a "planned series of interrelated actions progressing, because of the interplay of one force upon another, through a series of opposing forces to a climax and a denouement."[13] In fiction plot forms a major part of structure. It is not so necessary to poetry, since plot requires narrative and poetry need not have narrative. Also, as already indicated, narrative in poetry often works to set up certain lyric moments, not necessarily to move us toward a climax and denouement. But because the writer is always working against the reader's anticipation, the future has to be made uncertain, and the poet creates this uncertainty through surprise. Suspense is the foremost method of creating tension in fiction; surprise is the foremost method of creating tension in poetry.

Consider this tiny piece of fiction by Lon Otto called "A Very Short Story."

> A man is at a party with his former lover and her new husband. She is in one part of the room with her husband, talking with some old friends. He is a little way off, telling a story. And then he starts making a peculiar kittenish, rhythmical crying sound, then continues with his story.
>
> She and her husband do not look at each other. It is the sound she makes while making love. He does not pay any attention to them. The story is not about her; it is just that the woman in his story makes the same sound in bed as she makes. There is a certain tension in the room.[14]

William Trevor defined the short story as "the art of the glimpse,"[15] and that is what Otto has given us: a glimpse. Of course he is making a joke with his title, but he is also setting up certain expectations. The first sentence creates suspense by giving us a triangle. That suspense depends a great deal on our own life experience. We know that triangles are potentially dangerous. The second and third sentences give us the scene and the beginning of the action. The fourth sentence gives us a very detailed and strange action, the "peculiar kittenish, rhythmical crying sound." It is moderately surprising but what we mostly feel is curiosity.

Otto heightens this curiosity with the first sentence of the second paragraph: the fact that the husband and wife refuse to look at each other. The sentence delays us and we are also uncertain whether it is secondary or primary information. The next sentence identifies the peculiar sound. Then Otto seems to pull away from the triangle. The former lover apparently isn't aware of what he is doing, although he may be aware and this ambiguity itself creates tension. In the last sentence, Otto glides out of his story with his remark about tension, a tension that is obviously felt by the newly married couple: The husband is aware that his wife had been involved with the storyteller, the wife is aware of this awareness and perhaps, too, is struck by how completely she has gone out of her former lover's head, that she has become invisible to him, and perhaps the husband is also struck that his wife is someone who has become invisible to her ex-lover, that this woman he loves, his new wife, is ultimately very forgettable. Furthermore, there exists the possibility that the ex-lover has created this situation on purpose—to suggest that he has forgotten when he has not forgotten—and that perhaps he does this out of revenge.

We could expand the Otto story, flesh out the characters, give more action, but that wouldn't change the "glimpse" that is at the heart of the story. Otto leaves out nothing that is necessary to that glimpse, and he creates the tension right at the beginning that propels us toward it.

Structure, then, has two parts. It consists of the formal elements of language, texture, pacing and tone imposed upon the informal elements of action, emotion, setting and idea. And it also consists of the creation of tension to make the reader want to know what is going to happen: the making and controlling of anticipation. Both parts are governed by purpose, which means that the writer must discover his or her intention, must discover the meaning of the work. Only after that discovery can the work be properly structured, can the selection and organization of the significant moments of time take place. The writer must know what piece of information to put first and why, what to put second and why, so that the whole work is governed by intention.

It is this perfection of structure that allows the work to transcend its author, allows the work to be complete by itself. If the structure is imperfect, then the work remains tied to the writer and dependent on his or her psychology for completion and interpretation. But the work belongs to the reader. Its hidden subject is the life of the reader. It is through structure that the writer moves the work from his or her life to the reader's life, that the metaphor is moved from the quirky specificity of the writer's life to the greater universality of the reader's life. We write, finally, to be free of things, not to express ourselves; to become articulate, not to mumble to ourselves; to drive our feelings and vague ideas into consciousness and clarity. Structure is our primary means of achieving articulateness and consequently of communicating our discoveries.

4 | Notes on Free Verse

CONSIDER TWO SYSTEMS OF POETRY. In the first, the reader anticipates the rhythmic direction of the poem, finds his or her anticipation verified by the reading experience and feels a sense of gratification. In the second, the reader either can't anticipate or anticipates incorrectly, while being constantly surprised with unexpected patterns and repetitions. The first system, generally speaking, is the system of traditionally metered verse. The second is the system of free verse. The study of "the elements and structures involved in the rhythmic and dynamic aspects of speech" is called prosody.[1] Free verse employs a prosody governed by the unexpected.

Even before we read the first line of a poem we have begun to anticipate: the poem's shape on the page, its title, the length of its lines, whether those lines are of similar or dissimilar lengths, whether the poem has stanzas, whether those stanzas are of similar or dissimilar length—all act as information that allows us as readers to anticipate the nature of the reading experience. In the 1920s, I. A. Richards wrote:

> Rhythm and its specialized form meter, depend upon repetition, and expectancy. Equally where what is expected recurs and where it fails, all rhythmical and metrical effects spring from anticipation. . . . The mind after reading a line or two of verse, or half a sentence of prose, prepares itself ahead for any one of a number of possible sequences, at the same time negatively incapacitating itself for others. The effect produced by what actually follows depends very

closely upon this unconscious preparation and consists largely of the further twist which it gives to expectancy.[2]

Richards defined rhythm as "the texture of expectations, satisfactions, disappointments, surprisals, which the sequence of syllables brings about."[3] Ezra Pound said, "Rhythm is form cut into TIME, as a design is determined SPACE."[4] Charles O. Hartman defined rhythm in poetry as "the temporal distribution of the elements of language."[5] But rhythm also depends on repetition, and so we can expand these definitions with one taken from the *Princeton Encyclopedia of Poetry and Poetics*: "The rhythm of speech is a structure of ordered variation in the quantitative aspects of the flow of sound in which contrast is balanced by a cyclic recurrence of some identity."[6]

Meter, which is the ordering of syllables according to number and/or stress (or length as in quantitative meters), is one of many factors that influence rhythm. The *Princeton Encyclopedia* defines it as "a fixed schematization of the cyclically recurring identity in a rhythmic series,"[7] meaning that certain types of sounds repeat in a way that can be anticipated and that create a recognizable pattern. We have four types of meter: quantitative, syllabic, accentual and accentual-syllabic. It is not necessary for a poem to employ traditional meters, but it must have a rhythm; otherwise it moves into the province of prose. Why a poem requires rhythm is a much larger question. Most simply, it can be said that rhythm is a texturing of language, but it is also argued that rhythm imitates and echoes the rhythms of the heart and lungs, creating a physiological link between the reader and poem. For now let us define a poem as a rhythmically ordered noise of indeterminate duration; it is rhythmically sculptured sound. Furthermore, this aural quality directly influences the poem's meaning. The fact that the poem is a sound—that it is meant to be heard—gives rhythm an importance that it doesn't have in prose.

Meter influences the rhythmic dynamics of a poem. I. A. Richards wrote, "In metrical reading the narrowness and definiteness of expectancy, as much unconscious as ever in most cases, is greatly increased, reaching in some cases, if rime is used, almost exact precision. . . . With every beat of the meter a tide of anticipation in us turns and swings, setting up as it does so extraordinary extensive sympathetic reverberations."[8]

Although a skilled craftsman of metered verse will tease the reader's anticipation with metrical substitutions, enjambment and other devices to increase tension, a traditional sonnet still unwinds itself through its prescribed form. When we begin to read a sonnet, we anticipate that form and the moments of tension or uncertainty only heighten our expectation and pleasure.

A reader proceeds through a poem on many different levels. One of these levels is concerned with experiencing patterns of tension and release. A basic form of tension is the anxiety created in the reader when the writer apparently frustrates what the reader has anticipated to be the direction of the poem both in form and content: the higher the anxiety, the greater the tension. Tension can be created in many ways. One way is to establish a pattern and then seem to depart from it. Another is to delay or avoid natural points of rest—that is, places of punctuation or syntactical pauses—by enjambment or by frustrating the development of the sentence by holding back a particular part of speech: for instance, by delaying the subject, verb or direct object. Tension can also work to direct the reader's attention to particular parts of the poem by threatening to frustrate what he has begun to anticipate.

Even though "Leda and the Swan" is a sonnet unlike any other, its uniqueness heightens our appreciation of the form. We begin by anticipating certain patterns and essentially we turn out to be correct, even though Yeats has challenged our expectations and given them a rocky ride. But at the end, our correctness in anticipating the rhythmical direction of the poem is one of the pleasures we take from the reading experience.

Free verse or nonmetrical poetry works differently. Still, we are, as Robert Hass wrote, "pattern-discerning animals,"[9] and so we begin a free verse poem looking for and anticipating certain patterns and symmetries. In both metrical and free verse poetry, the poet manipulates the expectations of the reader. In much free verse, however, the poet consistently tries to keep the reader from correctly anticipating the direction of the poem. It is partly for this reason that "surprise" became a major tool of twentieth-century poetry.

To understand this we need to go beyond poetry to consider the society and how the society sees itself. The character of any historical period is reflected in its art, which is, in fact, a microcosm of that period. Consider these 12 lines from Pope's "Essay on Criticism":

> True ease in writing comes from art, not chance,
> As those move easiest who have learn'd to dance.
> 'Tis not enough no harshness gives offence,
> The sound must seem an Echo to the sense:
> Soft is the strain when Zephyr gently blows,
> And the smooth stream in smoother numbers flows;
> But when loud surges lash the sounding shore,
> The hoarse, rough verse should like the torrent roar:
> When Ajax strives some rock's vast weight to throw,
> The line too labours, and the words move slow;
> Not so, when swift Camilla scours the plain,
> Flies o'er th' unbending corn, and skims along the main.[10]

The controlled rhythms, the symmetrical form, the logical unfolding of the argument, even the calm and orderly syntax—all reflect Pope's definition of the cosmos: a definition that he shared with the social class and society to which he belonged. Here is a society that believes in a supreme being and the benevolent order of the universe; a society that believes that a person's life is guided by a clear set of principles and virtues. This is the Age of Reason and the major poetic unit of the period, the heroic couplet, is a microcosmic model of that age.

The twentieth century, on the other hand, has been typified by constant disruption and speed both in the physical and metaphysical aspect of people's lives. It has seen extreme violence, uncertainty and the disintegration of the class system. Instead of a clear system of values and a benevolent supreme being, we have a wide range of relative values and deep agnosticism. Indeed, the twentieth century, for all of its discoveries, could be called the Age of Unknowing.

As Pope's "Essay on Criticism" is, in form and content, a microcosm of the Age of Reason, so is Robert Creeley's "I Know a Man" a microcosm of our own age.

> As I sd to my
> friend, because I am
> always talking,—John I
>
> sd, which was not his
> name, the darkness sur-
> rounds us, what
>
> can we do against
> it, or else, shall we &
> why not, buy a goddamn big car,
>
> drive, he sd, for
> christ's sake, look
> out where yr going.[11]

Even though the shape of the poem—four three-line stanzas—presents a clear symmetry and sets up certain expectations, the poem progresses by frustrating those expectations, by surprising the reader with abrupt and unanticipated turns. Those surprises are not only in the form, with its violent enjambments and neo-spellings, they also occur within the content, where the hypothetical situation that is wished for in the third stanza, turns out already to exist in the fourth. Governing these surprises is the phrase "the darkness sur / rounds us," which suggests a condition responsible for both form and content.

Most eighteenth-century poetry reflected an ordered world. This was one of poetry's pleasures: the microcosm that the poem presented was reassuring. Perhaps one of the reasons poetry is less popular in the twentieth century is that as a microcosm it reflects the confusion of the age: a confusion that people find distressing. The end of William Carlos Williams's poem "To Elsie" from "Spring and All" typifies this uncertainty—"No one / to witness / and adjust, no one to drive the car."[12]

In his essay "Listening and Making," Robert Hass wrote,

> Every metrical poem announces a relationship to the idea of order at the outset, though the range of relationships to that idea it can suggest is immense. Free-verse poems do not commit themselves so soon to a particular order, but they are poems so they commit themselves to the idea of its possibility, and, as soon as recurrences begin to develop, an order begins to emerge. The difference is, in some ways huge; the metrical poem begins with an assumption of human life which takes place in a pattern of orderly recurrence with which the poet must come to terms, the free-verse poem with an assumption of openness of chaos in which an order must be discovered.[13]

A metrical poem creates an order that the poet may imagine as reflecting some greater order. The free verse poem is often set against the idea of disorder, the idea of darkness. Paul Fussell in *Poetic Meter and Poetic Form* argues that accentual syllabic meters are most popular during periods "committed to a sense of human limitation and order."[14] This is because the idea of order within accentual syllabic meters reflects the idea of order found within the society. We can expand Fussell's argument to say that the political and social beliefs of any poet are reflected in the form of his or her poems. In that a person's political beliefs are partly determined by psychology, the way a person writes not only reflects his or her politics and view of the world, but the writer's whole psychological makeup. The poem is not only a microcosm of the society in which it was written, it is a microcosm of the psychology of the poet.

The roots of the changes that influence twentieth-century free verse begin many centuries ago, but the use of surprise as a tool, although it is foreshadowed by Whitman, seems directly connected to the speed and change of the twentieth century itself. In his autobiography, *The Lost Grove*, Raphael Alberti tells how he and other Spanish poets of the 1920s learned much about poetic form and strategy from the "cinematographic speed" of American films, especially the slapstick films of Max Sennett.[15] But ten years before, in 1917, Apollinaire was describing how poets, whom he called "the sole dispensers of the true and the beautiful,"[16] were taking their place in the vanguard of scientists and inventors and that many of the inventions of the twentieth century had been foretold by poets. Hadn't it been a poet who had told the story of Icarus? he asked. Here was the airplane to prove him true. Apollinaire wrote: "The new spirit which will dominate the poetry of all the entire world has nowhere come to light as it has in France. . . . What is new exists without being progress. Everything is in the effect of surprise. The new spirit depends equally on surprise, on what is most vital and new in it. *Surprise is the greatest source of what is new.* It is by surprise, by the important position that has been given to surprise, that the new spirit distinguishes itself from all the literary and artistic movements which have preceded it."[17]

Apollinaire developed his idea of surprise both from his study of the cubist painters and from the poetry of Rimbaud. On one level it meant violent juxtapositions and nonlinear transitions. On another it meant the general effect of free verse, of not allowing the reader to anticipate correctly the rhythmic direction of the poem. Surprise for Apollinaire became a prosodic device. It kept the reader from ever resting or gaining his balance as he was sent tumbling down the page. The results of Apollinaire's thinking about surprise appeared in his first book, *Alcools*, which was published in 1912.

At the same time Apollinaire was developing surprise as a prosodic device, other poets were reaching similar conclusions. In

1913 in his essay "Morning of Acmeism" Osip Mandelstam wrote, "The capacity for astonishment is the poet's greatest virtue."[18] The same year in his essay entitled "On the Reader" he wrote, "The fresh air of poetry is the element of surprise."[19] The following year in "Remarks on Chenier," Mandelstam compared classic and romantic styles of poetry, concluding "Romantic poetics presupposes an out-burst, unexpectedness. . . . Romantic poetry affirms the poetics of the unexpected."[20]

Although Ezra Pound may have read Apollinaire, it is doubtful that he read Mandelstam. Yet, during these same years, 1912 to 1914, he, too, was developing a sense of poetry partly based on surprise and unexpectedness. From his dictum "Make it new" to even his definition that an image "presents an intellectual and emotional complex in an instant of time,"[21] Pound was constantly concerned with startling the reader. Even rhyme, he wrote, "must have in it some slight element of surprise if it is to give pleasure."[22] Metaphor, like image, depends on surprise. "Aristotle," wrote Pound, "will tell you that 'the apt use' of metaphor, being as it is, the swift perception of relationships, is the true hallmark of genius. . . . By 'apt use,' I should say it were well to understand, a swiftness, almost a violence, and certainly a vividness."[23]

However, the main way that Pound used surprise as a prosodic device was in his rejection of metered verse. By violating and finding alternatives to the iambic line, Pound ensured that the traditional pattern of anticipation-verification-reward would be set aside or at least challenged by this new system of anticipation and surprise.

In making similar statements about poetry in 1912, Apollinaire, Mandelstam and Pound were responding to weaknesses inherent in late Symbolist poetry, but they were also responding to the essential nature of the twentieth century. This is not to say that the twentieth century caused free verse, but it provided a climate that encouraged free verse to develop. Free verse could not have happened during the Age of Reason. It required a time of uncertainty and rapid change. Free verse also required certain changes in the use of metered verse, and to understand these changes we need to look briefly at its development. In his "Reflections on *Vers Libre*," T. S. Eliot wrote that "the decay of intricate formal patterns has nothing to do with the advent of vers libre."[24] In this we shall see that he was incorrect.

In the earliest poetry, meter had a function separate from content. Coleridge and others argue that meter was a mnemonic device that helped the speaker to memorize the content, which might not be poetry but history or the laws of the city. The Greek quantitative meters were sacred dance meters, according to Robert Graves, who wrote, "Greek verse-craft is linked to the ecstatic beat of feet around a rough stone altar, sacred to Dionysus (or Hermes, or Eros, or Zeus Cronidas), probably to the sound of the dactylic drum played by a priestess or priest. . . . A metrical line in Greek poetry represents the turn taken by a dancer around an altar or tomb, with a caesura marking the halfway point: the meter never varies until the dancers have dropped with fatigue."[25]

The English iambic foot, Graves claimed, derived from the Irish where the iamb imitated how the smith, a quasi-religious and magical figure, hammered the hot iron. As for the four-beat Anglo-Saxon line, it is "linked to the pull of the oar."[26] The Nordic poet had the job "of persuading a ship's crew to pull rhythmically and uncomplainingly on their oars against the rough waves of the North Sea, by singing them ballads in time to the beat. . . . Anglo-Saxon poetry is unrhymed because the noise of the row-locks does not suggest rhyme."[27]

Despite counterarguments to these theories, there are still two points to consider. First, meter had a clear function apart from content. Second, because of that function, there could be no variation within the meter. If meter is a mnemonic device, you cannot allow metrical substitutions. If 100 men are pulling their oars to a four-beat chant, you cannot insert a fifth beat without creating chaos.

The Norman invasion of England in 1066 and the imposition of the French language on the native Anglo-Saxon meant the eventual death of the Anglo-Saxon four-beat line. In his history of English prosody, George Saintsbury wrote, "The differences . . . of English verse of 1000 and English verse of 1300 are differences of nature and kind; the differences of English verse in 1300 and 1900 are mere differences of practice and accomplishment."[28]

French poetry of the year 1000 counted syllables; Anglo-Saxon poetry counted stresses. When Chaucer began to write in the late 1370s, he was well acquainted with the French decasyllabic line, and what he developed in English was the five-stress decasyllabic line. In the sixteenth century, the admiration for the Greek meters and the desire to legitimatize English meters led prosodists and poets to apply the Greek terms to the English metrical forms, and Chaucer's line became iambic pentameter. This has never been an entirely comfortable fit. The Greek quantitative meters measured long and short syllables—a long syllable being equal to two short syllables—and although English poets have attempted to write in quantitative verse, the accentual nature of English, plus a difference in the nature of the syllable, has made those attempts never fully successful.

It may have been this uncomfortable fit that led to the increased use of metrical substitutions just at a time when the French line was becoming increasingly rigid and defined. Another possibility is that the invention of the printing press made meter no longer important as an aid to memory. In any case, in the sixteenth century meter became less rigid. With this change came another: Meter was no longer thought to have a primary function apart from content. What developed instead was the theory that content chose meter, that certain meters were appropriate for certain subjects and that to write an elegy in dactylic hexameter, for instance, would be scandalous. This idea is important to the development of free verse. It ties form directly to content, and it allows form to be controlled by the needs of content. It can be argued that when the first metrical substitution was made, free verse became inevitable.

The seventeenth century saw further experiments with form and an increased subtlety with metrical variations. Poets found that metrical substitutions affected tension, created variety and made rhythm more intricate. Milton's use of irregular meters in the Chorus in "Samson Agonistes" is sometimes put forward as the first example of free verse in English, while his use of enjambment is cited as precedent for the violent enjambments found in twentieth-century poetry. The eighteenth century, however, brought a stop to this experimentation. Instead, it "advocated a rigid regularity."[29] Paul Fussell writes,

> This lust for regularity—"smoothness" the age was pleased to call it—seems to constitute one expression of the orderly and rationalistic impulses of the period. Although the best poets of the early eighteenth century . . . largely maintained the Renaissance tradition of expressive variation, even though they could not help responding to the regularistic climate, they carefully observed a uniformity in the number of syllables per line . . . and they generally rejected the enjambed line in favor of a strict line integrity.[30]

The reaction against this regularity began in mid-century as critics argued that the regular iambic line was becoming monotonous. "The arguments of these critics," writes Fussell, "issue from a new and revolutionary aesthetic, one favoring impulse, spontaneity, and surprise rather than the Augustan values of stability, predictability, and quietude."[31]

The emerging Romantic poets developed two theories that directly affect the future of free verse. The first was that the rigid forms and heightened diction of early eighteenth-century poetry formed a distortion of reality. Arguing that the object of poetry is truth, Wordsworth wrote, "The principal object . . . proposed in these poems was to choose incident, and situations from common life, and to relate or describe them throughout, as far as was possible in a selection of language really used by men."[32]

Wordsworth also attacked the idea that there is any *"essential* difference between the language of prose and metrical composition." "The poet," he wrote, "thinks and feels in the spirit of human passions. How, then, can his language differ in any material degree from that of all other men who feel vividly and see clearly?"[33]

Although Wordsworth didn't attack meter, he attacked its arbitrary use to help create what he calls *poetic diction*. A poet is a man speaking to men, and poetic diction interferes with the act of communication. In the twentieth century this idea has become a common argument against meter: that by distorting language, meter distorts the truth. This argument mostly occurs, however, when a special value is attached to verisimilitude. When it is claimed that a poem should be judged entirely on its own terms, this argument against traditional meters and heightened diction becomes rarer.

The second theory derived from the Romantic poets is that content determines form. In part this is a return to the idea that theme determines meter, which had fallen into disfavor in the early eighteenth century. The Romantics, however, expand the idea: They believe that content determines the very shape of the poem. As Keats wrote in a letter of February 27, 1818, "if Poetry comes not as naturally as the Leaves to a tree it had better not come at all."[34]

The most important argument for this theory was formulated by Coleridge in his essay "Shakespeare's Judgement Equal to His Genius," where he combated the charge that Shakespeare's apparent ignorance of classical form meant that his plays were formless.

> The true ground of the mistake lies in the confounding mechanical regularity with organic form. The form is mechanic, when on any given material we impress a pre-determined form, not necessarily arising out of the properties of the material; as when to a mass of wet clay we give whatever shape we wish it to retain when hardened. The organic form, on the other hand, is innate; it shapes, as it

develops, itself from within, and the fullness of its development is one and the same with the perfection of its outward form. Such as the life is, such is the form.[35]

Even though Coleridge may have been speaking specifically about Shakespeare, the term "organic form" has been used ever since to describe the way in which form can evolve out of content and how both can spring from the personality of the poet. The increased sensitivity to form among the Romantic poets led to many innovations besides simply rejecting the heroic couplet in favor of blank verse and a loosening of the iambic line. Most, however, existed on the stanzaic level: inventing new stanza forms or returning to stanza forms long out of use, such as those used by Spencer. Apart from some nonmetrical poems by William Blake, the possibility of giving up meters altogether was hardly considered.

To better understand the development of the idea of organic form, we should also look at it within the larger context of the American and French revolutions and the political thought of the period. Wordsworth was, for a time, quite excited by the French Revolution, and both Shelley and Byron were involved in the Greek war for independence. During the early eighteenth century, the heroic couplet was the form of choice, but the revolutionary ideas on the rights of man and what it meant to be an individual certainly worked against the doctrine of one approach for all poets. For that reason the idea of organic form perhaps derives as much from Thomas Paine as it does from Coleridge.

Ralph Waldo Emerson shared this enthusiasm for the idea of revolution, and he understood the political roots of the Romantic movement. In his essay "The Poet," he took Coleridge's idea of organic form and expanded upon it. For Emerson, however, poetry was not a matter of craft and idle invention. "For poetry was all written before time was, and whenever we are so finely organized that we can penetrate into that region where the air is music, we hear those primal warblings and attempt to write them down, but we lose ever and anon a word or a verse and substitute something of our own, and thus miswrite the poem. The men of more delicate ear write down these cadences more faithfully and these transcripts, though imperfect, become the songs of the nations."[36]

This idea puts Emerson in the same company as Plato and Robert Graves: that poetry is received, not constructed. Even Osip Mandelstam believed that the writing of a poem "involves the recollections of something that has never before been said."[37] This quasi-mystical approach to poetic composition is also at the root of many populist theories about poetry: the poet does not make or create poetry, he or she transmits it. Some find this absurd but we have to see that it connects to Coleridge's statement that organic form is innate. It is perhaps the dark side of the organic form theory. Even Pound may in part subscribe to this theory when he says "the poetic fact pre-exists."[38]

For Emerson, "the poet is the Namer or Language-maker." He is "a liberating god." The quality of the poem depended on the poet's purity and saintliness. "The sublime vision," he wrote, "comes to the pure and simple soul in a clean and chaste body."[39]

Even though the poet, for Emerson, was a semireligious figure, it was in his poems that all men find themselves. Therefore, he wrote, "the poet is representative. He stands among partial men for the complete man, and apprises us not of his wealth, but of the common wealth."[40] Because of this, the poet could not satisfy himself or herself with fixed and arbitrary forms; and here again one discovers the idea of organic form. "For it is not metres, but a metre-making argument that makes a poem,—a thought so passionate and alive that like the spirit of a plant or an animal it has an architecture of its own, and adorns nature with a new thing. The thought and the form are equal in the order of time, but in the order of genesis the thought is prior to the form."[41]

The poet's thought, wrote Emerson, was expressed "in a manner totally new. The expression is organic, or the new type which things themselves take when liberated."[42]

The form of the poem grew out of the vitality of its content; the argument makes the meter, instead of the meter being a predetermined form acting as a constraint on the content. Although Emerson was not suggesting that meter be abandoned, he was treating it with great liberty, as can be seen in his own poems "Threnody" and "Terminus."

Emerson closed his essay by claiming that America had yet to find its poet. "I look in vain for the poet whom I describe. . . . Our log-rolling, our stumps and their politics, our fisheries, our Negroes and Indians, our boasts and reputations, the wrath of rogues and the pusillanimity of honest men, the northern trade, the southern planting, the western clearing, Oregon and Texas are yet unsung. Yet America is a poem in our eyes; its ample geography dazzles the imagination, and it will not have to wait long for metres."[43]

When Emerson delivered his lecture "The Poet" at The New York Societal Library in Manhattan on March 5, 1842, Walt Whitman was in the audience. He was almost 23, and he wrote that the lecture was "one of the richest and most beautiful compositions, both for its matter and style, we have heard anywhere, at anytime."[44] Elsewhere he wrote, "I was simmering, simmering, simmering; Emerson brought me to a boil."[45]

It is edifying to compare Emerson's essay to the 1855 preface to Leaves of Grass. In the former, Emerson carefully describes the sort of poet America needs. In the latter, Whitman seems to have tailored his words to match those of Emerson. "The greatest poet hardly knows pettiness or triviality. If he breathes into any thing that was before thought small it dilates with the grandeur and life of the universe. He is a seer, he is individual, he is complete in himself. The others are as good as he, only he sees it and they do not. He is not one of the chorus. He does not stop for any regulation. He is the president of regulation."[46]

In his preface, Whitman also addressed the idea of organic form in a way reminiscent of Emerson and Keats. "The poetic quality is not marshalled in rhyme or uniformity. . . . The rhyme and uniformity of perfect poems shows the free growth of metrical laws and bud from them as unerringly and loosely as lilacs or roses on a bush, and take shapes as compact as the shapes of chestnuts and oranges and melons and pears, and shed the perfume impalpable to form."[47]

Whitman's explanation of his unmetered technique, according to Gay Allen Wilson, was that "the thought and the form must always exactly coincide."[48] With this Whitman became the first to use the idea of organic form as a reason for abandoning traditional meters.

In developing the form of his poems, Whitman was influenced by the rhythmical prose of such essayists as Emerson and Carlyle, but also by the oratory of preachers heard in his childhood, specifically the Quaker preacher Elias Hicks whose "powerful human magnetism" communicated "an unnameable something behind oratory, a fund within or atmosphere without, deeper than art, deeper even than proof."[49]

The form Whitman modified for his uses was the verset, which derives from the King James version of the Bible, specifically The Song of Songs, Psalms and Prophets. It is typified by the long line "corresponding roughly to one out-pouring of breath from full lungs."[50] Within the line can appear rhyme, assonance, alliteration, plus "anaphora and other types of repetition, rhetorical figures like antithesis and parallelism."[51]

What replaces the metrical rhythm of the line is cadence, a word defined in a variety of ways but which here means the symmetrical balancing of phrase units of similar length. Although the relationship between stressed and unstressed syllables is still important, cadence tries to replace the syllable with the phrase unit as the basic unit of poetry. The exact nature of that phrase unit will depend on the individual voice of each poet.

After Whitman the idea of cadence often appears as an explanation and rationalization for free verse. We find it among the French symbolists and in Pound's rule: "Compose in the sequence of the musical phrase, not in the sequence of a metronome."[52] We find it in Gertrude Stein and we find it William Carlos

Williams, where cadence becomes the basis for his theories concerning the variable foot. We also find it in Charles Olson's explanations about projective verse.

Other aspects of Whitman's poetry also became factors in twentieth-century free verse, such as his declamatory style and his rejection of the Romantic description of the poet as a melancholy outsider. Also influential was the enthusiasm with which Whitman anticipated the future and his insistence that the poetry of the future must "adapt itself to comprehend the size of the whole people . . . to the modern, the busy 19th century . . . with steamships, railroads, factories, electric telegraphs, cylinder presses"[53] and by so doing to take over as its subject areas that had previously belonged to prose. Whitman's enthusiasm and declamatory energy can be seen as influencing poets as diverse as Apollinaire, Carl Sandburg, William Carlos Williams, Charles Olson, Frank O'Hara and Gerald Stern.

Another point is that all of Whitman's lines are end-stopped. Instead of using enjambment to affect rhythm, he matches the cadence to the line.

In rejecting meter, however, Whitman is not opting for surprise. Even without meter, Whitman is attempting to create the same patterns of anticipation-verification-reward, but in place of meter, he uses cadence. Whitman believed that his rejection of metered verse had rendered it obsolete. He wrote: "In my opinion the time has arrived to essentially break down the barrier of form between prose and poetry. I say the latter is henceforth to win and maintain its character regardless of rhyme, and the measurement-rules of iambic, spondee, dactyl, etc., and that . . . the truest and greatest Poetry . . . can never again, in the English language, be expressed in arbitrary and rhyming metre. . . . The day of such conventional rhyme is ended."[54]

In England, Whitman's cause was taken up by Swinburne and William Rossetti, brother of the poets Christina and Dante Gabriel Rossetti. Apart from his own poetry, Swinburne was significant because of the poets he championed. Blake, for instance, had been completely forgotten since his death in 1827, and it was Swinburne's critical essay on him in 1868 (in which he compared Blake to Whitman) that brought him back to public attention. Baudelaire was another whose poetry and aesthetic theories Swinburne had publicized. Ranking Whitman with Victor Hugo, Swinburne became involved with Rossetti in publishing *Leaves of Grass* in England. English obscenity laws, however, didn't permit its complete publication and Rossetti was forced to select from the poems and do an expurgated version of the 1855 preface, all of which appeared in London in February 1868. Although Whitman had granted his permission, he called the selection a "horrible dismemberment of my book."[55]

Turgenev, then living in France, translated some of Whitman's poems into Russian. Other translations appeared in Germany and Scandinavia. But let us put aside Whitman for the moment in order to discuss free verse as it developed in France.

At the breakup of the Roman Empire, the Greek and Latin quantitative meters began to change and in the evolving Romance languages, what became important in the poetic line was the number of syllables with one clear accent falling at the end of the line and at least one more falling someplace within it. The accents or stresses in Romance languages are less pronounced than in the Germanic languages, and their placement was governed by strict rules of pronunciation. Furthermore, the polysyllabic nature of the Romance languages meant there were fewer accents than in the more monosyllabic Germanic languages. However, one of the reasons given by French free verse writers for the overthrow of the established line in the late nineteenth century was the need to recognize the importance of stressed syllables.

In France, the 12-syllable alexandrine emerged as the standard line in the sixteenth century, although it took its name from a twelfth-century poem by Lambert le Tort called *Roman d'Alexandre*, which concerned the adventures of Alexander the Great. Like other French meters, it became subject to strict rules. For instance, in the classical alexandrine, the sixth and twelfth syllables were stressed and the sixth syllable was followed by a caesura. The placement and/or number of other accents was allowed to fluctuate. The French Romantic poets altered the classical alexandrine with the use of enjambment and by introducing the *alexandrin ternaire* in which caesuras followed the fourth and eighth syllables.[56]

When Baudelaire began to write in the late 1830s, the alexandrine was the line he used. Essentially, he was a Romantic poet, although he appeared at a time of reaction against the extreme subjectivity of the French Romantics. His own model was Theophile Gautier, ten years his senior, whom we mostly remember as having coined the phrase translated as "art for art's sake." Although Baudelaire disliked the superficiality of the phrase, he believed that a work of art had to be judged solely on its own terms. He wrote:

> Poetry will be seen to have no other air but itself; it can have no other, and no poem will be as great, as noble, so worthy of the name "poem" as the one written for no purpose other than the pleasure of writing a poem. Let there be no misunderstanding: I do not mean to say that poetry does not ennoble manners—that its final result is not to raise man above the level of squalid interests; that would be clearly absurd. What I am saying is that, if the poet has pursued a moral aim, he will have diminished his poetic power; nor will it be incautious to bet that his work is bad.[57]

Perhaps Baudelaire's major influence and one of the reasons that modern poetry begins with him is that in his work the metaphor and image become primary carriers of information instead of basically serving an adjectival role, of modifying or giving examples of the stated subject. This use of metaphor generally evolved from three different sources: first, the use of symbol and allegory in painting; second, the theories of the utopian socialist Charles Fourier, who believed in what he termed "'the principle of analogy'; [that] the cosmos is built upon a series of analogous patterns; perception of those patterns means perception of its hidden ordering principle."[58] Consequently, metaphor in poetry, instead of simply modifying the object of the metaphor by saying that A is like B, is actually describing the fabric of the cosmos. This was also directly related to the ideas of Swedenborg, whom Baudelaire admired.

The third source of Baudelaire's use of metaphor was a combination of ideas deriving from Edgar Allan Poe and the schizophrenic poet Gerard de Nerval: that is, that the perceived world is a metaphor for the self, that what you tell about what you see reveals more about you than about the object you are ostensibly describing. This, too, connects with and modifies Fourier's system of analogous patterns.

In terms of the development of free verse, a major influence on Baudelaire was Poe, whom Baudelaire idealized as a soulmate, a fallen angel, a misunderstood aristocrat and pioneer of poetry who drank and deranged his senses not from weakness but in search of new images for his writing. Baudelaire called him "the best writer I know"[59] and learned English to translate his stories.

Baudelaire took ideas that he found in Poe's essays, such as "The Poetic Principle," and fashioned them into a new aesthetic. Rejecting the idea that the end of poetry is truth, he agreed with Poe that the end of poetry is beauty. Then he carried this further: "Rhythm is necessary to the development of the idea of beauty, which is the greatest and noblest aim of the poem. But the artifices of rhythm are an insurmountable obstacle to that detailed development of thoughts and expressions whose purpose is truth."[60]

Elsewhere he wrote: "Truth has nothing to do with song. The things which go to make the charm, the grace, the compelling nature of a song would rob truth of its authority and power."[61]

Baudelaire rejected Wordsworth's idea that a poet is a man speaking to men. Verisimilitude was not a goal of poetry. Nor did Baudelaire accept Emerson's theory that the poet transmits poetry from someplace in the ether. Poetry was made. However, the poet first approached that making, approached beauty and knowledge, through the imagination. Again he turned to Poe. "For Poe, the imagination was the queen of the faculties. . . . Imagination is a virtually divine faculty that apprehends immediately, by means lying outside philosophical methods, the intimate and secret relations of things, the correspondences and analogies."[62]

It was by imagination, not reason, that the cosmos was to be understood. The poet, by potentially having the greatest imagination, was potentially the wisest man. It was the exaggeration of this theory that led to the egoistic solipsism of the late French Symbolists. For Baudelaire, however, after this first act of imagining, of intuition, it was all hard labor. Still discussing Poe, he wrote:

> . . . having allotted the due share to the natural poet, to innateness, Poe goes on to apportion another to knowledge, hard work, analysis, a share that will appear exorbitant to the pride of the unscholarly . . . he subjected inspiration to the strictest method and analysis. . . . He dwells, with informed eloquence, on making means correspond with effects, on the use of rhyme, on perfecting the refrain, on adaption of rhythm to feeling. . . . Everything for final impact! he often repeats. Even a sonnet needs a plan, and construction, the framework, so to speak, is the most important surety of the mysterious life that informs the works of the spirit.[63]

Another idea that Baudelaire found in Poe was the rejection of the long poem, that the long poem was a contradiction in terms. A poem attempted to "excite and ravish the soul" of the reader, but since any such excitement can be only "fleeting and transitory," the length of the poem must be limited to match this experience. But neither can the poem be too short. "However brilliant and intense the effect, it will not last; the memory will not retain it; it is like a seal too lightly and hastily applied, which has not had the time to impress its image on the wax."[64]

The ideal length, wrote Baudelaire, was about 100 lines. The result was a highly crafted short poem that attempted to engage emotionally the reader, partly through rhythmic effects, and that had no didactic purpose. "Thus the poetic principle," he wrote, "is strictly and simply the human longing for a superior form of beauty."[65]

Although these ideas were first Poe's, it took Baudelaire to make them influential. Graham Hough wrote, "Baudelaire neither falsifies nor adds; he merely removes Poe's aesthetics from their journalistic context, ignores the sciolism and bravado and omits the limelight rhetoric."[66] Even the statement that the long poem is a contradiction in terms isn't as eccentric as it first seems. Hough argued that by rejecting the long poem, Poe ". . . foresees a change in the function of poetry that was really taking place. Its narrative and expository functions were to pass over to other forms, and poetry was to come nearer to a state of chemical purity than ever before."[67]

This prohibition against the long poem appears to be the single point of agreement between Poe and Walt Whitman. Although Whitman disliked Poe's poetry, arguing that Poe had "an incorrigible propensity for nocturnal themes," he claimed to have learned much from Poe's "The Poetic Principle," particularly ". . . that (at any rate for our occasion, our day) there can be no such thing as a long poem. The same thought had been haunting my mind before, but Poe's argument though short, work'd the sum out and proved it to me."[68]

The ideas that Baudelaire developed from Poe guided the writing of *Les Fleurs du Mal*, made up entirely of highly controlled formal poems. "Rhythm and rhyme," wrote Baudelaire in his introduction, "answer the immortal need in man for monotony, symmetry and surprise."[69]

But despite the formality of the poems, Baudelaire still used some rhythmic innovations. Specifically, he used what is known as *vers impair*, an impaired or damaged line, a line with an uneven number of syllables, so that among the alexandrines will sometimes occur an 11-syllable line. This may seem a trivial change, but considering the rigidity of the alexandrine line, *vers impair* was mildly innovative.

If Baudelaire had done no more than to modify Poe and write *Les Fleurs du Mal*, he still would have been a major influence on free verse. But toward the end of the 1850s his theories on beauty began to change. The values that had guided the first half of the nineteenth century, the classical values that defined men's actions, their culture and their religion, values that guided the painting of David and Delacroix: It seemed to Baudelaire that these were disappearing during the reign of Napoleon III. Instead, value was placed on expediency, fad, fashion and material reward. The moral and orderly world had grown hedonistic. The permanent gave way to the ephemeral. In explaining this, Baudelaire was forced to redefine his sense of beauty to include reasons why an artist's approach to beauty could drastically change from one period to another. "Beauty is made up, on one hand, of an element that is eternal and invariable . . . and, on the other, of a relative circumstantial element, which we may like to call . . . contemporaneity, fashion, morality, passion. Without this second element, which is like the amusing, teasing, appetite-whetting coating of the divine cake, the first element would be indigestible, tasteless, unadapted and inappropriate to human nature."[70]

In this same essay, "The Painter of Modern Life," he wrote, "Modernity is the transient, the fleeting, the contingent; it is one half of art, the other being the eternal and immovable."[71] As a result, artists must be entirely creatures of their times, must write in the idiom of their times and take their subjects from the world around them. "Woe betide the man who goes to antiquity for the study of anything other than ideal art, logic and general method! . . . Nearly all our originality comes from the stamp that time impresses upon our sensibility."[72]

The ostensible purpose of this essay was to celebrate Constantin Guys (1805-1892), a Dutch illustrator who had been a correspondent for the *Illustrated London News* during the Crimean War and whose illustrations of contemporary life appeared in newspapers all over Europe. Baudelaire wrote, "He is looking for that indefinable something we may be allowed to call modernity. . . . The aim for him is to extract from fashion the poetry that resides in its historical envelope, to distil the eternal from the transitory."[73]

Guys was not just an artist, he was "a man of the world," entirely at one with his time; "the painter of the fleeting moment" whose governing passion was a curiosity about the world around him. And Baudelaire quoted Guys as saying "Any man who is not weighed down with a sorrow so searching as to touch all his faculties, and who is bored in the midst of the crowd, is a fool! A fool! and I despise him."[74]

The arguments in "The Painter of Modern Life" cover many areas, but the important point is that Baudelaire used these same arguments to justify turning from formal poetry to the prose poem. Guys "had gone everywhere in quest of the ephemeral, the fleeting forms of beauty in the life of our day,"[75] in order to find subjects for his drawings, which were themselves ephemeral. Baudelaire came to see the prose poem as an equivalent form.

We might ask why Baudelaire didn't simply loosen his formal meters and develop his own version of free verse. But that might have suggested an espousal of realism, and Baudelaire still felt it wrong for art to aim at verisimilitude. Guys's sketches might be ephemeral but they were also highly stylized; Baudelaire's prose poems, in that they were carefully crafted quick pieces, resembled Guys's work.

Baudelaire began to write his prose poems in the late 1850s and began to publish them in the early 1860s under the general title of *Le Spleen de Paris* or *Petits Poemes en prose*. They finally appeared as a group in 1869, two years after his death.

The idea for the prose poems came to Baudelaire from reading the earlier prose poems of Aloysius Bertrand called *Gaspard de la Nuit*, published in 1842, but the results were quite his own. "From the beginning," he wrote, "I perceived that I was not only far

away from my mysterious model, but was, indeed, doing something . . . singularly different."[76]

Other influences were DeQuincey's *Confessions of an Opium
Eater*, which Baudelaire had translated, and the prose of Gerard de
Nerval.

Baudelaire wanted to make each prose poem "musical
without rhythm and without rhyme, supple enough and choppy
enough to fit the soul's lyrical movements, the undulations of
reverie, the jolts of consciousness."[77] He wrote, "The obsessive
ideal came to life above all by frequenting enormous cities, in the
intersection of their countless relationships."[78]

Here is Baudelaire's first prose poem, "The Stranger,"
(translated by Laure-Anne Bosselaar and myself):

> Who do you love best, enigmatic man? Say, your father,
> your mother, your sister or your brother?
> —I have no father, no mother, no sister, no brother.
> —Your friends?
> —You use a word the meaning of which remains unknown
> to me to this day.
> —Your fatherland?
> —I don't know in what latitude it lies.
> —Beauty?
> —I would gladly love her, goddess and immortal.
> —Gold?
> —I loathe it as you loathe God.
> —Hey! What do you love then, extraordinary stranger?
> —I love the clouds . . . the passing clouds . . . over there
> . . . over there . . . the marvelous clouds!

That attempt to capture the ephemeral, of there being
nothing to believe in but surfaces and appearances, of the values of an
earlier age having disappeared, the sense of being lost in a world
without worth—all of this, which is found in "The Painter of Modern
Life" and also in the prose poems, links Baudelaire to the twentieth

century. The *Petits Poemes en prose* are not only a prototype for subsequent prose poems, they are a step in the development of free verse. By stressing that form and craft were the poet's principal concern (after the imagination has done its work) and by rejecting the alexandrine, Baudelaire set in motion a series of ideas that lead directly to Pound.

PART TWO

In 1871, four years after the death of Baudelaire, the 16-year-old Arthur Rimbaud wrote to a friend: "Baudelaire is the first seer, king of poets, *a real God!* And yet he lived in too artistic a world, and the form so highly praised in him is trivial. Inventions of the unknown call for new forms."[79]

Rimbaud's youth, his rebellion, his perversity and ambition gave him little respect for literary precedents. In the space of three years, he moved from highly crafted alexandrines to the development of a new kind of prose poem and free verse. Then he stopped writing. Some poems were published, most were left in the keeping of the poet Paul Verlaine and were not published until the late 1880s, when most people assumed Rimbaud was dead and not trucking around Ethiopia trying to sell weapons.

In between the first regular poems and the prose poems, Rimbaud tried a variety of rhythmic innovations, using *vers impair* and developing with Paul Verlaine what came to be called *vers libére*, or liberated verse, which we will look at shortly. His typical prose poem, in the words of his biographer Enid Starkie, "is generally stripped of all its anecdotic narrative and even descriptive content and it becomes highly concentrated and short."[80] Rimbaud's prose poems seem to lack transitions, as if he had originally written them as longer narratives, then erased the connecting links. Starkie also points out that the form of Rimbaud's *Illuminations* resembles the manner in which Chinese poems were translated toward the end of the Second Empire—

those short isolated phrases—especially the versions made by Judith Gautier, the daughter of the Romantic poet.[81]

Here is Rimbaud's prose poem "Departure" in my translation.

Seen enough. The vision encountered itself in every air.
Had enough. Sounds of cities in evening, in sunlight and
    always.
Known enough. The pauses of life. —O! Sounds and
    Visions!
Departure into new affection and noise.

Among the *Illuminations* are two poems clearly written in free verse—"Marine" and "Mouvement." Both are short poems with end-stopped lines and are apparently the first free verse poems written in France. Even though they weren't published until 1886, their appearance, as we shall see, was influential.

A common question that arises concerning Rimbaud is whether he had read Whitman's poetry or not. Although there is some disagreement about this, it appears he had not. At least there are no references to it. On the other hand, he was in London in 1872, where he began the *Illuminations*, and might easily have seen the selection of Whitman's poems edited by Rossetti. But there is no influence of Whitman in the work, no sign that even if Rimbaud had read Whitman, it meant anything to him or that he had learned from it. In any case, by 1872, although he was only 18, Rimbaud was done learning about poetry.

Another element in Rimbaud worth noting is his juxtaposition of extremely sharp yet seemingly disparate and even contradictory descriptive phrases, of removing connecting links, stripping away any narrative to leave one stark image fixed next to another. In their preference for suggestion and for an indirect approach to their subject, both Rimbaud and Verlaine are strongly influenced by Baudelaire. But, writes Anna Balakian, "Whereas Verlaine seeks the infinite possibilities of the vague and the uncertainties of nuance, Rimbaud provides in his landscapes stark, concrete details—disconnected yet juxtaposed, so as to remain even more tantalizingly ambiguous than vague language. This is true even when he is conveying biographical experiences. . . . The sotto voce suggestiveness of Verlaine's images conveyed a sense of *intimacy*; the naked fragments communicated by Rimbaud were to give him an almost total *privacy* of meaning."[82]

Rimbaud swept into Paris in 1871, mocked and made enemies of most of the established poets, swept up Verlaine, who became his friend and lover, then fought with him and the relationship came to an end with Verlaine shooting Rimbaud in the wrist and spending two years in a Belgian jail. Rimbaud then rushed around Europe, tried to enlist in the American navy, joined the Dutch army and deserted, was expelled from Austria, worked as a foreman in a stone quarry on Cyprus, then went to Africa as a trader of coffee and guns in 1880.

If Verlaine has any claim to being a great poet, it is probably Rimbaud who should be thanked. The poetic innovations for which Verlaine is famous were begun under Rimbaud's tutelage. Although certainly gifted and intelligent, Verlaine was also self-indulgent and his rebellion at times seems to consist of his inability to resist temptation. In describing Verlaine, Arthur Symons wrote:

> Social rules are made by normal people for normal people, and the man of genius is fundamentally abnormal. It is the poet against society, society against the poet, a direct antagonism; the shock of which, however, it is often possible to avoid by a compromise. So much license is allowed on one side, so much liberty foregone on the other. The consequences are not always of the best, art being generally the loser. But there are certain natures to which compromise is impossible; and the nature of Verlaine was one of these natures.[83]

Symons, who knew Verlaine, was giving a definition of the poet now out of fashion. However, it is also a definition that

Verlaine himself embraced. Verlaine's importance to free verse was in the development of *vers libére*. This is a form that doesn't usually occur in English primarily because the rules governing English metrical verse were never as strict as those governing French verse. The closest in English would be simply loose blank verse. A poem in *vers libére* often begins by establishing the norm, for instance, an exact alexandrine line, then through *vers impair* and other methods the poet begins to vary the alexandrine. In the background, however, is always the regular line, while the actual line moves farther away, then closer, then farther away, creating tension by increasing and decreasing the distance from the norm.

T. S. Eliot was very fond of *vers libére* and uses it in "The Love Song of J. Alfred Prufrock." The iambics are established, then partly abandoned until they become almost as an echo in the background. Philip Larkin was another poet who used *vers libére*. Often he began a poem with an exact iambic line, then slowly departed from it, reestablished it, then departed from it again.

During the 1870s *vers libére* was considered quite radical, and Verlaine was often ridiculed for using it. From the late 1860s until the arrival of the Symbolists in the 1880s, French poetry was dominated by a group called the Parnassians who were led by the poet Leconte de Lisle. Their poetry was typified by extreme formalism and a complete rejection of personal themes, often taking their subjects instead from history or philosophy. The appearance of Symbolism in the late 1880s was as much a reaction against the Parnassians as it was an outgrowth of the work of Baudelaire, Rimbaud, Verlaine and Mallarmé. For the Parnassians, the artistic ideal was classical sculpture; for the Symbolists, it was music.

Rimbaud and Verlaine consistently attacked the Parnassians. P. Mansell Jones writes:

> Together the vagrant poets seem to have aimed at undermin-
> ing the prestige of the alexandrine. They increased the num-
> ber of verse-forms in use and revived lines of unequal numbers
> of syllables. They attacked the rhythmical unity of the classi-

cal verse and surpassed the Romantics in dislocating rhythms, practicing enjambment, ignoring the regular fall of the cae-sura. They simplified rhyme and tried assonance in its place. They broadened the rule of alternative masculine and femi-nine rhymes by admitting sequences of rhymes of the same sex, and they allowed rhyme between similar sounds spelt differently. All this tended to destroy the regularity of tradi-tional French verse and the type of music that went with it, and to impart mobility, fluidity and a new music of a more uncertain character.[84]

But Rimbaud stopped writing in 1873, and although Verlaine's first poems in *vers libére* appear in book form in 1874, the book was ignored. Verlaine, for all his experimentation, was no radical. As P. Mansell Jones remarked, Verlaine never forgot to count syllables. And when free verse began to appear in the late 1880s, Verlaine dismissed it, writing "It is not verse any more, it is prose, and sometimes it is only nonsense. And above all, it is not French. We are French, for God's sake!"[85]

But in addition to his use of *vers libére*, Verlaine influenced the development of free verse with his book *Les poetes maudits*, or *The Accursed Poets*, published in 1884. These were essays on such little-known poets as Rimbaud, Corbiere and Mallarmé, whom Verlaine saw as being forgotten and victimized because society feared their superior qualities. "Is it not true," he wrote, "that *now and forever* the sincere poet sees, feels, knows himself *accursed* by whatever system of self-interest is in power?"[86] By introducing a new generation of French writers to these generally unknown poets, Verlaine turned their attention away from the Parnassians and began them on a new path of rhythmic innovation.

Mallarmé's role in the development of free verse is less defined. Some of his early poems in the 1860s resemble Baudelaire's. In the 1870s he translated Edgar Allan Poe's poetry, which Baudelaire had called untranslatable. He maintained an avuncular relationship with the Symbolist writers of free verse in the 1880s and 1890s, saying that "whenever there is effort towards style, there is versification."[87] His own poems in *vers libére* are far less innovative than Verlaine's. Then in the 1890s he began to write prose poems, and in 1897 he published his last poem "Un Coup de des," which was the most ambitious free verse poem to appear in France.

Even though Mallarmé chose to work in regular forms, what he said about music and the nature of the word was often cited as precedent by the Symbolists who wrote in free verse. As Anna Balakian wrote in her book on Symbolism, Verlaine was Symbolism in practice and Mallarmé was Symbolism in theory.[88] And she quoted Mallarmé on symbol: "Where there is symbol, there is creation. . . . It is the perfect use of this mystery that constituates symbol: to evoke an object, little by little, in order to show a mood or, conversely to select an object and to extricate a mood from it, by means of a series of decodings."[89]

But Mallarmé was so private and idiosyncratic, so unwilling to be seen as part of any group, that his exact position is hard to calculate. Although he felt that free verse had a certain charm and potential, he was against abandoning the alexandrine altogether, arguing that it should remain the official line and be brought out on serious occasions like the national flag.

By 1886 Verlaine's *vers libére* had been accepted by the more radical poets as their "standard medium." "It represents," wrote Jones, "not a revolution in versification but what might be called the stage of penultimate dislocation."[90] The revolution itself was to begin during the summer of 1886, but before we discuss it, let's return briefly to Whitman.

The first attention given to Whitman's work in France were two reviews that appeared in 1872: one favorable, one unfavorable. He was seen as an especially American phenomenon and too peculiar to be considered important. The first large critical essay on Whitman in France appeared in 1884. The author, Leo Quesnel, found Whitman essentially untranslatable and "not enough of an artist to appeal to the French." *Leaves of Grass*, he argued, weren't poems but poetic prose.[91]

Two American poets, however, Stuart Merrill and Francis Viele-Griffin, had settled in Paris and knew Whitman's work. Viele-Griffin introduced *Leaves of Grass* to the young poet Jules Laforgue, who began to translate the poems around 1885.

Laforgue had been born in Montevideo in 1860 of French parents, was raised in France and from 1880 to 1886 he had been reader to the Empress Augusta in Berlin, reading her French newspapers and novels twice a day. He returned to Paris in 1886, married an English woman, lived in extreme poverty and died the following year of consumption. Arthur Symons wrote, "Laforgue died at twenty-seven: he had been a dying man all his life, and his work had the fatal evasiveness of those who shrink from remembering the one thing which they are unable to forget."[92] Pound, who according to T. S. Eliot, ignored Mallarmé and was uninterested in Baudelaire,[93] admired Laforgue immensely. Pound even compared him to Eliot, saying that Eliot was the best poet in England, France or America since the death of Laforgue.[94]

In a period with the sparse Parnassian poetry on one side and the lush musical poetry of Verlaine on the other, Laforgue cuts directly between with the clear, direct, occasionally colloquial language of common speech written in formal meters. Ironic, even cynical, sometimes comic, his intention was to "annotate his sensations as directly as possible."[95] He described himself as "bowing piously before the unconscious"[96] and wrote of "the inner Africa of our unconscious realm."[97]

But the unconscious mind of 1885 was not the carefully defined entity that it became under Freud. Laforgue took many of his ideas from Eduard von Hartman's book *Philosophy of the Unconscious*, published in 1868. Hartman had been a student of Schopenhauer's, and his definition of the unconscious derived from what Schopenhauer called the Will to Live. Hartman and Laforgue both subscribed to Schopenhaurer's pessimism: "that the totality of life's misfortune always outweighs any happiness that man can achieve, and that any pleasure he can experience is purely negative, since it consists solely in a temporary cessation of suffering."[98]

The Will or Will to Live created the illusion that man had a chance for happiness, but its function was simply the propagation of the race. The only way to free oneself from the will was "a total renunciation of the passions."[99] Hartman, in defining the unconscious, "identified it as the essential factor in the ceaseless and also futile proliferation of life . . . and was of the opinion that the human race, once convinced of the absurdity of existence, would renounce self-reproduction and continued survival of its own accord."[100]

These were popular beliefs among French writers of the 1880s and often led to the accusation of spiritual decadence. One of the most quoted lines from the period is from de Isle Adam's play *Axel's Castle,* where the hero, Axel, remarks, "As for living, our servants will do that for us."

Laforgue in particular often found his subject in Hartman's theories: "the absurdity of existence prolonged without reason . . . ; the illusoriness of love; the chaining of the individual to the will of the species; the superiority of the void into which humanity ought voluntarily to return."[101]

Devoid of rhetoric and decoration, written in the language of the moment, full of urban settings, the work of Laforgue seems almost contemporary. Arthur Symons wrote of him, "[t]he old cadences, the old eloquence, the ingenuous seriousness of poetry, are all banished, on a theory as self-denying as that which permitted Degas to dispense with recognizable beauty in his figures. Here, if ever, is modern verse, verse which dispenses with so many of the privileges of poetry, for an ideal quite its own."[102]

Arthur Symons's *The Symbolist Movement in Literature,* first published in 1899, remains important to us mostly because it was through this book that Yeats, Eliot, Pound and Wallace Stevens were first introduced to these new French writers, with the result that not only was the form of their poetry influenced by *vers libére* and French free verse, but their sense of metaphor, image and symbol was deeply affected by French examples. And although all four ended up disagreeing with Symons and went off in their own directions, their ideas about the Symbolists remained colored by Symons early writing on the subject.

Here is a prose poem by Laforgue, "Twilight," translated by William Jay Smith.

> Twilight . . . From houses I pass come the smell of cooking and the rattle of plates. People are preparing to dine and then go to bed or to the theater. . . . . Ah, too long have I hardened myself against tears; I can be a terrific coward now in the face of the stars! And all this without end, without end. Beaten-down horses drag their heavy carts along the streets—women wander by—gentlemen greet one another with polite smiles. . . . And the earth whirls on. Noon. One half of the earth lit by the sun, the other half black and spotted with fire, gas, resin, or candle flame. . . . In one place people are fighting, there are massacres; in another, there is an execution, in another, a robbery . . . Below, men are sleeping, dying . . . the black ribbons of funeral processions winding toward the yew trees . . . endless. And with all this on its back, how can the enormous earth go on hurtling through eternal space with the terrible rapidity of a lightning flash?[103]

Laforgue's first two books appeared in 1885 and 1886. Both were written in *vers libére*. In 1886 he began writing poems exclusively in free verse. The first were published in the magazine *La Vogue* on August 16, 1886. He wrote a dozen poems in free verse before his death in 1887, and all were rhymed. In 1885, he began translating Whitman, whom he read passionately for the last two years of his life. There is a certain irony that his own pessimism found such comfort in Whitman's optimism. Laforgue's translations of Whitman's "Inscriptions" appeared in *La Vogue* between June 28 and August 2, 1886.

Incidentally, the poet Stuart Merrill happened to be back in New York in 1887 and attended a lecture on Abraham Lincoln given by Walt Whitman in the Madison Square Theater on the twenty-second anniversary of the president's assassination. Afterward, Merrill gave Whitman Laforgue's translation of Whitman's "Children of Adam." According to Merrill, Whitman smiled and said, "I was sure a Frenchman would hit upon that part."[104]

In May 1886, Rimbaud's *Illuminations* began appearing in *La Vogue*. Rimbaud's poem "Marine" appeared in the May 29 issue and was the first publication of a free verse poem in France. Notice its similarity to later Imagist poetry. The translation is mine.

> Chariots of silver and of copper—
> Prows of steel and of silver—
> Batter the foam—
> Lift up the stumps of bramble.
> The currents of the earth,
> And the immense ruts of the ebb tide,
> Flow circularly toward the east,
> Toward the pillars of the forest,
> Toward the posts of the jetty,
> Whose angle is buffeted by whirlwinds of light.

Rimbaud's other free verse poem "Mouvement" appeared in the issue for June 21. On June 28, the editor of *La Vogue*, Gustave Kahn, began publishing his own free verse poems in the magazine. Later he claimed to be the inventor of free verse, and for the next 30 years he swore that he had been in no way influenced by the poems of Rimbaud.

The Greek poet Jean Moreas, who had settled in Paris and whose Symbolist Manifesto officially inaugurated the movement in September 1886, also began publishing free verse poems in *La Vogue*. He, too, at a later date, claimed to have invented free verse, adding that Kahn had refused to publish his free verse poems until after he had published his own.[105]

Although Kahn is remembered as a minor poet, it was through his energy and enthusiasm that many of the writers who saw themselves as Symbolists adopted free verse. In fact, if the Symbolists have any legacy it is not in their use of symbol, which under them became obscure and hermetic, but in their use and advocacy of free verse. Among the Symbolists the image stops being a carrier of information and becomes important for its own sake, becomes, in fact, decorative. It was primacy of the symbol over the whole of the poem that Pound, Apollinaire and Mandelstam were partly rejecting in 1912.

We tend to think of the Symbolists as Rimbaud, Verlaine and Mallarmé, but they were rather the precursors of Symbolism. Mallarmé, in 1891, refused any credit for beginning the movement, writing he was "an individualist and solitary man." Instead he pointed to Verlaine: "the father, the real father of the young is Verlaine, that magnificent Verlaine."[106]

Anna Balakian wrote:

> One could say that every poet of the 1880s, and right up to the 1920s, has tried his hand at being Verlaine. . . . Verlaine supplied the form, the vocabulary, the themes, the major symbols, the specific sources of animism in nature; he set the mood of ennui and bittersweet melancholy; he suggested the need for an air of mystery in the poetic setting. His great fault was his failure to supply depth beyond the obscurity. . . . He used "mourir" (to die) with a voluptuousness which makes one suspect that he did not feel the impact of the event, so much as the sound of the word.[107]

But Mallarmé's theories on the relationship of poetry to music also had a great influence on Kahn and the other Symbolists with the exception of Laforgue. Kahn himself traced the development of free verse from Baudelaire's *Petits Poemes en prose*, through the *vers libére* of Verlaine and the theories of Mallarmé to his own work, which, he said, "developed out of experiments in poetic prose"[108] during the late 1870s and sprang from a desire for a new music.

In his own poetry, Kahn rejected the line in favor of the stanza: "What is a verse [by which he meant a single line]? It is a simultaneous stop in the thought process. What is a stanza? It is the development by means of a sentence in verse form, of a completed point in the idea. What is a poem? It is the focusing, by means of the prismatic facets that the stanzas become, of the idea as a whole, which the poem wants to evoke. Free verse, instead of being, as in old verse, lines of prose cut up into regular rhymes, must be held together by the alliterations of vowels and related consonants."[109]

One of Kahn's main contributions, according to Remy de Gourmont, was to emphasize the syllable accent, to insist that in French poetry there was a clear difference between stressed and unstressed syllables and that those accents could no longer be ignored.[110] Distinguishing between rhythm and meter, Kahn argued that traditional meter was only one of many possibilities of rhythm. Then he continued with what became his most influential idea: "that the true poet's rhythms are always personal."[111] Poets must discover the source of their rhythm within themselves, which will be determined by their psychology and by their speech patterns. By rejecting the line in favor of the strophe or stanza, the poet is able to develop an absolutely personal rhythm. Arguing for his own version of organic form, Kahn wrote, "The importance of this technique . . . besides giving prominence to certain harmonies hitherto neglected, will be to enable every poet to realize his own type of verse, or rather an original strophe of his own, and to write an individual rhythm, instead of adopting a ready-made uniform which reduces him to being the pupil of some glorified predecessor or other."[112]

Let us list the various types of "new" verse to be found in France in the 1890s. First, there is the prose poem tradition deriving from Baudelaire. Second, there is Rimbaud's *Illuminations*. (The first edition of Rimbaud's poems appeared in 1891.) Third, there was the *vers libére* of Verlaine. Fourth, there was the work of Mallarmé. Fifth, there was the rich and musical free verse of Kahn and the Symbolists. One poet claimed that "language is scientifically music" and argued that they should not call themselves poets but "Instrumentalists."[113] Sixth, there was the free verse of Laforgue, written in the language of the day. Seventh, there were the translations of Whitman. Last, there were a variety of other translations, which, by being unrhymed and unmetered line-by-line versions, created examples of free verse that were influential much in the way that translations have been influential during the last 30 years, by showing at best a functional language that attempts not to call attention to itself.

There remains a final question about Whitman's influence. Although Whitman's poetry had appeared in French magazines, no complete translation of *Leaves of Grass* was published until 1909. The Americans who introduced him, Merrill and Viele-Griffin, never wrote like him or translated him. Kahn and his associates also wrote an entirely different kind of poetry. Still, there are times when Whitman sounds very much like a Symbolist. For instance, in a preface to the 1876 edition of *Leaves of Grass* Whitman wrote, "Poetic style, when address'd to the soul, is less definite form, outline, sculpture, and becomes vista, music, half-tint and even less than half-tints."[114] P. Mansell Jones dismisses Whitman's similarity to the Symbolists, writing

> On both sides of the Atlantic it seems to have been dis-
> tinctly realized that poetry was akin to music and that the
> essential power of each was to suggest. But such coinci-
> dences are of too general a nature to furnish of themselves
> anything definite in support of a literary influence. The
> effect they seem to imply is not that of Whitman's own
> experiments and ruminations so much as the pervasive
> influence of E. A. Poe. The question arises whether the
> French poets, on the one hand, and Whitman, on the other,
> were not more or less simultaneously attracted by the
> example and theories of Poe.[115]

Laforgue's poems come a little closer to Whitman's but the resemblance is hardly noticeable. Although he occasionally uses anaphora and repetition, neither Laforgue nor any of the French adapt Whitman's declamatory style. Nor did they share Whitman's optimism. Laforgue's translations were mostly ignored. Whitman was thought to be too idiosyncratic, too American.

Two other poets were clearly influenced by Whitman. The first was the mystic Maurice Maeterlinck, who began publishing Whitmanesque poems in 1888, but who in outlook and personality was completely different from Whitman. The second was Paul Claudel, who adopted the verset form but never credited Whitman and claimed to have invented the form himself. Although Whitman was an influential figure, writes Jones,". . . his importance for the French must not be fixed at too early a date. It would be safer to say that when the first *vers libres* were being written, the poets who knew Whitman, and they were few, were attracted mainly through the appeal made by his brusque originality to their pronounced taste for literary novelties."[116]

There is one final poem that, if you will, becomes the ninth French influence on modern free verse, and that is Mallarmé's last poem, "Un Coup de des," which appeared in the magazine *Cosmopolis* in Paris in May 1897, a year before Mallarmé's death. The title comes from the first phrase—"A Throw of the Dice Will Never Abolish Chance"—which is also the statement of its major theme: that is, a creative act can never triumph over death. Four themes appear in the poem, and a different typeface is used for each one. The line is completely destroyed and instead the words seem scattered across the page. Daisy Alden writes in her notes to her introduction, "Each page of the poem (there are twenty) forms an ideogram—an image of whiteness of sky and ocean, storm waves, crests, and troughs, male and female, wing and bird, sail and boat, the Dipper or Septentrion, etc. The four themes introduced by the title are equivalent to the four-phase movement of a symphony. That number, representing many phases of life and time—four divisions of a day, four seasons, four stages of total time, etc., is an important part of the pattern which unifies the poem."[117]

In his own notes for the poem, Mallarmé said that by placing the words about the page and by using the white space around them, he hoped the entire page would be seen at once. He is, in fact, trying to replace the line with the page. Mallarmé wrote, "Narrative . . . is avoided. Add that this unadorned use of thought with doubling back, goings on, runnings away, or the very portrayal of it, results for those who will read aloud, in a musical score. The different type faces between the principal motif, a secondary and adjacent ones, dictates their importance to oral delivery and the pitch on the page."[118]

The poem, Mallarmé wrote, attempts to merge both the prose poem and free verse, bringing them under the influence of "music heard in concert." Comparing his poem to a symphony, he wrote that in the future this genre he has invented will be appropriate for handling "subjects of pure and complex imagination and intellect." This in no way rejects or supplants "the ancient line of verse, to which I still pay my vows and attribute sovereignty of passion and dreams."[119]

Although Gustave Kahn claimed that Mallarmé had written the poem at Kahn's own instigation, "Un Coup de des" was in part a reaction against Kahn and the Symbolists and their extreme emphasis on music, which Mallarmé saw as decreasing the value of the word by placing exaggerated emphasis on musical effect. For Mallarmé this implied a lack of understanding of the relationship between poetry and music. Poetry for Mallarmé aimed at a purity, which meant liberating it "from all reference to the actual world."[120] Graham Hough wrote, "Mallarmé endeavors to make poetry a paradigm for an experience, without the actual content. He tries to give with the minutest delicacy, the structure of an experience without the actual experience; a structure that might be filled out, if we insist on filling it out, with many actual experiences. But the poem does not commit itself to any of them, or concern itself with them except in a minimal unavoidable way."[121]

Music can be imagined as a paradigm for experience, and this is what Mallarmé felt poetry should aspire to. But Kahn and the Symbolists were attempting to create music for its own sake, separate from experience, and by doing so they were ultimately rejecting the word. In disagreeing with them, Mallarmé wrote, ". . . it is not by means of the elemental sonorities of the brasses, the strings, the woodwinds—undeniably not—but from the individual (spoken) word at its apogee that Music must result, with plenitude and evidence, as the totality of the relationships that exist in all things."[122]

By being a paradigm for experience, the poem allows the reader to see the relationships between all things, but the reader's precise sense of those relationships depends on the precise use of the word. To make the word secondary to musical effects is to destroy the purpose of the poem.

"Un Coup de des" tried to present a paradigm for experience that joined poetry and music without succumbing to musical effects. Indeed, the words Mallarmé chose were particularly strident and "disturbingly ungainly in their sound."[123]

Anna Balakian wrote, "In this verbal calculation . . . the image or symbol has become vestigial; rather, the words chosen are now self-contained images, used not in logical relationships but as notes that form a chord in music. In a generalized way Mallarmé represents man's challenge of the void . . . whatever evocations we may personally have in reading or reciting the poem are purely private dimensions, unshared by others, even as no one can know how things look to other eyes than his own."[124]

"Un Coup de des" is one of the most extreme examples of organic form, of form and content being so joined that each becomes a metaphor for the other. It is also a supreme example of Mallarmé's idea that we can neither share nor take much interest in the specific experiences of our fellow human beings, that the role of a poem is not to relate such experiences but to relate the shape of them so that each reader can impose upon this shape, this paradigm, his or her own personal experiences.

"Un Coup de des" is clearly idiosyncratic and obscure. As a direct influence, it must have affected Apollinaire's *Calligrams* and e.e. cummings's experiments with typography. It is, however, more a poetic artifact than a living poem. It so precisely entwines form and content that its existence tends to force other poets to justify their own formal choices, instead of accepting a set form or giving little thought to what form a poem will take. Another result of "Un Coup de des" is that by being a direct attack on the lush music of the Symbolists, it stressed the importance of the single word as opposed to the accumulated music of many words.

With Mallarmé's "Un Coup de des," we have a ninth strand to influence the development of free verse. There are also more distant influences, such as the late poems of Holderlin written during his insanity as well as translations of Asian poetry, but the main influence is French. It must be understood, however, that the concept of free verse in France was not what it was in English. It meant no longer counting syllables. It meant rejecting the alexandrine, abolishing the medial caesura and rejecting heavy rhyme in favor of assonance and ignoring the division of rhyme into masculine and feminine. These are basically negative rules. Where it created a new poetry and influenced English free verse is more difficult to calculate.

But let us make another list. First of all, French *vers libre* helped foster a spirit of rebellion and an almost automatic questioning of established forms. Second, it laid great stress on the very question of form. Third, by emphasizing music, it led poets to seek new ways to be musical. Often this was no more than an attempt to replace an old system with a new one, but although such systems eventually failed, they still forced poets to experiment and seek out new methods. Fourth, by disrupting the old system of anticipation-verification-reward, *vers libre* prepared the way for surprise to become a major prosodic tool. Fifth, it drew new attention to the relationship between stressed and unstressed syllables. The fact that the accents were not entirely fixed in both French free verse and metrical verse made the French line more flowing and melodic. This created a model for English poets to envy. Even Yeats said in 1924, "We would seek out those wavering, meditative, organic rhythms which are the embodiment of the imagination."[125] Sixth, French *vers libre* often presented a system where rhythmical groups of words were made to correspond with syntactical groups. The effect of this use of cadence meant that nearly all the lines were end-stopped. Even Pound copies his French models. Most of his earlier poems proceed down the page by balancing phrases of similar length. The use of the line break as a rhythmical device, as we shall see, was an American development. Last, French *vers libre*, gave a slightly different emphasis to the idea of organic form, that the true poet's rhythms are always personal.

In criticizing the Symbolists and their use of *vers libre*, Remy de Gourmont said that the inventor of a tool is usually not the one who uses it on a masterpiece.[126] The best Symbolist poet is probably Laforgue and his work never had the chance to develop. None of the actual Symbolists ever equaled their teachers. The first great French poet to use free verse was Apollinaire, and the first great free verse poem in France was Apollinaire's "Zone," published 26 years after the appearance of the first free verse poems in *La Vogue* in the summer of 1886. What is particularly striking about Apollinaire's free verse is that he makes use of and synthesizes all the strands, even *vers libéré* and the prose poem. What also seems striking is that he rarely used enjambment. A third point about Apollinaire is that he rejected the voice of Verlaine, which had dominated French poetry and even his own earlier poems, and turned to the methods of Rimbaud: the abrupt juxtaposition of sharp but seemingly disparate details. And from Apollinaire forward, Rimbaud becomes a guiding force, not only in the poets who espouse surrealism and Dada but in seemingly realistic poets such as Jean Follain. A fourth point is that Apollinaire clearly knew the work of Whitman, and his "Poème lu au mariage d'André Salmon," published in 1909, the same year that a complete edition of *Leaves of Grass* appeared in French, shows an obvious Whitman influence in his rhythms and repetitions.

The influence of the French Symbolists on English poetry toward the end of the nineteenth century was primarily in the areas of subject matter and aesthetic theory. Free verse hadn't caught on. It should be noted, however, that the iambic line under Browning and others had become progressively looser and what was being published in the 1890s was often a kind of *vers libère*. After the appearance of Symon's *The Symbolist Movement in Literature*, a more serious attention came to be focused on the Symbolists and pre-Symbolists, if that term may be used to describe Baudelaire, Verlaine, Rimbaud and Mallarmé. In describing the aims of Symbolism, Symons wrote, "It is all an attempt to spiritualize, to evade the old bondage of rhetoric, the old bondage of exteriority. Description is banished that beautiful things may be evoked, magically; the regular beat of verse is broken in order that words might take flight, upon subtler wings."[127]

At worst, this resulted in a vague musical poetry in which words were heaped up for effect. At best, it introduced Yeats, Eliot, Pound and Stevens to a kind of thought and attention in writing that stayed with them all of their lives. Still, the regular beat of verse was slow to be broken, and at the beginning of the century the vast number of poets writing in English were using traditional meters.

In 1908, however, T. E. Hulme published an essay on modern poetry in which he discussed Gustave Kahn. Claiming that Kahn was the inventor of free verse, Hulme argued that its use indicated "the desire for greater individual expressiveness and spontaneity."[128] He went on then to paraphrase Mallarmé on the function of metered verse and free verse. Describing Hulme's approach, Graham Hough wrote, "He equates traditional verse with passion for permanence, eternity, and absolute beauty; and free verse with what he describes as the modern search for the fluid, and for the maximum of individual and personal expression. Fixed forms are suited to the themes of the older poetry—heroic action for example; modern poetry, according to Hulme, is small-scale and intimate."[129]

These small-scale, intimate, musical free verse poems that Hulme was looking for led him directly to Imagism and constitute part of his influence on Pound. But at the turn of the century, Hulme is just one of many English poets who were expressing the need "for a new musical articulation of verse."[130]

It is within this activity that we have to look at Pound's Imagist manifesto of 1912. Pound knew the current French writers, as did Amy Lowell and Hulme. On the other hand, Pound's sense of clarity and the flexibility of language was also influenced by Yeats and Ford Madox Ford. It was Ford who insisted that poetry should be as well written and as clearly written as good prose. One more item influencing Pound needs to be glanced at before we discuss his work.

In 1910, a small book on free verse called *Notes sur la technique poetique* was published in Paris by the poets Georges Duhamel and Charles Vildrac. For them free verse drew its strength and rhythm from the syntactical manipulation of phrases, which they divide into three types—the rhythmic constant, rhythmic balance and rhythmic symmetry. The use of the rhythmic constant entails the placement of different phrases of the same number of syllables throughout the poem. Their effect on the reader is like a refrain. Rhythmic symmetry could be the use of parallelism. "Rhythmic balance is not determined solely by the number of syllables"[131] but is created by syntax, grammatical forms and vocal rests. "Syntax and vocal rests are of great assistance in these matters. Words of the same type, their syntactical quality, determine the balance of the phrase, giving to certain corresponding phrases the color value of adjectives, the weight of nouns or the driving energy of a verb."[132]

Duhamel and Vildrac set down their ideas in a series of short phrases: "Today, the people who defend regular versification with the dogmatism and yapping intolerance of a Dorchian are blind men or imbeciles. . . ."

"The old-fashioned rhythms over-emphasize such matters. Now we are able to dance without heavy boots, we're able to sing without the metronome."[133]

Both Amy Lowell and Pound admired the poetry of Duhamel and Vildrac. Pound's 1912 essay "A Few Don'ts" was clearly influenced in style and content by *Notes sur la technique poetique*, which Pound urged the reader to study for further elucidation of his subject. This is not to negate Pound's role in developing American free verse but to suggest that he must be seen within the context of the period. Many of his rules, for instance, deal specifically with types of writing to be found at the turn of the century. Let's look at some.

"Direct treatment of the 'thing' whether subjective or objective."[134] Here Pound was reacting to the indirect approach favored by the Symbolists, who argued that you do not show the thing but show the effect of the thing. Notice that even Pound's method of presenting these rules—short, direct phrases—resembles Duhamel and Vildrac.

"To use absolutely no word that does not contribute to the presentation."[135] This was a reaction to the Symbolists' tendency to pile up words for musical effect, to use language not to communicate but as an end in itself. Actually Pound is responding to the lush language of the Symbolists in the same way the Symbolists responded to the sparse language of the Parnassians. "As regarding rhythm: to compose in the sequence of one musical phrase, not in the sequence of the metronome."[136]

Besides seeming to combine Mallarmé and the words of Duhamel and Vildrac, Pound was making a statement that had been repeated in France for 26 years and echoes the first stanza of Verlaine's poem "Art poetique," which in my translation reads:

> Music before everything else,
> Prefer the uneven verse *l'Impair*
> Vaguer and more fluid than air
> With no ponderousness or pretence.

As for image, Pound wrote, "An 'Image' is that which presents an intellectual and emotional complex in an instant of time."[137]

By "complex" Pound would seem to mean a momentary joining of intellectual and emotional elements perhaps through the use of sense data or physical description, as in his little poem "In a Station of the Metro":

> The apparition of these faces in the crowd;
> Petals on a wet, black bough.[138]

In the introduction to *The Symbolist Movement in Literature*, Symons takes his main definition of symbol from Thomas Carlyle, who wrote that the symbol was the distinct and direct embodiment of revelation of the infinite and finite, or, in other words, a symbol presents the finite and infinite in an instant of time.

Although these are not Pound's words, they come pretty close. Graham Hough has written, "With Pound and his school, the symbol is disenchanted and called an image. It is then supposed to be efficacious simply by its own configuration."[139]

Hough was specifically referring to the paragraph where Pound wrote, "Don't use an expression as 'dim lands *of peace.*' It dulls the image. It mixes an abstraction with the concrete. It comes from the writer's not realizing that the natural object is always the *adequate* symbol."[140]

The words "of peace" are unnecessary since the image within its context should be sufficient to convey peacefulness. For the late Symbolists, the use of symbols became a kind of code where nearly every object had its specific symbolic referent. But this is not how the symbol was used by Rimbaud, Laforgue or even Verlaine; and Pound is partly demanding a return to that earlier method, while also demanding that the symbol be cleansed of its patina of Swedenborgian mysticism. This reaction to a codified symbolism was very common in Europe at this time. It appears in Apollinaire and it appears in Mandelstam, who wrote in 1912, "Let's take for example a rose and the sun, a dove and a girl. To the Symbolists, none of these images is interesting in itself: the rose is a likeness of the sun, the sun is a likeness of the rose, a dove—of a girl, and a girl—of a dove. Images are gutted like scarecrows and packed with foreign content. . . . Acmeism arose out of a sense of repulsion: 'Down with Symbolism! Long live the living Rose!'"[141] At this same time, Pound was writing, "A hawk is a hawk."[142]

Pound's emphasis on craft also echoed the French, and in this he is rejecting many of the English poets of the 1890s for whom the poem was something that the poet experienced, rather like a bolt of lightning. Actually, Pound's sense of craft reminds one of Baudelaire, although in 1912 he had no interest in Baudelaire. For instance, on one hand, we have Baudelaire discussing how Poe redoubled "the pleasure of rhyme by adding a new element to it, strangeness, which is like the indispensable condiment of all beauty,"[143] while on the other, we have Pound writing "a rhyme must have some slight element of surprise if it is to give pleasure." Pound also echoed Baudelaire when he wrote, 'The touchstone of art is its precision."

And Pound echoed the French when he discussed rhythm. "Don't chop your stuff into separate *iambs*. Don't make each line stop dead at the end, and then begin every next line with a heave. Let the beginning of the next line catch the rise of the rhythm wave, unless you want a definite longish pause."[144]

Here Pound was discussing cadence, while attempting to adapt Duhamel and Vildrac's ideas concerning the rhythmic constant, rhythmic balance and rhythmic symmetry. Pound went on to write, "Naturally, your rhythmic structure should not destroy the shape of your words, or their natural sound, or their meaning."[145]

In the Credo part of his essay, Pound wrote, "I believe in an 'absolute rhythm,' a rhythm, that is, in poetry which corresponds exactly to the emotion or shade of emotion to be expressed. A man's rhythm must be interpretive, it will be, therefore, in the end, his own, uncounterfeiting, uncounterfeitable."[146]

This is Kahn's idea of organic form as it was picked up by T. E. Hulme: that the true poet's rhythms are always personal, that every poet has a rhythm of his or her own. Pound then continued with a remark that easily could have been made by Mallarmé: "I believe in technique as a test of man's sincerity." Then he paraphrased Keats: "I think . . . that some poems may have form as a tree has form." Then he paraphrased Mallarmé again: "I think . . . that most symmetrical forms have certain uses. That a vast number of subjects cannot be precisely, and therefore not properly, rendered in symmetrical forms."[147]

In another essay, Pound combined these ideas when he wrote, "The emotion and concomitant emotions of this 'Intellectual and Emotional Complex,' must be in harmony, they must form an organism; they must be an oak sprung from an acorn."[148]

And here is one final paragraph where Pound combined and paraphrased several ideas already mentioned. "I think one should write vers libre only when one 'must', that is to say, only when the 'thing' builds up a rhythm more beautiful than that of set metres, or more real, more a part of the emotion of the 'thing', more germane, intimate interpretive than the measure of regular accentual verse; a rhythm which discontents one with set iambic or anapestic."[149]

In Pound's Imagism the form of a poem is a metaphor for its content. To force the poem into some formal arrangement of words is to violate that metaphor. It is by apprehending that metaphor that the reader partly understands the poem. This idea develops further when Pound became involved with Chinese poetry. In any case, such theories are an outgrowth of the belief that content determines form and of the theories of organic form then current in England, France and the United States.

One could continue through Pound's essays showing how he was influenced by other writers, but this should be enough to indicate his place in the stream, as Mallarmé was a place in the stream, as were Rimbaud, Baudelaire, Whitman, Coleridge or any other writer. Literature is a process with one writer leading to and influencing another. To see Pound outside of his historical context stops the process, damns up the flow.

Imagism was a small, short-lived movement. Even before Pound was writing "A Few Don'ts," Gertrude Stein was writing *Tender Buttons*, which in its use of the paragraph as the rhythmic unit was influenced by Gustave Kahn. Discussing that time, Stein wrote, "I remember . . . looking at anything until something that was not the name of that thing but was in a way that actual thing would come to be written. Naturally, and one may say that is what made Walt Whitman naturally, that made the change in the form of poetry, that we who had known the names so long did not get a thrill from just knowing them. . . . This that I have just described, the creating it without naming it, was what broke the rigid form of the noun the simple noun poetry which now was broken."[150]

Stein was looking for a new way to make language fresh again, as were other writers. It was shortly after writing "A Few Don'ts" that Pound was introduced to the Chinese use of image, which altered his own use of image and language. But by then other poets were writing who were to become more influential. For all his radical talk about rhythm and image, during this second decade of the century Pound was still conservative in matters of diction and enjambment. His use of end-stopped lines, archaic diction and the second-person familiar form separated him from other American writers who wrote in a contemporary idiom and were beginning to use enjambment to create tension in a free verse line.

William Carlos Williams's first poems had combined Keats and Whitman, but under Pound's tutelage he became interested in free verse. Consider "To Mark Anthony in Heaven," written in 1912.

> This quiet morning light
> reflected, how many times
> from grass and trees and clouds
> enters my north room
> touching the walls with
> grass and clouds and trees.
> Anthony,
> trees and grass and clouds.

Why did you follow
that beloved body
with your ships at Actium?
I hope it was because
you knew her inch by inch
from slanting feet upward
to the roots of her hair
and down again and that
you saw her
above the battle's fury—
clouds and trees and grass—

For then you are
listening in heaven.

The diction remains contemporary and the enjambment, especially in lines 5, 12 and 16, seems new. Although Williams is almost the first to use the line break to create tension in free verse, the development of the line break at this time was also influenced by Marianne Moore, whose use of syllabic verse led her to break the lines after articles, prepositions, all parts of speech.

Because of the accentual nature of English, the syllabic poem as used by Moore is basically free verse placed under the arbitrary pressure of number. The syllabic system, as she used it, is neither noticeable when we read the poem nor when we hear it read out loud. At times it creates a visual effect. The actual effect was on Moore herself, who used this number system to discipline her free verse.

The third poet who influenced our contemporary use of line breaks was e.e. cummings, who manipulated line breaks to create a kind of syncopation, a rhythm of line breaks to replace the missing meter. These three—Williams, Moore and cummings—developed the line break as it is known today, and in that respect they were as influential as Pound in determining the course of contemporary poetry. Even though they didn't always honor the ends of their lines as artificial pauses within the movement of the sentence, it was their use of enjambment that led to the pause that for over 50 years we have understood to exist at the end of a poetic line.

Actually it was Pound and his Cantos, as well as Eliot, who, for a time, brought a stop to the development and dammed up the stream. This is why Williams hated Eliot. Williams wrote, "*The Waste Land* . . . wiped out our world as if an atom bomb had been dropped upon it. . . . Critically Eliot returned us to the classroom just at the moment when I felt we were on the point of an escape to matters much closer to the essence of a new art form itself. . . . I had to watch him carry my world off with him, the fool, to the enemy."[151]

After 1920, free verse developed in too many ways to enumerate, but the dominating idea was that the true poet's rhythms were personal. The various theories that emerged, such as Williams's variable foot and Olson's projective verse, were attempts by poets to define their personal rhythms and turn them into prosodies for all poets. This could not happen. Their effect, however, was to keep poets defining their craft.

In his *Autobiography*, Williams attempts to explain the change in poetry that occurred around 1912. Vaguely, he ties it to the Armory Show, where the public discovered the role of surprise in the new painting and aesthetics. He wrote, "There had been a break somewhere, we were streaming through, each thinking his own thoughts, driving his own designs toward his self's objectives. Whether the Armory Show in painting did it or whether that was also no more than a facet—the poetic line, the way the image was to lie on the page was our immediate concern. . . . I was tremendously stirred."[152]

This returns us to our beginning: that along with the discoveries of specific poets, changes in poetic form are linked to events in the world. At the turn of the century everything was ready for the appearance of free verse. But it needed something else. The very nature of the twentieth century with its constant rush and uncertainty had to declare itself. Whatever happened, 1912 seemed the important year. As Williams said, "There had been a break somewhere, we were streaming through."

PART THREE

Free verse, since its first appearance in France in 1886 and through much of the twentieth century, has often been seen as a form falling midway between metered verse and prose, able to dip into either yet inferior to both. Most usually it is defined negatively, as being not metered verse, not prose, as having lines of irregular length, as being without rhyme. Charles O. Hartman, in his book *Free Verse*, writes that "the prosody of free verse is rhythmic organization by other than numerical modes."[153]

Let us define some governing characteristics of free verse that show it as a form in its own right. As indicated earlier, free verse rejects the old system of anticipation-verification-reward for a system of anticipation and surprise. Certainly the degree of surprise varies with each free verse poem, but because there is often an attempt to thwart the anticipation of the reader, surprise has been called the main prosodic tool of free verse. So far we have discussed the background of free verse and how it was encouraged by the social and political life of the turn of the century. Abrupt change, a flood of information, immense energy—these remain common in the 1990s. Free verse still reflects our times, although we have lost the sense of promise and enthusiasm found early in the century. On the other hand, the popularity of metered verse in the 1940s and 1980s perhaps bears out Paul Fussell's claim that metered verse is more popular during politically conservative periods.

Two other aspects of free verse need to be stressed before continuing. First of all, free verse develops out of the idea of organic form—that the true poet's rhythms are always personal—an idea that we have seen evolve from Coleridge, through Whitman and the French Symbolists and wind up as Pound's idea of absolute rhythm. The extreme effect is to make a different prosody for every poet, which is what formalist critics dislike. It keeps free verse from being sufficiently accountable; it makes free verse impossible to categorize and codify. Indeed, this apparent lack of accountability is a common complaint against free verse.

The second important aspect of free verse is that through its diction and syntax, it often aims for verisimilitude. Although clearly artificial speech, it attempts to capture the realism and apparent spontaneity of natural speech. One of the criticisms that advocates of free verse make against metered verse is that stylized language is a distortion of reality. Remember that Baudelaire wrote that "the artifices of rhythm are an insurmountable obstacle to that detailed development of thoughts and expressions whose purpose is truth."[154] He was attempting to prove that the end of poetry was not truth but beauty. But later we find those values reversed; perhaps this was partly due to the nature of the society. Whitman and Apollinaire found the world so exciting that they wanted to chart it inch by inch. Baudelaire found the world so ugly that he wanted to set something else in its place. In any case, in free verse we often find Baudelaire's argument turned against metered verse: that the artificiality of metered verse makes it seem false.

Having touched upon these two issues, let us also set aside *vers libére*. For Eliot there are only two ways to approach free verse—by starting with a regular meter and moving away from it or by starting without meter and moving toward one. As Graham Hough points out, this is not the method of free verse but of *vers libére*.[155] Certainly the division between the two can be very fine, but in *vers libére* we always hear an echo of metered verse, while free verse, even though it manipulates stressed and unstressed syllables, can operate independently of metered verse.

Vers libére may also show a desire for a new music, may also reflect the political-social structure of the twentieth century and may aim for verisimilitude—as it does in the work of Philip Larkin—but it is not free verse. That is not to suggest that it is deficient, but simply that it is not our immediate focus. Continuing his discussion about Eliot, Hough writes, "Mr. Eliot has himself remarked that the peculiar task of the poetry of the early part of this century was the development of a proper modern poetic idiom, related to the living speech of the day, not merely related, as so much contemporary poetic language was, to a rather tired selection of recent literature."[156]

Hough is attempting to embrace the conclusion that free verse is a temporary phenomenon that should now be set aside. To justify this return to formal verse, he continues to quote Eliot to argue that "when the modern idiom has been established a period of musical elaboration can follow."[157]

This is indeed what happened, but in the United States this musical elaboration was not in most cases a return to formal verse, "which will have learnt much by the practice of free verse."[158] Rather it was a more active embracing of free verse. Generally, it can be said that while twentieth-century British poetry has followed the path of *vers libére*, American poetry has increasingly committed itself to free verse. Our question is how did free verse become such an American product?

Robert Hass has pointed out ". . . that we are pattern-discerning animals, for whatever reason in our evolutionary history. We attend to a rhythm almost instinctively. . . . This process is going on in us all the time, one way or another. It is the first stage, wakeful, animal, alert, of the experience of rhythm. And it is the place to which we are called by the first words of any poem or story."[159]

The pleasure we get from discerning patterns is one of the pleasures of poetry. The system of anticipation-verification-reward ultimately soothes us. But the system of anticipation and surprise may soothe us as well. Consider the last stanza of Creeley's poem "I Know a Man":

> drive, he sd, for
> christ's sake, look
> out where yr going.

This also soothes us, but it does so by pointing to the random violence of the cosmos and warning us against it. We read the Creeley poem constantly expecting it to go out of control, to whirl us into chaos. But it doesn't. It spins us around, then sets us back on our feet, having reassured us about the nature of the world by imposing order upon it. A similar process makes horror movies so popular: By describing the abyss, they show themselves to be superior and in control. And the further irony that we know the abyss to be uncontrollable makes such movies even more pleasing. The roller coaster, the horror movie and the extreme forms of free verse are all ways of thumbing our nose at our collective destiny. Furthermore, surprise is another aspect of verisimilitude. That's what life is like.

The effect of surprise and the other prosodic elements in free verse is that they allow the writer to manipulate the degree of tension within the poem. Tension, in part, is anxiety; it is the fear that the whole structure will plunge into chaos, and it can be created by apparently frustrating one or more of the patterns that the reader has begun to anticipate. Tension also works to direct the reader's attention to different parts of the poem. Consequently, it affects not only form but meaning. The three primary prosodic elements we will look at all work to increase or decrease tension.

The first such element is the line break. The traditional metric poem contains two clear rhythms: the rhythm of the sentence and the rhythm of the line. Hough writes, "It is a commonplace that the most powerful effects of traditional verse are achieved by playing off the syntactical movement against the metrical movement—making them coincide very closely as in the Augustan couplet, or making them diverge very widely as in Miltonic blank verse."[160]

This mixture of the rhythms of lineation and syntax is often called counterpoint, and it forms a major difference between the metered poem and the prose poem—that by not having the rhythm of the line, the prose poem is unable to create counterpoint. For a long time, it was argued that this was also a failing of free verse. Even a major British critic like Graham Hough, whose essay on free verse was written in 1957, refuses to see that the line break in a free verse poem affects rhythm, and he claims that because of this apparent lack of counterpoint, "a powerful range of effects is closed to free verse since there is no ideal metrical norm to appeal to."[161]

Free verse from Whitman to Apollinaire and early Pound attempted to match the syntactic to the rhythmic phrase in order to create cadence. The result was a series of end-stopped lines carefully balanced against each other. William Carlos Williams, Marianne Moore and e.e. cummings, however, rejected end-stopped cadence in favor of a mild counterpoint created by enjambment. The basic premise is that the line break, by being a brief pause, interrupts the rhythm of the sentence. The exact duration is unimportant. It lasts about as long as it takes to move one's eyes back to the beginning of the next line. The theory is that the poet is able to manipulate these artificial pauses to create a sufficient force to set against the rhythm of the sentence. It was by a similar use of enjambment that Milton was able to create a mild counterpoint within his blank verse.

One of the purposes of counterpoint is to create tension. When a line is broken at a piece of punctuation or a natural pause, that break creates a rest. When a line is broken between pauses or pieces of punctuation, that creates tension. Tension can be further affected by what part of speech is used as the last word in the line, whether the line is broken before or after the subject, verb or direct object, whether it is broken after an article, conjunction, preposition or adjective. Another element affecting the tension of the break is the amount of time or breath that has elapsed since the last rest. Another element concerns what the French call *rejet* and *contre-rejet*: that is, whether a lesser or greater amount of the grammatical phrase unit continues after the break.[162] The tension of the line break is also affected by the relationship between stressed and unstressed syllables within the line, the length of the line, the length of the sentence and the speed of the syllables within the line: that is, how the poet arranges mono- and poly-syllabic words, whether he or she uses short or long vowels, sharp or soft consonants, masculine or feminine word endings. It is further affected by pitch, rhyme, ascending, descending rhythms, assonance, alliteration—in fact, all the poetic elements we are accustomed to seeing. All work to create a rhythm that the line break may disturb, and all work to affect the tension created by that disturbance.

The poet, by moving his or her line breaks between tension and rest, creates a rhythm to set against the rhythm of the sentence. The poet also manipulates the degree of our anticipation by manipulating the flow of information. In Creeley's poem "I Know a Man," the sense of impending chaos is partly created by violently enjambing the first eight lines. This gives a breathless quality to the flow of information that increases the degree of our anticipation.

Lineation not only affects rhythm, it affects meaning. Line breaks can give stress to words that would not ordinarily be stressed, and they can also remove stress. They can create irony, suspense, humor, doubt and various multiple meanings. They can become a major tool in making form a metaphor for content.

Line breaks also influence cadence. By breaking the line during a phrase unit, the poet can vary the speed or pacing and again put pressure against our anticipation by threatening to interrupt the cadence or overthrowing it altogether.

The weakest free verse is that which does not attempt to set up a rhythmic system against the rhythm of the sentence. As Hartman writes, every line in a poem must "justify its individual existence."[163] Where one breaks the line can never be a matter of accident since the line break is so much a part of both form and content. Indeed, it is often here that the poet's most personal rhythms are clearest. Consider James Wright's poem, "Petition to the Terns."

> I have lived long enough to see
> Many wings fall
> And many others broken and driven

To stagger away on a slant
Of wind. It blows
Where it pleases to blow,
Or it poises,
Unaccountably,
At rest. Today, sails
Don't move.
In the water,
In front of my eyes,
The huge dull scarlet men-of-war loll, uncaring and slobbish,
And stain
All the shore shallows
That men may hope to become
Green among.
The sea
Is already unfriendly.
The terns of Rhode Island
Dart up out of the cattails, pounce on the sunlight,
Claim it,
And attack.
They must be getting their own back,
Against the wind. But the wind is no angrier
Than any wing it blows down,
And I wish the terns would give it
And me a break.[164]

The first four line breaks and the way they interrupt the
rising rhythm not only reflect the meaning of the sentence but
give a small example of that meaning. Similarly, in line 8 the
word "unaccountably" gives an example of something being
poised, unaccountably, at rest. In line 10 the placement of the
words "Don't move" creates a metaphor for the immobility of
the sails. In line 13, the lolling and slobbish nature of the
men-of-war is reflected by the length of the line. The breaks in
lines 11 through 16 all increase a tension that is relaxed only by

the words "Green among," which conclude the sentence. The words suggest an almost spiritual yearning for something that people can't have, and the line breaks through that center section help create that sense of yearning and frustration. The next two line breaks—lines 18 and 19—give further emphasis to the frustration. The poem then appears to become a kind of joke, a bitter joke about the futility of the protest. The remaining line breaks imitate the terns' futile attack, while the last line break and joke seem to emphasize the whole process.

Beyond these effects, the line breaks seek to duplicate the process of thought, the process by which a questioning man defines his surroundings—hesitant, pondering, melancholic. And we realize, partly because of the way the lines are broken, that the "wings" in line 2 are not just the wings of birds; rather the word suggests the spiritual aspiration of his fellow human beings, his friends and finally himself. The end of the poem is not just about terns but about the fight against something that can't be changed and about the fact that the fight itself, which can simply mean not surrendering to life, is what causes the wings to fall or be broken or to stagger away. This is the use of metaphor as a primary form of communication; the symbol as Baudelaire intended it: the realization that the perceived world is a metaphor for the self.

If the poem were rewritten in prose or had simplified line breaks, its meaning would be diminished. What we see here, after we return to the poem a second time, after we have been pushed through the process of tension and rest, is that what at first seemed to lead toward dissolution and surprise actually leads toward definition and reward: "reward" in the sense that this very poem is like the terns' attack—a gesture of rebellion against the omnipotent—and that the final address is made not just to the terns; it is the poet addressing himself.

A second prosodic device to be found in free verse is the manipulation of stressed and unstressed syllables. Poetry is not natural speech; it is artificial speech stylized in such a way to evoke a sense, perhaps a new sense, of the natural. Manipulation of stresses is one of the ways that stylization occurs.

English is an accentual language with a high percentage of monosyllabic words. In any ten syllables, whether by accident or design, there is a contrast between stressed and unstressed syllables. This is one of the reasons why syllabics and quantitative verse are less successful in English: the sound of the accent tends to override other considerations.

In any ten syllables of prose, there tend to be from four to six stresses, depending on how Latinate or Germanic is the style of the writer. Educated British may have only three or four stresses per ten syllables; nonacademic American, which uses a higher quantity of monosyllabic words, tends to have six. These stresses may not be as strong as the stresses in poetry and they may shift from speaker to speaker, but they are still clearly heard within the sentence.

Iambic pentameter takes existing stresses and orders them according to a pattern. It may also increase the tension in the line by adding an extra stress; that is, if the average is three or four stresses and a writer creates a pattern with five, then he or she is putting a certain tension against an existing norm. It is also argued that the decasyllabic line corresponds to the length of an average phrase or the average time between breaths.

Educated British English, as opposed to American English, is an ascending language; the rhythms rise during speech. The rhythm of iambic pentameter, by moving from rest to stress, duplicates this process. Furthermore, it should be realized that educated British has undergone little change during the past 400 years. The model of Oxford-Cambridge British has been maintained. To some degree the language has become less Latinate and sentences are shorter, but a more substantial change—the removal of terminal unstressed syllables—has reinforced the ascending rhythms of the language.

Iambic pentameter takes the ascending rhythms of educated British and heightens their natural movement by arranging them in a set pattern. American English, however, has no pure or privileged form and consequently has undergone more changes. Here is a paragraph quoted by Charles Hartman: "John Erskine has pointed out that there are even now (1929) diverging language movements in English poetry. The cadence of American speech is no longer that of the English, and since it was from the English models that the best American poets fifty years ago learned the cadence of both their speech and verse, it is not surprising that the American ear today detects a strange, almost foreign note in the fall of the lines of such poets as Tennyson, Lowell and Longfellow."[165]

American English has no model like Oxford-Cambridge English that rises above regional differences and imposes a consistent rhythm upon the language. Philip Larkin's line, "I work all day and get half drunk at night,"[166] is a perfect blend of his Oxford-Cambridge English speech patterns and iambic pentameter. Consider this iambic tetrameter stanza from Larkin's poem "At Grass."

> The eye can hardly pick them out
> From the cold shade they shelter in,
> Till wind distresses tail and mane;
> Then one crops grass, and moves about
> —The other seeming to look on—
> And stands anonymous again.[167]

Here is another Larkin stanza in loose iambic pentameter from "I Remember, I Remember":

> Coming up England by a different line
> For once, early in the cold new year,
> We stopped, and, watching men with number-plates
> Sprint down the platform to familiar gates,
> "Why, Coventry!" I exclaimed. "I was born here."[168]

And here are some looser iambics from Larkin's "High Windows":

> When I see a couple of kids
> And guess he's fucking her and she's
> Taking pills or wearing a diaphragm,
> I know this is paradise. . .[169]

The rhythms are ascending rhythms, and this joining of iambic pentameter to Oxford-Cambridge English makes it possible for him to use the *vers libére* so successfully.

The language of Robert Hass, on the other hand, is made up of descending rhythms. Consider the first stanza of "Heroic Simile."

> When the swordsman fell in Kurosawa's *Seven Samurai*
> in the gray rain,
> in Cinemascope and the Tokugawa dynasty,
> he fell straight as a pine, he fell
> as Ajax fell in Homer
> in chanted dactyls and the tree was so huge
> the woodsman returned for two days
> to that lucky place before he was done with the sawing
> and on the third day he brought his uncle.[170]

The stanza is like a long slide, letting the reader descend bit by bit.

The regional differences in American English, the fact that it is less Latinate than Oxford-Cambridge English, the fact that there is no controlling standard in American English, all this has contributed to the discomfort that many American poets feel about using metered verse. It is not simply a matter of breaking the iamb. For many poets the iamb doesn't feel appropriate. If the writer begins with the premise that the true poet's rhythms are personal, and his or her own speech patterns form themselves, for instance, among descending rhythms, then, like Hass, he or she might develop a descending line that reflects those rhythms. Clearly there are many poets who write comfortably in a loose iambic line—poets such as Heather McHugh and Ellen Bryant Voigt and many others—but the rejection of metered verse by so many American poets cannot be attributed to perversity or ignorance. It has to be seen as a reflection of their belief that the strict iambic pentameter line feels uncomfortable to their voice.

William Carlos Williams wrote, "We have had a choice: either to stay within the rules of English prosody, an area formed and limited by the English character and marked by tremendous masterwork, or to break out, as Whitman did, more or less unequipped to do more. Either to return to rules, more or less arbitrary in their delimitations, or to go ahead, to invent other forms by using a new measure."[171]

Elsewhere he wrote, "A language . . . which will not conform to rigid prosodic rules is forced to break those rules if it is to be retained in its own character. . . . It is the refusal of English (especially American English) to conform to standard prosody which has given rise to free verse."[172]

Williams's solution was to discover a poetic rhythm that matched his own voice. The unit of measurement that he developed for this rhythm he called the variable foot. He wrote:

> The crux of the question is measure. In free verse the measure has been loosened to give more play to vocabulary and syntax—hence, to the mind in its excursions. The bracket of the customary foot has been expanded so that more syllables, words, or phrases can be admitted into its confines. The new unit thus created may be called the "variable foot" . . . It rejects the standard of the conventionally fixed foot and suggests that measure varies with the idiom by which it is employed and the tonality of the individual poem. Thus, as in speech, the prosodic pattern

is evaluated by criteria of effectiveness and expressiveness rather than mechanical syllable counts.[173]

These ideas don't seem particularly outlandish, but the variable foot, as Williams developed it, defined his own personal rhythm. While we may learn from it, to use it would be like using another person's prescription glasses. This returns us to an idea found in Whitman: that is, the pursuit of organic form leads to the situation where each poet has an individual prosody—a prosody circumscribed by his or her individual voice.

American English with its regional differences and lack of a single clear standard has ascending rhythms, descending rhythms and whatever may lie in between. It might be argued that Hass, if he wishes to use descending rhythms, could write in trochaic pentameter, but the trochaic form remains tied to English prosody, which, we come to realize, reflects a specific class system. When Philip Larkin chooses to write a poem about uneducated miners, the form he uses is trochaic tetrameter:

> Down the lane came men in pitboots
> Coughing oath-edged talk and pipesmoke
> Shouldering off the freshened silence.[174]

One of the reasons he writes in trochaic tetrameter is because of his subject, because the trochees best capture the sense and feeling of "coughing oath-edged talk." This is also a reason why "Hiawatha" was written in trochaic tetrameter: The Indians may be noble but they are still savages.

These distinctions lack validity in contemporary American English, partly because we no longer have an ideal form of the language and partly because of our theories of egalitarianism. The British have always had difficulty making sense of Williams's poetry. They have judged the rhythms and language according to their standards and have seen it as little more than dumb people's talk. They claim they can't hear the rhythms; they have no way to measure the skill of his metrical performance. It remains for them unaccountable, and that lack of accountability—that the stressed and unstressed syllables don't aspire to any prescribed measure—is viewed as weakness.

Think again of Creeley's poem "I Know a Man." The poem uses ascending rhythms and a large number of anapests often found in British comic verse. Although an American might find the poem funny, what would amuse him or her most would be the wit, the use of surprise and syncopation. The fact that the speech patterns and diction indicates something about the social class of the speaker would be irrelevant. To an educated Britain, it could be one of the sources of humor. This vague egalitarianism on our part and the fact that most of our free verse does not reflect a class system becomes another example of an attempt at verisimilitude. The poetry aspires to duplicate not only casual speech but common speech.

In both British and American English, however, the line is an accumulation of stressed and unstressed syllables that the line break interrupts. And in both dialects, if we may call them that, rhythm is caused partly by the dynamic relationship between stressed and unstressed syllables. Also, that relationship is a factor in determining where the line is broken.

Our guide is still the more or less equal division between stressed and unstressed syllables. If the number of stresses is increased in a line, then the tension is increased. If the number of stresses falls below half, then tension is decreased. When a line is called flaccid, what is usually meant is that the unstressed syllables outnumber the stressed. Whitman attempted to give his lines a liquid flow by lengthening them and decreasing the proportion of stressed syllables. The unfortunate result is sometimes a sense of flaccidity. Gerard Manley Hopkins often decreased the proportion of unstressed syllables, thereby causing a density that at times becomes impenetrable.

The reader has in mind an ideal balance based on experience of the language. How a poet manipulates that balance is a major source of rhythmic tension. Further tension can be created by obstructing the rhythm of the line. In iambic pentameter, the ascending rhythm can be obstructed with the use of trochaic and dactylic substitutions. With free verse the process is harder and leads to another reason for its unpopularity among formalist critics. If the relationship between stressed and unstressed syllables and ascending and descending rhythms derives from the writer's own voice, then he or she must learn the nature of that voice in order to manipulate its rhythms. This is what Williams did. Robert Hass, when he uses descending rhythms, can put pressure against those rhythms and manipulate surprise by occasionally reversing the pattern and inserting rising rhythms.

But doesn't this create a separate system of prosody for each poet and so create confusion? No, it does not. These are not major differences and language has never been an exact tool. We have no serious trouble in appreciating the rhythms of Whitman or Gerard Manley Hopkins, while their differences remain examples of their uniqueness. What free verse poets deprive us of is a metrical grid that can be placed over their poems so we can see how well they are doing their metrical job. This is what critics miss. But the moment you admit what Coleridge said 200 years ago about organic form, then the present state of affairs seems inescapable: "The organic form . . . is innate; it shapes, as it develops, itself from within, and the fullness of its development is one and the same with the perfection of its outward form. Such as the life is, such is the form."[175]

We are looking at three different factors: the number of stresses per line, the relationship between stressed and unstressed syllables and the matter of ascending or descending rhythms. All affect anticipation and surprise, affect tension, affect rhythm and ultimately affect meaning.

For a poet, not to control the relationship between stressed and unstressed syllables means to take decreased responsibility for the poem. This, too, can be a possible strategy—to create random rhythms—but not to be conscious of it as a strategy means also to take decreased responsibility. Unfortunately, the proliferation of translations has influenced this weakening of control. The language of a good translation is functional and does not call attention to itself. As a result, even the best translations lack the dimension that Graham Hough calls "radiance," which is "the requirement that literature . . . shall satisfy and illuminate by its verbal surface."[176] This is a great loss. To imitate the language of translations is to waste a major tool. The free verse poem doesn't simply use less or no meter; the free verse poem differs from the metered poem not in degree but in kind.

If we compare James Wright's "Petition to the Terns" to a sonnet and read both out loud, we find that each is a sound lasting about 30 seconds. But while the traditional sonnet tends to move forward in 14 clear steps, the Wright poem seems all of a piece; while the hesitations caused by the line breaks, instead of stopping us, shape the direction of the flow, creating a more fluid gesture. Certainly every poem will be different. Certainly there are exceptions. But this may be a partial basis for those comparisons between free verse and music: both free verse and metered verse constitute sounds of varying duration, but, for the most part, the line breaks in free verse are not used as divisions but as rests, silences, within the total flow of sound.

The devices of metered verse are more obvious. That desire for verisimilitude on the part of the free verse poet tends to make the devices of free verse more subtle, as assonance can be more subtle than rhyme. Indeed, as we shall see, many structural effects operate barely at the threshold of consciousness.

Let's consider two free verse poems to see how stressed and unstressed syllables can be used to create tension. The first is Philip Larkin's "Coming," one of his few free verse poems.

> On longer evenings,
> Light, chill and yellow,
> Bathes the serene
> Foreheads of houses.
> A thrush sings

Laurel-surrounded
In the deep bare garden,
Its fresh-peeled voice
Astonishing the brickwork.
It will be spring soon,
It will be spring soon—
And I, whose childhood
Is a forgotten boredom,
Feel like a child
Who comes on a scene
Of adult reconciling,
And can understand nothing
But the unusual laughter,
And starts to be happy.[177]

In the first four lines we find a pattern established between
masculine and feminine endings or trochees and iambs. The first
two lines are rhythmically the same; both conclude with two
trochees: "longer evenings" and "chill and yellow." However, it is
not clear that this is a pattern until the third line interrupts it by
interjecting an ascending rhythm: "bathes the serene." This creates
a slight tension, which is relieved in the fourth lines by a return to
a descending rhythm, a dactyl and trochee, "foreheads of houses."
These four lines create a pattern that will be repeated throughout
the poem: rhythmically similar lines, followed by a deviation,
followed by a return to the original rhythm. The fifth line again
creates tension by returning to an ascending rhythm, but we
anticipate a return to what has become the norm and we are right.
Line 6 repeats the dactyl and trochee of the fourth line. The next
three lines continue this pattern. Then, with the repeated line—"It
will be spring soon"—Larkin changes the pace and threatens to
throw over the pattern by inserting seven ascending lines. This
greatly increases the tension, which is further increased by delaying the phrase "of adult reconciling" by the parenthetical "whose
childhood / is a forgotten boredom." We don't know what will

happen to the child, if it will be a good or bad, and this switch to ascending rhythms not only creates tension and anxiety but also suspense. Without its various modifiers the sentence is simply "And I feel like a child who starts to be happy." Or, without the simile, "I start to be happy." The modifiers and simile create tension by delaying the relative clause and keeping us from learning what will happen to the child.

The rhythm of "of adult reconciling" is barely ascending. Read by itself, it is descending, but the assonantal rhyme with the last word of the previous ascending line, "scene," brings it up and the tension is continued. The next two lines ("And can understand nothing / but the unusual laughter") continue to be ascending because we are still waiting for the conclusion of the relative clause and for some verb. Then Larkin releases the tension with the last line, which is descending: "And starts to be happy." It comes as a physical exhalation, a release that is heightened by the appearance of the verb "starts," because basically everything between the initial "I" and the verb "starts" has been simile and because of the syntax we have understood that a verb must be coming. Our experience of the rhythm of that line is like the sudden awareness of happiness, a release of tension. We feel what the child felt, but Larkin has created the physical sensation of that feeling by a manipulation of rhythm.

These are not the rhythms of metered poetry, and although we use the terms of metered poetry—iamb and trochee—it is for convenience rather than technical appropriateness.

Consider Michael Ryan's poem, "When I Was Conceived."

It was 1945, and it was May.
White crocus bloomed in St. Louis.
The Germans gave in but the war shoved on,
and my father came home from work that evening
tired and washed his hands
not picturing the black-goggled men
with code names fashioning an atomic bomb.

Maybe he loved his wife that evening.
Maybe after eating she smoothed his jawline
in her palm as he stretched out
on the couch with his head in her lap
while Bob Hope spoofed Hirohito on the radio
and they both laughed. My father sold used cars
at the time, and didn't like it,
so if he complained maybe she held him
an extra moment in her arms,
the heat in the air pressing between them,
so they turned upstairs early that evening,
arm in arm, without saying anything.[178]

The rhythmical effects are less obvious than Larkin's but the poem still begins with a pattern that is established in the first two lines. Tension is then created by approaching and moving away from that pattern. In this case, the term "pattern" is somewhat inaccurate; perhaps the words "touchstone" or "tonic" would be more appropriate.

In any case, the repetition of "it was" turns those two syllables into a faint double stress. That sibilant double stress is amplified by two sibilant double stresses in the second line: "White crocus" and "St. Louis." That double stress forms a kind of tonic note and by the end of line 2 we anticipate its recurrence. Line 3 presents two more double stresses but it varies them, dropping the sibilant: "gave in" and "war shoved on." Understand that these are relative stresses. "Gave in" would normally be a trochee but the rhythm of the line turns it into a double stress. As Otto Jespersen wrote in his "Notes on Meter," "It is the relative stress that counts."[179]

By the end of the third line we have had six double stresses and we begin to anticipate a pattern: a tonic note now exists that will be approached and moved away from. In line 4, we have "came home," in line 6 "black-goggled," in line 7 "code names fashioning." Lines 8 and 9 add a new element with the repetition of "maybe," while giving us another double stress with "jawline. In line 10, we have "stretched out," line 12 "Bob Hope," line 13 "both laughed" and "used cars." Then the next four lines seem to drop the pattern, which increases the tension, although we are relieved by the second repetition of "maybe" and by the faint double stress of "held him" in line 15 and "air pressing" in line 17. The result of this delay is to greatly emphasize the end, an emphasis that would not be so strong if this pattern of double stresses didn't exist within the poem. In the penultimate line, the phrase "turned upstairs early" reads as four stresses, partly because that pattern of double stresses had been briefly removed; while the third repetition of the phrase "that evening" tends to stress the "that." In the last line ("arm in arm, without saying anything"), that same departure from the norm leads us to stress seven of its ten syllables. Again this is relative stress and it would be probably more apparent with a four-stress system, but within the last line the words "in," "with" (in without) and the second syllable of "any" are weak and all the rest are stronger.

We could also go through this poem looking for ascending and descending patterns, but the point should be clear: both the Larkin and Ryan poems create a relationship between stressed and unstressed syllables that seems to differ in kind from the way stresses are used in metered poetry. Certainly we can find in metered poetry the use of double stresses as a sort of touchstone (Yeats's "Leda and the Swan" for example), but the manner in which they are used and why they are used seems essentially different.

A third prosodic device governing the free verse poem is the manipulation of repeating elements. Our desire for repeating elements goes back to our being "pattern-discerning animals," since the effect of repetition is to present us with a pattern. We find repeating elements pleasurable. Besides suggesting a pattern and allowing us to anticipate correctly, even a single repetition presents us with the familiar and therefore with the known world. This comforts us.

There are two general ways of using repetition. The first is to set up patterns that the reader will correctly anticipate. This is the method of traditionally metered verse. We correctly anticipate many of the various kinds of repetition found in a traditional sonnet. The second way is to surprise the reader with repetitions—rhyme where he or she didn't expect it, alliteration, unanticipated repetitions of stressed and unstressed syllables. This second method has become one of the major devices of free verse, and it is one of the major ways of manipulating surprise. Of course any poem may have dozens of repeating elements occurring in both predetermined and seemingly random positions. In free verse, however, the placing of those elements appears to be more unpredictable, which is not to say that it is arbitrary.

Repeating elements may be part of the content or form, while elements influencing content may be divided into intellectual, emotional and physical: that is, a particular idea, emotion or physical description is put in a symmetrical relationship with another that is either the same or slightly different. This can be seen in a refrain like Yeats's "a terrible beauty is born" or Eliot's "in the room the women come and go," or it can be a slightly different repetition, as in Yeats's "Sailing to Byzantium," where he pairs "monuments of unaging intellect" with "monuments of their own magnificence." By intellectual, emotional and physical, I mean that the basic content at that point can be roughly placed into one of those three categories of information.

Repeating elements that primarily affect the form can be either visual or aural. Our sense of visual repetitions derives from the appearance of the poem on the page: the shape of the poem and whether there are lines and stanzas of equal length. A metered poem, like a sonnet, often presents a symmetrical shape, and this leads us to anticipate certain qualities even before we begin to read. A free verse poem will often have a meandering and apparently arbitrary shape, although carefully symmetrical shapes are also common. Creeley's poem "I Know a Man" is very symmetrical in appearance: four three-line stanzas with the lines of more or less equal length. And perhaps one of the reasons we accept the rush and violence of Creeley's poem is because we have already been reassured by its visual symmetry.

But the most common repeating element is aural. In free verse and formal verse there may be dozens of repeating aural elements vying for the attention of the reader. Not only do they help create the music of the poem, the degree of radiance or texture, but they increase and release tension and emphasize content. In free verse, the placement of these elements may appear arbitrary, less governed by some predetermined scheme; and because of that general desire for verisimilitude, these elements tend to be subtler. Furthermore, because a metered poem puts greater emphasis on the individual line, the repeating elements, such as end rhyme, usually work to emphasize the line.

The use of repeating elements may entail the balancing and/or repetition of syllables, words, phrases, sentences, lines and stanzas of similar length. It may also entail the recurrence of elements of pitch, quantity, assonance, rhyme—in fact, all aspects of form that can be used to give the reader a sense of symmetry. Stressed and unstressed syllables, ascending and descending rhythms can also be used in repeating patterns.

Consider Donald Justice's poem, "Absences."

It's snowing this afternoon and there are no flowers.
There is only this sound of falling, quiet and remote,
Like the memory of scales descending the white keys
Of a childhood piano—outside the window, palms!
And the heavy head of the cereus, inclining,
Soon to let down its white or yellow-white.

Now, only these poor snow-flowers in a heap,
Like the memory of a white dress cast down . . .
So much has fallen.
                    And I, who have listened for a step
All afternoon, hear it now, but already falling away,

> Already in memory. And the terrible scales descending
> On the silent piano; the snow; and the absent flowers
>   abounding.[180]

Approaching the poem, we first notice its symmetrical shape: two six-line stanzas, one with a wrinkle. The lines seem of similar length and, looking farther, we find they average about 12 syllables. In the first line are a disproportionate number of low-frequency vowels—especially the long *o* but also *oo* and *ow*. The use of these vowels is continued in the second line which establishes a pattern. This repetition of the long *o*, plus the *oo* and *ow*, then continues through the poem, is decreased in lines 10 and 11, then comes back very strongly in the last line. Justice is using his pattern of vowels somewhat as Larkin used his pattern of ascending-descending rhythms and Ryan used his double stresses. All three introduce an aural element, use it to create a pattern, threaten to remove it, then return to it strongly.

Another example of symmetry in the Justice poem is the alliteration of the *s*es and *f*s in the first two lines. Both alliterations emphasize key words—"sound," "snow," "falling," "flowers"—while the *s* alliteration is continued through the poem, occurring a total of 30 times. The only place where it lets up is in lines 10 and 11, then it returns strongly in line 12. In fact, its movement through the poem is almost exactly like the long *o* sound.

Additionally, those key words at the beginning are further emphasized by the "ing" rhyme. That rhyme occurs five more times in the poem and is especially strong at the end. Full or partial rhyme is also used to connect the end words: remote/white, keys/heap/step, palms/down, inclining/descending/abounding. The two unrhymed end words—"flowers" and "away"—are rhymed within the body of the poem. A further rhyming occurs with the repetition of key words: snow, flowers, falling, descending, white, memory, afternoon, piano, scales, already. "White" is used four times, and "snow" and "flowers" both appear three times.

We also find in the poem a balancing of content, a balancing of the segments of information dealing with idea, emotional evocation and description. An additional symmetry is seen in the fact that the lines are end-stopped. Only three lines—3, 9 and 11—are slightly enjambed.

If we look at the rhythms of the poem, we find further examples of repetition. The first line is made up of four units: (1) "It's snowing"; (2) "this afternoon"; (3) "and there are no"; (4) "flowers." These are what Williams meant by variable feet, where "the bracket of the customary foot has been expanded so that more syllables, words, or phrases can be admitted into its confines."[181] Justice certainly isn't basing his rhythm on Williams, but the term remains applicable. However, what should be noticed about these units is that the first three are ascending and the last shows a descending rhythm. Lines 2 and 3 repeat this pattern. Line 4 breaks the pattern by introducing two descending units. Line 5 returns to the norm with two ascending and one descending. Lines 6 and 7 have three ascending and one descending. Line 8 has two ascending and one descending. Line 9 repeats line 4 with two descending units. Lines 10, 11 and 12 have the first three ascending and the last descending. Or possibly line 10 has four ascending and one descending. This arrangement repeats the pattern we have seen with trochees and iambs, double stresses and repeating vowels and consonants: a norm is established, departed from briefly and returned to with emphasis.

The rhythms in Justice's lines are even more complicated. The first three have a similar rhythm, which the fourth line interrupts. Lines 5 and 6 return to it. Line 7 interrupts. Line 8 returns. Line 9 strongly interrupts, completely destroying the rhythm, which is never returned to. That breakup of the rhythm matches the shock of the emotional epiphany ending the poem.

The rhythm and the ascending/descending units are quite similar and move together for most of the poem, then they separate at the end to create the sense of dislocation testified to by the narrator. If we look at the relationship between stressed and unstressed syllables, we see how Justice achieves this separation. The first four lines each have five stresses. This establishes the norm. Line 5 has four stresses, line 6 has either four or six, lines 7 through 9 have six stresses, line 10 has seven, line 11 has five and the last line has six. Again, the norm is established, moved away from and returned to. However, if we look at the unstressed syllables, we see another process occurring. Line 7 has five unstressed syllables, line 8 has four, but then they increase sharply so that the last three lines are nine, nine, twelve. It is this sharp increase in unstressed syllables in the last three lines that disrupts and throws over the established rhythm.

All these elements control our sense of repetition and symmetry. Because they do not seem predetermined and imposed on the poem, as are traditional rhyme scheme and meter, their presence and placement can appear arbitrary, even if it is not. There are many kinds of repeating patterns, but a common poetic technique, as we have seen, is to surprise the reader with the pattern, establish it, threaten to remove it and then return to it. What makes the closing of some of these poems so strong, apart from meaning, is that they suddenly reemphasize symmetrical patterns that the reader had feared had been abandoned.

We have looked briefly at three prosodic devices found in free verse: the counterpoint created by lineation and syntax; the manipulation of stressed and unstressed syllables; and the manipulation of repeating elements. There may be other devices as well, such as the sharp juxtaposition of seemingly unconnected concrete details, which was the method of Rimbaud and which is common in many twentieth-century art forms. But the three devices presented here are to be found in varying degrees in many free verse poems. Some hardly use any, others are packed. The determining factor is often the degree of verisimilitude sought by the writer. What these devices do, however, is influence our response to the poem. Charles O. Hartman defines prosody as "the poet's method of controlling the reader's temporal experience of the poem, especially his attention to that experience."[182] The three devices described here all attempt to achieve this aim.

I. A. Richards wrote that meter "is the means by which words may be made to influence one another to the greatest possible extent."[183] Free verse also has its ways of making words influence one another, and it is not, as Graham Hough and Robert Graves have claimed, simply a blurring of the boundaries between verse and prose. One of the difficulties, as has been indicated, is that the use of apparently individual prosodies denies critics a metrical grid to enforce accountability. Each poem has to be analyzed on its own terms. But hasn't this also been true of metered poetry?

There are perhaps two other rules that may be applied to free verse, although both were originally used for metered verse. The lesser comes from Robert Graves, who wrote, "there should be no discrepancy between the sound and sense of a poem."[184] The second and greater rule returns us to Coleridge, who wrote that a work of art must contain "in itself the reason why it is so, and not otherwise."[185]

Poets must constantly measure not only their poems but each word against that rule, for it is by that rule that any poem is ultimately judged.

5 | Pacing: The Ways a Poem Moves

A WORK OF ART IS SOMETHING THAT EXISTS independent of all people, all value systems, that does not need, is not needed and has as much importance as a rock floating through outer space. Contrariwise, it is also a conduit passing between artist and audience, the half-open door standing between them. Yet it is more than a means of communication, it is also what is being communicated. It contains the essence, the very spirit of its creator, but if the audience cannot find its way within it, then the work of art will fail. A work of art is about the artist, about the audience and about nothing at all at the same time. It is irrational, mysterious and attempts to touch the emotions, the senses, the intellect, even the spirit of its audience. It does this not only with what it communicates, its apparent subject, but also with its form. A poem, for instance, communicates as much through the manner of its telling as through what is told.

　　The moment we write about form apart from content we engage in a deception: The two cannot be divided. This doesn't mean that we can't write about form and content separately, but to emphasize we are writing about something that is impossible. Given that warning, I would like to suggest that the linguistic qualities that make up a poem's form can be divided into four categories: (1) the relation between stressed and unstressed syllables; (2) the aural qualities of language, that is varieties of rhyme, alliteration, vowel pitch, consonant quality and so on; (3) pacing; and (4) tone. As well as working separately, these elements often mix and overlap, while certain devices such as the line break play a strong role in all four.

　　Our immediate subject is pacing, which may be defined as controlled variations in the forward momentum of the poem.

Pacing is equally influenced by the reader's anticipation and desire to know, as well as by the natural forward movement of the English sentence and the speed of the flow of information from the poem to the reader. In both fiction and poetry, the writer is always playing off what the reader knows against what he or she does not know. This was argued in chapter 3 but now I would like to deal with it more specifically.

By making the reader want to know, the writer can use the reader's ignorance as energy to move down the page. Given this desire to know, the writer is always balancing the reader's expectation against his or her frustration—the former being that the reader will learn the answers, the latter being that he or she won't. If frustration overwhelms expectation, or if the reader grows indifferent, then the writer has lost the reader.

One of the hardest tasks in calculating expectation is to imagine a reader, but without doing so the poem's success is left to chance. The poet must imagine the reader picking up the poem, looking at it, reading the first line, then deciding to read the second. He or she must imagine the reader moving from indifference to curiosity to interest to anticipation. As Philip Larkin wrote, "poetry is emotional in nature and theatrical in operation."[1] The poet has to create in the reader a desire to know. This means more than having a subject that is intrinsically interesting and conveying it in an earnest and sincere manner; it is a matter of choosing and arranging the language in the most effective way possible. If the poet has written because he or she was driven to write by emotional need, then we automatically have a degree of interest, since we are interested in whatever arouses passion in our fellow creatures. But even the most passionate concern can be made tedious by obscurity and trivial form. Although we are talking about the form of a poem, the four categories mentioned earlier are equally a matter of content. Unless a poet's language is precise and interesting, exact pacing is impossible.

The poet most likely should have in mind a reader who resembles himself or herself or is a faceless composite of friends, and the poet must get to know this ideal reader as well as he or she knows anyone. We, as readers, pick up the poem to be moved and entertained. We do not read it to learn about the poet, or if we do, then it is for the reasons we pick up *People* magazine, and these have little to do with poetry. Such reasons may be part of the means of the poem, part of the theater, but they can have nothing to do with its ends. No matter the subject of a poem, we always read to learn about ourselves. Even when we read to be taken out of ourselves, we are in fact seeking new perspectives on ourselves. We read partly to discover new tools, new methods for seeing into our own future.

One reason why content must be equal to form is that we as readers, must be secure in the belief that we are touching another human being who is speaking out of passion or at least because he or she was unable to remain silent. When the form is more important than the content, when it exists to convince or dazzle or decorate or distract, then the form is not rising out of the needs of the content but is being used rhetorically; that is, to convince for its own sake. The eventual effect will be to frustrate us, because we are looking, ultimately, to be moved out of ourselves, to be able for a second to step away and see ourselves in relation to the world. When a poem's effects are used rhetorically, there may be a momentary uplift while we feel we are on a new road to understanding, but this is followed by frustration or ultimate indifference when we discover that the road leads nowhere.

Parenthetically, it should be noted that the writer's apparent desire for information affects the reader's desire. The stronger that desire, then the less chance the reader has of becoming frustrated. If the reader cannot feel the writer's passion, he or she will have none. This is partly a matter of clarity; it must become clear to the reader what drove the writer to make the poem. But it is also a matter of how the information is presented. It is always dangerous for the reader to think the poet is giving answers rather than seeking them. What we partly look for in a piece of writing is discovery. That discovery cannot be imparted, it must be enacted. This is a great strength in Whitman, Neruda and Yeats, and a weakness in many of the later poems of William Wordsworth. In the first three poets, the search is enacted; in late Wordsworth, the results of the search are passed out like improving pills.

Unless the reader has some prior feeling about the writer, a willingness to trust is the one thing the reader may give the writer for free, and it is based on nothing the writer has done but on the reader's whole relationship to literature. But the dark side of the willingness to trust is suspicion. If the poet does not reward this trust in the first few moments of the poem, he or she is in trouble, because the longer the poet takes to reward it, then the harder it will be to keep it. Most of our willingness to trust is based on the expectation that the poem will speak to us about our own lives. If we cannot find this, we must find something else: humor, beauty of structure or language, intelligence, eccentricity and so on. But no matter the strength of these elements, they will be basically decorative unless the poem speaks first to the life of the reader.

In making the poem important to the reader, it may be necessary for the writer to think not only about the poem, but what lies outside the poem competing for the reader's attention. We readers are constantly concerned with our past, present and future, and we are surrounded by a flurry of entertainments and activities that either seek to distract us from or speak to us about our private concerns. We live in a time when, because of the wide variety of public entertainment, the nature of the advertising industry and the size of the news media, we are bombarded with spectacle. The writer must consider this when seeking to capture our attention, while avoiding the use of spectacle. It may be that the reader turns to poetry in relief from the noise of the other. It may be that the writer must be more aggressive.

We can begin reading a poem with enthusiasm or mild interest, skepticism or downright disbelief. This expectation is partly affected by where we find the poem (the quality or nature of the publication), by our knowledge of the writer, the visual appearance of the poem on the page, and those elements in the title and first few lines that take our interest and/or make us think that what follows will be made meaningful.

The writer needs to be careful about trying to influence where the reader finds the poem. While it is necessary to imagine an ideal reader, the moment the writer begins to think of a specific reader, say the editor of magazine X, then his aesthetic choices begin to be influenced by matters outside the poem. This can be harmful. The writer has to write without worrying if future readers will like or dislike the end result. The writer may worry about clarity but not about good or bad reviews. When asked about the writer's role during a period of repression, the Polish poet Zbigniew Herbert said: "To see things with illuminating clarity— and, if they are simple, to describe them simply and to learn to live with everyday despair, telling oneself that perhaps one must write but that it is not necessary to publish."[2]

As for the reader's prior knowledge of the writer, there is little the writer can do about this. The best he or she can do is not violate the reader's willingness to trust. If the reader approaches the poem with distrust, then the poet must work all the harder to regain that trust. I am not talking about the quality of the poet's personality. After all, it is not necessary to the poem for the poet to be a good human being but a complete human being. At some point, the poet will fall away and leave only the poem, but if the poet is dishonest in his or her writing, then the poem will never have a chance of transcending the poet.

The reader's approach to the poem is greatly influenced by the poem's visual shape on the page. If the poem is long or short, symmetrical or asymmetrical, has long or short lines, this affects the reader's expectation. As readers, we not only bring our attention to the poem, we also bring a sense of how much effort will be required to read the poem, as well as some sense of possible reward. If the poem is large, long and blocky, it is even more necessary to make the poem interesting to the reader as soon as possible. If the poem is thin, short and looks easy to read, then the writer has more time to work with the reader's expectations.

The reader is mostly propelled through the poem by energy. This comes from many sources, but the earliest comes from the reader's interest and sense of expectation. It may not be a particularly strong element and the poet may choose to do nothing with it, but he or she must acknowledge it. Many contemporary poems have a rather dull symmetrical shape—lines from 8 to 12 syllables proceeding down the page with an even left-hand margin. This is the shape of many of my own poems. Whatever a poem's shape, there must be a reason for it; not to have a reason means leaving one of the effects of the poem to chance.

After taking in the size and shape, as well as estimating the effort needed to read the poem, the reader takes in the title. Clearly, these are split-second apprehensions, but they influence the reader's sense of expectation. By combining the information provided by the shape of the poem with the title, the reader is either nudged forward in a willingness to trust or grows more suspicious. A title can simply be a label, or it can create tone, or it can give information that either immediately locates the poem when we read the first line or clarifies the focus farther on. A title can direct the reader and establish a context, giving the reader a sense of what is important; or it can create tension by using emotionally charged language. If the poem is named "Song," we begin to read it in a different manner than we would if it were named "The Rape." Or think of these titles: "The Widow's Lament in Springtime," "Why Should Not Old Men Be Mad?" "Depressed by a Bad Book of Poetry, I Walk Toward an Unused Pasture and Invite the Insects to Join Me," "Frogs Eat Butterflies. Snakes Eat Frogs. Hogs Eat Snakes. Men Eat Hogs." Some poets, such as Theodore Roethke, used titles that were hardly more than labels ("The Lizard," "Root Cellar," "The Waking"); others, such as James Wright, have titles that do a lot of work: setting the tone, locating the poem and creating suspense. Consider Wright's titles "As I Step Over a Puddle at the End of Winter, I Think of an Ancient Chinese Governor" and "A Message Hidden in an Empty Bottle that I Threw into a Gully of Maple Trees One Night at an Indecent Hour."

Along with the poem's visual appearance and title its initial few words must be included. The combination of these three factors influence the reader's expectation and decision to trust. After that, expectation is joined by the forward moment of the sentence to create what truly may be calling pacing.

Think of Yeats's "Leda and the Swan." When we approach the poem for the first time, we see it is a sonnet. That knowledge creates one kind of expectation. The title creates another. There is the sense of dealing with a traditional subject in a traditional manner. But then we have the first words: "A sudden blow: the great wings beating still . . ." The violence of that line is at such variance to the expectations created by the poem's title and visual shape that it creates an energy that rushes the reader through the initial stanza. Yeats further affects the speed by the syntax of the single sentence that makes up the first quatrain, by the use of short vowels and hard or plosive consonants and a series of spondees or double stresses. He then brings that rush to a halt in the second quatrain by the different syntax of the two questions, and by using long vowels and soft consonants, by which point the reader is completely controlled and directed by the language.

A poem has emotion, idea, physical setting, language, image, rhythm and tension. The degree that the poem is successful is the degree to which all these elements are made important to the reader, and at least one must be made important as soon as possible, either in the title or in the first line or two. Even the most gentle poem must be aggressive. Although expectation leads us into the poem, once the first sentence is begun, it is the momentum of the language that carries us along, while both form and content create further energy and expectation to propel us through the poem. In order to control pacing, the poet must have an awareness of the reader's sense of expectation on one hand and frustration on the other; trust on one hand and suspicion on the other.

Once the poet has created in the reader a desire to know, then pacing requires tension and the language must never go slack. As readers, we must have a sense of trying to catch up, of being on the verge of understanding. This requires an exact gap between the language and our understanding. The poem must stay ahead of us and never let us relax into our own pace. If for any one of many reasons (obscurity, complexity, density, speed) the poem gets too far ahead and we feel we won't understand or that the poem won't be made meaningful to us, then we may become frustrated and give up. If we too easily encompass or grasp what the poem is attempting to say, because the writer has been too slow or too obvious, our energy level will drop and we will lose interest.

Let's focus briefly on pacing before looking specifically at language. Pacing is controlled by tension, and tension is energy. This energy comes from language and the reader's anticipation. Even the reader's trust is a form of energy. The writer is balanced between making us want to know and not letting us feel that the poem's effects exist primarily to create this desire. Pacing is like a hand pressed in the middle of our backs, pushing us along. Although we must occasionally be allowed to rest, those places of rest must be of the writer's choosing. The reader also moves forward by a process of asking questions and finding the answers. We need to be teased a little with our ignorance; we must be made to want to know more. Even at the end of the poem it is best to leave the reader with questions that can be answered only by returning to the page. The writer should also be wary of giving us the answer or even the word we anticipate, and often he or she should shift the scene or subject while we are still satisfied and want to know more.

If our questions, as readers, are answered too easily, we will lose interest. Consequently, one of the writer's most effective tools in pacing is surprise, which is a shift in form or content un-anticipated by the reader. This can be simply a shift in attention or a more radical juxtaposition. A major pleasure in a poem using traditional form is the linguistic surprises that occur within that defined framework. All poems are visually finite. Part of the pleasure of surprise in any poem is its suggestion of the infinite within the finite, that even when all apparent possibilities have been anticipated, change is still possible. But what is imperative with surprise or any of these effects is that they must arise out of the needs of content. For the reader to think they exist for their own sake is to jeopardize the reader's trust.

If the poet can get us to believe about a small thing, we will be more likely to believe the poet about a big thing. One of the quickest ways to establish the reader's trust is through precise description of physical setting. More difficult are precise descriptions of emotional and spiritual conditions. All three mean giving us a combination of the familiar and unfamiliar, what we know with what we do not know. These three types of description are best communicated with the help of metaphor. And it is probably through the quality of metaphor that the poet most quickly achieves or loses the trust of the reader.

When we pick up a poem for the first time we are a wonderful paradox. We have our defenses, opinions, prejudices. We have our complacency. Yet we want them challenged and even overthrown, possibly so we can make them even stronger. Our complacency is held in place by a series of linguistic defenses that say we are who we are for a variety of good reasons. These defenses are intended to stand against counterarguments. But a metaphor is nonanalytical. It uses words to make something nondiscursive, something pre-word (in that direct statement may not yet exist to describe it). In *Problems of Art*, Suzanne Langer wrote, "A metaphor is not language, it is an idea expressed by language, an idea that in its turn functions as a symbol to express something. It is not discursive and therefore does not really make a statement of the idea it conveys; but it formulates a new conception for our direct imaginative grasp."[3]

Because it creeps beneath the barriers of argument, metaphor is a tool to breach our linguistic defenses and topple our complacency. Even though a poem may not contain metaphor, it in itself is a metaphor, standing for an aspect of a human being's relations between the self and the world.

One of the requirements of a writer and especially a poet is to see things in relation to one another, to observe phenomena in terms of how they link with other phenomena, to be always in quest of metaphor, since to seek metaphor is to seek underlying pattern. To expect pattern among apparently random phenomena is part of the Romantic condition, since it requires a belief if not in unity, then in connection. As human begins, we are problem solvers, imposers of form (our dark side is the destroyer), and part of the pleasure of poetry is that it imposes pattern. The way a poem is created is a metaphor for the ordering of chaos, not only through the use of pattern, but also through structure, which is the presence of a beginning, middle and end. Pattern in poetry is the repetition of two verbal elements to create the expectation of a third. Indeed, the perception of beauty is in part the perception of pattern above the randomness of the world where the only constants are human violence and selfishness, while a perfect joining of form and content may become if not beautiful itself, then a metaphor for the nature of beauty—beauty being concrete evidence of the possibility of perfection.

It is partly the anticipated pleasure of discovering pattern, shape and what Graham Hough calls "radiance" ("the requirement that literature . . . shall satisfy and illuminate by its verbal surface"[4]) that leads us to begin reading a poem. In the ordering of chaos, these qualities stand against randomness, formlessness and cacophony. Additional qualities are harmony, which is the working together of these three elements, and grace, which is blending these elements in a form that is equal to the content. Pacing is constantly influenced by this expectation of pattern, shape and radiance, since the reader's fear is that the whole structure will collapse back into chaos. It is the poet's constant occupation to control this fear, creating tension to speed or slow the pacing.

In Count Basie's piano trio recordings, part of the pleasure comes from hearing how far Basie can depart from the melody until he is doing only a few plink-plinks in the upper register. The fear is that the whole business will fall apart and just when the tension is greatest, Basie again picks up the melody. Poems may use a similar device. After a subject has been established in the title and/or first few lines, the writer can move away from it, while the farther he or she gets, the greater becomes the tension, unless the bond is actually broken. Again, the writer is playing what we know against what we don't know. What is necessary is that the writer occasionally connects with the subject and of course eventually returns to it or so changes the terms of the poem that the original subject becomes irrelevant.

In a narrative poem, pacing is influenced by the clarity of the narrative and its development. In a lyric poem, it is influenced by the clarity of whatever it was that drove the poet to make the poem. Since all poems contain lyric and narrative elements, these two types of clarity are constantly being juggled to affect the pacing of the poem. Clarity must be a constant concern. It is one of the tools the poet uses to move back and forth between the reader's ignorance and knowledge, and without this pacing is hardly possible.

The interworkings of these elements to affect pacing should be, if not obvious, at least imaginable. For instance, one of the effects of surprise is to seem to jeopardize the establishing of pattern, shape and radiance. This heightens the tension and so speeds the pacing. Given the reader's original sense of expectation, anything that the poet does to vary the speed of the flow of information will increase or decrease the tension, which in turn speeds or slows the pacing.

We can observe this in line breaks. To break a line at a piece of punctuation or a normal syntactical pause creates a rest; to break the line where there is not normally a pause, that is, to enjamb the line, creates tension and so speeds the pacing. This tension is further affected by what part of speech is used as the terminal word in the line, what part of speech follows the break, whether a larger or smaller portion of the sentence follows the break, whether the poet is using an ascending or descending rhythm or meter, whether the poet is using some kind of rhyme, line length, what kind of consonants and vowels are used, what kind of sentence is being used as well as its structure and syntax. The greater the tension, the faster the pacing, which can be further affected by using words with initial or terminal letters that either elide or bang against each other. If the reader, however, is not given a chance to rest, he or she will grow frustrated and break away from the poem.

More important than line breaks in controlling pacing is the natural momentum of the English sentence. It is this that most directly affects the flow of information and, consequently, the reader's expectation and desire to know. The potentially fastest sentence is a simple sentence of eliding one-syllable words using short and high-pitched vowels and hard or plosive consonants— "Tim needs sex." Polysyllabic words, longer vowels and softer consonants slow that movement—"Harry hungers for women."

A compound sentence can move more slowly than a simple sentence and a complex sentence more slowly than a compound sentence. In any sentence, the primary information is carried by the subject, verb and direct and indirect objects. The complex sentence also has a load of secondary information carried by subordinate clauses, prepositional phrases, parenthetical phrases, interjections and whatever. The moment the primary information is delayed or interrupted by secondary information, there is a chance to influence the movement of the sentence and so increase or decrease pacing. Furthermore, pacing is affected by the kind of sentence that is used, whether exclamatory, declarative or interrogative; how these sentences are varied; how the simple, compound and complex sentences are varied; and how the length of the sentences are varied within the entire text. It should also be seen that primary and secondary information exists not only in the sentence, but also in the line, stanza and poem. How secondary information is used to delay primary information is a major device of pacing.

Let's look at this process in four contemporary poems. The first is by Philip Larkin, written in 1955.

REFERENCE BACK

That was a pretty one, I heard you call
From the unsatisfactory hall
To the unsatisfactory room where I
Played record after record, idly,
Wasting my time at home, that you
Looked so much forward to.

Oliver's *Riverside Blues*, it was. And now
I shall, I suppose, always remember how
The flock of notes those antique negroes blew
Out of Chicago air into
A huge remembering pre-electric horn
The year after I was born
Three decades later made this sudden bridge
From your unsatisfactory age
To my unsatisfactory prime.

Truly, though our element is time,
We are not suited to the long perspectives
Open at each instant of our lives.
They link us to our losses: worse,
They show us what we have as it once was,
Blindingly undiminished, just as though
By acting differently we could have kept it so.[5]

The narrative situation may be paraphrased as follows. The narrator, whom we assume is Larkin, goes home to visit his mother. He has little relationship with her and he sits in his room listening to records, specifically King Oliver's "Riverside Blues." His mother, trying to connect with him, responds to the song by saying "That was a pretty one," and Larkin realizes that now the song will always remind him of this failed relationship. Furthermore, he thinks that at any moment we can see what we now have as it once was, see the change and realize that perhaps if we had acted differently we could have kept it bright, wonderful and undiminished.

This reading is not easily given and we have to extract it from the page. Looking at the poem, we see a somewhat balanced shape, three stanzas of different length (six lines, nine lines, seven lines), an AA, BB, CC rhyme scheme, a loose iambic meter in lines of 6 to 12 syllables and a title that makes no immediate sense. We are drawn through the poem by asking questions and seeking answers, and we are drawn through by the syntax. The poem has five sentences, the first, third and fifth of which are so complicated that the pacing constantly changes speed. The second and fourth sentences, especially the second, function as rests.

The meaning of the first line by itself is obscure, although we may see that the spoken phrase is actually making a reference back to something else and by doing so connects to the title (a title that becomes ironic once we understand the full meaning of the poem, that almost everything in life becomes "a reference back"). Larkin follows the first line with two prepositional phrases, a relative clause and two adverbial clauses. The third and fifth lines are severely enjambed and only the last, the sixth, breaks at a complete rest. The effect is to constantly vary the pacing, which is also influenced by line breaks, rhyme and the reader's questions concerning what Larkin is talking about. The final effect is of a completely balanced stanza held together by an internal tension governed primarily by syntax.

The second stanza makes a different yet similar movement. Larkin halts the momentum with a short sentence, surprising our expectations by the reverse word order and answering one of our questions by giving us the referent to "that" from the first line. He then slowly begins his longest sentence, again using enjambment and rhyme to affect the pace, but mostly manipulating the clauses and five prepositional phrases, inserting three of them between the subject and the verb "made" to build tension.

The third stanza is syntactically the simplest and least enjambed. Beginning with the adverb "truly," Larkin delays the subject and verb with an adverbial clause, then he hurries the movement with two fairly simple lines, coming to an abrupt halt with the word "worse," which is balanced against the "truly" that began the stanza. The word "worse" slows us before we fall away again into the second half of the compound sentence. "Blindingly undiminished" slows us again, then we stagger forward through the three phrases that make up the last adverbial clause, reaching a sense of release and rhythmic completion with the "though-so" rhyme in the final couplet. There is nothing static in this poem, no place to rest that is not of Larkin's choosing. The changes and juxtapositions constantly pull us forward. Moreover, the three longer sentences all accumulate meaning, saving the most important words to the end: "looked forward to," "unsatisfactory prime" and "kept it so."

Let's consider a free verse poem by Louise Glück.

HAWK'S SHADOW

Embracing in the road
for some reason I no longer remember
and then drawing apart, seeing
that shape ahead—how close was it?
We looked up to where the hawk
hovered with its kill; I watched them
veering toward West Hill, casting
their one shadow in the dirt, the all-inclusive
shape of the predator—
Then they disappeared. And I thought:
one shadow. Like the one we made,
you holding me.[6]

We have twelve lines and five sentences, although the fifth sentence is technically part of the fourth and given its own unit for rhetorical stress. Three lines are severely enjambed, three others make complete rests and the remaining six are partial rests. The sentences are complicated, the first teasing us with four adverbial clauses before we realize we are dealing with an interrogative sentence that reverses the movement begun in the first three and a half lines. In addition, the first three clauses of the first sentence have a descending rhythm or inflection, while the enjambed "seeing" becomes ascending, as does that following clause and the interrogative. Also pushing us through the sentence is the increasing dread and the reader's question as to what constitutes the threat.

The second sentence is a compound sentence, the first part of which functions as a rest; the second half speeds and slows with each adverbial clause, ending with the appositive phrase. The third sentence forms a rest, but it, and the four short phrases that follow, while standing in contrast to the longer phrases earlier in the poem, force the poem to stumble to its close, a stumbling that implies an anxiety that we also infer from the words. This anxiety takes on greater impact when we return to the poem and understand the double meaning of the second line ("for some reason I no longer remember"), which leads us to see the shadow as an omen and that the poem is not about an embrace but about an impending separation and the reason for it. Again, the movement is never static. One has the sense of moving ahead not on one's own, but of being pulled along by the syntax.

The third poem is David Bottoms's "On the Willow Branch":

Now the pond is still and the softest paddle stroke eases
the boat into the cove. Over the floating stars
you drift, the water settles around you.

The eyes widen as the body remembers,
the stars flare over the pines.

Down cove the tree frogs line their favorite hymns
and the wood drake listens.
At your fingertips the water strider performs
his nightly miracle.

Then a branch above the jon boat rustles like breath
and you look up. Nothing,
then the rustle again, and you shine the light.

Red eyes spark on the willow leaves,
flare, selfless,
and suddenly you're ashamed of your loneliness.

The wind gusts hard at the pond, and the branch sways
out of your beam. The jon boat tosses
easy in the wave-slap, and the old brain clings
to the spine.[7]

The poem describes someone at night paddling a boat into a pond, becoming aware of an animal up on the branch of a willow tree—perhaps a raccoon—and experiencing an epiphanic moment. I don't wish to comment on the content but to point out that the tension in the form comes from the line breaks, charged imagery and language. The poem's ten sentences are nearly all compound sentences of similar structure, while the exceptions start with propositional phrases and make an equivalent shape. The sentence with the greatest tension is in the fourth stanza, and that tension is caused primarily by the short line "flare, selfless." All ten sentences are nearly the same length, and in each compound sentence the first half moves quickly and the second half slowly. The effect is a sense of dullness. The pacing and movement of the poem—its very form—seem at odds with its subject. It can also be argued that the charged imagery and diction are inappropriate. They are not tied to the needs of the content, but exist to create expectations that are not satisfied.

What are those tree frogs lining their favorite hymns, what is the water strider's nightly miracle? To create more expectations than the poem satisfies will frustrate the reader.

Bottoms has written fine poems but perhaps this is not one of them. What should be noticed is that the ten sentences with their repetitive structure create a form that is not integrated with the poem's content. Previously we defined grace as the blending of pattern, shape and radiance in a form that is equal to content. In "On the Willow Branch" one feels that form and content pursue their own ends, each free of the other.

Here is a last example of pacing in a poem by James Wright.

A FISHING SONG

I have never killed anybody
Except a gopher, and some fish.
I blatted fine gold hair all over hell's half acre
With a shotgun beside a road.
And one fish among many, a sunfish, I liked.
I cut his throat, and I ate him.
Whatever is left of the gopher's little ratface,
So far more sensitive than a song-thrush's face
When you see it up close,
Blows on a prairie somewhere.
Minnesota's dead animals are too many
For me to remember.
Yet I live with and caress the body
Of the sunfish. One out of many,
I caught him out of sheer accidental daring
As he tried to hide in the sunlight.
Leaping toward the Marsh Lake Dam,
He pretended he was merely a little splinter
In the general noon.
I knew better about his life.

Sweet plum, little shadow, he feeds my brother,
My own shadow.[8]

Even though the syntax and diction of the Wright poem
are simpler than the previous poems, we are always aware of
Wright's control over the pacing, beginning with the expectations
caused by the juxtaposition of the title with the first line, to the
direct address and surprise at the end. Much of the tension comes
from the syntax. The poem's 22 lines are broken mostly as natural
pauses and only two are slightly enjambed. Of the eleven sentences, only the fifth ("What is left . . .") and the eighth ("One out
of many . . .") have any real complexity. The rest are fairly simple
and all, with one exception, use different syntax, length and
rhythms. The exception is the first two sentences in the first four
lines. These have almost the same structure, but when we read that
very different third sentence ("And one fish among many, a sunfish,
I liked."), the result is surprise and increased momentum.

The jazz saxophonist Ben Webster had a way of varying
the quality and texture of nearly every phrase of music he played,
which gave each phrase the added quality of surprise. Wright, too,
uses such constant variety. Speed, length, rhythm—each line is
different and each contains its surprise. Additionally, Wright uses
syntax, punctuation and the pauses as pointers, to first show us
this, then that, and to keep us moving forward.

There remains one last element of pacing to touch upon:
proportion. Language is information and information is energy. If
pacing is the force of that energy, then proportion is its distribution. Proportion is primarily affected by the arc the poem makes,
the fact that it has a beginning, middle and end—parts that may
not be understood as beginnings, middles and ends until the poem
is finished. Proportion is also affected by the poem's length and the
need for every word, sound, effect, et cetera to contribute to the
purpose of the poem. "Purpose" is certainly an inexact word, but
within it lurks the idea that any poem has an ideal number of words
of a certain quality and that to go over or under by even one

syllable is to violate the laws of proportion and so weaken the poem. Where the poet starts the poem and the reason for the placement of every successive word is partly controlled by this need for proportion. If the poem is too long or too short, then exact pacing is impossible, because the movement of the language becomes separated from the requirements of content.

Proportion is not a technique but a quality that influences not only pacing but also the other three categories of form—tone, the aural qualities of the language and the relation between stressed and unstressed syllables. At the close of the poem, we must not only feel that our expectations have been met but that our lives have been increased, if only to a small degree. We read in part to lose consciousness of our surroundings and to be a different person when we return to them. This rarely happens, but how the poem spins us through it, how it manages our expectations and interest without finally frustrating us, is also how it draws us away from our complacency and self-obsession. To learn to control pacing is one of the many ways a poet learns to control the poem. As Baudelaire said, "There are no *minutiae* in matters of art."[9] If something works, the poet must determine why it works—(1) to prove he or she isn't deceiving himself or herself and (2) so that it can be done again.

6 | The Function of Tone

ONE OF OUR FIRST QUESTIONS when we pick up a poem is: What brought this poem into being? This is not nosiness on our part. Most poetry written over the past 200 years has tried to give the impression that it was driven into existence by forces impossible for the poet to resist. Rainer Maria Rilke wrote in a letter to his wife (June 24, 1907), "Works of art are indeed always products of having-been-in-danger, or having-gone-to-the-very-end in an experience, to where one can go no further . . . and the work of art, finally, is the . . . most valid possible expression of this uniqueness."[1] And Philip Larkin described the first stage of writing a poem as "when a man becomes obsessed with an emotional concept to such a degree that he is compelled to do something about it."[2] What he does is write a poem that attempts to re-create that same emotional concept in the reader.

As a result, the question of why was the poem written is one of the most important we can ask because it provides access to part of the poem's intention. "Part" because the author's intention controls both the means of the poem (how it was written) and its ends (why it was written) and our first question deals with why, not how.

The poem's intention is found both within the meaning of its words and in its sound: that is, in the individual sound of the words and in their relation to one another. Let's first look at the meaning of the words.

The three types of meaning are denotative, connotative and intonative. Denotative is a word's primary meaning. Bread, for instance, is a comestible made up of flour, yeast, water and so on. A word's connotative meaning includes its secondary meanings as well as its symbolic and cultural dimensions. Bread is the staff of life as well as a word for money. Intonation is the emotional shading given by the word's stress and pronunciation. It also indicates whether the sentence is interrogative, declarative or exclamatory. In a piece of writing, such as a poem, intonation must be inferred from the context and/or from mechanical or formal devices such as typeface, punctuation marks, line breaks, meter, rhyme, the onomatopoeic values of sound and pitch and so on. It is through a piece of writing's intonation that we discover the intention of the writer. Tone controls how we read a word's denotative and connotative values.

Tone is one of four general linguistic qualities making up a poem's form. The others are the relation between stressed and unstressed syllables; the aural qualities of language, that is varieties of rhyme, alliteration, vowel pitch, consonant quality and so on; and third, pacing, which is controlled variations in the forward momentum of the poem.

Of these four qualities, tone is the most difficult to analyze because it is intangible. Like a person's emotional mood, it cannot be precisely measured. Yet if we do not correctly recognize the poem's tone, then we will be unable to discover its meaning and consequently its intention. Further, the tone of the poem and the tone of the speaker of the poem may be different, as in T. S. Eliot's "The Love Song of J. Alfred Prufrock" or Robert Browning's "To His Last Duchess."

Of these four qualities that make up a poem's form, we can say that tone is the way in which *the manner of the telling is included in what is told;* the manner of telling becomes part of the subject matter. *The Princeton Encyclopedia of Poetry and Poetics* states that tone, "on which the effectiveness of a discourse largely depends, consists in the tactful selection of content and in the adjustment of style to influence a particular audience."[3] I question the word "particular" since I think a poem should address as wide an audience as possible, but the more important question is: What is a tactful selection of content?

The process of writing is a process of discovery. One never begins writing knowing what the end product will be. It is found along the way. The end product is the poem's intention and how that intention is communicated: what Coleridge called the best words in the best order. All else—emotion, description, idea, beauty of language—are aspects of that tactful selection because that selection affects more than content, it is also the way the poem is told: it is form. The reader seeks to discover what led the writer to break silence. The writer in giving us a poem is presenting us with a metaphor that represents some aspect of his or her emotional relation to the world, what Suzanne Langer called "his *insight* into the nature of sentience, his picture of vital experience, physical and emotive and fantastic."[4]

The metaphor has been a great discovery on the part of the writer, and we, as readers, want to share in that discovery, not only because we hope to be entertained but also because that discovery may be useful in the living of our lives. The metaphor may be the transcription of a remembered event, it may be totally invented or it may fall someplace in between. What is important is the truth of the metaphor, not what gave rise to it.

At some point in the writing process, the poet discovers the tone of his or her telling perhaps even before he or she discovers the connotative and denotative meaning of the words. In fact, it is tone that often allows us to expand a word's special denotative meaning to the wider connotative meaning. And again from the *Princeton Encyclopedia*, we say that tone is the work's "pervading 'spirit' or 'atmosphere' or 'aura.'"[5] Beyond that immediate tone lie "more complex descriptors which attempt to map onto the text larger blocks of a given version of literary history: such attributes as 'sentimental,' 'classical,' 'romantic.'"[6]

Most simply tone is the emotional distance between speaker and subject matter. It also indicates the writer's emotional distance to the reader. This is not style but the greater umbrella of intention, which includes style, structure, all those elements that the writer wants to affect the reader.

We go to a work of literature for the emotional life within it, and tone becomes our guide within that labyrinth. Clearly, in a restaurant menu tone matters little, but in a newspaper article the tone indicates the reporter's (or editor's or newspaper's) particular slant. It can be a personal slant indicating that the reporter wishes us to see these events in a particular way (good, bad, horrifying, benign), or it can be a cultural slant, as in a *New York Times* article that takes for granted cultural assumptions that may or may not be true.

When we look just at the meaning of words, we find that tone has four governing aspects. Try to imagine the diagram of an atom. The subject matter is the nucleus. Swirling around it, let's say on a north-south axis, is the entire range of possible emotion: love, hate and everything in between, scorn, envy, jealousy, adoration. We can imagine these graded, put side by side and forming a circle, just as colors are shaded from one hue to the next. We may call these the qualitative aspects of tone.

Now imagine another circle, this one swirling on an east-west axis. On this circle we have different types of voice: the ironic, the sincere, the cynical, the gullible and so on. These, too, can be arranged like colors, shade by shade.

Now imagine a third circle that cuts across the other two. Call it aspects of conditionality. I do feel sad; I should feel sad, I could feel sad, I might feel sad and so on.

The fourth aspect is intensity or distance. Are emotion, voice and conditionality weak or strong? In our model this can be represented by how far from the nucleus these circles rotate. In a newspaper article they may be distant. In an editorial they come closer. In a restaurant menu they may seem absent. In a descriptive menu (an enticing concoction of anchovies, capers and cream) our rotating circles come a little closer.

Emotion, voice, conditionality and intensity are the primary elements determining tone in the denotative and connotative meaning of words. Any writer has to come to terms with all four before the piece of writing is done. Take word choice. A word like "sad" has dozens of synonyms, ranging from a hint of emotion to the histrionic. This is true of all adjectives, adverbs, nouns and verbs. The synonym a writer chooses is partly determined by the tone he or she wishes to employ.

It would be pleasant if degree of emotionality were the only factor affecting synonyms, but it is not. English has more synonyms than any other Western language, and the reason for this is historical. William the Conqueror, Duke of Normandy, invaded England in 1066 and brought with him tens of thousands of Latinate words. The French, obviously, were the conquerors. The resident Anglo-Saxons became the lower class.

After a few hundred years, the two groups merged, but the combined language retained classist characteristics. The French perspire; the Anglo-Saxons sweat. The French ate beef; the Anglo-Saxon ate meat. The upper classes have professions; the lower classes have jobs. They work. To return to the word "sad," we have grim, unhappy, bleak, which are Germanic. We have unfortunate, lamentable, miserable, which are Latinate. The difference between Latinate and Germanic often indicate a difference in class and education. The Latinate tend to be more refined. I feel sad tonight; I feel melancholy tonight. In England, with a more rigid class system, these differences become even more important.

So two factors influence diction: the degree of emotion and the Latinate-Germanic element, which is classist and may suggest the speaker's degree of education. And we can have a classist aspect where we don't have an emotional one, as in I bought a new car or I bought an automobile. We can emotionally shade diction just as we shade voice and conditionality, and this shading may be a prime factor in intensity, as in I dislike you, I hate you, I detest you.

When we approach a poem, we try to find its emotional center and to discover why the poem was written. It is through tone that we make these discoveries. When I read Spanish—my Spanish is poor—I can often understand meaning but I can't understand tone. Consequently, I can read a newspaper but I have no sense of poetry; or rather, I can say that a poem is about a particular event or emotion but I have little sense why the writer decided to write about the event. It is tone that tells us this.

Think of the first line of Philip Larkin's poem "Talking in Bed": "Talking in bed ought to be easiest." The word "ought," the conditional, is the primary establisher of tone. It contains elements of wonder, desire, regret, fatalism. But the sentence is also affected by the nonemotional quality of the other words. "Talk" is the least emotional and descriptive of all the verbs for human speech: intone, orate, chatter, prattle. "In bed" is also nonemotional and could have been replaced by after fucking, after sex. The word "easiest" obviously could have been replaced by more descriptive words. But the word that Larkin wants to emphasize is "ought." In order to make it resonate, he must make it stand out in the line.

Larkin does that by making the other words emotionally neutral and with the halfrhyme with "talking." Indeed, the poem becomes about how things ought to be. By flattening the other words, Larkin is able to begin making this declaration. It would be wrong to say that he establishes the poem's tone in this line, but he suggests what the tone will be. We read by anticipating what will come next, and the word "ought" leads us to anticipate a certain tone. Reading on, we see we are correct. In fact, it is tone that often lets us anticipate because it controls our emotional understanding of the whole.

So tone is not only about the emotional value of key words but also of surrounding words. Often one can argue that the more aggressive the word's denotative and connotative meanings, then the more neutral should be the tone. Conversely, the more neutral the word's denotative and connotative meanings, then the more aggressive should be the tone. When the three types of meaning are equally aggressive, the work becomes strident. When the three types of meaning are equally passive, then we can't discover intention and we read simply to discover event, rather than emotional shading, again, as in a newspaper article. But a poem is not passive; it is meant to communicate emotion. In the *Princeton Encyclopedia* a poem is defined as "an affective or expressive instrument: i.e., a piece of rhetoric meant to move its audience."[7] A newspaper article is not primarily intended to move its audience but to inform. When it tries to move, it becomes yellow journalism.

Anton Chekhov once wrote to a young woman friend, Lydia Avilova, about a story she had sent him (March 19, 1892). "I read your story *On the Way*. If I were the publisher of an illustrated magazine I would publish it with great pleasure. Only let me give you some advice as a reader: when you describe the miserable and unfortunate, and want to make the reader feel pity, try to be somewhat colder—that seems to give a kind of background to another's grief, against which it stands out more clearly. Whereas in your story the characters cry and you sigh. Yes, be more cold."[8]

Lydia Avilova didn't like Chekhov's comment, and a month later Chekhov wrote to her again (April 29, 1892). "I wrote to you before that you have to be cold when you write touching stories. But you didn't understand me. You can cry over your stories and groan, and suffer together with your characters, but I think it must be done in such a way that the reader never notices it. The more objective you are, the stronger will be the impression you make. That's what I wanted to say."[9]

Chekhov's remark about objectivity leads us to a second function of tone. Not only does tone establish the author's emotional involvement with subject matter, it also establishes the author's credibility. If the tone of the writing is strident or keeps changing unaccountably, we stop believing the writer. Credibility is based on trust. We trust what comes next will make sense and contribute to the whole. If we don't trust the writer, we stop reading. Again, there may be two tones here: the tone of the piece and the tone of the speaker of the piece. It is just because we distrust the tone of the speaker of "To His Last Duchess" that we discover Browning's intention.

We begin a poem or a piece of fiction searching for its tone. We do this even with some anxiety because it is tone that allows us to anticipate and have a sense of what will come next. Until we discover the tone, we remain, as it were, up in the air. Tone grounds us. When we come upon the word "ought" in Larkin's first line, "Talking in bed ought to be easiest," we experience something like comfort. We have a sense where the poem will go.

Within the language itself, as separate from the sound of the language or the imposed embellishments of meter, rhyme and so on, tone can be established both by the manner of the telling—that is, choice of diction, syntax, pacing, conditionality—and by what is told: that is, the denotative and connotative meaning of the words. One can divide subject matter into descriptive, intellectual and emotional. All three establish tone. For instance, Chekhov's short story "Gusev" begins, "It was getting dark; it would soon be night." The story concerns a Russian soldier who has been released from the service, is going home by ship and is dying. The first sentence not only details the time of day but presents us, as we come to realize, with a symbol that refers to the fact that Gusev is dying.

Not only do we read by anticipating what comes next, we read through the lens of what we have read. Our life experience shows us that phenomena have metaphoric value and therefore tonal value. Morning, afternoon, evening, night. These words also connect to hope, aspiration, life and to the end of those things. The same is true of spring, summer, fall, winter. Our medium is time. Not only do we constantly measure that time, but everything around us contributes to that measurement. Consider the emotional value given to colors: red, pink, blue, white, gray, black. Each has a tonal shading derived in part from emotion (the passion of red, the coolness of blue), in part from purity (white and black) and in part from age (pink and gray). These are the connotative values of any word. They are established by our experience and may be different in different cultures and in different periods.

As a result, the sentence "It was getting dark; it would soon be night" makes us attentive to the possibility that a certain tone will be established, just like the word "ought" in the line "Talking in bed ought to be easiest."

Conditionality affects tone, but so does certainty and uncertainty. What does the qualifier do in the first sentences of Albert Camus's *The Stranger*: "Mother died today. Or, maybe, yesterday; I can't be sure" Immediately we know something important about the speaker. This, too, is an example of how the tone of a text may be different from the tone of the speaker of the text. When Camus inserts "Or, maybe, yesterday," we know he is telling us something crucial about his character.

Read the beginning of Raymond Chandler's story "Red Wind": "There was a desert wind blowing that night. It was one of those hot dry Santa Anas that come down through the mountain passes and curl your hair and make your nerves jump and your skin itch. On nights like that every booze party ends in a fight. Meek little wives feel the edge of the carving knife and study their husbands' necks. Anything can happen. You can even get a full glass of beer at a cocktail lounge."[10]

Something nasty is going to take place, although Chandler deflates the possibility of the horrible with the joke at the end. The speaker also displays an intelligence that lets us believe he will remain in control no matter what. The paragraph establishes suspense. Conditions exist for extreme violence but the violence has not yet occurred. Suspense then is an element that affects tone. What we know of the writer, what we feel about where we find the story, what we think about its beginning: we conclude this will be an adventure with murder and mayhem.

Now consider this beginning from P. G. Wodehouse's *Uncle Fred in the Springtime*: "The door of the Drones Club swung open, and a young man in form-fitting tweeds came down the steps and started to walk westwards. An observant passer-by, scanning his face, would have fancied that he discerned on it a keen, tense look, like that of an African hunter stalking a hippopotamus. And he would have been right. Pongo Twistleton—for it was he—was on his way to try to touch Horace Pendlebury-Davenport for two hundred pounds."[11]

The paragraph creates certain expectations. Suspense is established. But because of the humor (the names, the simile, the descriptions, the language), our expectations differ from those created by the Chandler story. In the Chandler, we expect to be made apprehensive; in the Wodehouse, we expect to laugh.

So tone is more than establishing an emotional relationship with the material. It is also anticipating how that relationship will evolve, whether fearful, humorous, romantic and so on.

We find some occasions, however, when the tone does not declare itself so quickly. In the same way that obscurity in content can be used as a tool to make the reader ask why and to become a participant in the creative process, so may tone be obscure. In such an instance we read in part to seek out the tone, which again means we read to discover the writer's intention. Look at the beginning of Kafka's *The Metamorphosis*. "As Gregor Samsa awoke one morning from uneasy dreams he found himself transformed in his bed into a gigantic insect. He was lying on his hard, as it were armor-plated, back and when he lifted his head a little he could see his domelike brown belly divided into stiff arched segments on top of which the bed quilt could hardly keep in position and was about to slide off completely. His numerous legs, which were pitifully thin compared to the rest of his bulk, waved helplessly before his eyes."[12]

The words are reportorial, almost scientific. Although we find comic elements, it is not funny. Although we find horrible elements, it is not fearful. The paragraph doesn't have a clear emotional direction. What we find is surprise, which provides us with the energy to keep reading. The surprise coupled with the very matter-of-factness of the language (itself a tone) propels us forward.

Tone, as said before, is the intangible element, while the apparent absence of tone may itself constitute a version of tone.

The American poet Charles Simic also has many poems where the tone is diminished. Here is "Drawn to Perspective."

> On a long block
> Along which runs the wall
> Of the House of Correction,
> Someone has stopped
> To holler the name
> Of a son or a daughter.
>
> Everything else in the world lies
> As if in abeyance:
> The warm summer evening;
> The kid on roller skates;
> The couple about to embrace
> At the vanishing point.[13]

The word "abeyance" does wonderful work because it has a tonelessness not shared by its synonyms: dormancy, standstill, limbo. The poem's actions and descriptions ("The warm summer evening; / The kid on roller skates") are potentially jam-packed with tone, but because of the word "abeyance" no action has as yet begun. We have only potential. We are on the threshold of action. What this diminished tone can do in a poem is to give it the appearance of existing without an author, which in turn gives it the appearance of permanence, as if it had always existed, in the way that the Bible exists or that laws exist. It tries to separate itself from a human maker. And isn't that also a tone? Doesn't it make us ask why Simic choose this as a strategy?

The apparent tonelessness of a piece of journalism tries to testify to the writer's objectivity. The grief expressed in an elegy creates a tone that makes us believe the material is truly heartfelt and, again, that the writer was driven into speech by the strength of his or her feelings. The tones we have been discussing all emerge from content. But we can also have tone that is imposed on top of the content as a rhetorical device meant to convince us of something. This, too, is a strategy.

Sentimentality is such a device. We distrust it because the emotion seems to have been imposed from without rather than arising from within. We say in such a case that the emotion is not deserved. Often this is manipulation on the part of the writer, but sometimes the writer simply has not done enough preparation. Consider the poem "B.C." by William Stafford, a poet who has written many fine poems.

The seed that met water spoke a little name.

(Great sunflowers were lording the air that day;
this was before Jesus, before Rome; that other air
was readying our hundreds of years to say things
that rain has beat down on over broken stones
and heaped behind us in many slag heaps.)

Quiet in the earth a drop of water came,
and the little seed spoke: "Sequoia is my name."[14]

We feel manipulated by the adjectives, the simple rhyme and a plot that resembles the plot of Hans Christian Andersen's "The Ugly Duckling." But mostly we feel the emotion at the end—the tone—is not deserved. It is not integrated with the whole. It is imposed.

We find many instances of tone being imposed from without. For instance, a piece may be overdramatic or sensational or may have an undeserved sense of foreboding or jocularity. Once these false strategies are mentioned, then many become obvious. But there is a more insidious imposed tone that is harder to spot and that has become common in contemporary poetry. I am referring to earnestness.

We cannot pick up a poetry magazine without coming upon examples of earnestness. What is earnestness? It is a tone meant to convince the reader of the truth of the speaker's feelings in the absence of sufficient evidence. It is an attempt through the manipulation of tone to convince the reader that the material is indeed heartfelt and that the writer was indeed forced to write because he or she was unable to remain silent. It is a form of propagandizing. But if we analyze the event described by the poem and the writer's description of his or her emotions and the tone imposed on the relationship between the two, then we may come to think that the tone is undeserved. It is imposed from without rather that arising from within.

Look at "From a Childhood" from Rainer Maria Rilke's *The Book of Images* published when he was in his 20s.

> The darkening was like treasures in the room
> in which the boy, so deeply hidden, sat.
> And when his mother entered as in a dream,
> a glass trembled on the silent shelf.
> She felt how the room was giving her away,
> and kissed her boy: Are you here? . . .
> Then both gazed fearfully toward the piano,
> for many an evening she had a song
> in which the child got strangely, deeply caught.
>
> He sat stock still. His wide gaze hung
> upon her hand, which, all weighed down by the ring,
> as if it trudged through deep snowdrifts,
> traveled over the white keys.[15]

The translation is by Edward Snow, to my mind the best of the contemporary translators of Rilke. The tone is earnest and portentous. It is made that way by the diction, the similes—*like treasures in the room, as in a dream, trudged through deep snowdrifts*—by the adjectives and adverbs—*deeply, silent, fearfully, strangely, deeply, stock still, wide, deep, white*—and by the actions—*so deeply hidden, sat; entered as in a dream; a glass trembled on the silent shelf; gazed fearfully toward the piano; in which the child got strangely, deeply caught; His wide gaze hung / upon her hand, which, all weighed down by the [wedding] ring, [the hand] traveled over the white keys.* These elements seem added rather than arising from the content. A discrepancy exists between the event and the description of the event. The purpose of this is to convince us of something about which the poem gives us insufficient evidence.

In the *Poetics* Aristotle wrote that tragedy has six elements that determine its quality: plot, character, diction, thought, spectacle and song. Of these six he calls spectacle "the least artistic and connected least with the art of poetry" because it is imposed from without. An imposed tone such as sentimentality or earnestness is a minor form of spectacle. It is a rhetorical device imposed from without in order to convince the reader of the value of what is within.

So far our subject has been tone as it results from the meaning of words. But tone is also affected by the sound of the words as well as elements imposed on the language. These can be divided into (1) elements that emphasize specific words, such as rhyme, alliteration, assonance, consonance, pitch and the onomatopoeic value of words; and (2) elements that affect the whole poem, such as meter and line length. Clearly these may overlap. A spondee, for instance, calls attention to a specific word or pair of words while also being an aspect of meter. Line breaks can emphasize a word not normally emphasized.

Some of this we can get rid of quickly. It is obvious how rhyme can give emotional emphasis to a word that otherwise might not receive such emphasis. The ending of Stafford's poem "B.C." with its "came" and "name" rhyme is such an example. And we can imagine how alliteration, assonance and consonance can do the same. As for line breaks, the line can be broken in such a way as to make the first word of the next line into a surprise, that is, something not anticipated. That, too, is emphasis. Moreover, the strongest places in the line are at the beginning and end, and so the lines can be broken in order to put key words into those positions. All this is fairly self-evident.

Tone is also influenced by vowel pitch and the onomato-poeic value of words. Vowel pitch runs from low *oo* to high *ee*. Some argue these sounds by themselves carry emotional value. Others argue it is through historical association that the words using these sounds receive their emotional value. (These matters are discussed at length in George Steiner's *After Babel*.) But it seems true that high-pitched vowels are disruptive and low-pitched vowels are soothing. For instance, the high-pitched vowel and soft and hard consonants of the word "shriek" seem to duplicate the act of shrieking. This is also true of the Spanish words for he yells or shrieks—*grita, chilla*—both of which have the same high-pitched *ee* sound. On the other hand, the word "feather" has the soft sound of the object it describes. This is also true of the Spanish word for feather: *la pluma*. Again, the question is whether our response is physiological or historical. I prefer only to say that certain sounds lend themselves to the expression of certain emotions. In a good poem the tone comes equally from the sound and the sense. If you take a sonnet jam-packed with emotion and replace the words with similar sounding nonsense words, its tone is greatly reduced. If you rewrite the same sonnet in prose and insert synonyms that lack the sound value of the original language, the tone will also be greatly reduced. Look at Yeats's sonnet "Leda and the Swan."

> A sudden blow: the great wings beating still
> Above the staggering girl, her thighs caressed
> By the dark webs, her nape caught in his bill,
> He holds her helpless breast upon his breast.
>
> How can those terrified vague fingers push
> The feathered glory from her loosening thighs?
> And how can body, laid in that white rush,
> But feel the strange heart beating where it lies?
>
> A shudder in the loins engenders there
> The broken wall, the burning roof and tower

> And Agamemnon dead.
>   Being so caught up,
> So mastered by the brute blood of the air,
> Did she put on his knowledge with his power
> Before the indifferent beak could let her drop?[16]

Many aspects of this poem's sound contribute to its tone, but I only want to look briefly at the vowels and consonants in the first two quatrains. The first stanza describes the attack of the swan. The consonants are plosives, hard sound after hard sound until the fourth line: *ds, bs, ts, gs,* hard *cs, ks* and *ps.* The vowels are (1) of short duration—*great wings beating still*—and (2) from middle to high pitch: *wings, still, ing, girl, his breast.* The effect is to create a metaphor for the attack itself. It is fast and violent, and this greatly contributes to the violence of the tone.

The second stanza changes. The consonants are fricatives, labials and much softer: *bs, ths, fs, shs, ls, ghs, whs.* The vowels are long in duration: "those terrified vague fingers push" and "strange heart beating where it lies." We have more low-pitched vowels. From the sound of these words, we realize Yeats wants us to think the attack has stopped being a terror for Leda and that she is being sexually and emotionally caught up. The vowels and consonants create a sensuous, hypnotic tone.

The manipulation of vowels and consonants in the first two quatrains show how the onomatopoeic value of words can be used to influence tone, which controls our sense of the poem's meaning. The use of the consonants and vowels in the second quatrain help indicate that the experience has stopped being horrible for Leda. And, undoubtedly, the tone in these two quatrains is also deeply influenced by the meter and the pauses or caesuras.

A good poet working in either traditional forms or in free verse always has this tonal attentiveness to the sounds of the language. A factor making bad translations so bad is when the translator lacks this attentiveness and uses sounds at odds with the poem's meaning, which creates a kind of cacophony. But we also find this in many inferior poems written in English: the tone of the sounds and the poem's meaning are in conflict.

An equally subtle way of influencing tone is through meter: either in formal meter or in the rhythms created by the relationship between stressed and unstressed syllables found in free verse. Hearing the line "There was a young lady named Cranston," you prepare to be amused. The anapestic line of three feet suggests a tone apart from any meaning of the words. Further, you may recognize this, by sound only, as the first line of a limerick, a light verse form that first appeared in print in 1821. The first line of a limerick introduces the character. The second line gives the background: "who was rogered six times in a hansom." The third and fourth lines are anapestic dimeter, which serve to introduce the action: "when she cried out for more / a voice from the floor . . ." And the fifth and last line in anapestic trimeter provides the comic resolution: "Said, 'Lady, the name's Simpson, not Sampson.'" Apart from the sound of the words, the combination of meter, line length and strategy create emotional expectations that in turn create tone.

It is a commonplace of English prosody to say that each of the major meters has subject matters suitable and unsuitable to it. The dactylic and anapestic meters are more suited to comic verse. Trochaic meters are more suited to semicomic narratives concerning the lower classes, although Philip Larkin challenges this when he uses trochaic tetrameter for his poem "The Explosion." Iambic is the one meter suited to serious subjects in formal poems and the suitable length is pentameter, although within the line there may be trochaic and anapestic substitutions.

Many prosodists argue that specific meters cause specific physiological effects, as if the very sound of a limerick could tickle us. Others argue that this is historical: that through our experience of the form we come to anticipate certain emotions with certain meters. Be that as it may, it would be hard to write a serious elegy using limericks. The meter itself prepares us for a certain tone. Additionally the meter can also be used to emphasize certain words. The two quatrains of "Leda and the Swan" use five spondees—"great wings," "dark webs," "nape caught," "white rush" and "strange heart"—which work to accent Leda's strange ordeal.

We can also have cases where we are given an apparently prosaic line, then realize that the line is in perfect iambic pentameter. The first line of Larkin's "Aubade" is such an example: "I work all day and get half drunk at night." The combination of the prosaic and the meter leads us to anticipate certain effects, even emotions. We feel ourselves to be under an artistic control that is not prosaic at all.

Given these distinctions, it is easy to see how different meters affect tone. What is harder to see is how free verse rhythms affect tone. All poetry explores the relationship between stressed and unstressed syllables: This is simply a condition of the English language. A free verse poet can ignore traditional meters yet still use the relationship between stressed and unstressed syllables to affect tone. Consider once again Robert Creeley's "I Know A Man" (printed on page 57 of this volume).

The rhythms and line breaks emphasize the first and last words of the lines, the single exception being "why not, buy a goddamn big car," which shows the speaker's highest aspiration and desire for escape. The rhythmic relationships between the words joined with the rhythm created by the line lengths and line breaks create a sense of the frantic, almost desperate, almost fearful, which derives from a sense of existential isolation. This is a clear tone. If one wrote this poem out in prose and in full sentences that frantic tone would be severely diminished.

Consider the poem entitled "Flirt" by Roger Fanning from his first book *The Island Itself* published in 1991.

> Picture a butterfly balanced on a pith helmet
> that sits on quicksand, the struggler gone
> under (lungload of oat meal, no oxygen):
> so lyrical nature and agony man coexist.
>
> Let the butterfly be a certain enticing gesture
> impossible to forget: bra strap fidget

on a first date, eye contact maintained
as an abacus clacks countless, long kiss expected.

Let the quicksand be the grave, patient
for every one of us, a succulent mouth
muttering the truth: death, death. What do we get
meanwhile? Lies and lays, moments only.[17]

The tone, which we eventually discover, is one of stoical resignation tinged with a sense of paradox bordering on the comic. The poem presents a surprising analogy: that one's first exciting sexual encounter perches on top of one's mortality as a butterfly perches atop the pith helmet of a man who has just drowned in quicksand. Certainly this is peculiar, but once it is presented we cannot quarrel with it. What does life give us? Only deception and sexual encounters, the latter taking our minds off the former, while the poem itself, we see, is also a kind of deception, but a pleasurable one: a jape. Although a free verse poem, the rhythms caused by the relationship between stressed and unstressed syllables are as surprising as the content. In 12 lines we find 14 double stresses and 4 triple stresses. Also, the stressed syllables are strongly stressed, while the weak syllables are very weak. For instance, the poem uses articles 11 times and two-letter words 13 times. The rhythm caused by the relation between stressed and unstressed syllables is loud, assertive, constantly changing and energetic. That energy is further heightened by off rhyme, alliteration and the aggressive use of consonance and assonance that begins with the very first line: "Picture a butterfly balanced on a pith helmet." This noisy forceful rhythm does not make the tone but greatly contributes to it. The analogy presented by the content and the form of the poem work to surprise and engage the reader, while presenting one of life's unpleasant truisms in an original way.

If we look again at the Simic poem, which has a subtle tone, we find a slight rhythm caused in part by end-stopped lines and by a smaller range of difference between stressed and unstressed syllables. Just as the tone is flat, so is the rhythm flat, while the vowel pitch is mostly in the middle range. In fact, we can argue that the flatness of the rhythm contributes to the flatness of tone. As with the Fanning and Creeley poems, there is a consistency between the manner of telling and what is told. That consistency is one of the primary elements that makes the poem credible. If the manner of telling and what is told were at variance, credibility would be weakened.

No element of a poem's construction can be accidental unless the poet is using accident as a strategy. Just as meaning affects emotion, voice, conditionality and intensity, so can they be affected by the physical aspects of language. Not to integrate the poem's sound and sense is to jeopardize the poet's credibility with the reader. If the tone of a poem is meant to testify to the poet's sincerity, that the poet was moved to write because he or she was unable to remain silent, then the tone of the content and the tone of the form must be mutually consistent.

The reason for this returns us to the poem's function. Suzanne Langer wrote: "All art is the creation of perceptible forms expressive of human emotion."[18] Tone in a work of art is the primary indicator of that emotion. Langer also wrote:

> What discursive symbolism—language in its literal use— does for our awareness of things about us and our own relation to them, the arts do for our awareness of subjective reality, feeling and emotion; they give inward experiences form and thus make them conceivable. The only way we can really envisage vital movement, the stirring and growth and passage of emotion, and ultimately the whole direct sense of human life, is in artistic terms. . . . Self-knowledge, insight into all phases of life and mind, springs from artistic imagination. That is the cognitive value of the arts."[19]

The arts civilize us, not by making us "cultured" but by educating our feelings, by helping us live in the human community and realizing that others have interior lives similar to our own. We go to art because it is pleasurable and because of the human emotion expressed within it. As Langer says, "The aim of art is *insight*, understanding of the essential life of feeling."[20] Our first question is "Why was this thing made?" Until we understand the poem's tone, we can gain no sense of the poet's intention. Until we gain a sense of intention, we have no understanding of the poem itself. If the poem remains obscure, then we cannot care about it except as a puzzle or as a piece of decoration. The work won't touch our own emotions. We will glance at it, put it down and forget it.

7 | The Voices One Listens To

THERE ARE TWO QUOTES I KEEP returning to that touch upon the constraints I put on myself as a writer. The first is by Anton Chekhov, who wrote in a letter to his editor in the spring of 1888 "My only job is to be talented, that is to know how to distinguish important testimony from unimportant."[1]

The second quote comes from Rainer Maria Rilke, who wrote to his friend Lou Andreas-Salomé, in the summer of 1903, describing his inability to write new poems. He had just fled Paris where he had originally gone to make his poetry stronger but he had been swamped with confusion. He wrote, "Perhaps it is only a kind of clumsiness that hinders me from working, that is, from accumulating from all that happens; for I am equally perplexed when it comes to taking what is mine from books or from contacts; . . . and I no longer know how to separate the important from the superfluous and am bewildered and intimidated by all there is."[2]

Chekhov and Rilke are pointing to a kind of arbitrariness, that in the failed work the writer has not been able to distinguish between what is important or unimportant, what is necessary or superfluous. Given the choice between two words or two images, the writer chooses blindly.

True arbitrariness is choice without restriction, to choose without a sense of value or standard or a sense of limit, to choose randomly. Although a writer may suffer from this, what Chekhov and Rilke specifically point to is a confusion of value, that the writer cannot decide what makes one word better than another, what ideas or emotions are guiding the whole, and so everything appears arbitrary.

What makes a word the right word to use in a particular context? We might say that the correct word needs to be part of the author's ordering design. And there is a sentence in an essay of Charles Baudelaire's on Edgar Allen Poe that I often think about: "In the whole composition, not a single word must be allowed to slip in that is not loaded with intention, that does not tend, directly or indirectly, to complete the premeditated design."[3]

But what affects our sense of that design? And how much of what affects that design lies outside the work?

We write in privacy and we write totally enmeshed in the world. This paradox makes literature useful, because it means even the most idiosyncratic writer can tell us about our lives. But it is also what makes this question of the important versus the unimportant difficult to calculate. If we wrote only in privacy and only for ourselves, then word choice wouldn't matter. Any word could do. But we also write knowing that someone is listening. Not only is the world listening, but we are listening, our superego is listening: meaning the part of our-selves that judges our actions within society and finds them wanting. It is often this knowledge of someone listening that interferes with the writer's ability to calculate the sense of value that controls his or her work. Instead of seeing the work on its own terms or trying to discover those terms, the writer has some outside criteria influencing his or her choices.

So we have many considerations affecting our choice of a single word. Does the word fit seamlessly into the whole? Does it pass muster with the superego? Will it pass muster with the world? But when we imagine the word fitting into the whole, is it possible to do this without interference from the superego? Both Chekhov and Rilke spoke of measuring the word against the conscience, by which they meant impartiality and freedom from bias. But con-science is close to superego—that voice in the head that likes to impose moral value—and this is an area fraught with self-decep-tion. Are our choices purely aesthetic, or is there a psychological bias? When we imagine a word being accepted or rejected by the world—that is, by the reader—we are always in the area of potential psychological meddling. The confusion that comes from such an anxiety leads to the sense of arbitrariness described by Rilke: we feel unable to choose the right word or even what is meant by the word "right."

If we fear that the reader will reject a word, is it because the word does not fit into the whole, or because the word violates some system of value or idea of limit? Is the word potentially sentimental or strident or ugly or obscene? Those categories affect tone. Is there some way the word has made the tone of the piece unacceptable? When a writer rejects a word, to what degree is he or she second-guessing the reader and engaging in self-censorship? And what is the writer's fear?

Perhaps the fear is twofold. Perhaps it is not only a fear that the work will be rejected, it is a fear that the self will be rejected. To what degree is the writer afraid that he or she will be found lacking not only as a writer but as a human being?

Unfortunately, the considerations affecting the choice of a single word can occur in a split second. The psychological is mixed with the aesthetic, and it is hard to keep them separate, and then, perhaps, they cannot be kept separate entirely. Also, although we are discussing the individual word, we could say the same about image, idea, description, entire sentences. What lets us feel that our choices are correct?

When we write, we imagine a reader's response to what we have written. We think of a reader because we constantly judge the clarity and possible effect of language, image, idea and so on. Has the reader understood? What are the reader's expectations in terms of the development of the story or poem? How has the reader been moved? Naturally we writers want to be understood. After all, we are engaged in communication. But additionally we want the words to be convincing. And beyond that—and here is authorial quicksand—we often want the reader's agreement and approval, or, perhaps more important, we want to avoid the reader's disagreement and disapproval. What a small step this is. It is a minuscule movement from the desire to convince, to the desire for agreement and approval, but what a confusion may exist within that space.

Within it the writer's concerns shift from the work to the world outside of the work, from the thing to the effect of the thing.

In that same 1888 letter to his editor, Chekhov wrote, "You write that neither the conversation about pessimism, nor Kisochka's story ["Lights"] help to solve the problem of pessimism. In my opinion it is not the writer's job to solve such problems as God, pessimism, etc.; his job is merely to record who, under what conditions, said or thought what about God or pessimism. The artist is not meant to be a judge of his characters and what they say; his only job is to be an impartial witness."[4]

This is an example of what is called Chekhov's freedom; that is, he was free of the need for approval, that he had no moral, political or social expectations for the work. He saw his approach to the world and to his subject matter as completely empirical; "the scientific method," he called it. For Chekhov what was important was fidelity to his subject; the story was more important than what people thought about the story.

In praising the painter Cézanne, Rilke wrote, "No one before him ever demonstrated so clearly the extent to which painting is something that takes place among the colors, and how one has to leave them alone completely, so they can settle the matter among themselves. . . . Whoever meddles, arranges, injects his human deliberation, his wit, his advocacy, his intellectual agility in any way, is already disturbing and clouding their activity."[5]

Among other things, Rilke describes how artists must ignore their superegos, their ambitions that lie outside the work and their desires to have some kind of response from the world. All are destructive. It should also be seen that this meddling mostly occurs after the intuitive faculties have done their job. Both Chekhov and Rilke believed that the elements of the work—whether they be words or colors—need to establish a dynamic relationship between one another, a relationship that their creator's ambitions about how they function in the world will destroy.

But let's return to simple word choice. The writer measures the word against the work, against the premeditated design. The writer also measures the word against his or her superego and ambitions for the work. Third, the writer measures the word against the potential response of the world. Here is an example of the word being measured against the work: the first, untitled draft of the poem "Amaryllis" by Ellen Bryant Voigt, followed by the published version, which appeared in her book *The Lotus Flowers*.

Having been a farmer's daughter,
she didn't want to be a farmer's wife, didn't want
the perpetual flies in her kitchen, the stale
manure in all his clothes, cows
mewling at the barn door twice a day,
his bright white forehead above the hatbrim
as white as the pillow. So she nagged him toward
a job in town; so she sulked at her mending
as he unfolded the pocketknife to shave a callous
from his palm; so she sprang from the table,
weeping, when he swore at the children
and picked his teeth. If she'd married a doctor,
how forbearing she would be, arranging
the magazines in the waiting room; or a lawyer,
bringing his lunch to the courthouse, in the latest
pumps and a small blue sheath. Or the preacher
who smelled so good, his wife smelled good,
and smiled and smiled. She could have had her own life,
arranging flowers—glads and ——————,
Wednesdays over lunch. But she goes to bed
when he is tired, gets up when he gets up
Even now, she is wide awake and listening
to the man breathing who lies stretched out
beside and over her, an arm across her breast,
who had, that morning, loped into the pasture
with an icepick and plunged it into the bloated cow,
its several stomachs failed, too full
of sweet wet clover.

And here is the published version of "Amaryllis."

Having been a farmer's daughter
she didn't want to be a farmer's wife, didn't want
the smell of ripe manure in all his clothes,
the corresponding flies in her kitchen,
a pail of slop below the sink,
a crate of baby chicks beside the stove, piping
beneath their bare lightbulb, cows calling at the gate
for him to come, cows standing in the chute
as he crops their horns with his long sharp shears.
So she nagged him toward a job in town;
so she sprang up from the table, weeping, when he swore;
so, after supper, she sulks over her mending
as he unfolds his pearl pocketknife
to trim a callus on his palm.
Too much like her mother, he says, not knowing
any other reason why she spoils the children,
or when he comes in from the combine with his wrenches
to find potatoes boiled dry in their pot,
his wife in the parlor on the bench
at her oak piano—not playing
you understand, just sitting like a fern
                         in that formal room.
So much time to think,
these long hours: like her mother,
each night she goes to bed when her husband's tired,
gets up when he gets up, and in between tries
not to move, listening to the sleep of this good man
who lies beside and over her. So much time alone,
since everything he knows is practical.
Just this morning, he plunged an icepick
into the bloated side of the cow unable to rise,
dying where it fell, its several stomachs having failed—
too full, he said, of sweet wet clover.

Several points should be made before discussing these two versions. Ellen Bryant Voigt is no beginner. She has been passionately writing poems for over 30 years, and "Amaryllis" appears in her third published volume. By this I mean she has already done a fair amount of choosing and rejecting even before she starts her first draft. Second, we don't know how quickly she produced the first draft: whether it took hours or came quickly. Third, 34 more drafts were necessary before she arrived at the finished poem. But what strikes me about her first draft is that it not only has the first and last lines of the final poem, but also its structure and much of its strategy.

After she finished the first draft, Voigt eventually decided it contained a number of ideas she didn't need. For instance, the thoughts about marrying a doctor, lawyer or priest are already implied in the lines "she didn't want to be a farmer's wife" and "so she nagged him toward a job in town." The lines about other possible husbands repeat a gesture the poem has already made. They may be graceful, interesting and perceptive, but they don't move the poem forward, so she cuts them.

Another change is in point of view. Voigt doesn't want the woman to seem to be the farmer's victim or to suggest the farmer is in any way bad. This is an ambiguity in the first draft, and Voigt corrects it by including those new lines from the husband's point of view, by describing him as "this good man" and by indicating that if he has a fault, it is that he is practical rather than imaginative. The result is an even-handed treatment of husband and wife. Who is at fault? Neither is at fault. In the final version the farmer no longer swears at the children and picks his teeth. While what is expanded is not a description of his personal habits, but details of farm life, especially the cows, since Voigt needs to set the cows up for the end. She has to place them in the reader's memory.

So Voigt cuts back on the woman's fantasies and builds up the character of the man. Do you see what a difference it makes for the pocketknife to become a "pearl pocketknife," how the word "pearl" blunts and civilizes the pocketknife?

Another change comes at the end of the poem. In the first version the icepick is suggestively phallic. The woman is lying wide awake listening to the man breathe as he lies stretched out beside and over her and she thinks how that morning he loped into the pasture and stuck an icepick into an ailing cow. Voigt doesn't get rid of the phallic entirely, but she weakens it. She adds the description of the husband as a "good man" and exchanges the verb "stretched out" for the less descriptive "lies." She takes the man's arm off the woman's breast. And she inserts the sentence "So much time alone, / since everything he knows is practical" between the reference to the man's body and the reference to the icepick. In the final version the icepick is less aggressive. The phallic suggestion is weakened.

A final important change is the title. The first draft had no title, but one can perhaps see "amaryllis" in the blank space after "glads." Amaryllis is the name of a shepherdess in Virgil's *Eclogues*. She is a rustic sweetheart and so the title becomes ironic. The woman is caught between the idealized farm and the actual farm with all its ugliness. This again brings to mind the icepick and its phallic suggestion.

In the revision of "Amaryllis," we see how Voigt has excised the unimportant and heightened the important. Governing these choices is a clear idea of the entire design, which she arrived at only through the writing process: a process that was plainly a process of discovery. The final poem gives no answers, as perhaps the first draft did. We are left considering the impossibility of the situation: a situation in which the only culprit is the woman's imagination, her own dreams.

Voigt, in revising "Amaryllis," tries to create a wholly balanced structure, and her changes are aimed at that end. But we can also hypothesize that certain changes were affected by her superego and how she wanted the poem to function in the reader's mind. In the first draft the husband "lopes" into the pasture with the icepick. In the next revision "lopes" is changed to "strode," then the verb is removed entirely. "Lopes" suggests an animal, "strode" the masculine. To remove both is in keeping with Voigt's intention not to show the husband at fault for the wife's condition. Also in an early draft, she inserts the phrase "a heavy leg across her legs" after the phrase "an arm across her breast." This clearly heightens the sexual, which is a dimension Voigt later decides to downplay.

It is possible to speculate that Voigt downplayed the sexuality for other than aesthetic reasons. Perhaps she was uncomfortable with the more aggressive sexuality of the father and worried about how the phallic icepick might be received. It is in areas of potential taboo that a writer is most likely to engage in self-deception, to confuse psychological restrictions with aesthetic restrictions. I don't mean to suggest that Voigt has done this. After all, a good husband is in keeping with the poem's overall intention, which is not to find anyone at fault, not to have a villain. But we see how easy it would be to make the poem suggest that the husband destroyed the wife's ambitions by sexually dominating her, by plunging the icepick into the bloated stomach, by cropping her "horns with his long sharp shears." As it is, the cow's hankering for "sweet wet clover" still echoes the wife's hankering for a life in town.

Had Voigt written that poem, she would have made a lesser poem. She would have been giving answers rather than carefully formulating the question, which is "How do we live?" She would have been writing a partisan poem in which she would be trying to gain sympathy from the reader for a poor woman dominated by her husband's brutish nature.

How does the writer tell what is important and necessary to the work? How does the writer avoid meddling with his or her intuition or with the reader? How does he or she avoid this sense of arbitrariness, this uncertainty as to what is important? What system of value or sense of limit guides the writer's choices?

Let's look at two more quotes by Chekhov and Rilke. In January 1887, Chekhov wrote to a young woman friend who had criticized his story "Mire" as being in bad taste, arguing that it shouldn't exist and would corrupt the people who read it. "To a chemist there is nothing impure on earth. The writer should be just as objective as the chemist; he should liberate himself from everyday subjectivity and acknowledge that manure piles play a highly respectable role in the landscape and that evil passions are every bit as much a part of life as goods ones."[6]

Again we see Chekhov's refusal to be daunted by what the reader might view as politically correct. He didn't use that term, of course; instead he says "everyday subjectivity." But is there a difference? "Human nature is imperfect," wrote Chekhov in the same letter, "so it would be odd to describe none but the righteous." Again what Chekhov was demanding is that the writer be free from the bullying of his own superego, free from his fear of the reader's disapproval.

Rilke's position was even stronger. In a letter to his wife in 1907, he described the debt writers owed to Baudelaire, who showed them that subject matter needs to be taken from the entire range of life without worrying about what might be improper. "Artistic perception had to overcome itself to the point of realizing that even something horrible, something that seems no more than disgusting, *truly exists*, and shares the truth of its being with everything else that exists. Just as the creative artist is not allowed to choose, neither is he permitted to turn his back on anything: a single refusal, and he is cast out of the state of grace and becomes sinful all the way through."[7]

Material comes to the creative artist through the intuition; he or she rarely chooses it consciously. And when the material comes, the creative artist is not allowed to reject some part of it because it is horrible or disgusting; the writer cannot refuse it by imposing upon it an everyday subjectivity. If he or she does, then the writer becomes sinful all the way through.

This action of turning the back on a particular subject matter or word choice: Doesn't it come from psychological and perhaps political values rather than aesthetic ones? Isn't the writer afraid of the superego and of the reader's response? Alternatively, the writer may want to please or win favor or impress or be approved of. These, too, are psychological concerns that destroy the work. This is not a matter of clarity, whether the reader understands or not, but of a false morality, whether the reader approves or disapproves.

All literature is political, whether the writer is responding to a sunset or expressing indignation over the world's many injustices. It is political because not only does it make us aware of the world, it helps us live within the world. But a distinction can be made between the political and the partisan. This is a distinction I first heard made by the poet Joan Aleshire. Partisan art, instead of posing questions, gives answers. It tells us how to think and feel. We have seen antiwar poems of this nature, radical feminist, black, gay and Marxist poems. Every belief has its partisan art, which either speaks to those already convinced of its truth or bullies those who aren't. The difficulty is that while extreme partisanship is easy to spot, its subtle forms can be insidious. Any kind of bias is a form of partisanship and if it enters the work, it then weakens it unless the work's avowed purpose is to be propagandistic or didactic or to curry favor. Isn't the writer attempting to curry favor when he or she writes something that tries, even in part, to win the reader's approval?

If we go back to why one word is chosen over another, we can make a distinction between internal and external decisions as to what is important. By internal, I mean what works on the page, what works within the whole of the design: the activity that occurs among the words themselves. The external is everything outside the work, the philosophies, the intellectual constraints, the ambitions the writer has for the work, the everyday subjectivity, what comes after the writing and reading: the accolades and rewards. Does the writer choose a word because it is correct inside the work or correct outside the work?

Any creative writing teacher will admit that the poems of undergraduates are often more original than those of graduate writers, even though they may be terrible in a thousand other ways. The undergraduate writer has not yet been told what he or she can or cannot do. Nor is the undergraduate writer, in his or her wonderful modesty, aware that anyone is listening. But graduate writers have developed the beginnings of a critical sense. They are intent on learning the rules and trying not to go off the rails. They look for models. They grow conservative. They develop an outside standard that affects their aesthetic choices. The question of what is important and unimportant is influenced by how their work will be seen by others. They grow timid and defensive. The work becomes dull.

There are benefits to be derived from graduate workshops. They help a writer to gain objectivity, and they help the writer spot alternative and unintended readings; that is, they help the writer to write more clearly. They also help the writer take the work out of the head, of having it refer to some unshared memory, and put it on the page where it can become an experience shared by writer and reader. But graduate workshops are also a conservative force in that they exert peer pressure to be tidy and correct. Where does this sense of correctness come from?

It is no coincidence that the major British and American poets of the nineteenth and twentieth century were outsiders. Keats, Wordsworth, Whitman, Dickinson, Poe, Yeats, Hardy, Lawrence—Wordsworth was the only one to go to a major university, and everyone laughed at his bumpkin accent. These writers matured with no one telling them what they could and could not do. There were plenty of other writers who came out of the universities and tried to write within some supposed tradition. They were as smart as the more famous writers and probably had their potential, but they wrote under an intellectual and psychological constraint. They were bullied by a sense of correctness. Nowadays we hardly know their names.

It is very difficult to judge the quality of contemporary writing. On the one hand, we are caught up in the everyday subjectivity that Chekhov warns against, all the isms, all the ideas of correctness. These become a filter that colors everything we read. On the other hand, we read the work through our own historical context. We recognize the references that are true of our time: the idiosyncratic usages, the mannerisms, even the silences. Raymond Carver is a writer I love, but will there come a time when his exact dialogue will sound as strange as the dialogue in a novel by Sir Walter Scott?

Sometimes in workshop we read a poem from a student that by all rights should be completely obscure. Let's say it refers to a divorce that is never mentioned within the poem. Because we know the student and the student's other work, we have a context that allows us to understand that the poem is about a divorce. Consequently, we misread the poem, even though we understand it correctly. We see in the poem something that nobody without that outside knowledge could see.

We read our contemporaries through a similar knowledge. We share the same time and space. We understand their particular air. We flesh out their work from our own experience. It sometimes astonishes me how I can give poems of the 1950s and 1960s to intelligent graduate students—poems that moved me and still move me—and their response is blank incomprehension. In almost every case what is missing for the graduate student is a sense of historical, social or cultural context. The poems seem foreign to them. This is a context that I supply when I read the poem; a context that is not on the page. This is not true of the best work of Eliot or Williams or Yeats or Neruda or Rilke, whose poems can contain within them everything needed for their understanding and appreciation.

This meddling within the work to affect the world's response imposes criteria that the work cannot and should not support. It is not surprising that some of our best writers have been outsiders, people not so vulnerable to peer pressure or worried what others think. And our literature is moved forward by these people: Rimbaud, Apollinaire, Whitman, Dickinson and others. We call a work original when it surprises our opinions and expands our preconceptions of the limits of the form. These opinions and preconceptions are biases, and the less one listens to the world and the superego, with its question "Don't you want to be liked and admired?" then the less one is influenced by such biases.

The writer must make certain the writing is capable of being understood. The writer must make certain that the reader can find his or her way within the poem. But the writer cannot try to influence the reader as to what the reader thinks about what he or she finds within the poem. The writer's concern must be the work itself, not the world outside of the work.

The most original poet of my generation, Bill Knott, is also the greatest outsider. Consider his sonnet "The Sculpture," which was dedicated to Star Black.

> We stood there nude embracing while the sculptor
> Poked and packed some sort of glop between us
> Molding fast all the voids the gaps that lay
> Where we'd tried most to hold each other close
>
> Under the merge of your breasts and my chest
> There remained a space above the place our
> Bellies met but soon that clay or plaster
> Of paris or state of the art polymer
>
> Filled every hollow which we long to fit
> Then we were told to kiss hug hug harder
> And then our heat would help to harden it
>
> We stood there fused more ways than lovers know
> Before the sculptor tore us away
> Forced us to look at what had made us so whole

The peculiarity of this poem is in the originality of its idea, a strange parable that makes sense due to the clarity of its telling. The final paradox—that there is always distance between two people, but that this very distance creates wholeness—makes a complicated statement about our intrinsic isolation as human beings. Here is another sonnet of Bill Knott's, "An Obsolescent and his Deity (Polyptych)."

> Bending over like this to get my hands empty
> Rummaging through the white trashcans out back
> Of the Patent Office, I find a kind of peace
> Here, in this warm-lit alley where no one comes.
>
> For even the lowest know that nothing new
> Is going to be thrown out now—no formula.
> Never not one blueprint will show up in these
> Bright bins, their futures are huge, pristine.
>
> Old alleymouth grabbags my attention at times
> I see the world flash by out there, furtive as
> The doors of decontamination chambers—
>
> I return to my dull, boring search, foraging
> For the feel it gives me of the thing which has
> Invented me: that void whose sole idea I was.[8]

The humor of these sonnets is deceptive. What the poems indicate is that a writer can be serious without being earnest, yet it is earnestness that critics often look for, confusing it, as they often do, with sincerity. When we work through this second sonnet it becomes tremendously sad. The narrator feels himself to be such a complete outsider that human birth had to be, in his case, an impossibility. Consequently, he had to be invented. And what could invent a Knott (Knott constantly puns on his name)? Only a void could invent a Knott.

In language, imagery, ideas and strategy, Knott's poetry is surprising and energizing. He has dozens of obscure poems, but he also has dozens that are clear and extremely moving. Knott is outside the tradition of American poetry, although not outside the tradition of world poetry. The everyday subjectivity of the critical establishment doesn't know what to make of him. They hope he will go away.

Years ago on National Public Radio the South African writer Nadine Gordimer was asked how she could continue to write when faced with imminent censorship. Her answer was that one must write as if one were already dead. If it is necessary that one must write, then one must write regardless of the consequences, even if it means not publishing. That is what Bill Knott does.

It is frightening to face a blank piece of paper, and it is common for our choices at that point to seem arbitrary. That sense of arbitrariness often leads us to turn to what we know best: the prejudices, opinions and everyday subjectivity. It isn't just subject matter that seemingly displays the nature of the writer, it is also tone, which indicates the emotional distance between the voice and the subject. Voice is often confused with the writer: that the voice of the piece is the writer's voice. Sometimes it is, sometimes it isn't. But when a writer worries that something may be sentimental or strident or ugly or obscene, it is from a fear that those qualities will be attributed to his or her voice and ultimately to the self. I know a novelist who only writes in an ironic voice to shield himself from all possible accusations. And I had a teacher in college, a poet who was able to show emotion only in a series of lovely elegies. He was a very emotional man, but it was only to the dead that he felt capable of showing his feelings. This psychological bias hurt his work. It meant that he could not be impartial.

Rilke wrote in a letter, "[One has] to take one's impartiality to the point where one rejects the interpretive bias even of vague emotional memories, prejudices, and predilections transmitted as part of one's heritage, taking instead whatever strength, admiration, or desire emerges with them, and applying it nameless and new, to one's own tasks. One has to be poor unto the tenth generation."[9]

By poor, Rilke meant free of the interpretive bias that is part of our cultural conditioning. We all have it; we must learn to recognize it. Only in such a way can we be free of everyday subjectivity. "One has to be able at every moment to place one's hand on the earth like the first human being,"[10] wrote Rilke. By which he meant that the writer must write with a sense of complete freedom, as if he or she were already dead or as if no one else existed. Only when Rilke reached these conclusions was he able to get past his fear that he couldn't distinguish between the important and unimportant, to get past his arbitrariness.

8 | The Traffic between Two Worlds

THE WORLD WE SEE, HEAR, TOUCH, TASTE AND SMELL, the world reported in newspapers—this is what we think of as common reality. It is the world into which politicians are elected, a world of tools, of pragmatism, of daily work and eating, the world where we spit, breathe and move our bowels. This world surrounds us like a shell, sometimes pressing close and sometimes, if we have money or are simply fortunate, giving us a little room to amuse ourselves. Yet the walls are always there. It is the temporal, finite, measurable world and we take that measurement with our five senses.

But there is another world that we attempt to measure not with our senses but with our emotions. In fact, emotions have no place in the world of common reality, unless as tools. Tears have pragmatic value only as a means of coercion. Nor do the senses have any function in this other world. They can lead us to the edge but they can no more take us across than we can see in utter darkness. This other world is not literal but mysterious, not measurable but immeasurable, not temporal but infinite. Because we chart this other world not with our five senses but with feelings and acts of faith, we find much disagreement as to its nature. Many wars are fought over that disagreement, and there are endless arguments.

As a result of this disagreement, we can define this other world only with a range of possibility. At one extreme is the place where God exists, all sorts of gods, spirits, magic and mysterious forces. At the other is the place where beauty exists and love is possible, where the objects of the literal world are seen through an element of emotion. To appreciate a sunset, for instance, or a rose or a rainbow—those emblems of hackneyed beauty that the newspaper world tries to turn into commodities—means to approach it with the senses and then there is a further reaction, an emotional reaction, which as human beings we deem significant. Moreover, in experiencing beauty or any aspect of this other world, we think of ourselves as most human. Because while we take our physical definition from common reality, we derive our spiritual definition from this other world, and we take our sense of self-worth mostly from this spiritual definition.

It is also argued that there is no other reality, it is only appearance and metaphor and wishful thinking, there only *seems* to be another world: beauty is a matter of taste and love a matter of glands. But what is important is perhaps not whether this other reality exists but that there is another sense of reality, a reality different from the common reality around us, a reality measured by our emotions. Whether this is appearance or fact is another issue. What concerns us is that we have this perception, even if that perception is false. For whether this other reality is fact or illusion, we still respond to it.

Because of the disagreement over the nature of this other reality, we have to keep it in mind as a range of belief with a variety of gods at one end and perhaps the concepts of beauty and love at the other. But here are further comparisons. Morality, which is basically pragmatic, belongs to the world of common reality. A philosophy of life belongs to this other reality. One world is objective and the other subjective—the rational exists on one side, the irrational on the other; wit on one side, humor on the other; action on one side, contemplation on the other; the probable on one side, the possible on the other; the decorative on one side, beauty on the other; the analytical on one, the intuitive on the other; the mortal on one side, the immortal on the other.

To make these comparisons is not to say that this other reality is better than common reality, although some would argue that. Personally, it seems the one could not exist without the other, that it is the joining of the two realities that allows us to be most human. "But Love has pitched his mansion in / The place of excrement," as Yeats writes.[1] The point, I think, is to accept both realities: the one we objectively measure with our senses, the other that we subjectively chart with our emotions, because in order to explore and understand this other reality, we need to be well anchored to the literal, and in order to lead a tolerable existence in the literal, we need to keep a constant sense of the other. We most value the person who appears to live balanced between these two worlds—the spiritual and the corporal—and we tend to criticize those people who lean more toward the corporal (they are somehow more bestial and soulless, we say) and those who lean more toward the spiritual (he is too ethereal, too monkish, there is no meat on him).

Clearly, my terminology is flawed, but I want to avoid words suggesting soul or spirit because of their religious dimension, while terms like physical reality and emotional reality or objective and subjective reality seem too limiting. The very vagueness of the terms common reality and other reality makes them sufficient for these purposes.

In that we cannot see and touch this other world, we at times forget about it or doubt it or lose our appreciation for it. After all, it has no direct value in the marketplace of common reality. It tends to be a weekend or after-hours world. But without a sense of this other world, we become diminished and our attention focuses too much on the pragmatic, hedonistic and temporal. When our sense of value becomes entirely material, then we treat other people as commodities and ourselves as consumers. The result of being too much of one world or too much of the other is to lose a sense of contrast and to become too centered on the self and to be less able to see ourselves in relation to the world around us. We become isolated.

As journalism tries to describe this literal world, so does art try to describe this other world: the former being of the day, the moment, the latter trying to be outside of time. Journalism documents and so helps to create physical links between those of us slogging our way through three-dimensional reality. It allows us to place ourselves in the physical world. Art creates emotional links between us by putting a limit on our subjectivity and showing us that our most subjective feelings are capable of being shared. We are at our worst in isolation; we lose our capacity for objective measurement and drift toward solipsism. As journalism confirms our existence in the literal world, so does art confirm our existence in this other world. Further, as a knowledge of the literal grounds and protects us in our wanderings through this other world, so does art expand and enrich our sense of common reality. Both journalism and art help to create a sense of community; they show us that our actions and feelings are part of a communal world. Both allow us to define ourselves in relation to reality—the common and the other, the reality of the senses and the reality of the emotions.

In her collection of lectures entitled *Problems of Art*, Suzanne Langer defines a work of art as "a perceptible form that expresses the nature of human feelings."[2] It tries "to make an outward image of this inward process, for oneself and others to see; that is, to give the subjective events an objective symbol. . . . It is an outward showing of inward nature, an objective presentation of subjective reality."[3]

Art helps to take us out of our isolation by showing us the commonalty of our feelings, by precisely reflecting our emotional and spiritual life, by showing us how we resemble one another, by creating links between human beings and also perhaps by showing the responsibility we bear each other. It also takes us out of our isolation by challenging our complacency—which I would define as the tendency toward spiritual solipsism, physical stasis and emotional vacancy. As humans we strive to reach a place without worry or anxiety, a place of comfort where all our needs are cared for, a place without threat, a place where we no longer have to think, improve or judge ourselves. Art functions to jar us out of this place by engaging our emotions and showing us in relation to the rest of the world and to this other reality, which, ideally, will lead us to reconsider the terms of our lives and to resume our roles in the greater community.

So far in our discussion, art affects us in four ways: (1) it objectifies subjective life; (2) it coerces us into thinking about our own lives; (3) it helps us to see our lives in relation to the lives of others; and (4) it helps to establish a balance between common reality and this other reality, the one that we are defining as a range from the theological to the lyrical. And there is the fifth way that can't be forgotten: it gives us great pleasure. Art civilizes us; that is not to say it makes us cultured or refined, but it teaches us to live within a civilization—that larger community that tends to our physical and spiritual needs.

But it is not just feelings that are the subject of art. Art also takes the literal world, takes what is mundane, and makes it fresh again. It takes something which we have grown so used to that we can hardly see and makes it new to us. Here again we have to consider a range of belief that lifts us into the province of this other reality. At the extreme end is a sort of Platonism—that each object, such as a chair or bed, has its ideal or eternal form. Poetry, said Shelley, "strips the veil of familiarity from the world, and lays bare the naked and sleeping beauty, which is the spirit of its form."⁴ By showing us the eternal forms, poetry allows us to tolerate the mundane.

At the other end of this range is the simpler idea that a poem makes us see the mundane as new by retranslating it into fresh language, symbols, metaphors, and by adding to it a degree of emotion. Riddles do this. They take a common object or idea and create an image that makes it fresh again. If we think of a simile as being made up of an object and an image, what a riddle does is present us with the image and tease us into guessing the object. Here are some Serbian riddles with the answer given. Man: earth digging earth. Eyes: two pillars hitting the sky. Comb: one dead pulls a hundred live from a mountain. Trousers: I jumped into a pit and came out at two gates. Gun: hangs on a nail, thinks evil. Boat: the dead carries the living over a field of unrest. The sound of a bell: I shake a tree here, but the fruit falls half an hour away.⁵ In each case, the image expands our sense of the object. It is as if we have had a momentary flash showing us this other world, so much huger than our own place of shadow. Plato makes this comparison is his parable of the cave in Chapter Seven of *The Republic*, that this greater world is different from our world as a chair, say, is greater than the shadow of a chair. Certainly this may be illusion, but then the image at least creates the illusion that it is describing some other place. It may be a big place—the place where God exists—or a smaller one—the place where love is possible.

In the same way that art can take the objects of this world and make them new again, so it can do the same for ideas—big ones such as truth and justice or smaller ones such as hospitality and charity. And again we approach this process with a range of beliefs with the eternal forms on one side and perhaps no more than new and original language on the other.

Most simply art takes ideas and objects that have faded into the general gray of common reality and brightens them with new language and by infusing a degree of emotion into the new definition, by creating a definition that helps us to see the object or idea in relation to feeling. "All art," says Langer, "is the creation of perceptible forms expressive of human feelings."[6] The riddle "the dead carries the living over a field of unrest"[7] is describing in terms of feeling what a boat does. No work of art presents idea or object by itself, rather they are presented, to a greater or lesser degree, through the medium of emotion, as if emotion were that field of unrest over which travels the object and the idea, the dead bearing the living, the boat bearing the human being.

The purpose of art, says Langer in one lecture, is no more than enjoyment.[8] And in another: "The aim of art is insight, understanding of the essential life of feeling."[9] And in another: "Self-knowledge, insight into all phases of life and mind, springs from artistic imagination. That is the cognitive value of the arts."[10] But I would also repeat that art helps establish community, it takes us out of our isolation and helps us to see ourselves in relation to the physical, emotional, spiritual and intellectual world around us; and furthermore, it helps us define our responsibility to that world, not by twisting our arms or foisting some philosophy upon us, but by reminding us of that relationship and by being in itself evidence of the necessary balance between the literal and the other. A work of art presents us with an example of how to live not by what it says but by what it is—a perceptible form balanced equally between the two realities.

One of the functions of poetry is to chart this other world. Poetry explores the world of feeling just as an explorer charts the physical world. And both send back maps: one being a matter of latitude and longitude coordinates, the other being a matter of emotions and metaphors. Although a poem tries to convince, it isn't an argument; although it tries to be exact, it isn't analytical; although it tries to be consistent, it isn't logical, even though it can contain elements of argument, analysis and logic within it. A poem approaches its truth not through what Keats called "consequitive reasoning" but through metaphor. Langer writes, "The principle of metaphor is simply the principle of saying one thing and meaning another, and expecting to be understood to mean the other. A metaphor is not language, it is an idea expressed by language, an idea that in its turn functions as a symbol to express something. It is not discursive and therefore does not really make a statement of the idea it conveys; but it formulates a new conception for our direct imaginative grasp."[11]

A metaphor, she says in another lecture, makes us conceive "things in abstraction; the bloodless abstract language we usually associate with abstract ideas only [names] them after they have long been conceived, and have grown familiar."[12] This gives an additional value to poetry, that it allows for the discovery and expression of ideas/concepts/emotions for which there is not yet language. Langer writes: "Sometimes our comprehension of a total experience is mediated by a metaphorical symbol because the experience is new, and language has words and phrases only for familiar notions. Then an extension of language will gradually follow the wordless insight, and discursive expression will supersede the nondiscursive pristine symbol. This is, I think, the normal advance of human thought and language in that whole realm of knowledge where discourse is possible at all."[13]

A poem both uses metaphor and is metaphor. By combining words, sounds, ideas and emotions, a poem gives a sense of this other world, not by describing it but by being a metaphor for it. The poem attempts to enact it. And not only does the language work to create the metaphor, but the way the language is presented is also part of the metaphor. For in poetry the manner of telling is as important as what is told. Language is not the end of poetry, rather language is to poetry what noises are to music or paint is to painting. The poetic use of language is not communicative, says Langer, but formulative. "Poetry as such is not discourse at all, it is the creation of a perceptible human experience which, from the standpoint of science and practical life, is illusory."[14]

So it is the metaphor that charts this other world, not by telling us about it but by enacting it, by being a paradigm for it. In the world of common reality, we can measure, describe, argue and define. We use language discursively, as it is used in journalism. But when we deal with this other reality, which we can explore only with our emotions and for which we have no objective standard, it is only through metaphor that we can measure, describe, argue and define, since metaphor, as Langer said, "formulates a new conception for our direct imaginative grasp." Additionally, what the metaphor allows us to realize is that the experience of the poem is a shared experience, because what the successful poem does is to express verbally something that we have felt but have not tried or have not been able to articulate, something that we now realize was not our own private feeling but a shared feeling, and by doing this it forges one of these links that helps remove us from our isolation.

In the short essay "The Pleasure Principle," Philip Larkin describes how a poem comes into being.

> It consists of three stages: the first is when a man becomes
> obsessed with an emotional concept to such a degree that

he is compelled to do something about it. What he does is the second stage, namely, construct a verbal device that will reproduce this emotional concept in anyone who cares to read it, anywhere, any time. The third stage is the recurrent situation of people in different times and places setting off the device and re-creating in themselves what the poet felt when he wrote it. The stages are interdependent and all necessary. If there has been no preliminary feeling, the device has nothing to reproduce and the reader will experience nothing. If the second stage has not been well done, the device will not deliver the goods, or will deliver only a few goods to a few people, or will stop delivering them after an absurdly short while. And if there is no third stage, no successful reading, the poem can hardly be said to exist in a practical sense at all.[15]

The most important sentence for our present consideration is that the successful poem must reproduce the "emotional concept in anyone who cares to read it, anywhere, any time." Why is this? Is it so we can sympathize with the poet or think him or her sincere or tender or perceptive or brave or admirable? No, it is none of those things. It is so we, as readers, can take the emotional concept and make it our own. We recognize the emotional concept as something within our own experience, something that we have felt or can imagine or empathize with, and as this linking takes place, the metaphor of the poem becomes no longer an articulation of the writer's feelings but of ours as well. Indeed, the writer's feelings are important only to the degree they lead us to confront our own feelings. What began as the symbolic presentation of the writer's subjective reality becomes the symbolic presentation of the reader's. So the fact that the writer has suffered or felt deeply is incidental to the potential impact of the poem, which must be the articulation of an emotional concept true and meaningful to the reader. Seen this way, the subject of the poem is never the writer but the reader. "Sailing to Byzantium" isn't about Yeats's ambivalence about aging; rather, it is a metaphor articulating the reader's ambivalence. The poem is about the reader, and the writer, if he or she is there, is only there as the reader's stand-in or representative.

Certainly all poetry is not directly autobiographical. Plenty of poetry lacks the first-person voice of the poet, in plenty of poetry the poet distorts, lies or invents, since fidelity to the world of common reality is not one of the poet's concerns. But just as the poem is a microcosm of this other reality, so is it a microcosm of the poet. "Paradise Lost" is not about Milton, but it is completely *of* him. It has his flesh and blood, his psychology, personality, essence. This, too, is incidental to the poem. It is important that the poem be made of the stuff of life, but it doesn't matter whose life. The question as to whether "Skunk Hour" is exactly true of Robert Lowell's life is a matter of gossip. But whether true or not true, the poem is still a microcosm of Lowell's life; yet even that is irrelevant. What is important is that he was "obsessed with an emotional concept to such a degree that he [was] compelled to do something about it" and that he had the ability to "construct a verbal device that [could] reproduce this emotional concept in anyone who [cared] to read it, anywhere, any time." The poem, if it is successful, stops being a metaphor for Lowell's emotional life and becomes a metaphor for the emotional life of the reader.

The successful poem is a microcosm of this other world and a microcosm of the poet. In addition, it is a microcosm of the time and society in which it was written. "Paradise Lost" is not about the seventeenth century but it is *of* that century. *The Iliad*, "The Rape of the Lock" and Ginsburg's "Howl" are all microcosms of the time and societies in which they were written. They reflect the society's sense of the cosmos, of the known and unknown world. Langer describes a work of art "as both a product and an instrument of human insight."[16] A poem is jointly a product of its author and of the time in which it was created, as well as an instrument of human insight into this nonrational world of feeling and spirit, aesthetic perception and intuition, the so-called other reality of my argument. So we can call a poem a microcosm of the time and society in which it was written, a microcosm of the poet and a microcosm of this other reality that the poem tries to express. And the degree to which the poem is successful is affected by the degree to which these three microcosms overlap, because the more perfectly they overlap the better we, as readers, can find our way within the poem and discover our own life—that creature waiting at the end of the labyrinth.

What besides inferior talent could keep this overlapping from taking place? Possibly the poem can fail to be a microcosm of this other world if the poet has not been "obsessed with an emotional concept." Clearly this is a Romantic notion and echoes Wordsworth, who wrote: "I have said that poetry is the spontaneous overflow of powerful feelings; it takes its origin from emotion recollected in tranquillity: the emotion is contemplated till, by a species of reaction, the tranquillity gradually disappears, and emotion, kindred to that which was before the subject of contemplation, is gradually produced, and does itself actually exist in the mind. In this mood successful composition generally begins."[17]

We find many statements like this by many poets, and I would emend Wordsworth's with a statement by C. Day Lewis, who wrote that a poet's task "is to recognize pattern wherever he sees it, and to build his perceptions into a poetic form which by its urgency and coherence will persuade us of their truth."[18] There is also Coleridge, who wrote that the metaphor-making skills of the poet "become proofs of original genius only as far as they are modified by a predominant passion; or by associated thoughts or images awakened by that passion; or when they have the effect of reducing multitude to unity, or succession to an instant."[19]

Possibly the poem will fail if it is not a microcosm of the time and society in which it was written. This has nothing to do with whether the poet lives in or out of society. Both Whitman and Rilke were children of their times, and we breathe their world through them. So it would seem that whether the poem is a microcosm of a particular time or not is not a matter of how the poet lived, but a matter of attitude. And the controlling factor of that attitude is empathy: The poem will be a microcosm of a particular time if the poet is emotionally engaged with his or her time, and that engagement would seem to be empathy in its most extended form. Baudelaire, for instance, expressed great scorn for the time in which he lived but beneath that scorn existed an empathy for the basic human creature half suffocated under a blanket of materialism and false value.

Possibly the poem will fail if it is not a microcosm of the poet. Am I, as a poet, projecting who I am or how I would like to be seen, or perhaps I just have no sense of myself? But no matter what the answer, the poem will still reflect me. It is still *of* me. Good or bad, the poem is always a microcosm of the poet, and yet the poem may fail. It may even fail when the poem is written with brilliance and originality. So there seems to be an additional requirement, and that might be how the poet sees himself or herself, sees the poem's audience and, again, his or her degree of empathy.

Before discussing empathy, let me define two types of narcissism: petite narcissism and grand narcissism. We see evidence of petite narcissism when the poem plainly exists to show off the poet as, say, intelligent, sensitive, perceptive, brave, kind, long-suffering, and so on. We know these poems and they don't concern us. We can't find ourselves within them: (1) there is no sense of audience or rather the only role of audience is adulation; (2) there is no expression of empathy (it is irrelevant to the purpose of the poem); and (3) since the poem consists of one person's self-absorbtion, there is little or no distinction between possibility and probability. Many poems fail because the writer has failed or refused to draw the line between the probable and the possible. But for the solipsist all possibility *is* probability—something becomes true because the poet desires it to be true. He or she wants a metaphor to work, so it does work; he or she wants the poem to be beautiful, so it is beautiful. This puts a barrier between the poem and the reader, who, without sufficient proof, remains unconvinced. Petite narcissism is extremely common in a period of uncertainly, anxiety, self-doubt and introspection. Not having a clear sense of himself or herself within the society, the writer replaces this with narcissism and solipsism. He or she becomes his or her own private society.

Grand narcissism is where the narcissism is so great that to look at one's self and to look at the world are the same. One encompasses the world and wherever one looks one sees oneself. To love the world is to love oneself. To caress the world is to caress oneself. Much fine poetry derives from grand narcissism—Whitman, Neruda, even Rimbaud, whose self-obsession took the form of self-hatred. Instead of empathy there is self-love on a mammoth scale with the result that to love one's neighbor is to love oneself, since one's neighbor is an extension of one's self.

We can do little with grand narcissism. It is a phenomenon, and because the poet sees himself or herself as the world, there may be a perfect overlapping of the three microcosms. Also, the grand narcissists tend to burst on the world very young or with wonderful suddenness. Although their work may show great craft, there may not be the sense of working and improving over a long period of time. But at the moment we are considering those poets who were not grand narcissists, poets who thought long about their work and whose work became increasingly better as they learned their craft, poets such as Baudelaire, Yeats, William Carlos Williams.

One of the qualities we see in these great poets is empathy, which is the ability to feel and experience another person's feelings and experiences as our own. Empathy helps us to see ourselves in relation to our fellows and to draw a line between the possible and probable. It is partly through empathy that a poem can be overlapping microcosms of the society, the self and that world of feeling. It is something a person has or hasn't, but different people have different degrees of it and we can have different degrees of it toward different things. It is even possible to make a scale with solipsism and self-obsession on one end and empathy and disinterestedness on the other. It is empathy that lets the poet take subjects from the world, then lets the reader find himself or herself within the subject and become a participant within the poem, since, after all, it is the reader's world, too. Some writers have such an abundance of empathy they never have to think about it; others must remind themselves constantly.

Perhaps this is a matter of Universality, but I think that is an overblown idea. Certainly a fear of aging is a universal fear, but it is Yeats's empathy that makes it work, that creates the bond between the writer and reader, not just the expression of Universality. Without empathy there can be only a weakened sense of Universality, since empathy not only controls subject matter but how the reader will react to it. The narcissists who write about losing their looks and ask us to mourn may have the same subject as Yeats's "Sailing to Byzantium," but their sense of audience is so self-oriented that we are excluded from the work. We are there to admire, not participate. Their stage has room for only one dancer, so their theater comes to hold only one fan.

Along with empathy, that perfect overlapping of the three microcosms is influenced by the poet's sense of audience and a sense of what it is to be a poet. Here, too, we finds a range of belief, extending from the classic to the Romantic. The classic places the least stress on the relevance of this other reality since, in many cases (think of Alexander Pope), such poetry attempts exactly to define common reality, or, in Friedrich von Schlegel's definition, classicism is "an attempt to express infinite ideas and emotions in finite form."[20] Classicism often means describing common reality in uncommon language with the hope that the thing described will transcend the literal and take on a level of glitter, which in turn engages our own emotions and sense of beauty. Failure occurs when the thing described doesn't transcend common reality and remains mundane. Instead of being beautiful, it remains decorative; instead of becoming universal, it remains trivial; instead of becoming meaningful to the reader, it remains tied to the taste of the writer; instead of becoming significant, it remains anecdotal;

instead of being able to respond emotionally, the reader can respond only intellectually.

The Romantic view of the poet, which has dominated poetry for several centuries, puts great emphasis on this other world, and it, too, has to be treated as a range of belief. At its most extreme is the idea of the poet as hero—a solitary wanderer in the shadow-land of emotion who, because of his or her superior intuition, imagination and quality of feeling is best able to chart the landscape of the heart. Unfortunately, such a view may be riddled with petite narcissism, where the function of the reader is to applaud the poet rather than to find his or her own life within the poem. Most often the poem, in all its obscurity, is something like a lion skin or rhino's horn—not something for the reader but evidence of the poet's dangerous adventures.

The late Symbolists were such poets and many of the modernists. But to some degree poets such as John Berryman, Sylvia Plath, Anne Sexton and Robert Lowell were also influenced by this sense of the poet as hero. That they suffered and wrote fine poems is not to argue the theory. The main reason this sense of self damages the poet is that it violates the poet's relationship with audience. Instead of audience and poet being in the same boat, the attitude of the poet as hero creates a situation where the poet is in a special boat. It keeps the poet from being the reader's representative and lessens the poem's chance to create a sense of community. It also puts little importance on empathy—we, as readers, become receivers, witnesses, onlookers. We don't join, we accept and stand in awe. Although there are different degrees of this position, even in the best poems of Lowell and Berryman we may feel that the poets want the attention on themselves and their troubles. These are not poems where we are encouraged to discover our own lives, and while we may be moved and experience pity and fear, we are not moved to the extent that we would be if we felt the poem was also about us.

It would seem that any definition of the poet that makes the poet essentially different from the reader will weaken the poet-reader relationship. It will make the poet less able to act as reader representative, to weaken this feeling of empathy, to decrease any sense of community, and to violate the requirement that there be a balance between common reality and this other reality. The emotional concept that has been deeply experienced by the writer can be exactly reproduced in the reader only if the writer feels that he or she and the reader are more or less in the same boat and, perhaps, that the reader is an extension of the writer. For the grand narcissists, of course, this is no problem.

To my mind, the most successful poets are the ones who fall between the classic and Romantic, who draw from both sets of ideas, who try to create a balance between craft and feeling, sense of artist and sense of audience, empathy and introspection, consciousness and intuition: poets such as Keats, Baudelaire, Yeats, Rilke, Mandelstam, Williams and Elizabeth Bishop. It is that balance between the poet and the world, of trying to exist equally in the world of the senses and the world of feelings, that allows the poet to establish the line between the probable and possible, helps the poet achieve the necessary empathy, lets him or her think in terms of relation, in terms of audience, and enables the poet to act as the reader's stand-in or representative.

Parenthetically, I should say that even though the poem may exist as an example of the balance between the two worlds, the artist, especially a Romantic artist, is forced to violate the balance by constantly focusing on the emotional. Even the classical artist is damaged by the constant need to subject the emotions to scrutiny. To endlessly dissect one's emotional life, to push it into consciousness, to muck around in those dark areas where there is not yet language does not necessarily lead to happiness. Shifting from objective reality to subjective reality diminishes one's ability to see oneself in relation to the world. It leads toward solipsism. The poet may not be a hero but I can think of many who have been heroic, since certainly it is heroic to put the ego in jeopardy. Unless the poet is a grand narcissist, being an artist does damage. It oversensitizes the emotional part of one's life, which upsets the balance and makes it difficult to live in the world of objective reality.

For the extreme position of the poet as hero, the poet makes little barks and these are deemed significant. Little value is placed on communication and understanding, while the reader is improved simply by being in proximity to the noise. But for the poet whom Larkin describes, there is the requirement that the emotional concept be experienced by the reader. Poetry, wrote Larkin, "is emotional in nature and theatrical in operation."[21]

A poem might begin with intuition and a vague feeling, but finally it is made, while the need for the reader to experience the emotional concept requires cunning on the part of the writer, in the same way that theater demands cunning. You not only want your readers to be swept away and draw pleasure from what you have written, you want them convinced. After all, the poet is trying to present the nature of this other world, and if the reader isn't convinced, isn't able to make the experience a personal experience, then the poem won't succeed.

The poet's task, as C. Day Lewis wrote, is to recognize pattern. This requires looking into the world as well as into the self. It requires seeking links between human beings and between this common and other reality. Lewis also wrote that "poetry's truth comes from the perception of a unity underlying and relating all phenomena, and that poetry's task is the perpetual discovery, through its imaging, metaphor-making faculty, of new relationships within this pattern, and the rediscovery and renovation of old ones."[22]

The poet can discover pattern only if he or is not separate from but joined to the surrounding world. Equally, the poet can't forget the reader but must endlessly measure his or her effects and language against the reader's response. Not because the poet is seducing the reader through cheap tricks but because once we see that the subject of the poem is ultimately the reader, then any poem that excludes the reader through obscurity, vagueness, indifferent form, triviality, self-obsession, narcissism—any of a thousand reasons—will fail.

Too often the artist feels his or her work is important because it expresses feelings he or she has had, but really the work is important, writes Langer, because it expresses "feelings and emotions which the artist *knows*, his *insight* into the nature of sentience, his picture of vital experience, physical and emotive and fantastic."[23] Having experienced the feelings may lead to knowledge, but otherwise the "having" is irrelevant.

But to many poets it is the having that is important, and that creates a division between the poet and audience. Such a division destroys the poet: It makes the knowledge drawn from the experience of secondary importance to the experience itself. The poet learns partly by observing the effects of what he or she has written, and if the poet is indifferent to his or her audience, then no effects can be observed. The result of this indifference, wrote Larkin, can be found throughout the poet's work.

> He will forget that even if he finds what he has to say interesting, others may not. He will concentrate on moral worth or semantic intricacy. Worst of all, his poems will no longer be born of the tension between what he non-verbally feels and what can be got over in common word-usage to someone who hasn't had his experience or education or travel grant, and once the other end of the rope is dropped what results will not be so much obscure or piffling (though it may be both) as an unrealized, "undramatized" slackness, because he will have lost the habit of testing what he writes by this particular standard. Hence, no pleasure. Hence, no poetry.[24]

To return to Schlegel's definition of classicism, that it is "an attempt to express infinite ideas and emotions in finite form," the poet tries to construct something perceived by the senses that will express a portion of the inexpressible and unencompassable. The poem is a conduit between the worlds of common and uncommon reality. It passes through the poet's self, his or her nature and personality. It is *of* the poet but must not be *about* the poet, must not be limited by his or her psychology. A work of art, says Langer, "is neither a confessional nor a frozen tantrum; it is a developed metaphor, a non-discursive symbol that articulates what is verbally ineffable—the logic of consciousness itself."[25] The result, ideally, is to link us together in an apprehensible community of feeling.

Art increases our knowledge about this other world, this world of uncommon reality, by making it less mysterious, less immeasurable. Earlier I claimed that poetry mapped this other world much as an explorer maps the physical world. By reducing our ignorance about this other world and by making us more conscious of our feelings, poetry increases the emotional territory in which we live. But to do this, the poet must think of the poem not as a vehicle of self-expression but of communal expression, not private property but public property. Seen in this light, the poem isn't the poet's servant or chattel to do with as he or she might wish. On the contrary, the poet emerges as servant of the poem.

9 | Rilke's Growth as a Poet

TALENT IN A WRITER IS CHEAP. Many have it: the ability to make metaphor, to be imaginative, to be passionate about language, to have a bent for solitude. Does it exist equally among children? But in some children it gets encouraged, or other talents are frustrated, and eventually they may reach a point in their teens when they decide that they, too, want to write. They have a certain promise, ambition, gall. If Keats could do it, why can't they? In the same way that Keats once said, If Milton can do it, why can't I?

But talent is only potential. A writer with promise is a person with a hankering. How can promise be achieved? For half a century it has been argued that a poet's success can be given a boost if he or she attends a graduate creative writing program, and, clearly, good writers have emerged from these programs. But having observed and taught in such programs, I have seen that even the most talented can fail to achieve their promise, while lesser talents have apparent success.

Talent isn't enough. Determination, ambition, energy and gall are also needed, as well as the need to have one's ego serve the writing and not the reverse. Knowledge is required, not general knowledge but knowledge in the service of the writing. In fact, everything must be in the service of the writing, which means sorting through one's life and getting rid of what is inessential to the work. Very few can do this, but a striking example of someone who did it successfully is Rainer Maria Rilke, who pushed through the limitations of his talent to become perhaps the greatest lyric poet of the twentieth century.

Rilke's first major work, *New Poems* [1907], appeared when he was 32 years old. It was followed the next year by *New Poems, The Other Part*. Although Rilke wrote many fine poems before these books, it is in *New Poems* that he went beyond his talent. His development until then can be divided into three stages. The first two are fairly similar to any young poet who has gone through a course of study like a Master of Fine Arts program. But it was through the third stage that Rilke became a major writer.

Rilke was born in Prague on December 4, 1875, and baptized René Karl Wilhelm Johann Josef Maria Rilke. His father, Josef, a retired army officer, was inspector and later head of personnel for the North Bohemia railway. His mother, Sophie, was the daughter of a Prague merchant and Imperial Councillor. René Maria was their only child, although an earlier daughter had died shortly after birth.

> My childhood home was a cramped rented apartment in Prague [Rilke wrote in a letter at age 27]; it was very sad. My parents' marriage was already faded when I was born. When I was nine years old, the discord broke out openly, and my mother left her husband. She was a very nervous, slender, dark woman, who wanted something indefinite of life. And so she remained. . . . I had to wear very beautiful clothes and went about until school years like a little girl; I believe my mother played with me as with a big doll. For the rest, she was always proud when she was called "Miss." She wanted to pass for young, sickly, and unhappy. And unhappy she probably was too, I believe we all were.[1]

Prague belonged to the Austro-Hungarian Empire, and Rilke's family formed part of the 7 percent of the city who were native German speakers: civil servants and upper middle class who lived in a small enclave surrounded by Czechs. Rilke's mother read him poetry and had him memorizing poetry when he was seven. She referred to him as her little poet, and his first known poem was written in honor of his parents' wedding anniversary when he was eight. After his parents' separation Rilke was sent to the Militar-Unterrealschule at St. Polten. "After the worst coddling," wrote Rilke, "I . . . found myself among fifty boys who all met me with the same scornful hostility."[2]

Despite his misery, he at first did well at St. Polten and he continued to write. Indeed, poetry was his main consolation. Many times at the beginning of German class, he would give copies of his poems to the teacher, who asked him to read them out loud. A fellow student later wrote, "We knew little about poetry, and were silent, for us a sign of great respect, and no one poked fun. He was a personality."[3]

After five years at St. Polten, Rilke left for reasons of physical and mental health and entered the Commercial Academy in Linz, where he lived with an aunt. At this point he resembled any other adolescent with a strong desire to write. But what Rilke also had was a high degree of energy, ambition and an intensely focused will. Socially, he was known for his ability to improvise carefully rhymed poems as a parlor game, and he flattered himself about these abilities and thought he knew something about the craft. Like other young writers, he studied contemporary magazines to see what was fashionable. He sent out his poems and wrote flattering letters to the editors. He also sent copies of his poems to other contemporary writers, calling them Master, asking for their opinion. His poetry was florid, Romantic and obscure. He tried every genre and his poems were written in every style: naturalism and symbolism, historical verse, narrative verse. He tried everything. "[I] believe . . . every artist," he wrote at the time, "must struggle through the misty fumes of crass materialism to those spiritual intimations that build for him the golden bridge to shoreless eternities."[4]

In 1895 he entered Carl-Ferdinand University in Prague ostensibly to read law but actually to take courses that would benefit his writing: history of art, literature and philosophy. He was deeply into self-expression and intent on "being" a poet, on looking like a poet. Often he walked through Prague "dressed entirely in black and carrying a single long-stemmed iris."[5] He edited magazines and published his first books: *Life and Songs* and *Offerings to the Lares*. The draft of his entry in a nineteenth-century lexicon of German poets and prose writers read: "René Maria Caesar Rilke . . . currently editor of 'Young Germany and Young

Austria.' My motto: patior ut potiar. For the present I nourish a striving toward light; for the future, one hope and one fear. The hope: inner peace and joy of creation. The fear (burdened as I am with an hereditary nervous condition): madness! I am active in the fields of drama . . . , the novella and sketch (many scattered in over 20 journals, soon to be collected), lyric poetry, psychodrama, criticism, etc."[6]

In 1896 Rilke moved to Munich to be at the center of the literary scene. He was totally self-absorbed and deeply involved in self-advertisement. Despite his apparent confidence, he was also full of doubt. In an autobiographical fragment, he wrote, "Really—I lie awake sometimes the whole night, with folded hands, and torment myself with the question: 'Am I worthy?'"[7]

Part of his doubt came from separating himself from the wishes of his family. His mother wanted him to be a poet, but even her desire made him suspicious because he felt that she lacked credibility. His father tried to be understanding but didn't see why Rilke couldn't be a clerk and write poetry, as well. As a result, Rilke came to view himself as the Prodigal Son. He had left the conventional world. Now he would either be a poet or nothing. This only increased his intention and desperation. When he was still 21, he wrote to a friend. "I feel that this is my belief: Whoever does not consecrate himself wholly to art with all his wishes and values can never reach the highest goal. He is not an artist at all. And now it can be no presumption if I confess that I feel myself to be an artist, weak and wavering in strength and boldness, yet aware of bright goals, and hence to me every creative activity is serious, glorious, and true."[8]

This was Rilke at the end of the first stage of development: the stage that defined his intentionality. The second stage began when Rilke was still 21 when he met Lou Andreas-Salomé. She was 14 years his senior, very beautiful, had published three novels, a book on Ibsen and a book on Friedrich Nietzsche, who had unsuccessfully courted her and complained about her "animal-like egoism."[9] She scorned physical love and claimed that "every man, no matter when I met him in my life, always seemed to conceal a brother."[10]

Rilke pursued her and they had a brief sexual relationship—apparently her first—which she broke off for fear of hurting her husband. She and Rilke remained close and twice went to Russia together. Later she wrote that the two of them had "developed a private life in which we held everything in common."[11] And she felt that his first trip to Russia when he met Tolstoy was "the creative breakthrough, [his] turning point as a poet."[12] Eventually she pushed him away, feeling too overwhelmed by him, but throughout his life they occasionally met and continued to correspond. After his death, she wrote, "We were not two halves seeking the other: we were a whole which confronted that inconceivable wholeness with a shiver of surprised recognition. We were thus siblings—but from a time before incest had become sacrilege."[13]

That summer of 1897, they both lived in the country outside Munich and saw each other daily. Lou Andreas-Salomé was very attracted to Rilke but felt that his effect "arose primarily from his human qualities, and not from a sense of the great poet he would become."[14] Writing to him after his death, she confessed, "I couldn't appreciate your early poetry, in spite of its musicality (you consoled me back then by saying that you would repeat it so simply someday that I would understand it after all)."[15]

But she could also see that he was spoiled and "suffered if even the slightest limits were imposed on what he wanted."[16] She proceeded to take him in hand, and one of the first changes was to make him change his name from René to Rainer. She also made him curb the illegibility of his handwriting and develop the clear Italianate German script that became his hallmark. They studied Italian Renaissance art together and rose at dawn to look for deer and walk barefoot in the dew. She urged him to take control of all parts of his life. He stopped drinking, became a vegetarian and began importing Quaker Oats from California. In order to improve his circulation while he wrote, he purchased a standup desk.

More important, Lou Andreas-Salomé made Rilke look at his poetry in a disciplined manner. She criticized his obscurity and flowery language and words used for padding or effect. She urged him not to be concerned with critical acclaim but to direct every action toward the work itself. He stopped feeling the need "to mark each period of his development" with a new book.[17] She urged him to take longer with a book, to downplay inspiration, to be more precise, to commit himself to hard work, to put the work before the life. What became important was the work itself, not publication and possible success. She also urged him to go back to the university. In a diary he began for Lou, he wrote, ". . . what becomes laughter or tears for you, the artist must form with his struggling hands and raise above himself . . . his material is of this world and so he must set his works in the world. But they are not for you. Touch them not, and stand in awe."[18]

Here we still find elitism and a Symbolist stance, but also a sense of a relationship to clarity and to the reader. There is also an emphasis on hard work. Two summers later he wrote from St. Petersburg, "At bottom one seeks in everything new (country or person or thing) only an expression that helps some personal confession to greater power and maturity. All things are there in order that they may, in some sense, become pictures for us. And they do not suffer from it, for while they are expressing us more and more clearly, our souls close over them in the same measure."[19]

What is important is the "personal confession": that is, the work. All experience feeds that confession. The world exists to create pictures for the artist. It exists to express the artist; the artist exists to express the world. Rilke's Russian studies, his trips to Russia (which he called his spiritual home), his study of art, all were done for the work. And it was chiefly because of Lou Andreas-Salomé that he wrote the best work of this period: *Stories of God*, *The Book of Images*, *The Book of Hours*.

One also finds in this early work the rudiments of an idea that Rilke would develop more fully: that of pictures or images.

Who creates these pictures, the world or the artist? And what is the role of seeing and observing precisely?

In August 1900, on returning from his second trip to Russia, Rilke visited the painter Heinrich Vogeler at Worpswede, an artist colony near Bremen. He wanted to learn more about painting, about seeing precisely, and he felt that the artists at Worpswede could teach him. "Everything truly seen *must* become a poem!"[20] he had told Lou in Moscow. On this visit he met a young sculptress, Clara Westhoff, who was about to go to Paris to study with Rodin. She told him about Rodin's sculpture and also about Cézanne. Later, in February, when Rilke was in Berlin studying Russian at the university, Clara visited him. She became pregnant and they were married at the end of April. But right from the start, Rilke's sense of marriage entailed separation. That summer he wrote to a fellow poet, "It is a question in marriage . . . not of creating a quick community of spirit by tearing down and destroying all boundaries, but rather a good marriage is that in which each appoints the other the guardian of his solitude. . . . A *togetherness* between two people is an impossibility, and where it seems, nevertheless, to exist, it is a narrowing, a reciprocal agreement which robs either one party or both of his fullest freedom and development."[21]

We find here Rilke's wish to protect his own writing but also an indication of his peculiar psychology, a psychology that led him to say that the story of the Prodigal Son—which he saw as his story— was "the legend of a man who didn't want to be loved"[22]; that to love a person was to assault that person's freedom, and that love's highest fulfillment was abnegation: a denial of love. "To be loved," he wrote, "is to be consumed in flames."[23] Nevertheless, Rilke and Clara established a house in Worpswede and he continued to write. In December 1901, their daughter Ruth was born. But added to their problems was a lack of money. Rilke wrote many reviews, wrote a study on the artists at Worpswede, considered going back to school, considered a job as a clerk and began to think about doing a book on Rodin.

He was also trying to finish the *Book of Images*, and he put more effort into that book than into any of his previous books: working on the binding, paper, typeface and deciding to have the whole book printed in uppercase lettering. Even the smallest word, he said, "must stand like a monument." But the writing was still based on inspiration. It was subjective, personal and self-indulgent. Six years later, looking back to this time, Rilke wrote to his wife, ". . . in those days Nature was still a general incitement for me, an evocation, an instrument on whose strings my fingers found themselves again; I did not yet sit before her; I let myself be carried away by the soul that issued forth from her . . . I went along with her and saw, saw not Nature, but the faces she inspired in me."[24]

In April 1902, Rilke and his wife decided to separate in order to protect their solitude and to live more cheaply. Rilke also wanted to go to Paris to do a book on Rodin. He wanted to learn from Rodin, to train his eyes and learn how to look at the objects of the world. On August 1, he wrote to Rodin, "Your art is such . . . that it knows how to give bread and gold to painters, to poets, to sculptors: to all artists who go their way of suffering, desiring nothing but that ray of eternity which is the supreme goal of the creative life."[25]

Rilke arrived in Paris a month later. He was well on his way to being a poet, but what he had achieved at the end of this stage was what many young poets achieve. He had explored the limits of his facility. He had developed a style, which, as he said later, he could easily have used for the rest of his life. But he knew something was wrong. In a second letter to Rodin on September 11, 1902, he wrote that he had come to him to ask "how must one live? And you replied: by working. And I well understand. I feel that to work is to live without dying."[26]

What Rodin meant by "working" and its implications for Rilke was what led him to the third stage of his development, but the path wasn't easy and it took him to the edge of a nervous breakdown, which he later described in his novel *The Notebooks of*

Malte Laurids Brigge. What he saw in Rodin was a great artist who had achieved his full potential, and what nearly broke Rilke was that he didn't know how to follow Rodin's example. As he wrote to Lou a year later, "I suffered from the too great example which my art offered no means of following."[27] Six years later, in the sonnet "Archaic Torso of Apollo," Rilke created a metaphor for this experience.

> We never knew his head and all the light
> that ripened in his fabled eyes. But
> his torso still glows like a candelabra,
> in which his gazing, turned down low,
>
> holds fast and shines. Otherwise the surge
> of the breast could not blind you, nor a smile
> run through the slight twist of the loins
> toward that center where procreation thrived.
>
> Otherwise this stone would stand deformed and curt
> under the shoulders' invisible plunge
> and not glisten just like wild beast's fur;
>
> and not burst forth from all its contours
> like a star: for there is no place
> that does not see you. You must change your life.[28]

The broken statue of Apollo was for Rilke a metaphor of the potential of art and for the artist himself. He had seen the statue in the Louvre during the fall of 1902. Scattered around Rodin's grounds and studio were many partially finished pieces that had the same effect. Also, the image of "star" represented for Rilke Rodin's own power and the power of the artist: a power that Rilke had yet to achieve. Describing Rodin in a letter to his wife on September 15, 1905, Rilke wrote, "He moves like a star. He is beyond all measure."[29] This image existed for Rilke as a confrontation, a challenge truly to become an artist, and with it came the single demand: "You must change your life."

In his first letter to his wife on September 2, Rilke was primarily descriptive, saying how much he liked Rodin, describing the difficulty of speaking French and the huge amount of unfinished work lying around the grounds. But in his second letter three days later, he told of two "lessons." The first was Rodin's contention that the subject matter isn't important; that everything resides in *le modelé*, that is, in "the character of the surfaces" of the sculpture, "the law and relationship of these surfaces" that are comprised "of infinitely many meetings of light with the object, and it became apparent that each of these meetings was different and each remarkable."

A piece of sculpture does not simply have one surface; it has many, and its strength comes from the relationship between those surfaces and the play of light upon them. Rilke continued, "What must it have meant to him when he first felt that no one had ever looked for this basic element of plasticity! He had to find it: . . . above all [in] the nude body. He had to transpose it, that is to make it into *his* expression, to become accustomed to saying *everything* through the *modelé* and *not otherwise*. Here, do you see, is the second point in this artist's life. The first was that he had discovered a new basic element of his art, the second, that he wanted nothing more of life than to express himself fully and all that is through his element."[30]

Le modelé used style, strategy and form as a vehicle for the artist's most complete expression. Subject matter was only pretext. Rilke attempted to find some counterpart for the *modelé* in poetry, and he fixed his attention on syntax and language. The language of his earlier work had been functional, and its musicality had been often unconnected to content. No matter how formally elaborate, the poem had been a vehicle to convey a subject. Now Rilke began to look at it more closely. He began reading books on German grammar and syntax, to study the dictionary of the brothers Grimm. He began to see language as more than a vehicle but a thing in itself: the unwinding of information, the relationships between the sounds and stresses, the varieties of rhythm. It was here that true self-expression resided and with it a true image of the world.

The second point or lesson Rodin described by saying "Yes, one must work, nothing but work. And one must have patience." And Rilke went on to say

> One should not think of wanting to make something, one should try only to build up one's own medium of expression and to say everything. One should work and have patience. Not to look right nor left. Should draw all of life into this circle, have *nothing* outside of this life. Rodin has done so. "I have given my life to it," he said . . . It all points to the same thing: that one must choose either this or that. Either happiness or art. "One must find happiness in one's art," [Rodin said] . . . The great men have all let their lives become overgrown like an old road and have carried every-thing into their art. Their lives are stunted like an organ they no longer need.[31]

As for inspiration, Rodin dismissed it. He had no time for it. Instead he replaced it with the habit of daily work. "Thus everything always became real. That is the principal thing—not to remain with the dream, with the intention, with the being-in-the-mood, but always forcibly to convert it into things. As Rodin did. . . . One can imagine a man who had felt, wanted all that in himself, and had waited for better times to do it. Who would respect him; he would be an aging fool who had nothing more to hope for. But to make, to make is the thing. . . . [Rodin's] work stands like a great angel beside him and protects him."[32]

A few days later he wrote to his wife how Rodin "is so tremendously balanced"[33] in his life and work. And to Rodin he wrote that he was the only man in the world who "is building himself in harmony with his work," while work for Rilke had been "a festival connected with rare inspirations; and there were weeks when I did nothing but wait with infinite sadness for the creative hour. It was a life full of abysses. I anxiously avoided every artificial means of evoking the inspirations. . . . But in all this which was doubtless reasonable, I didn't have the courage to bring back the distant inspirations by working. Now I know that it is the only way of keeping them."[34]

Rilke understood what he had to do but he was a long way from being able to do it. Added to his frustration was his fear of Paris itself with its dirt, noise and crowds of people. He took long walks to teach himself how to look at things, but what he saw filled him with despair. He found Paris "unspeakably dismaying. It has lost itself utterly, it is tearing like a star off course toward some dreadful collision."[35]

Additionally there was the difficulty of the task he had set himself, of taking experience and turning it into a "thing," a poem, in the way that Rodin turned experience into sculpture. He made lists of topics for poems and put aside time every day for writing, but most of his attempts ended in frustration. In November 1902, however, he wrote the first of his thing-poems, although a long time passed before he wrote a second. Rodin had suggested that Rilke go to the zoo to look for subjects, and in the panther Rilke found an image to serve as a metaphor for his own sense of entrapment within Paris and his inability to write. And it was also linked in Rilke's mind to a small plaster cast of a tiger that Rodin kept in his studio and that was the perfect example of *le modelé*. "There, in this animal, [he wrote to his wife at the end of September] is the same lively feeling in the modeling, this little thing . . . has hundreds of thousands of sides like a very big object, hundreds of thousands of sides which are all alive, and animated, and different. . . . And with this the expression of the prowling stride is intensified to the highest degree, the powerful planting of the broad paws, and at the same time, that caution in which all strength is wrapped, that noiselessness."[36]

The poem doesn't need this explication, but it is also a clear example in Rilke where subject matter exists as pretext, while the language, syntax and rhythms combine with the emotional energy from this other hidden subject of personal frustration to create a powerful thing, an image of "The panther."

In the Jardin des Plantes, Paris

His gaze has from the passing of the bars
become so tired, that it holds nothing more.
It seems to him there are a thousand bars
and behind a thousand bars no world.

The supple pace of powerful soft strides,
turning in the very smallest circle,
is like a dance of strength around a center
in which a great will stands numbed.

Only sometimes the curtain of the pupils
soundlessly slides up—. Then an image enters,
goes through the limbs' taut stillness—
and in the heart ceases to exist.[37]

In German the poem is intricately rhymed while the strong iambic meter enacts the pacing of the beast. Rodin is the freed panther; Rilke, unable to follow Rodin's example in art or life, resembles the caged panther. And, just as Rilke felt imprisoned by Paris, so was the panther imprisoned within its cage.

But this was the single new poem he wrote that fall. The others were the old "mood-images" that he was trying to get away from. As soon as Rilke finished his essay on Rodin, he fled to Italy to find a way of imitating Rodin's great example. But the months of frustration continued and with it came his rejection of his own earlier work. Writing to his wife at the end of April 1903 about his book *Stories of God*, he said, "There wasn't enough patience in me when I shaped it, that is why it has so many blurred and uncertain places; but perhaps I shall come again soon to such a book, and then I will build it with all the reverence I have in my hands, and will not let go of any passage as long as it is less than I myself, and will make each into an angel and will let myself be overcome by him and force him to bend me although I have made him."[38]

And to a young poet, Franz Kappus, with whom he had begun to correspond that spring, Rilke wrote on this same day that he wrote to his wife, "*Everything* is gestation and then birthing. To let each impression and each embryo of a feeling come to completion, entirely in itself, in the dark, in the unsayable, the unconscious, beyond the reach of one's own understanding, and with deep humility and patience to wait for the hour when a new clarity is born: this alone is what it means to live as an artist . . . *Patience* is everything."[39]

One of Rilke's gifts was unrelenting self-analysis, and his brooding about Rodin and his own failings led him to a series of remarkable letters to Lou Andreas-Salomé in the summer and fall of 1903. He wrote in clear desperation (on July 18, 1903) after a two-year silence. "I would like to tell you, dear Lou, that Paris was for me an experience similar to military school; as a great fearful astonishment seized me then, so now again terror assailed me at everything that, as in an unspeakable confusion, is called life."[40]

He told her he had tried to make things out of his fear, but had succeeded only once (presumably the writing of "The Panther") before the fears again broke loose and overwhelmed him. He also told her much about Rodin and the amazing example of his work. "And this work could only come from a worker, and he who has built it can calmly deny inspiration; it doesn't come upon him, because it is *in* him, day and night, occasioned by each looking, a warmth generated by every gesture of his hand"[41] (August 8, 1903).

Rodin had given him a clear idea of his path, but Rilke didn't know how to follow it. "Only things speak to me. Rodin's things . . . they directed me to the models; to the animated, living world, seen simply and without interpretation as the occasions for things. I am beginning to see something new . . . but I still lack the discipline, the ability to work"[42] (August 8, 1903).

Lou answered, telling him that of course he suffered from Rodin's example. Rodin was a mature artist while Rilke was still young. She urged him to write down his fears and to make work out of them. Her letter calmed him but didn't diminish his passionate intention. "Somehow I too must manage to make things; written, not plastic things,—realities that proceed from handwork. Somehow I too must discover the smallest basic element, the cell of my art, the tangible medium of presentation for everything, irrespective of subject matter. . . . The subject matter would lose still more of its importance and weight and would be nothing but pretext; but just this apparent indifference to it would make me capable of shaping all subject matter, to find and to form pretexts for everything with the right and disinterested means"[43] (August 10, 1903).

Rilke's success in the third stage of his development grew out of these letters. Several months later, in February 1904, he began the book about the fears he had experienced in Paris: *The Notebooks of Malte Laurids Brigge*. He also worked to change himself so that chance events wouldn't overwhelm him. He reserved his ideas for his work and stopped expending himself in conversation. He learned to free his unconscious, to allow it to settle on an image without any interference from his conscious mind. In April 1904, he wrote to a friend, "I believe that the best figures are those which come into being for their creator without ulterior motive, simply as figures."[44] This didn't mean that he wouldn't work on them, but their beginnings had to be unconscious. He also continued his study of German grammar and syntax and the German dictionary of the Grimm brothers, "[about which he wrote on May 12, 1904] a writer can derive much wealth and instruction. For indeed one really ought to know and be able to use everything that had once entered into the language and is there, instead of trying to get along with the chance supply that is meager enough and offers no choice."[45]

Slowly new poems emerged and he began to grow secure in his path. "What is required of us," he wrote to a young girl, "is that we *love the difficult* and learn to deal with it."[46]

Several years later, he wrote a poem about this process of learning and discovery, although, as in most of the *New Poems*, the originating meaning is buried within the ostensible subject matter. The poem, "Falconry," describes how Emperor Frederick II increased his skills as a ruler through the study of falconry.

Being Emperor means outlasting many
things unmoved, through actions one keeps hidden:
when at night the chancellor stepped
into the tower, he found *him* there, saying
that bold princely tract on falconry

into a scribe bent in upon his words;
for he himself in that sequestered hall
had paced nights long and many times
with the unsettled creature on his arm,

when it was strange, new, and full of turbulence.
And whatever beckoned then—
plans which had sprung up in him,
or tender recollections'
deep, deep inner chiming—
he had spurned at once, for that frightened fledgling

falcon's sake, whose blood and worries
he taxed himself relentlessly to grasp.
In exchange he too seemed borne aloft,
when the bird, to whom the lords give praise,
tossed radiantly from his hand, above
in that all-embracing springtime morning
dropped like an angel on the heron.[47]

In the way Frederick II studied the workings of the falcon, so Rilke studied his craft. In the way that Frederick separated himself from all distractions ("plans which had sprung up in him") and emotional needs ("tender recollections' deep, deep inner chiming"), so Rilke put aside the university, his ambitions to be a critic, put aside even his own wife and daughter in order to concentrate on the work of poetry. And as the falcon drops like an angel upon the heron, so the poem drops upon the reader. You recall the letter to his wife in which Rilke wrote that he hoped to make each poem "into an angel and will let myself be overcome by him and force him to bend me although I have made him."[48] And behind this great endeavor lies a great ambition: "Being Emperor means outlasting many / things unmoved, through actions one keeps hidden." And behind that lies a greater ambition: "to be borne aloft," to become like an angel himself.

In the fall of 1905, Rilke returned to Paris as Rodin's secretary. They had become friends and in their eight months together, Rilke learned much from Rodin's example. The following summer, 1906, Rilke lived alone in Paris, and if his fear was not gone, it was at least under control. Moreover, new poems were coming quickly. Rilke also discovered Van Gogh, whose work led him to Cézanne. His study of these painters, especially Cézanne, enabled him to articulate what he felt he had learned about his own work and how he had been able to move that work forward from a subjective outpouring to the clear gazing that typified the *New Poems*. Indeed, in many of these poems we find the verbs: to look, to gaze, to see. This is one of the most important things which he felt he learned from Rodin: how to look at things. "Gazing is such a wonderful thing [he wrote to his wife on March 8, 1907], of which we still know so little; with it we are turned completely outward but just when we are most so, things seem to be going on within us that have waited longingly to be unobserved, and while they . . . achieve themselves in us *without our help*,—their meaning is growing up in the object outside, a name convincing, strong, the only one possible for them, in which we blissfully and reverently recognize the event within us."[49]

This describes the process of the *New Poems*. We gaze at something and in the intensity of that gaze we forget, for a moment, our passionate preoccupations. In that moment the thing being gazed at—say, a panther pacing in its cage—suddenly takes on our preoccupations and becomes a metaphor for them. The gazing, however, must be objective and free from conscious interference. Rilke would argue that subjectivity comes from the conscious mind, while the unconscious is objective. He continued this subject to his wife in a letter of June 24, 1907.

> Works of art are indeed always products of having-been-in-danger, or having-gone-to-the-very-end in an experience, to where one can go no further. The further one goes, . . . the more personal, the more unique an experience becomes, and the work of art, finally, is the . . . most valid possible expression of this uniqueness. . . . We surely have no choice then but to test and try ourselves out to the extreme, but also we are probably not bound to express . . . this extreme before it enters into the work of art: for as something unique that no one else would or should understand, as personal insanity so to speak, it has to enter into the work in order to become valid there and to show the law, like an inherent design which becomes visible only in the transparency of the artistic sphere.[50]

Several points can be made about this. One, it shows a willingness to face and forgive oneself for any nastiness that the unconscious mind dredges up. Two, it argues that one must go to the very end of the process, no matter how painful it may be. Three, it argues that the private material turned up by this process is irrelevant and probably uninteresting to a reader. It is a "personal insanity." We also find the inference that the poet is always writing about himself or herself, whether the poet writes about a panther or a German emperor. Four, the "personal insanity" must enter the work and be the organizing principal of the work ("to show the law"), to become an invisible drawing within the work.

This June 24 letter perfectly describes the poems that Rilke wrote during this time, sometimes writing as many as 40 in a month. The majority—no matter their apparent subjects—have a hidden subject drawn from Rilke's own life, his personal insanity. Many concern writing and ambition, many deal with a desire for personal transcendence. Those hidden subjects are of no real concern to us and are interesting now only when we see how these poems were made. But their passion—passion in poems about panthers and gazelles, Greek gods and biblical figures—is always a personal passion. Each poem gives a strong sense of this having been in danger, having gone to the very end, but the danger is the personal danger of facing one's personal insanity. It doesn't help us to appreciate the poem to know that the archaic torso of Apollo is Rodin and his example or that the cage surrounding Rilke the panther is the inhibiting nature of Paris, but his passionate involvement with these subjects energizes the apparent subject, which, as you remember, he calls a pretext.

During the summer and fall of 1907, Rilke completed the first volume of *New Poems* and wrote most of the second. He also completed a study of Van Gogh and discovered Cézanne. His letters to his wife about Cézanne articulate what he had learned about writing, because he felt he saw in Cézanne what he had been striving for himself. In many places, he simply fine-tuned ideas that he had introduced elsewhere. But he also made five points that have to do with the "gazing" and "hidden insanity" and that clarified what is necessary in order to create poems that "achieve the conviction and substantiality of things."[51]

The first point was that art arises from conflict. Rilke said, "without resistance there would be no movement."[52] There were two kinds of conflict: the wish to change one's own life or to transcend one's present state, and, second, the conflict that occurs between the looking and making: ". . . a mutual struggle between the two procedures of, first, looking and confidently receiving, and then of appropriating and making the personal use of what has been received; that the two, perhaps as a result of becoming conscious, would immediately start opposing each other, talking out loud as it were, and go on perpetually interrupting and contradicting each other."[53]

Rilke had also described this conflict—the conflict of making—as wrestling with an angel. The poet takes the things of the world and, through conflict, makes art of them—or, quoting Van Gogh, makes "saints" of them, or, like Cézanne, "forces them—*forces them*—to be beautiful, to stand for the whole world."[54]

The second point concerned the need to look at something without imposing one's prejudices, without any ulterior motive. For instance, for the work to succeed it must go beyond love. It's natural, wrote Rilke, to love each of these things as one makes it, but if one shows that love, then "one makes it less well; one *judges* it instead of *saying* it. One ceases to be impartial; and the very best—love—stays outside the work, is left outside, untranslated."[55] He said that was how sentimental painting came about—and of course sentimental writing. "They'd paint: I love this here; instead of painting: here it is."[56] To be concerned with telling the audience about one's loves and hates is not to make art. At worst it is propaganda, and at best it is yearning for a sympathetic ear. Rilke praised Cézanne for "This labor which no longer knew any preferences or biases or fastidious predilections, whose minutest component had been tested on the scales of an infinitely responsive conscience, and which so incorruptibly reduced a reality to its color content."[57]

The "conscience" became the third point. You measure the work against your conscience. Are you being truthful in your gazing? Are you being manipulative? Are you being influenced by outside concerns: fame, money or love? Does the work represent the totality of your craft? Are you lying to yourself when you imagine it to be completed? Cézanne's impartiality was an example of great conscience. "Sure one had to take one's impartiality to the point where one rejects the interpretive bias even of vague emotional memories, prejudices, and predilections transmitted as part of one's heritage, taking instead whatever strength, admiration, or desire emerges with them, and applying it nameless and new, to one's own tasks. One has to be poor unto the tenth generation."[58]

By poor, Rilke meant that the poet had to be free of interpretive bias, especially the bias that is part of his or her cultural conditioning. The poet has to recognize that conditioning in his or her language, value system and choice of subject matter. "One has to be able at every moment to place one's hand on the earth like the first human being."[59]

Even if that is impossible, the poet can approach such innocence by being completely unconscious in the making process, by being without ambition or constraint. This need of unconsciousness was Rilke's fourth main point, and again he turned to Cézanne. "No one before him ever demonstrated so clearly the extent to which painting is something that takes places among the colors, and how one has to leave them alone completely, so they can settle the matter among themselves. . . . Whoever meddles, arranges, injects his human deliberation, his wit, his advocacy, his intellectual agility in any way, is already disturbing and clouding their activity. Ideally, [an artist] should be unconscious of his insights . . . all his progress should enter so swiftly into the work that he is unable to recognize them in the moment of transition."[60]

Rilke was less than clear about this need for unconsciousness, but elsewhere he made a distinction between making and revising, seeing them as separate activities and that the making was the unconscious part. This unconsciousness was also necessary in the process of gazing if the "personal insanity" was to enter the work. Consciousness led to invented art, "to a great deal of intentionality and arbitrariness—in short to decoration."[61] But consciousness is also necessary in the process of revision.

Rilke's fifth and final point was that the artist must not turn his or her back on any subject. He wrote about Baudelaire's poem the "Carrion" in which the speaker tells his love that someday she will be like the rotten corpse they saw by the side of the road: "Artistic perception had to overcome itself to the point of realizing that even something horrible, something that seems no more than disgusting, *truly exists*, and shares the truth of its being with everything else that exists. Just as the creative artist is not allowed to choose, neither is he permitted to turn his back on anything: a single refusal, and he is cast out of the state of grace and becomes sinful all the way through."[62]

Just as the artist cannot repress anything inside of himself or herself, neither can the artist repress any subject that becomes the focus of his or her gazing. Any bias destroys the work and makes it decorative. Such biases come out of the conscious mind, while the true work comes from a meeting between the world and the unconscious mind, from that act of unconscious gazing, where the self—for example, the poet's frustration—enters something within the world—for example, the panther in its cage. The artist tests and tries himself or herself against the utmost, said Rilke, and that utmost is the artist's singularity, his or her uniqueness, "which no one would or even should understand" and which enters the work, must enter it, as a kind of personal insanity and so becomes the work's hidden design.

Rilke wrote about this conflict with one's own personal insanities in the poem "The Temptation" during this same summer of 1907. Ostensibly the poem is about St. Anthony, who claimed he could not be tempted and so was tested. But actually the poem is about turning one's personal insanities into art.

> No, it didn't help, that he drove sharp
> thorns into his lecherous flesh;
> all his pregnant senses threw forth
> amid shrill laboring, shrieking
>
> half-cocked births: lopsided, leeringly envisaged
> crawling and flying apparitions,
> nothings, whose malice, bent on him alone,
> united and had fun with him.
>
> And already his senses had grandchildren:

for the pack was fruitful in the night
and in ever wilder specklings
botched itself and multiplied by hundreds.
From the whole mix a drink was made:
his hands grasped the sheer handles,
and the shadows slid open like thighs
warm and wakened for embracing—.

And then he screamed for the angel, screamed:
And the angel came in his halo
and was present: and drove them
back inside the saint again,

that he might wrestle on within himself
with beasts and demons as for years now
and make God, the as yet far from clear,
out of the ferment inwardly distill.

The angel is the ability to turn personal insanity into art, to make God. It is also art itself. You recall the early letter where Rilke said that Rodin's "work stands like a great angel beside him and protects him."[63] St. Anthony struggles with his demons and makes God, makes an act of worship. He distills the ferment. Likewise the artist creates works of art out of his personal demons. It was Rilke's utilization of this truth that led him through the third stage of his artistic development, led him past his facility to some of his greatest achievements.

In the end, however, Rilke knew he couldn't live like Rodin or Van Gogh or Cézanne: a life where he was always in the work, where to live meant to work. "The tender recollections' deep, deep inner chiming" was too loud for him. "Ah [he wrote to his wife], if only one did not have comforting memories of times spent without working. Memories of lying still and taking comfort. Memories of hours spent in simple waiting, or leafing through old illustrations, or reading some novel or other."[64]

These memories created for him two worlds that were always in conflict with never any hope of peace. Rilke had learned that his poems arose from this conflict, out of constantly chewing at himself. How nice to give it up, he thought, although he knew he couldn't. How nice to buy a used bookstore and have a dog and sit behind the counter for 20 years and have a family, instead of having "to contend with all the worries, the great ones and the little ones." Then he added, "You know how I mean that: without complaining. After all, it's good the way it is, and it's going to get even better."[65]

10 | Mandelstam: The Poem as Event

I WANT TO CONSIDER A SMALL SYMBOLIST heresy that occurred in Russian poetry in 1911 as a way of looking into the aesthetics of Osip Mandelstam (1891-1938) to see what might be useful in his ideas about poetry for those of us writing today.

The two decades of Russian literature before World War I were known as the Silver Age to distinguish them from the Golden Age, 60 years before, which was the age of Pushkin. The Silver Age began about 1893 with the appearance of the first Russian poetry strongly influenced by Baudelaire, Rimbaud, Verlaine, Mallarme and the French Symbolists, as well as the German Symbolists, meaning Schopenhauer, Nietzche and Ibsen.

The best Russian Symbolists were Valery Bryusov and then, in the second generation, Alexander Blok, Andrei Bely and Vyacheslav Ivanov. Beyond these four were dozens of others who considered themselves Symbolists and whose work contained varying mixtures of French Symbolism and German Romanticism.

The period before this had been a dead period in Russian poetry dominated by the belief that the purpose of poetry was to make people into better human beings and citizens according to the liberal ideas of the 1860s. In fact, a poem was good only in so far as it "served goals extraneous to it."[1] The influence of Baudelaire and the French Symbolists changed this. In addition, Simon Karlinsky argues, in *Anton Chekhov's Life & Thought*, that these didactic critics had lost credibility by trying to show Chekhov's stories as politically incorrect. Chekhov's great popularity rendered these judgments questionable and the critics' power was diminished.

It was Charles Baudelaire who put forth the idea that the perceived world is a metaphor for the self. He also found a link in the philosophy of Emanuel Swedenborg, the Swedish mystic who lived from 1688 to 1772. Baudelaire's sonnet "Correspondences" is an espousal of Swedenborgian beliefs and a nod to his friend Eliphas Levi, the magician, occult historian and poet who had written a poem with the same title. Here is Baudelaire's poem translated by Laure-Anne Bosselaar and myself.

> Nature is a temple, where the living columns
> Sometimes murmur a mysterious language
> As man passes through its forest of symbols
> Which observe him with familiarity.
>
> Like faraway echoes, which in the distance
> Fuse into a oneness profound and deep,
> As vast as the night, and as clarity,
> So do sounds, colors and scents correspond.
>
> There are scents as sweet as a baby's flesh,
> As serene as oboes, green as meadows,—
> And others, corrupt, rich and triumphant,
>
> Possessing the vastness of infinite things
> Like ambergris, incense, benjamin and musk
> That cry the raptures of the mind and senses.

The poem describes a system of correspondences intuited by the poet who communicates the intuition to a reader by drawing on this "forest of symbols." Baudelaire was also influenced in these ideas by an older poet, and fellow Swedenborgian, Gerard de Nerval, who was often committed to mental hospitals and who suffered from a psychosis of reference, meaning that he felt all random events were not random but contained symbolic information capable of being understood. Here is Nerval's sonnet "Golden Verses" written ten years before Baudelaire's "Correspondences." The translation is by Laure-Anne Bosselaar and myself.

Everything is sentient!
Pythagoras

Free-thinker, do you imagine only man can think
When life bursts from everything in this world?
Your freedom lightly disposes of the powers you hold,
But from your intentions, the universe is absent.

In each and every animal respect the active spirit,
To Nature each flower becomes a blossoming soul,
The mystery of love inhabits every metal;
Everything has power over you. "Everything is sentient!"

Fear, in the blind wall, the eye that watches:
Even to matter itself a voice is attached.
Never permit it serve some unworthy need.

Often, in obscure beings, a God lies hidden,
And, like a nascent eye covered by its lid,
A pure spirit swells beneath the skin of stones.

It can be argued that all modern European, American and South American poetry derives from this poem. Although a Romantic, Nerval was also a realist and his poem described the world as he knew it. He completely believed in the eye watching from the blind wall. He had seen it often.

What Baudelaire realized, however, was that the eye in the wall is a projection of the self. He came to this idea partly through his study of Edgar Allen Poe. We recall in the story "The Tell-tale Heart" that the murderer imagines he hears the pounding of his dead victim's heart and wonders why the police don't hear it, as well. That heart, and there are many such examples in Poe, is the same as the eye in the blind wall. But in Poe the symbol is projected by the self.

For Baudelaire the world reflects self. When Baudelaire wrote "all nature in one temple," that temple was in part the human brain. But Baudelaire was not a Symbolist poet. He was a transitional figure who mixed Classicism and Romanticism. What also set him apart from other poets of the period was his emphasis on craft and his belief that a poem must be judged on its own terms. About craft he wrote: "Everything beautiful and noble is the result of reason and calculation."[2]

He also wrote, "Death or deposition would be the penalty if poetry were to become assimilated to science or morality; the object of poetry is not Truth, the object of poetry is Poetry itself."[3] But even though he argued that virtue should not be confused with printer's ink, neither did he accept the idea of Art for Art's sake put forth by earlier French Romantics. He wrote, 'The puerile utopia of art for art's sake, by excluding morality and often even passion, was inevitably sterile."[4]

Baudelaire felt that by writing clearly about the world and his relationship to the world, the poet described the truths of the world, but that did not mean the end of poetry was truth. From his reading of Swedenborg, he also believed in a universal rhythm and harmony. Through an awareness of symbol, of the correspondences connecting all things, the poet portrayed that harmony. Baudelaire wrote, "I do not think it is shocking to consider every infraction of morality, of the morally beautiful, as a kind of offense against the universal rhythm and prosody."[5] But the morality of a poem should be implicit, not explicit, and when Algernon Swinburne wrote Baudelaire to say that he had defended him as a moral poet, Baudelaire, with some irritation, answered: "Nevertheless, allow me to say that you take my defense rather too far. I am not such a *moralist* as you obligingly pretend to believe. I believe simply (as no doubt you do yourself) that every poem and every work of art that is *well made* naturally and perforce suggests a moral. It's up to the reader. I even feel a very decided hatred toward every exclusively moralistic *intention* in a poem."[6]

The theory of correspondences gave Baudelaire's poetry a tremendous emphasis on metaphor and symbol. If everything was connected and the way to understand the world was to understand those connections, then analogy became one of the highest forms of expression. For Baudelaire, these analogies could be used in allegorical poems that described the world. For the later Symbolists, the ability to compose these analogies made them into high priests, and often, unlike Baudelaire, they put little value on communication. Baudelaire's poem "The Albatross" is such an analogy. The translation is by Laure-Anne Bosselaar and myself.

> Often, to pass the time on board, sailors
> Will catch an albatross, that vast bird of the seas,
> Indolent escort of their journey, which drifts
> Above the ship gliding across the bitter gulfs.
>
> As soon as the sailors set the bird on deck,
> This heavenly king, awkward and ashamed,
> Lets his gigantic white wings drag
> At his sides, like immense oars, lingering.
>
> How clumsy and weak becomes this winged voyager!
> Once full of grace, now he's ugly and lame!
> A sailor sticks a burning pipe into his beak,
> Another mimics the cripple that once flew.
>
> The Poet is like this prince of clouds
> Who scorns the archers and haunts the storms,
> Exiled on earth among the jeering crowds,
> He cannot walk, dragged down by his giant wings.

We note the tremendous magnitude given to the poet, which is later found in the Symbolists, but in Baudelaire the poet was still a link between "all high things" and human beings, who were often unable to appreciate these high things. Among the late Symbolists, the link stopped being important.

Baudelaire's ideas about poetry were studied by Stéphane Mallarmé, who viewed the world as no more than "a brutal mirage."

He had had a breakdown in 1866 when he lost his religious faith
and for a time was in the grips of nihilism. Then he wrote in a letter,
"After I had found Nothingness I found Beauty."[7] And in 1867, in
another letter, "The only reality is Beauty and Its perfect expression
is Poetry. All the rest is a lie—except for those who live by the body,
by love, or by the mental love that friendship is."[8] From these
thoughts he developed his idea that all "experience must ultimately
be contained in a book."[9] Thirty years later in a lecture at Oxford,
Mallarmé repeated this idea: "Yes, Literature *does* exist and, I may
add, exists alone and all-exclusively."[10] He also said in that lecture:
"I suggest, at my own esthetic risk, the following conclusion . . . :
namely, that Music and Literature constitute the moving facet—
now looming toward obscurity, now glittering unconquerably—of
that single, true phenomenon which I have called Idea."[11]

Poetry makes the world understandable through analogy
and metaphor. It cuts through surface appearance to significance,
to the meaning of the symbol. We understand that meaning with
our intuition. Through the intuition we grasp the analogies that
describe the universal harmonies. As master of intuition the poet is
the person best able to understand these harmonies. But craft was
still paramount. As Mallarmé said to Degas: "It isn't with ideas but
with words that one makes a poem."[12]

The risk in the shift from Baudelaire to Mallarmé was the
importance given to a symbolism that didn't need to have logical
connection to the world. In fact, the only purpose of the physical
world, that brutal mirage, was to supply those correspondences
that led the poet to the spiritual world. The weakness was that
everything returned to the subjectivity of the poet, which was not
far from the madness of Nerval.

Graham Hough has written:

Symbolism moves in the direction of an autonomous art,
severed from life and experience by an impassable gulf. The
Symbolists share with the Romantics the reliance on the
epiphany, the moment of revelation; but they differ sharply

about its status in nature and relation to art. . . . For the Symbolist poet there is no question of describing an experience; the moment of illumination only occurs in its embodiment in some particular artistic form. There is no question of relating it to the experience of a lifetime, for it is unique and exists in the poem alone. . . . Symbolism therefore has strong transcendental overtones. The poet is a magus, calling reality into existence. Or he is the sole transmitter of a mysterious system of correspondences that actually pervades the universe, but only becomes apparent in art. Or he is capable of evoking from the Anima Mundi symbols of the profoundest import, but strictly unexpoundable, for their content is inseparable from the form of their first expression.[13]

Valery Bryusov was one of the founders of Russian Symbolism. He edited and published anthologies of Russian Symbolist poetry in the early 1890s, and he edited a magazine called *The Scales*, in which the best Russian Symbolists and translations from the French Symbolists were published. His own poems were imitations of French Symbolist poetry, and he probably did more than anyone to create a following for Symbolism in Russia. Bryusov was also a fairly orthodox Symbolist, emphasizing the importance of the integrity of the word and believing, with Baudelaire, that poetry has no end but itself. But, like Mallarmé, he thought of poetry as a sacred duty and the poet became a priest and seer. Here again was the possibility to expand the subjective into absurdity, but by stressing the value of the poem as a poem above all else, Bryusov was able to maintain a sense of craftsmanship. He liked to quote Gautier that the poet was "first of all a worker—a builder, a craftsman"[14] and said: "Poets may be evaluated by the worth and the flaws in their poetry, and by nothing else."[15]

The second generation of Russian Symbolists—Blok, Bely, Ivanov and others—expanded the role of the subjective and, instead of believing that poetry has no end but itself, they considered poetry important only insofar as it made links with the religious, mystical and metaphysical. Ivanov argued that "the highest calling of the poet is to serve God and help the reader experience a sense of union with the Divine Spirit."[16] He claimed that those who felt that "poetry has no end but itself" simply had "no knowledge of Symbolism."[17]

Among the Russian Symbolists of 1910, the idea of the poet as craftsman was quickly diminishing. Instead, the poet was a seer who "was to seek and record visions of eternal metaphysical truth rather than to concern himself with artistic form."[18] Because the poet was the master of intuition and because it was through intuition that the poet discovered the analogies with which to communicate the divine correspondences, the most subjective ideas were given as standing for universal harmony.

These later Symbolists in general mocked the physical world, arguing that nothing existed but the spiritual. They turned to other religions and types of mysticism, ranging from Theosophy to the belief that the present could be revitalized by a return to paganism. To some this meant worshipping Perun, the ancient Russian god of thunder, but even Ivanov "believed that a combination of Christianity and the cult of Dionysius could be fertile in new myths, which would be created by the whole of mankind."[19]

Everything arose from the personality of the poet; meaning was whatever the poet wished. Consequently, the meaning of a word could be distorted in order to stress its sound and to use it musically. This greatly increased the obscurity of already obscure poems, but the late Russian Symbolists claimed that the reader was not intended to understand but to witness. In fact, a poem was important only insofar as it recorded the experience of a superior human being. What the reader could hope for was to achieve a transcendent experience by being in the vicinity of the poem. In *Hope Abandoned*, Nadezhda Mandelstam wrote:

> The Symbolists, almost to a man, were under the influence
> of Schopenhauer and Nietzsche, and hence they either

rejected Christianity or tried to refashion it, adding elements of classical antiquity, a dash of paganism, the ancient Russian deities, or other things of their own divising. Even Blok, infinitely profounder than his brash contemporaries and the living embodiment of the Russian intelligentsia's tragedy, was marked by the times he lived in. But the main tempters and seducers were Bryusov and Vyacheslav Ivanov with their cult of art and the artist. Blok noted down something Ivanov said in a lecture: "You are free, Godhead—everything is permitted, only dare!"[20]

By believing that all is permitted to the man who dares, the late Russian Symbolists freed the poet from moral responsibility to society, making him responsible only to his own current theory. Nadezhda Mandelstam wrote: "Vyacheslav Ivanov proclaimed the idea of art as theurgy and, inviting us to follow him, . . . promised initiation, by means of symbols, into a 'world beyond.' Or, to quote Berdiayev [a Russian philosopher and religious thinker], who was close to the Symbolists: 'The world beyond is revealed to art only in its symbolic projection.' For Berdiayev the symbol was a link between the two worlds, a bridge between them."[21]

The break with the late Symbolists began quite simply. Ivanov held open Wednesday evenings in St. Petersburg (much like Mallarmé's Tuesday evenings) in his fifth-story apartment known as the Tower. Ivanov's group was called The Academy of Verse, and his followers addressed him as Vyacheslav the Magnificent. It was in the Tower that Osip Mandelstam met Nikolai Gumilev and his wife, Anna Akhmatova. Gumilev edited a magazine called *Apollo*, which he had started in 1909.

One Wednesday evening in 1911, Gumilev was invited to read a poem entitled "The Prodigal Son," which Ivanov and his followers attacked with such ferocity that Gumilev and some others quit the Academy of Verse and set up the Poet's Guild in opposition. The Symbolist writer Bely mocked them for being too sensitive and as a joke called them Acmeists. Gumilev accepted that term for his group, saying that in Greek "acme" meant the highest degree of something.

There were six of them. Three never were very successful, but Gumilev was a promising poet, as was Anna Akhmatova, who had just begun to write. She was made secretary of the Guild. Then Gumilev urged Mandelstam to join (he was 21 at the time and Gumilev was 27), and he soon became, as Akhmatova said, "first violin." Nadezhda Mandelstam wrote: "I have a feeling that Gumilev's break with the Symbolists was prompted in psychological terms, by his urge to have his own 'school.' As an associate of the Symbolists, he was himself in the position of a disciple, yet all the while his popularity was growing, his books sold out at once, his public appearances were invariably a great success and—in Akhmatova's words—the girls hung around his neck like garlands."[22]

Nadezhda Mandelstam also argues that the real reason for the break was not the poem "The Prodigal Son" or disagreements about poetic technique, but because "they had come to recognize the basic difference between their understanding of life and that of their late mentors."[23] Also, as an Orthodox Christian, Gumilev found Ivanov's ideas about theurgy blasphemous, as did Akhmatova. Even Mandelstam, a Jew who had toyed with becoming a Roman Catholic, disliked Ivanov's attempts to revise Christianity.

Gumilev's ideas had been moving away from Ivanov's for some time. In 1910, Gumilev had published an essay in *Apollo* called "The Life of Verse," which challenged the Symbolists with the heretical statement: "Poems written even by true visionaries in moments of trance have meaning only insofar as they are good."[24]

Gumilev admitted the debt poetry owed the French Symbolists, arguing that Symbolism "was the result of the maturation of the human spirit, which declared the world our own conception,"[25] but he mocked the subjective defenders of Art for Art's sake by making them say "For us, Princes of Song, sovereigns of castles of dream, life is merely a means of flight: the harder a dancer strikes the earth with his feet, the higher he soars."[26]

One of the Acmeists' criticisms of the Russian Symbolists, whom Mandelstam called Pseudo-Symbolists, was that for them the poem was nothing in itself, but took its importance from referring back to the superior personality of the poet. Gumilev attacked this idea in "The Life of Verse." "In any attitude toward anything, whether toward people, things or ideas, we require first of all that it be chaste. By this I mean the right of every phenomenon to be valuable in itself."[27]

Chaste seems an odd word, but Gumilev used it elsewhere to mean the right of something to be defined on its own terms.

Gumilev had a good knowledge of English and American poetry. In attacking the Symbolists for exaggerating the plastic quality of the word and ignoring its integrity, he drew on such English writers as Oscar Wilde and Coleridge, quoting Coleridge that poetry is the best words in the best order.

After a year of meeting together, Gumilev and his Acmeist friends formally attacked the Symbolists in a series of essays and poems in the magazine *Apollo*. Mandelstam also wrote an essay, but Gumilev refused to print it and the essay didn't appear until six years later. The reason isn't clear, although perhaps Gumilev, who saw himself as leader, felt critical of Mandelstam whose ideas somewhat differed from his own.

Gumilev's essay, "Acmeism and the Legacy of Symbolism," began with the claim that Russian Symbolism was dying and that Acmeism had arrived to replace it. Then Gumilev acknowledged his debt to French Symbolism.

> French Symbolism, the ancestor of all Symbolism as a school, moved purely literary questions into the foreground—free verse, a more original and vacillating style, metaphor elevated above all else and the notorious "theory of correspondences. . . ." Just as the French sought a new, freer verse, the Acmeists strive to break the chains of meter. The giddiness of Symbolist metaphors trained them in bold turns of thought; the instability of vocabulary . . . prompted

them to search in the living national speech for one with a more stable content; and a lucid irony . . . has now replaced that hopeless German seriousness which our Symbolists so cherished. Finally, while we value the Symbolists highly for having pointed out to us the significance of the symbol in art, we cannot agree to sacrifice to it other methods of poetic influence and we seek the complete coordination of all of them.[28]

Stressing that the use of symbols was a method and not the end of poetry, Gumilev wrote that no phenomenon should take its importance from referring to something else and that we must be aware of each phenomenon's intrinsic worth. He then attacked Russian Symbolism for concentrating on the unknown, mysticism and occultism.

"The first thing that Acmeism can answer . . . is to point out that the unknowable, by the very meaning of the word, cannot be known. The second, that all endeavors in that direction are unchaste. . . . The principle of Acmeism is always to remember the unknowable, but not to insult one's idea of it with more or less likely conjectures."[29]

Gumilev closed by talking about the four cornerstones of Acmeism. Taking a metaphor from Mandelstam, he had said that the Acmeists were attempting to build a cathedral, whereas the Symbolists were only building a tower (a gibe against Ivanov's penthouse apartment). Then he named the cornerstones: "Shakespeare showed us man's inner world; Rabelais—the body and its joys; Villon told us of a life which has not the slightest doubt in itself, although it knows everything—God, sin, death and immortality; Theophile Gautier found in art worthy garments of irreproachable form for this life. To unite in oneself these four moments—that is the dream which now unifies the people who so boldly call themselves Acmeists."[30]

The emphasis was on the world: that poetry must be of the world and show the world. In later essays, Gumilev wrote about the role of the reader, arguing that the reader experienced the poet's actions in order to discover himself or herself in the poem. He also discussed the need of the poet to be a craftsman. Quoting the French painter Delacroix, he wrote: "It is necessary to study tirelessly the technique of one's art, so as not to think of it in moments of creation."[31]

Although Gumilev's ideas have value in themselves, they are also important because of their influence on Mandelstam and Akhmatova. It would be wrong to argue that Gumilev made Mandelstam, but at a critical period he helped form Mandelstam's ideas. Mandelstam never changed those ideas, although he developed them, and it was as a result of those ideas that he died in a Russian prison camp near Vladivostok in 1938. His wife, Nadezhda, later wrote in her memoir *Hope Against Hope*: "Just as mystical experience gives rise to a religious view of the world, so the working experience of an artist defines his view of the material and spiritual world around him. It is probably this experience as an artist that explains why M.'s view about poetry, the role of the poet in the society and the 'merging of the intellectual and the moral' in an integrated culture (as well as in each of its individual representatives) never underwent any substantial changes."[32]

Elsewhere she wrote: "'Poetry is power,' he once said to Akhmatova in Voronezh [about two years before he died], and she bowed her head on its slender neck. Banished, sick, penniless and hounded, they still would not give up their power. M. behaved like a man conscious of his power, and this only egged on those who wanted to destroy him."[33]

And one more quote from *Hope Against Hope*: "How could this man living at bay in the isolation, emptiness and darkness to which we were consigned, think of himself as the 'factory whistle of Soviet cities?' . . . It can only be explained by that sense of being right without which it is impossible to be a poet. If one were to name the dominant theme in the whole of M.'s life and work, one might say that it was his insistence on the poet's dignity, his position in a society and his right to make himself heard."[34]

Gumilev, who was soon divorced from Akhmatova, never had much opportunity to develop as a poet. The Revolution overturned his life, as it did the lives of all of them. He was executed on charges of antirevolutionary activity in 1921.

Although Mandelstam learned much from Gumilev, he was a poet before the two had met. He had gone to a progressive school in St. Petersburg run by an early Symbolist poet (Nabokov went to the same school a few years later), and when he left at the age of 16 he had been writing for several years. He then visited Western Europe, attended classes in Paris and Heidelberg and toured Italy and Switzerland. At that point, he saw himself as a Symbolist poet. He knew Ivanov and sent him poems from France. When he was 18, Mandelstam wrote Ivanov:

> First allow me a few reflections on your book. It seems impossible to dispute—it is captivating and destined to win hearts.
>
> When a person steps under the vaults of Notre Dame does he really ponder the truth of Catholicism, and does he not become a Catholic merely by virtue of being under those vaults?
>
> Your book is magnificent in the beauty of its great architectural creations and astronomical systems. Every true poet would write just as you did if he could write books on the basis of the precise and immutable laws of his work.[35]

Then Mandelstam offered some criticism. "However, it seems to me that your book is too—how shall I say it?—too circular, without any angles. No matter which direction one approaches it from, it is impossible to cause injury to it or oneself, since it has no sharp edges."[36]

At this point, Mandelstam called Ivanov "my friendly enemy" yet signed himself "your pupil." Three years later, in "Morning of Acmeism," he was hardly friendly. He wrote: "A work of art attracts the great majority only insofar as it illuminates the artist's world view. The artist, however, considers his world view a tool and an instrument, like a hammer in the hands of a stonemason, and his only reality is the work of art itself."[37]

The Symbolists saw the expression of their worldview as the end of poetry. Mandelstam argued that his worldview was important only insofar as it helped him fashion the poem. The reality of the poem was "the word as such."[38] The poet used the word to raise a "phenomenon to its tenth power, and the modest exterior of a work of art often deceives us with regard to the monstrously condensed reality contained within."[39] He called "the word as such" "the Logos," signifying not just meaning but all elements of the word. He concluded his discussion of the word by arguing "For the Acmeists the conscious sense of the word, the Logos, is just as magnificent a form as music is for the Symbolists."[40]

The Acmeists were builders, taking joy in their own gravity. They celebrated the physical world and its physiology. "The architect says: I build, that indicates I am right. The consciousness of our rightness is dearer to us than anything else in poetry. . . . What madman would agree to build if he did not believe in the reality of his material, the resistance of which he knew he must overcome? A cobblestone in the hands of an architect is transformed into substance, but a man is not born to build if he does not hear metaphysical proof in the sound of the chisel splitting rock."[41]

As the individual stone was the foundation of the Gothic cathedral, so was the word the foundation of the poem. And as that stone was shaped and placed in a delicate balance with other stones, so were words arranged in a poem. It was to symbolize this process that Mandelstam gave the name *Stone* to his first book and included poems celebrating such great structures as Notre Dame and Hagia Sophia. In his essay, he wrote, "It was as if the stone thirsted after another existence. It revealed its own dynamic potential hidden within itself, as if it were begging admittance into the 'groined arch' in order to participate in the joyous action of its fellows."[42]

Mandelstam felt that the Russian Symbolists rejected the dynamism of the phenomenal world. The word to them was not stone but a bit of perfume, a note of music, while the poem was not an end in itself but a means to achieve a mystical experience. The Symbolists disliked the world, felt uncomfortable in their bodies and scorned three-dimensional space. Mandelstam attacked this: "Genuine piety before the three dimensions of space is the first condition of successful building: to regard the world neither as a burden nor as an unfortunate accident, but as a God-given palace. Indeed, what can you say about an ungrateful guest who lives off his host, takes advantage of his hospitality, all the while despising him to the depths of his soul, thinking only how to deceive him?"[43]

The poem, by being "monstrously condensed," was like a small cathedral, and like the cathedral, it contained the intellectual and moral, physical and spiritual, social and individual.

> We perceive what is particular in a man, that which makes him an individual, and we incorporate it into the far more significant concept of the organism. Acmeists share their love for the organism and for organization with the physiologically brilliant Middle Ages. . . . What in the thirteenth century appeared to be the logical development of the concept of the organism—the Gothic Cathedral—now has the aesthetic effect of something monstrous: Notre Dame is the triumph of physiology, its Dionysian orgy. We do not want to distract ourselves with a stroll through the "forest of symbols," because we have a denser, more virgin forest-divine physiology, the infinite complexity of our own dark organism.[44]

As a poem was like a cathedral, so was a human being in his or her complexity like a cathedral. When one had such a wealth of material, Mandelstam asked, why should a poet turn to a Baudelairian forest of symbols to explain it? The cathedral itself was already a forest of symbols.

The cathedral was the ideal. A few years before in an essay on François Villon, Mandelstam wrote: "In the Middle Ages a man considered himself just as indispensable and just as bound to the edifice of his world as a stone in a Gothic structure, bearing with dignity the pressures of his neighbors and entering the common play of forces as an inevitable stake. To serve meant not only to act for the common good. In the Middle Ages a man unconsciously recognized the plain fact of his own existence as service, as a kind of heroic act."[45]

Mandelstam's justification of the intellectual and moral in his poems gave him his sense of rightness and great dignity. It would be something the Stalinists could not tolerate. In the "Morning of Acmeism," Mandelstam concluded the section concerning the concept of the organism by exhorting: "Love the existence of the thing more than the thing itself and your own existence more than yourself: that is Acmeism's highest commandment."[46]

These ideas are also found in Mandelstam's poem "Notre Dame." The translation is by Robert Tracy.

> Where a Roman judge framed laws for an alien folk
> A basilica stands, original, exulting,
> Each nerve stretched taut along the light cross-vaulting,
> Each muscle flexing, like Adam when he first woke.
>
> If you look from outside you grasp the hidden plan:
> Strong saddle-girth arches watchfully forestall
> The ponderous mass from shattering the wall
> And hold in check the bold vault's battering ram.
>
> A primal labyrinth, a wood past man's understanding,
> The Gothic spirit's rational abyss,
> Brute strength of Egypt and a Christian meekness,
> Thin reed beside oak, and the plumb line everywhere king.
>
> Stronghold of Notre Dame, the more my attentive eyes
> Studied your gigantic ribs and frame
> Then the more often this reflection came:
> From cruel weight, I too will someday make beauty rise.[47]

The mention of Adam in the fourth line is a reference to Acmeism. One of the Acmeists, Sergey Gorodetsky, insisted they call themselves Adamists instead of Acmeists, writing in his own Acmeist manifesto: "a poet should look at the world with Adam's fresh eye, and Adam created words by giving names to things."[48] In the third quatrain we find a reference to Baudelaire's "forest of symbols," with Mandelstam arguing that the primal labyrinth of the cathedral is more complicated and rewarding.

Mandelstam was 21 when he wrote "Notre Dame," but it contained ideas that he kept all his life. It is interesting to compare this poem to Rilke's "Archaic Torso of Apollo" written seven years earlier. Both poems celebrated paradigms that Rilke and Mandelstam believed enabled them to write. For Mandelstam, the poem is made: The plumb line is king. The poem does not exist to argue an idea, nor does it refer back to its architect. Like a cathedral, it stands apart from its builder. A poem requires constant tension and intricate balance to hold it together. Just as the cathedral is held together by gravity, so the poem is held together by the relationship of its parts.

The Symbolist poem tried to achieve tension by referring back to the life of the poet, but as an Acmeist, Mandelstam stressed that the poem must be an event complete in itself, not dependent on anything outside of it. Since his poems are at times obscure and associational, Mandelstam would seem to contradict his own theories. But I expect he would argue that the poem isn't reality but a reality that has been "monstrously condensed", and it is a mistake to expect it to seem realistic. After all, he was not aiming for verisimilitude. The Russian Symbolists never cared if the reader understood. Mandelstam insisted that the poem must be capable of being understood, otherwise it cannot be considered an autonomous event.

The Symbolist poems were often written in free verse, and much of their tension was supplied by their reference back to the superior human being, even though this turned the reader into a bystander. But for the poem to be an event in itself, according to

Mandelstam, the poem's tension must be achieved by formal considerations. The Symbolist poem is basically Romantic. The ideal poem for Mandelstam was a mixture of Classic and Romantic. Discussing Mandelstam's work, Jane Gray Harris wrote: "As an Acmeist, as an admirer of Pushkinian 'Classicism' and of the French Symbolist tradition . . . , as a proponent of such basic Neo-Classical tenets as simplicity of outline and complexity of the thematic, Mandelstam sought poetic 'dynamism' in efforts to achieve balance and harmony through striking juxtapositions of human, architectural or natural images in verbal constructions which astonish the readers' intellect as well as his senses."[49]

In his essay "The Word and Culture," Mandelstam wrote, "Revolution in art inevitably leads to Classicism, not because David reaped the harvest of Robespierre, but because that is what the earth desires. . . . Poetry is the plow that turns up time."[50]

In an essay on Andre Chenier, the French poet executed during the Reign of Terror, Mandelstam argued for a mixing of the Classic and Romantic: "Chenier belonged to the generation of French poets for whom syntax was a golden cage from which they would not dream of escaping."[51] Poetry cannot come entirely out of Reason, but neither can it depend entirely on the irrational. "Romantic poetry," wrote Mandelstam, "affirms the poetics of the unexpected."[52] Chenier, like Pushkin, was able to combine the two, and Mandelstam holds up Pushkin's formula that poetry must unite the intellect and the furies.

Mandelstam admired Chenier throughout his life and particularly admired Chenier's "stress on the ideals of heroism and stoicism in the face of adversity." Jane Gray Harris wrote:

> Chenier never lost sight of the fact that the writer is both
> an individual with his own individual capacities, as well as
> a social creature, responsive to his society. Moreover, he
> was careful not to allow his views of contemporary society
> and the arts to falsify his historical sense. He sees the artist's
> role in society as related to the health or corruption of its

institutions balanced by the moral consciousness of the artist himself. Thus, the artist's role is posited as an active force in society through its opposition to, as well as through its reflection of, social values and institutions.[53]

These ideas became Mandelstam's own, and Chenier was one of his heroes. In the mid-1920s Mandelstam stopped writing poetry for about five years. His wife felt he stopped because he realized his ideas would lead to his destruction. But remembering the example of Chenier, he at last accepted whatever might happen. "Poetry came back to him," wrote his wife, "when he once more knew he was right and had taken the proper stand."[54] In an unfinished essay on Scriabin from about 1915, Mandelstam wrote: "I wish to speak of Scriabin's death as the supreme act of his creative activity. It seems to me that the death of an artist should not be excluded from the chain of his creative achievements but should be viewed as its final closing link."[55]

This was also how he saw the death of Chenier. In 1931, when Mandelstam resumed writing, it was also the death he accepted for himself. Referring to the fragment on Scriabin, Nadezhda Mandelstam wrote: "The death of an artist is never a random event, but a last act of creation that seems to illuminate the whole of his life under a powerful ray of light. M. steered his life with a strong hand toward the doom that awaited him, toward the commonest form of death, 'herded with the herd,' that we could all expect."[56] And she wrote, "I had the impression that death for him was not the end, but a kind of justification for one's life."[57]

In combining the Classic with the Romantic and emphasizing form and personal voice, Mandelstam argued that a poem still must astonish. "The fresh air of poetry," he wrote, "is the element of surprise."[58] By quick shifts and juxtapositions, the poem constantly kept the reader from anticipating its direction. This practice comes, Mandelstam wrote, from the poet's own desire "to be astonished by [his] words, to be captivated by [his] originality and unexpectedness."[59] And elsewhere he wrote, "The capacity for astonishment is the poet's greatest virtue."[60] By being able to be astonished himself, the poet is able to astonish his reader. But this astonishment isn't caused by the absurd or the fantastic. At the end of the "Morning of Acmeism," Mandelstam wrote:

> Logic is the kingdom of the unexpected. To think logically is to be perpetually astonished. We have come to love the music of proof. Logical connection for us is not some popular song about a finch, but a choral symphony, so difficult and so inspired that the conductor must exert all his energy to keep the performers under his control.
>
> How convincing the music of Bach! What power of proof! The artist must prove and prove endlessly. The artist worthy of his calling cannot accept anything on faith alone, that is too easy, too dull. . . . We cannot fly, we can ascend only those towers which we build ourselves.[61]

Here again is the Gothic cathedral. Surprise is best manipulated within a logical context. The Gothic arch and the seemingly weightless ceiling of the cathedral are astonishing only insofar as they are logical.

The poet can astonish the reader only if he or she is capable of being astonished; the poet can move the reader only if he or she is capable of being moved. Mandelstam felt that the poet's sense of being right derived from a sense of unity with his fellow human beings. As he wrote in his essay on Villon, man was to society as the stone was to the cathedral. It was the poet's constant contact with the physical world that let him be a source of truth and created his sense of rightness. In "On the Addressee," he wrote, "After all, isn't poetry the consciousness of being right?"[62]

To understand this, we must recall Mandelstam's statement that "a work of art attracts the great majority only insofar as it illuminates the artist's world view." We, as readers, go to the poem to find ourselves and the closer the poet tries to become united to his or her fellow creatures, the better we will be able to find ourselves within the poem. This is why the poet must consider his or her worldview as a tool, "like a hammer in the hands of a stonemason," because through that worldview the poet becomes united with the reader. Nadezhda Mandelstam wrote: "The work of the poet as a vehicle of world harmony has a social character—this is, it is concerned with the doings of the poet's fellow men, among whom he lives and whose fate he shares. He does not speak 'for them' but with them, nor does he set himself apart from them: otherwise he would not be a source of truth."[63]

In order to maintain a capacity for astonishment, the poet can never anticipate the identity of the reader. Once the writer knows for whom he or she is writing, then the writer becomes too conscious of trying to influence that person and to interfere with the intuitive process. "The prose writer," wrote Mandelstam in "On the Addressee," "always addresses himself to a concrete audience, to the dynamic representatives of his age. Even when making prophecies, he bears his future contemporaries in mind."[64] The poet, on the other hand, "is bound only to his providential addressee."[65] Later in the essay he wrote: "And so, although individual poems such as epistles or dedications, may be addressed to concrete persons, poetry as a whole is always directed toward a more or less distant, unknown addressee, in whose existence the poet does not doubt, not doubting in himself."[66]

What was the function of poetry for Mandelstam? We find that answer in his ideas about the Gothic cathedral, Andre Chenier and the integrity of the word. Beyond that, the poem expresses the eternal verities. That doesn't mean the end of poetry is truth. He would still think the end of poetry is poetry itself, but truths should be contained within the poem just as they are contained within the cathedral. Additionally, poetry increases the links between human beings. It reminds them and makes them think of what it means to be human, what it means to belong to a community just as a cathedral does.

Mandelstam scorned the idea of progress in literature. He felt it was suicidal and kept writers from thinking about how to accomplish their own tasks. In "On the Nature of the Word" he wrote: "The theory of progress in literature represents the crudest, most repugnant form of academic ignorance. Literary forms change, one set of forms yielding its place to another. However, each change, each gain, is accomplished by a loss, a forfeit. In literature nothing is ever 'better,' no progress can be made simply because there is no literary machine and no finish line toward which everyone must race as rapidly as possible."[67]

In this essay, "On the Nature of the Word," written in 1922, Mandelstam expanded his earlier definition of Acmeism. He had been strongly influenced by the French philosopher Henri Bergson, who described two different methods of knowing the world: simple intellect, which logically analyzes, and the intuition, which expresses itself through metaphor. The first must break up time, but the second participates in it, perceives duration and so is able to understand the flow or rhythm of life. We recall the Symbolists' emphasis on intuition: that it is through intuition one perceives the truth. Mandelstam had kept his belief in the intuitive power of the poet but justified his belief with Bergson's argument. Jane Gray Harris wrote: "Following Bergson's aesthetic theories, Mandelstam views the poet as the master of 'intuition.' The poet seeks to perceive the unity and continuity of life and to preserve that unity and continuity by shaping it, by giving it artistic form. He can do so, however, only by mastering the craft of poetry. In this way, the poet acts both spontaneously, in accord with his intuition, and rationally, in accord with the demand of poetic craft to give form to the objects of his spontaneous intuition."[68]

The pertinent ideas in "On the Nature of the Word" have already been discussed, but what is interesting is that Mandelstam chose to write the essay even though Gumilev was dead and Acmeism as a movement had ended seven years before. Also in 1922, the Soviets were not receptive to Mandelstam's attack on progress and civic poetry. He ended this essay by saying that poetry must not educate merely citizens but "Men," meaning the whole human being. Mandelstam had very mixed feelings about

Soviet Russia and was attacked for saying that human beings were more important than ideas. The Symbolists had a Strong Man theory, and even Gumilev emphasized the strong and manly. It may appear that Mandelstam was making a similar argument. Instead he argues for the endurance of man against theories and philosophies. "The ideal of perfect manliness is provided by the style and practical demands of our age. Everything has become heavier and more massive; thus man must become harder, for he must be the hardest thing on earth; he must be to the earth what the diamond is to glass. The hieratic, that is to say, the sacred character of poetry arises out of the conviction that man is harder than everything else in the world."[69]

Nadezhda Mandelstam wrote in *Hope Against Hope*:

> Culture, after all, is not something generated by the upper level of society at any given time, but an element passed down from generation to generation—a product of the continuity without which life would break up in chaos. What is thus handed down in the community often seems unbearably set in a conventional form, but it cannot be all that terrible if it had enabled the human race to survive. The threat to the human race comes not from its communal morality, but from the extravagant innovations of its more volatile elements. M. defined the poet as one who "disturbs meaning." What he had in mind, however, was not rebellion against inherited order, but rejection of the commonplace image and the hackneyed phrase by which meaning is obscured. This was another way of appealing for an art that faithfully recorded life and living events, as opposed to all that was deathlike.[70]

In the early 1920s, Mandelstam argued that the aim of Acmeism "was to be the conscience of poetry. It sat in judgement on poetry, but was not itself poetry."[71] At another time, he told an audience that Acmeism was "a yearning for world culture," by which he meant that it wasn't a school of poetry but a standard to which they aspired.

Although the movement broke up in 1915, Mandelstam called himself an Acmeist all his life, as did Gumilev, as did Anna Akhmatova, who died in 1966. On the seventh anniversary of Gumilev's execution, Mandelstam wrote to Akhmatova: "My dialogue with Kolia [Gumilev] has never broken off and never will be."[72]

Nadezhda Mandelstam wrote: "I can confirm that M. was always recalling what Gumilev had said about one or the other of his poems, or wondering what he might have made of new ones he would never be able to read. In particular he liked to repeat some words of praise that Gumilev had once spoken to him: 'This is a very good poem, Osip, but when it is finished, not a single one of the present words will remain.'"[73]

Nadezhda Mandelstam suggested that Mandelstam, Gumilev and Akhmatova were tied together not by theories of poetry but by a common understanding of life. They formed a community where they were able to test their ideas on one another, show one another their poems and develop as poets because of this common enthusiastic influence on each other.

> I think M. was lucky to have had a moment in his life when he was linked by the pronoun "we" with a group of others. His brief friendship with certain "companions, co-seekers, co-discoverers"—to quote a phrase from [his] "Conversations about Dante"—affected him for the rest of his life, helping to mold his personality. In "Conversation about Dante" he also says that time is the stuff of history and that, conversely, "the stuff of history is the joint tenure of time" by people bound together as "we." If a man is mindful of the fact that he lives in history, he knows he bears responsibility for his deeds, which, in turn, are determined by his ideas.[74]

Later in *Hope Abandoned* Nadezhda Mandelstam wrote that she felt the Strong Man theories of the Symbolists and Gumilev were rather comic and pretentious, and despite her understanding of Mandelstam's idea that "man must be the hardest thing in the world," she had laughed at his line "Only in battle do we find our allotted part." It made her think of the "doddering old knights" in the Eisenstein films.

> M. never had the faintest idea how to handle a rifle, hated firearms with all his being, and had never worn a military uniform. How was I to know that real battles with real bloodshed . . . would be found in such an unwarlike field as poetry, of all things. Luckily M. did not take offense, nor did he expect flattery from his wife. The "strong" men of our heroic age always demanded praise from their women-folk. This was by way of compensation for all the indigni-ties inflicted upon them in their public life. M. had no need of this, for a reason that is quite clear to me. His youthful association with the Acmeists had given him a genuine sense of community, helping him achieve a feeling of "self" which was *not* merely individualistic and thus not in need of constant affirmation.[75]

In November 1933, two years after he began writing poetry again, Mandelstam recited a poem about Stalin to a group of friends. Here it is in a translation by Clarence Brown and W. S. Merwin.

> Our lives no longer feel ground under them.
> At ten paces you can't hear our words.
>
> But whenever there's a snatch of talk
> it turns to the Kremlin mountaineer,
>
> the ten thick worms of his fingers,
> his words like measures of weight,

the huge laughing cockroaches on his top lip,
the glitter of his boot-rims.

Ringed with a scum of chicken-necked bosses
he toys with the tributes of half-men.

One whistles, another meouws, a third snivels.
He pokes his finger and he alone goes boom.

He forges decrees in a line like horseshoes,
One for the groin, one the forehead, temple, eye.

He rolls the executions on his tongue like berries.
He wishes he could hug them like big friends from home.[76]

A friend reported the poem to the authorities. Mandelstam was arrested, then sent into internal exile, constantly having to change his place of residence, constantly harassed by the authorities. This went on for four years. Then he was arrested again and shipped east to a prison camp where he died.

For Mandelstam to resume writing in 1931 meant rejoining the human community, no matter the consequences. During those frightening years after he wrote the "Stalin Epigram", he asked his wife, "Why do you complain? Poetry is respected only in this country—people are killed for it. There's no place where more people are killed for it."[77]

Near the end of *Hope Against Hope*, Nadezhda Mandelstam wrote, "For the sake of what idea was it necessary to send those countless trainloads of prisoners, including the man who was so dear to me, to forced labor in eastern Siberia? M. always said that they always knew what they were doing: the aim was to destroy not only people, but the intellect itself."[78]

11 | Chekhov's Sense of Writing as Seen through His Letters

ON JANUARY 7, 1889, a few weeks before his twenty-ninth birthday, Anton Chekhov wrote to his friend and publisher, the archconservative Alexei Suvorin:

> What aristocratic writers take from nature gratis, the less privileged must pay for with their youth. Try and write a story about a young man—the son of a serf, a former grocer, choirboy, schoolboy and university student, raised on respect for rank, kissing the priests' hands, worshiping the ideas of others, and giving thanks for every piece of bread, receiving frequent whippings, making the rounds as a tutor without galoshes, brawling, torturing animals, enjoying dinners at the houses of rich relatives, needlessly hypocritical before God and man merely to acknowledge his own insignificance—write about how this young man squeezes the slave out of himself drop by drop and how, on waking up one fine morning, he finds that the blood coursing through his veins is no longer the blood of a slave, but that of a real human being.[1]

The young man described here is Chekhov himself, and what he describes is how he developed in himself "a sense of personal freedom," by which he meant the ability to live and write without constraint, with nothing inhibiting the creative impulse except his own sense of duty, responsibility and definition of what it was to be a human being. It also meant a passion to free himself from all labels and philosophies. In a letter written three months earlier to the writer Alexei Pleshcheyev, Chekhov wrote:

> The [critics] I am afraid of are the ones who look for tendentiousness between the lines and are determined to see me as either liberal or conservative. I am neither liberal, nor conservative, nor gradualist, nor monk, nor indifferentist. I would like to be a free artist and nothing else. . . . I hate lies and violence in all their forms. . . . I look upon tags and labels as prejudices. My holy of holies is the human body, health, intelligence, talent, inspiration, love and the most absolute freedom imaginable, freedom from violence and lies, no matter what form the latter two take.[2]

But freedom for Chekhov required hard work. From his earliest writing, he carefully distinguished between freedom and license. License meant preying on the world and one's fellow creatures, to destroy without hesitation, to be entirely selfish. But freedom meant seeing oneself without self-deception, to understand one's duty to the world and to one's fellow creatures, to work to exercise one's potential as a human being and to improve the quality of life for not only the people now living but for those not yet born.

Freedom for Chekhov was a difficult place to reach. Born on January 29, 1860, in Taganrog, on the Sea of Azov in southern Russia, Chekhov's childhood was a misery. As he once said, "There was no childhood in my childhood." He was the third of six children, and his two older brothers, both alcoholics, were never able to free their minds from the ill treatment they had received in their youth.

Their father, Pavel Chekhov, had been born a slave whose own father had bought the family's freedom in the early 1840s. Pavel Chekhov was a religious fanatic who had a small general store in Taganrog. The store opened at five A.M. and closed at one A.M. Chekhov and his two older brothers were required to run the store as well as sing in their father's choir, attend church several times a week and otherwise remain quiet.

Here is the character Laptev in Chekhov's story "Three Years" describing his childhood. The description is thought to refer to Chekhov's own childhood. "I can remember my father beginning to teach me, or, to put it more simply, to beat me, when I was not yet five years old. He whipped me with birch rods, pulled my ears, hit me on the head, and when I woke up each morning, the first thing I thought of was: Will I be beaten today?"[3]

In a letter to a fellow writer dated March 9, 1892, Chekhov described his childhood. "I received a religious education . . . choir singing, reading the epistles and psalms in church, regular attendance at matins, altar boy and bell-ringing duty. And the result? When I think back on my childhood it all seems quite gloomy to me. I have no religion now. You know, when my two brothers and I would sing the 'Let my prayer arise' trio or the 'Archangel's voice,' everyone looked at us and was moved. They envied my parents, while we felt like little convicts."[4]

But Pavel Chekhov's tyranny extended to more than religion. In a letter to his older brother Alexander, Chekhov wrote, "Let me ask you to recall that it was despotism and lying that ruined your mother's youth. Despotism and lying so mutilated our childhood that it's sickening and frightening to think about it. Remember the horror and disgust we felt in those times when Father threw a tantrum at dinner over too much salt in the soup and called Mother a fool."[5]

Chekhov was writing to his brother on this occasion because he was shocked at how his brother was treating his family—yelling at his common-law wife and the children, being rude to the servants, drinking every day, turning the people around him into slaves. Alexander blamed his bad behavior on his life, but Chekhov would have none of it. "Your difficult situation, the bad disposition of the women it falls to your lot to live with, the idiocy of your cooks, your forced and loathsome labor and all the rest cannot serve to justify your despotism. It's better to be the victim than the hangman."[6]

It was that decision—that it was better to be the victim than the hangman—that led Chekhov toward a sense of personal freedom. What helped as well was his father's bankruptcy in 1876 and the departure of the family to Moscow, leaving Chekhov alone in Taganrog for three years to finish high school. During this time Chekhov reeducated himself. Not only did he spend most of his free time at the public library, but he worked to drive the slave from himself, to put aside violence, lies, sloth, vanity—all those faults he classified under the Russian word *posblost'*, which means, in part, vulgarity, ill-breeding, indecency.

Little is known about these three years, but toward the end of that time, Chekhov sent a letter to his 14-year-old brother Mikhail. He praised his brother's handwriting and grammar, but then said there is one thing he didn't like. "Why do you refer to yourself as my 'worthless, insignificant little brother.' So you are aware of your worthlessness, are you? . . . Do you know where you should be aware of your worthlessness? Before God, perhaps, or before human intelligence, before beauty or nature. But not before people. Among people you should be aware of your worth. You're no cheat, you're an honest man, aren't you? Well then, respect yourself for being a good honest fellow. Don't confuse 'humility' with 'an awareness of your own worthlessness.'"[7]

A sense of freedom required a sense of worth, and the young man who wrote this letter was a different person from the one his family had left three years before. When he came to Moscow to enroll in medical school a few months later, he brushed aside his father's attempts to control him and took over the family, including the education, feeding and clothing of his younger brothers and sister. The only rules he insisted upon were that there must be no more violence, no more lies.

What is also significant about Chekhov's letter to his young brother is that it is written by the son of a serf, the son of a bankrupt owner of a little store. In 1861, Alexander I had freed 52 million serfs, five-eighths of the population. Russia in the nineteenth century was an extremely rigid society in which the civil service was divided into 14 grades termed "the table of the ranks." The gentry and clergy made up just 2 percent of the population. For the 18-year-old Chekhov to tell his brother "Among people you should be aware of your worth" was practically a subversive remark.

But from this three-year period, Chekhov developed a scorn for class distinctions and saw them for what they were—the attempt of the minority to control the majority. What he had instead was a sense of correct behavior. Those who acted badly were guilty of vulgarity, ill-breeding, of *poshlost'*. A sense of decency was what governed Chekhov's actions for the rest of his life. What mattered was not intelligence, wealth, or class position but how a person treated his or her fellow creatures. In the letter to his brother Alexander quoted earlier, Chekhov wrote,

> During my very first visit I was repelled by your SHOCK-ING, completely unprecedented treatment of Natalia Al-exandrovna [Alexander's second common-law wife] and the cook. Forgive me please, but treating women like that no matter who they are, is unworthy of a decent, loving human being. What heavenly or earthly power has given you the right to make them your slaves? Constant profanity of the most vile variety, a raised voice, reproaches, sudden whims at breakfast and dinner, eternal complaints about a life of forced and loathsome labor—isn't all that an expression of blatant despotism?[8]

What Chekhov is talking about is not conventional morality but the need for people to treat each other with courtesy and consideration. In his writing this is the one judgment he makes—that someone treats the people around him badly. This is far more important than class position and all the rest. For Chekhov, it is far worse to be unkind than to be immoral.

What should be understood is that this behavior for Chekhov was learned behavior. Growing up in Taganrog, he was another sort of person. The examples he had before him as a child were examples of *poshlost'*, which Vladimir Nabokov defined as the "falsely important, the falsely beautiful, falsely clever, the falsely attractive."[9] Many of Chekhov's characters are guilty of *poshlost'*, but one of the guiltiest is Natalia, who marries Andrey in *The Three Sisters*.

Poshlost' leads people to treat others badly. It is a selfish complacency that argues that where we are now is the best place to be. It is against change, against education, against medicine, against art and against the belief that people are equal. It is the tendency to blame our troubles on outside forces, not on what is inside. *Poshlost'* for Chekhov was the natural drift of all human behavior.

When Chekhov was 26, he wrote a fierce letter to his older brother Nikolai, who had been treating his family badly. He explained his brother's behavior by saying "It's the bourgeois side of you coming out, the side raised on birch thrashings beside the wine cellar and handouts, and it's hard to overcome, terribly hard."[10]

To help his brother, Chekhov gave him eight rules of behavior, which he described as found in well-bred people.

1. They respect the individual and are therefore always indulgent, gentle, polite and compliant. . . .

2. Their compassion extends beyond beggars and cats. They are hurt even by things the eye can't see. . . .

3. They respect the property of others and therefore pay their debts.

4. They are candid and fear lies like the plague. They do not lie even about the most trivial matters. A lie insults the listener and debases him in the liar's eyes. They don't put on airs, they behave in the street as they do at home, and they do not dazzle their inferiors. They know how to keep their mouths shut and they do not force uninvited confidences on people. Out of respect for the ears of others they are often more silent than not.

5. They do not belittle themselves to arouse sympathy. They do not play on people's heartstrings to get them to sigh and

fuss over them. They do not say, "No one understands me!" or "I've squandered my talent on trifles!" . . .

6. They are not preoccupied with vain things. They are not taken in by such false jewels as friendships with celebrities. . . . When they have done a penny's worth of work, they don't try to make a hundred rubles out of it, and they don't boast over being admitted to places closed to others. True talents always seek obscurity. They try to merge with the crowd and shun all ostentation. . . .

7. If they have talent, they respect it. They sacrifice comfort, women, wine and vanity to it. They are proud of their talent. . . .

8. They cultivate their aesthetic sensibilities. They cannot stand to fall asleep fully dressed, see a slit in the wall teeming with bedbugs, breathe rotten air, walk on a spittle-laden floor or eat off a kerosene stove. They try their best to tame and ennoble their sexual instinct. . . . They don't guzzle vodka on any old occasion, nor do they go round sniffing cupboards, for they know they are not swine.[11]

Although this letter is directed to his brother Nikolai, it also describes the program of reeducation that Chekhov set himself during those three years alone in Taganrog. These rules not only govern Chekhov's life, they govern his writing. During his life, critics attacked Chekhov for not being didactic enough, but he was always didactic. He was always writing against vulgarity, indecency and ill-breeding: not by preaching against it, but by creating situations in his stories where the reader must judge for himself or herself.

When Chekhov moved to Moscow to enroll in Moscow University in 1879 as a medical student, he needed to earn money. His older brothers gave him no financial support, but some years before they had introduced him to the Moscow humor magazines. Alexander and Nikolai had been publishing in these magazines since 1876—Alexander as a writer and Nikolai as an illustrator. They encouraged Anton to write and helped with his first efforts.

After several years of trying, Anton published his first article in the magazine *Dragonfly* on December 23, 1879. In the next five years he published hundreds of articles in such magazines as *Dragonfly, Spectator, Fragments* and *Alarm Clock,* work ranging from one-line captions for cartoons to two full-length novels. Most he signed with the pseudonym Antosha Chekhonte, a nickname he had gotten in high school. Chekhov's work for these magazines became popular and he soon passed his brother Alexander in his ability to get published. On April 17, 1883, he wrote Alexander telling him how to do a story for the magazine *Fragments.* "1. The shorter, the better; 2. A bit of ideology and being up to date is most a propos; 3. Caricature is just fine, but ignorance of civil service ranks and of the seasons is strictly prohibited."[12]

These magazines had strict length and subject requirements, and by adhering to them, Chekhov learned much about writing. But by 1884, he began to chafe against these restrictions. He was tired of the stereotypes and caricatures. He wanted to write longer stories and to mix the humor with something else. He began to change his work. On May 10, 1886, he sent Alexander a new recipe for how to get a story published. He was again criticizing one of Alexander's stories, and he told him that his story would be successful

> only under the following conditions: 1) absence of lengthy torrents of a politico-socio-economic nature; 2) total objectivity; 3) honesty in the description of characters and objects; 4) extreme brevity; 5) daring and originality; shun clichés; 6) compassion.
>
> I think description of nature should be very short and always a propos. . . . You have to choose small details . . . , grouping them in such a way that if you close your eyes after reading it you can picture the whole thing. For example, you'll get a picture of a moonlit night if you write that

on the dam of the mill a piece of broken bottle flashed like a bright star and the black shadow of a dog or wolf rolled by like a ball, etc. Nature will become animated if you don't disdain comparing its appearance with human actions, etc.

In the realm of psychology you also need details. God preserve you from commonplaces. Best of all, shun all descriptions of the characters' spiritual state. You must have that state emerge clearly from their actions. Don't try for too many characters. The center of gravity should reside in two: he and she.[13]

Although Chekhov's work became fuller in the 18 years after this time, these precepts remained with him all his life: a refusal to take sides, honesty, brevity, originality and that paradox that typifies his work, objectivity and compassion.

As Chekhov took his writing more seriously, so other writers took it more seriously. They urged him to stop writing for the humor magazines and to develop more responsibility toward his own talent. These letters astonished Chekhov, and it became clear that he had never seen his talent as anything important. It was just a knack he had.

In a letter to the writer Dmitry Grigorovich, who had praised him, Chekhov wrote on March 28, 1886:

Your letter . . . struck me like a thunderbolt. I was so overwhelmed it brought me to the brink of tears, and even now I feel it has left a deep imprint on my innermost being. . . .

If I do have a gift that warrants respect, I must confess before the purity of your heart that I have as yet failed to respect it. I felt I had one, but slipped into the habit of considering it worthless. . . . All my friends and relatives have looked down on my work as an author, and they never stop giving me friendly advice against giving up my real life's work [medicine] for my scrawling. . . .

Until now I treated my literary work extremely frivolously, casually, nonchalantly, I can't remember working on a single story for more than a day, and "The Huntsman," which you so enjoyed, I wrote while I was out swimming. I wrote my stories the way reporters write up fires: mechanically, only half-consciously, without the least concern for the reader or myself.[14]

The letter from Grigorovich changed Chekhov. He began to write more seriously and to try longer pieces, the first being "The Steppe," published in 1887. But willing a change would not have been enough without two other factors. The first was Chekhov's sense of personal freedom, that it allowed him to write without constraint—that what governed the stories were the stories themselves rather than some outside idea or fear or grievance or ambition. The second factor was Chekhov's medical studies and his work as a doctor, which he took very seriously, even though it didn't pay as well as the writing. He joked about medicine and writing, calling medicine his "lawful wedded wife" and literature his "mistress," but it was clear to him that his writing benefited from his medical work. He described this more exactly in an autobiographical statement he wrote October 11, 1899, for his fifteenth class reunion. "There is no doubt in my mind that my study of medicine has had a serious impact on my literary activities. It significantly broadened the scope of my observations and enriched me with knowledge whose value for me as a writer only a doctor can appreciate. It also served as a guiding influence; my intimacy with medicine probably helped me to avoid many mistakes. My familiarity with the natural sciences and the scientific method have always kept me on my guard."[15]

It is difficult for writers to look at their work with a high degree of objectivity, but Chekhov's medical studies helped him achieve this. He taught himself to turn the same empirical method that guided his medical work to his writing and to remove from the writing any personal considerations. Once the subject was chosen, how a story or play was written was governed entirely by what worked and what didn't. He also trusted this pragmatism. Even after the poor reception of *The Seagull*, he didn't change his method but pushed forward using the tools he had developed. Chekhov was the most original, most experimental Russian writer of his time. Despite constant attacks from the critics and a lot of self-doubt, he never softened his aesthetic judgments or altered his work.

What writers influenced him? Although Chekhov read widely, there is no writer we can point to as a substantial influence. He admired Turgenev's novels but didn't read the stories until he was in his 30s. He liked D'Maupassant moderately, then came to dislike him. He loved Shakespeare. He disliked Dostoevsky and his emotional untidiness. He had huge admiration for Tolstoy, and in a letter written to another writer on January 28, 1900, when Tolstoy was sick, Chekhov described his feelings.

> His illness frightened me and made me very tense. I fear Tolstoy's death. His death would leave a large empty space in my life. First, I have loved no man the way I have loved him. I am not a believer, but of all beliefs I consider his the closest to mine and most suitable for me. Second, when literature has a Tolstoy, it is easy and gratifying to be a writer. Even if you are aware that you have never accomplished anything, you don't feel so bad, because Tolstoy accomplishes enough for everyone. His activities provide justification for the hopes and aspirations that are usually placed on literature. Third, Tolstoy stands firm, his authority is enormous, and as long as he is alive bad taste in literature, all vulgarity in its brazen-faced or lachrymose varieties, all bristly and resentful vanity will remain far in the background. His moral authority alone is enough to maintain what we think of as literary trends and schools at a certain minimal level. If not for him, literature would be a flock without a shepherd or an unfathomable jumble.[16]

Despite Chekhov's admiration for Tolstoy, the Russian writer whom Chekhov called greatest was Nikolai Gogol. What he admired in Gogol was his brevity and originality, the exactness of his description and how he could blend the serious, the bizarre and the comic. All these characteristics can be found in Chekhov, as well, but when Chekhov began reading Gogol, he had already been writing for some years.

Although Chekhov admired the works of a few contemporary Russian writers, he had little good to say about the writers themselves. In a letter to Suvorin (May 15, 1889), he wrote, "Russian writers are duller than their readers, their heroes are pallid and insignificant, and the life they portray is meager and uninteresting. The Russian writer lives in the drainpipe, eats sowbugs and has love affairs with hussies and laundresses; he knows nothing of history or geography or sciences or the religion of his country or its administration or its legal procedures . . . in short, he doesn't know a goddamn thing."[17]

Russian literary criticism at this time was extremely powerful, and Chekhov hated how his contemporaries were cowed by it. They wrote safely and were quick to criticize each other for not conforming. For Chekhov, this meant writing without freedom. Nor did he think much of the intelligentsia in general. In a letter to a fellow doctor on February 22, 1899, he wrote, "I have no faith in our intelligentsia; it is hypocritical, dishonest, hysterical, ill-bred, and lazy. I have no faith in it even when it suffers and complains, for its oppressors emerge from its own midst. I have faith in individuals, I see salvation in individuals scattered here and there, all over Russia, be they intellectuals or peasants."[18]

Chekhov's sense of what a writer should be was linked to his sense of freedom and decency. On April 10, 1890, he wrote a letter to an editor who accused him of unprincipled writing.

True, my literary career has consisted of an uninterrupted series of errors, sometimes flagrant errors, but that can be explained by the dimensions of my talent, not by whether I am a good or bad person. I have never gone in for blackmail, I have never written lampoons or denunciations, I have never toadied, nor lied, nor insulted. In short, I have written many stories and editorials that I would be only too glad to throw out because of their worthlessness, but I have never written a single line I am ashamed of today. . . .

I have always made a point of avoiding literary soirees, parties, conferences, etc. I never show my face in editorial offices without an invitation, I've always tried to have my friends think of me more as a doctor than a writer—in short, I was a modest writer and the letter I am writing you now is my first immodest act in the ten years of my career as a writer.[19]

Chekhov felt that literary theories constrained a writer. What guided him in his writing was his pragmatism guided by his sense of decency. Several weeks before the angry letter to the editor, he wrote a similar letter to a friend who had criticized his views on moral and artistic problems, claiming that Chekhov's writing wasn't properly artistic. Chekhov responded, "When people speak to me of what is artistic and what anti-artistic, of what is dramatically effective, of tendentiousness and realism and the like, I am at an utter loss, I nod to everything uncertainly, and answer in banal half truths that aren't worth a brass farthing. I divide all works into two categories: those I like and those I don't. I have no other criterion."[20]

This pragmatism is also seen in the textual criticism that Chekhov gave to other writers, and it goes back to those points that he detailed to his brother Alexander in 1886. Although he wrote to many writers, I want to look at the letters he sent to just one: Maxim Gorky, with whom he began to correspond in 1898. Gorky was very persistent in using Chekhov as a sounding board for his own work. Chekhov liked Gorky, but he was also quick to criticize. On December 3, 1898, he wrote:

I'll start by saying that, in my opinion, you lack restraint.
You are like a spectator in the theater who expresses his
delight with so little restraint that he prevents himself and
others from listening. This lack of restraint is especially
evident in the nature descriptions you use to break up your
dialogues. When I read them . . . I feel I'd like them to be
shorter, more compact, only about two or three lines long.
Frequent reference to languor, murmuring, plushness and
the like give your descriptions a rhetorical quality and
make them monotonous; they discourage a reader and
become almost tiresome. The same lack of restraint is
evident in your descriptions of women . . . and love scenes.
It is neither a majestic sweep nor bold strokes of the brush;
it is simply lack of restraint. Then the frequent use of words
that do not belong in the type of stories you write . . . is
annoying. . . . In your descriptions of intellectuals I feel a
tenseness somewhat akin to caution. That doesn't come
from not having observed intellectuals enough. You know
them, but you don't know exactly from what angle to
approach them.[21]

Chekhov's criticism resembles a doctor's description of a
patient. What was important was discovering the ailment and how
to make the patient better. A week or so later, Gorky wrote back
unhappy with the criticism and asking for amplification. On
January 3, 1899, Chekhov wrote again.

Your only fault is your lack of restraint and lack of grace.
When someone expends the least amount of motion on a
given action, that's grace. You tend to expend too much.

Your nature descriptions are artistic; you are a true
landscape painter. But your frequent personifications [of
nature] . . . make your descriptions a bit monotonous,
sometimes cloying and sometimes unclear. Color and ex-
pressivity in nature descriptions are achieved through sim-

plicity alone, through simple phrases like "the sun set," "it grew dark," "it began to rain," etc. . . . .

Don't ever write about land captains. There's nothing easier than writing about disagreeable men in power, readers love it, but only the most unpleasant, untalented sort of readers.[22]

On September 3, 1899, Chekhov sent Gorky more criticism.

Another piece of advice: when you read proof, cross out as many modifiers of nouns and verbs as you can. You have so many modifiers that the reader has a hard time figuring out what deserves his attention, and it tires him out. If I write, "A man sat down on the grass," it is understandable because it is clear and doesn't require a second reading. But it would be hard to follow and brain-taxing were I to write, "A tall, narrow-chested, red-bearded man of medium height sat down noiselessly looking around timidly and in fright, on a patch of green grass that had been trampled by pedestrians." The brain can't grasp all of this at once, and the art of fiction ought to be immediately, instantaneously graspable."[23]

What should be clear, along with the pragmatism, is Chekhov's attentiveness to the reader, that he doesn't put down a single word without calculating its effect upon the reader.

Finally, on October 22, 1901, Chekhov wrote to Gorky about his play *The Philistines*. After praising it, Chekhov said, "I have so far found only one [fault], a fault as irreparable as red hair on a redhead—its conservatism of form. You have new, original people singing new songs from a score that has a second-hand appearance."[24]

For Chekhov, conservatism of form was a triple sin. One, it bored the reader or audience with what had been done already. Two, it signified that the writer was writing lazily. Three, it signified that the writer was trying to attach his or her work to a kind of writing that had already received critical approval, which indicated that the writer was not writing with complete freedom.

The criticism Chekhov gave to Gorky makes up one kind of textual criticism found in Chekhov's letters. The other kind deals with the writer's relation to his or her own work and to the reader. Here, too, Chekhov was innovative. And here he received the greatest abuse from the critics of his time.

One of Chekhov's literary protégé's was Yelena Shavrova, a young woman who began giving him stories when she was 15. In one story, she makes the villain a cynical, fat, stupid and skirt-chasing gynecologist and further burdens the character with medical stereotypes. Chekhov criticized the character (September 16, 1891), then went on to tell her about Noah and his son Ham. "All Ham could see was that his father was a drunkard; he completely disregarded the fact that Noah was a genius, that he had built the Ark and saved the world. Writers must avoid imitating Ham. Mull that one over for a while. I don't dare ask you to love the gynecologist . . . , but I do dare remind you of justice, which is more precious for an objective writer than air."[25]

Chekhov was accusing Shavrova of attacking members of an older generation for personal reasons. These prejudices kept her from writing freely, which in turn kept her from writing justly. In "The Duel," Chekhov has a character say "To criticize is the act of a slave," meaning that a person who criticizes is always subjectively bound to that which he or she is criticizing.

Several years later (February 28, 1895), Chekhov again criticized Shavrova for a story she wrote about syphilis. "The ladies in your story regard syphilis as if it were hellfire and brimstone. Well, they're wrong. Syphilis isn't a vice, it isn't the product of ill will, but a disease, and the people who have it need warm, human care. It's wrong for a wife to desert her sick husband with the excuse that the disease is contagious or disgusting. She is free to react to syphilis however she likes, of course, but the author must remain humane to the very end."[26]

Chekhov's subject was always how should we live and how should we treat our fellow human beings. On January 14, 1887, Chekhov wrote to his friend Maria Kiselyova, who had criticized his story "Mire" as being in bad taste. She argued that literature should present only exemplary characters, not ugly ones, and that Chekhov had failed in his duty. Chekhov charged her with advocating censorship and for using literature as a soapbox for the fashionable ideas of the time. "Everything in this world is relative and approximate," he wrote. "There are people who can be corrupted even by children's literature."[27]

Then he said:

> Your statement that the world is "teeming with villains and villainesses" is true. Human nature is imperfect, so it would be odd to describe none but the righteous. Requiring literature to dig up a "pearl" from the pack of villains is tantamount to negating literature altogether. Literature is accepted as an art because it depicts life as it actually is. Its aim is the truth, unconditional and honest. . . . A "pearl" is a fine thing, I agree. But the writer is not a pastry chef, he is not a cosmetician and not an entertainer. He is a man bound by contract to his sense of duty and to his conscience. Once he undertakes this task, it is too late for excuses, and no matter how horrified, he must do battle with the grime of life. . . .
>
> To a chemist there is nothing impure on earth. The writer should be just as objective as the chemist; he should liberate himself from everyday subjectivity and acknowledge that manure piles play a highly respectable role in the landscape and that evil passions are every bit as much a part of life as good ones.[28]

The rule to be objective led Chekhov to argue that the writer must not judge, manipulate, or take sides. Clearly, the writer cannot be 100 percent objective, and Chekhov wrote stories, such as "The Grasshopper," where he fails at objectivity. But his attempt to treat his characters even-handedly is what typifies his work. It was also what led to his being dismissed by critics who demanded that art be didactic.

In a letter to the editor Pleshcheyev, Chekhov wrote on October 9, 1888, "Is there really no 'ideology' in the last story? You once told me that my stories lack an element of protest, that they have neither sympathies nor antipathies. But doesn't the story protest against lying from start to finish? Isn't that an ideology? It isn't? Well, I guess that means either I don't know how to bite or I'm a flea."[29]

To Chekhov, being objective and compassionate and refusing to judge was an ideology. He was in the business of showing his readers the nature of the world. Wasn't there some ideology in that? In a letter to Suvorin on May 30, 1888, Chekhov wrote:

> You write that neither the conversation about pessimism nor Kisochka's story [in the story "Lights"] help to solve the problem of pessimism. In my opinion it is not the writer's job to solve such problems as God, pessimism, etc.; his job is merely to record who, under what conditions, said or thought what about God or pessimism. The artist is not meant to be a judge of his characters and what they say; his only job is to be an impartial witness. I heard two Russians in a muddled conversation about pessimism, a conversation that solved nothing; all I am bound to do is reproduce that conversation exactly as I heard it. Drawing conclusions is up to the jury, that is, the readers. My only job is to be talented, that is, to know how to distinguish important testimony from unimportant.[30]

In another letter written to Suvorin in October of that same year, Chekhov continues in a similar vein. "You are right to demand that an author take conscious stock of what he is doing, but you are confusing two concepts: answering the questions and formulating them correctly. Only the latter is required of an author."[31]

In order to formulate the questions correctly, the author has certain requirements: a sense of humanity and justice, objectivity and compassion, a personal sense of freedom and that sense of decency and breeding that he had outlined to his brothers. Against this is *posblost'*: ignorance, vulgarity, selfishness and complacency. Chekhov had little faith in human speech as a means of communication since speech is so full of hidden meanings and disguised intentions. Our speech is where we whine and complain. It is only through art, Chekhov felt, that emotion, suffering and what it is to be a human being can be communicated. He sets this down very clearly in stories such as "Rothchild's Fiddle" and "The Student." Art helps us to live by helping to teach us what it is to be a human being. But to do that, the writer must stand up for all people, both good and bad.

In a letter to Suvorin about the Dreyfus trial (February 6, 1898), Chekhov praised Zola for attacking the French government which he claimed had framed Dreyfus. "Let us assume that Dreyfus is guilty—even so Zola is right, because the writer's job is not to accuse or persecute, but to stand up even for the guilty once they have been condemned and are undergoing punishment. 'What about politics and the interests of the state?' people may ask. But major writers and artists should engage in politics only enough to protect themselves from it. There are enough accusers, prosecutors and secret police without them, and in any case the role of Paul becomes them more than that of Saul."[32]

Although Chekhov was criticized for not being political, probably no writer of his time was more political. For isn't the first question, How should one live? And the next, How should we treat our neighbors? For Chekhov these questions were based on the ideas of decency and breeding that guided his behavior throughout his life. In a late letter to one of his editors (December 17, 1901), he wrote, "It's not forgotten words or idealism that matters; it is a consciousness of your own purity, that is, the perfect freedom of your soul from all forgotten and unforgotten words, idealisms and all the rest of those incomprehensible words. One should either believe in God, or if faith is lacking, one should do something other than fill the void with sensationalism, one must seek, seek on one's own, all alone with one's conscience."[33]

Such a search guided Chekhov's life, and it was fueled by a knowledge of his own purity, which doesn't mean he was saintly but that he strove to identify and be free of the world's prejudices. That purity and those prejudices he discovered by driving the slave out of himself, by developing a sense of personal freedom. It let him write while ignoring the pressures from outside and by ignoring the pressures from his own psychology. He pursued his craft as a scientist pursues his research. What is it to be a human being? His stories weren't meant to answer to that question; they were the question itself, precisely formulated. It was up to the reader to answer the question, to be the jury, because, after all, it was the readers' life and health that Chekhov cared most about.

12 | Ritsos and the Metaphysical Moment

CONSIDER THE FOLLOWING poem by Yannis Ritsos.

TRIPLET

As he writes, without looking at the sea,
he feels his pencil trembling at the very tip—
it's the moment when the lighthouses light up.[1]

Consider the poem without thinking of it as a translation from the Greek, without considering its merits as a poem. The "he" of the poem is the poet, probably Ritsos himself, and what the poem gives us is a metaphysical connection between the poet and the world. The lighthouses light up and the poet—because of the very fact of being a poet—feels his pencil tremble: a trembling caused by the lighting of the lighthouses. We call the moment itself metaphysical. It is neither rational nor scientific. It is not governed by what we might think of as logical systems of cause and effect. It suggests a series of sympathetic affinities and a sensitivity to these affinities on the part of the poet.

Consider another poem by Ritsos.

MARKING

Sometimes in the whole forest there is only one tree
all of whose leaves stir, without any breeze at all. And
    right away
it turns marble-still again like an unlit chandelier
in the night's center, quickening
the breathing of shepherds, horses, stars.[2]

The stirring of the leaves is another metaphysical moment, something impossible to understand by our rational—one might say Aristotelian—processes of thought. Indeed, the poem is anti-Aristotelian. It posits a world beyond scientific measurement. Again we have a world, a universe, of sympathetic affinities: The very stars have quickened their breathing. A mystery has occurred and this mystery communicates itself with the ripple effect of a stone dropped in a pond. The poem doesn't explain the mystery, it bears witness to it and to these affinities, connections, correspondences. The simile ("like an unlit chandelier / in the night's center") attempts to widen the scope of these affinities beyond the existing world to the imagined world. More important, it blurs the boundaries between what exists and what can be imagined. One could say: It extends the parameters of the existing world to what cannot be imagined.

Here is another poem by Ritsos.

THE DAY OF A SICK MAN

All day, a smell of rotting, wet floor boards—
they dry and steam in the sun. The birds
glance down momentarily from the roof tops and fly away.
At night, in the neighboring tavern, sit the grave-diggers,
they eat whitebait, they drink, they sing
a song full of black holes—
a breeze starts blowing out from the holes
and the leaves, the lights quiver, the paper lining his shelves
    quivers too.[3]

We have a metaphysical moment and a series of sympathetic affinities. But here the connections might seem logical. The sick man perceives around him evidence of the worst possible result of his sickness: the smell of rotting, the birds flying away, and a breeze—a wind of death—blowing through the holes of the song being sung by the gravediggers. The sick man hears the song and is reminded of his predicament. He quivers, everything quivers. The real and imagined worlds are blended together. To say the song is full of black holes is to make a metaphor. Technically, the holes may be the graves that the gravediggers dig; metaphorically, they may be references to death and destruction. But in the next line—"a breeze starts blowing out from the holes"—the holes exist, the breeze is presented as a real breeze.

Another poem: "Midnight Stroll." As with the first example, we can assume that the "he" of the poem is Ritsos himself. And the poem describes a momentary frustration and uncertainty about the process of writing poems. Then it concludes with a statement about the mystery and what poems are for, that is, testimony.

> In the end, afraid of the poems and the many cigarettes,
> he went out at midnight to the suburb—a simple, quiet
> walk among closed fruit stores, among
> good things with their true, vague dimensions.
> Having caught a cold from the moon, he wiped his nose
> now and then with a paper napkin. He lingered
> there before the pungent odor of fresh brick,
> before the horse tied to a cypress tree,
> before a barn's padlock. Ah, like this—he said—
> among things that demand nothing of you—
> and a small balcony shifting in the air
> with a solitary chair. On the chair
> the dead woman's guitar has been left upside down;
> on the guitar's back moisture sparkles secretly—
> it is sparks such as these that prevent the world from dying.[4]

Yannis Ritsos was born in Monemvasia, Laconia, on the southeastern tip of the Peloponnesos on May 1, 1909 and died in Athens on November 11, 1990. His first book, *Tractor,* published in 1934, consisted of poems written in meter and rhyme, as did his next two books, but by the late 1930s he had switched to free verse. All told, his creative output was 93 books of poetry, 3 dramatic works, 9 books of fiction, a book of essays and 11 volumes of translations. He also painted and composed music. He worked as a dancer and an actor. His poetry has been translated into about 50 languages, and he received practically every prize the world offers except the Nobel, which he might have received were he not a committed Communist. His political beliefs led to about 12 years of imprisonment and exile, first after the Greek civil wars, then during the military government of the late 1960s and early 1970s. Although much of his shorter work resembles what we have seen, he also has many long poems and many poems drawing from Greek history and mythology, as well as many political poems. The short poems are typically a series of precisely rendered images sometimes standing on their own and sometimes given a unifying context. He himself has defined this process.

APPROXIMATELY

He picks up in his hands things that don't match—a stone,
a broken roof-tile, two burned matches,
the rusty nail from the wall opposite,
the leaf that came in through the window, the drops
dropping from the watered flower pots, that bit of straw
the wind blew in your hair yesterday—he takes them
and he builds, in his backyard, approximately a tree.
Poetry is in this "approximately." Can you see it?[5]

Again, the "he" in these poems is often Ritsos. The process of writing a poem means joining things that don't normally fit to create the representation of a new thing: the approximation of the mystery. For Ritsos, this can happen only if there exists the possibility of sympathetic affinities between all that exists.

Here is another poem: "The Meaning of Simplicity."

I hide behind simple things so you'll find me;
if you don't find me, you'll find the things,
you'll touch what my hand has touched,
our hand-prints will merge.

The August moon glitters in the kitchen
like a tin-plated pot (it gets that way because of what I'm
  saying to you),
it lights up the empty house and the house's kneeling
  silence—
always the silence remains kneeling.

Every word is a doorway
to a meeting, one often cancelled,
and that's when a word is true: when it insists on the
  meeting.[6]

If we think of Ritsos as a committed Marxist, we can see within this poem a sort of Marxist aesthetic: the emphasis on a simplicity of detail that can be apprehended by anyone regardless of education; the emphasis on a connection between the writer and reader, and the writer's responsibility to the reader to create a "true" language so that the connection takes place. A word is not true unless it exists to communicate, until it exists for the reader. But in the second stanza, we also see the writer's responsibility to the mystery, to bear witness to the *it* and to present it through "true" language. As he says, "it gets that way because of what I'm saying to you." This is the poet's endeavor: to make something real with words. The language is a conduit through which the mystery is passed on to the reader.

Here is another. Again, the "he" is the writer.

MAYBE, SOMEDAY

I want to show you these rose clouds in the night.
But you don't see. It's night—what can one see?

Now, I have no choice but to see with your eyes, he said,
so I'm not alone, so you're not alone. And really,
there's nothing over there where I pointed.

Only the stars crowded together in the night, tired,
like those people coming back in a truck from a picnic,
disappointed, hungry, nobody singing,
with wilted wildflowers in their sweaty palms.

But I'm going to insist on seeing and showing you, he said,
because if you too don't see, it will be as if I hadn't—
I'll insist at least on not seeing with your eyes—
and maybe someday, from a different direction, we'll meet.[7]

The poet. He looks at the tired crowded stars, that is, the actual, and sees "these rose clouds in the night," that is, the mystery. The poet's job is to use language to make the reader see what he has seen—first, to reduce the intrinsic isolation of poet and reader by making a bridge between them; second, to validate what the poet has seen, because if the reader doesn't see what the writer had seen, then perhaps the writer has merely hallucinated; third, to bear witness to the mystery. The first reason is social; the second is psychological; and the third is moral. The poet's temptation is to diminish the mystery, to make it more mundane by seeing through the reader's eyes in order to guarantee a contact. But while this might mean a lessening of his intrinsic isolation, it also reduces the quality of the mystery. It is in fact a betrayal of the mystery. In the last stanza, the poet decides against diminishment, insists on seeing with his own eyes and making the reader see what he has seen. He rejects the limited meeting that might decrease the loneliness in hopes of a future more complete meeting where true understanding will occur.

Here again Ritsos discusses his creative process.

NECESSARY EXPLANATION

There are certain stanzas—sometimes entire poems—
whose meaning not even I know. It's what I do not know
that holds me still. You were right to ask me. But don't ask me.
I don't know, I tell you.
                    The parallel lights
from the same center. The sound of water
falling in winter from an overbrimming drain pipe,
or the sound of a waterdrop as it falls
from a rose in a watered garden
slowly, slowly on a spring evening
like a bird's sobbing. I don't know
what this sound means; even so, I acknowledge it.
I've explained to you whatever else I know. I've not been
    neglectful.
But even these add to our lives. I would notice,
as she slept, how her knees formed an angle on the
    bedsheet—
It was not only a matter of love. This corner
was a ridge of tenderness, and the fragrance
of the bedsheet, of cleanliness, and of spring supplemented
that inexplicable thing I sought—in vain again—to explain
    to you. [8]

The poet neither analyzes nor defines, he describes, bears witness, testifies. The details don't describe "the inexplicable thing" but the space around it. They show its footprints: evidence of its passing. The poet charts the mystery by giving its outline. In the face of the mystery, he is humble and full of frustration. He may not understand the mystery, but he acknowledges it. But beyond this is a moral purpose: Such testimony adds to our lives. This is not simply Marxist. It is part of the definition of the poet's job that has existed since earliest history.

In the next example, Ritsos presents this creative process more simply. The "it" in the first line would seem to be the process of writing a poem.

THE MORE SUFFICIENT

You can accomplish it rather easily—it's enough
not to want to persuade or deceive. Alone and alone
the birds, the children, the music, the couch, the curtains.
The sick woman is ironing. A last fly
almost ready to die wanders along the warm sheet.
And there are secret sequences with mild deaths
beyond our common death, beyond its statues
polite and laudatory within that fleeting miracle,
within the light of this mirror that knows how to copy
(however false and fragmentary) the glory of two naked
    bodies.[9]

To be a witness means to turn oneself over to what is being witnessed: the "fleeting miracle." For the writer to interfere by attempting to persuade or deceive is to destroy the testimony. It is hard not to tamper. One has hopes and expectations. One wants to be respected, loved, believed. One wants to be published, wants tenure, one wants a raise. Ritsos would call these peripheral desires a form of tampering and they destroy any chance of success. The writer submits to the mystery and at best holds up a false and fragmentary mirror to the mystery and mostly the writer fails. But what is the effect of the successful poem? The poem that succeeds briefly draws us out of our isolation, draws us out of the mundane, challenges our ideas of cause and effect, our ideas of what is real

and what isn't, challenges our very complacency. Ritsos
demonstrates this in the poem "Motionless Swaying."

> As she jumped up to open the door,
> she dropped the basket with the spools of thread—
> they scattered under the table, under the chairs,
> in improbable corners—one that was orange-red
> got inside the glass lamp; a mauve one
> deep in the mirror; that gold one—
> she never had a spool of gold thread—where did it come
>   from?
> She was about to kneel, to pick them up one by one, to tidy
>   up
> before opening the door. She had no time. They knocked
>   again.
> She stood motionless, helpless, her hands dropped to her
>   sides.
> When she remembered to open—no one was there.
>
> Is that how it is with poetry, then? Is this exactly how it is
>   with poetry?[10]

The reader is not only confronted with the fleeting
miracle but with helplessness before it. Briefly the reader even
becomes a participant in the miracle. But what is a miracle? It is
something that exists outside of known experience, something that
doesn't make sense in the ways we have been taught things should
make sense. It is evidence of the hidden fabric of the universe. In
its presence all our definitions are overthrown. The woman in the
poem is reduced to a motionless swaying. Nor can she say what has
happened, only that something powerful has taken place.

Ritsos tries to create this effect by joining together a series
of precisely rendered details—"things that don't match," as he says
in "Approximately"—sometimes bordering on what we might
think of as the surreal, although he would reject that word. What

makes the details powerful for Ritsos is this idea of sympathetic affinities: the idea that all things are connected. These ideas take us back to the very earliest definitions of poetry, and it is the area where, historically, poetry and magic have been intertwined. Let me first discuss it in terms of magic. Here is how it is defined by Georg Luck in his book *Arcana Mundi*:

> One important concept in all magic is the principle of cosmic sympathy, which has nothing to do with compassion but means something like "action and reaction in the universe." All creatures, all created things, are connected by a common bond. If one is affected, another one, no matter how distant or seemingly unconnected, feels the impact. This is a great and noble idea, but in magic it was mainly applied in order to gain control. Scientists think in terms of cause and effect, while *magi* think in terms of "sympathies" or "correspondences" in the sense defined above. The positions of the planets in the signs of the zodiac, as well as their aspects in relation to one another, govern the character and destinies of human beings, not by some sort of direct mechanical influence but rather by a hidden "vibration."[11]

And you will remember that in most of the Ritsos poems that we have looked at there exists a vibration: a trembling, a stirring, a quivering, a sparking, a swaying, a movement that testifies to the passing of the mystery.

For the Greeks, the three most important magicians or shamans were Orpheus, Pythagoras and Empedocles. Orpheus is more mythic than historic, but Pythagoras and Empedocles lived in the fifth century B.C. In his book *The Greeks and the Irrational*, E. R. Dodds wrote:

> A shaman may be described as a psychically unstable person who has received a call to the religious life. As a result of his call he undergoes a period of religious train-

ing, which commonly involves solitude and fasting and may involve a psychological change of sex. From this religious "retreat" he emerges with the power, real or assumed, of passing at will into a state of mental dissociation. In that condition . . . his own soul is thought to leave its body and travel to distant parts, most often to the spirit world. A shaman may in fact be seen simultaneously in different places; he has the power of bilocation. From these experiences, narrated by him in extempore song, he derives the skill in divination, religious poetry, and magical medicine which makes him socially important. He becomes the repository of a super normal wisdom."[12]

This is how Pythagoras and Empedocles described themselves and how Orpheus was described. Not only were they magicians, they were poets. Added to this was a belief in astrology and, in the case of Pythagoras, numerology. As Werner Jaeger wrote in *Paideia*, "Number meant much more to [Pythagoras] than it does to us. For he did not use it to reduce all natural phenomena to measurable *quantitative* relations, but held numbers to be *qualitative* essences of very different things, such as heaven, justice and so on."[13]

These ideas continued until the Hellenist age, kept alive by Orphic and Pythagorean cults, and given additional stature by the attention of Plato and Aristotle. But in the late Graeco-Roman world and early Christian centuries came an influx of new ideas: Stoicism, Neoplatonism, Zoroastrianism, the Christian and non-Christian Gnostic sects, the worship of Mithra, Isis, Attis and Cybele, the study of the Jewish Cabala, plus the texts attributed to Hermes Trismegistus. There was also a great revival in the practice of white and black magic, of superstition and a belief in astrology. In this amalgam of ideas, we can locate the beginning of what later came to be called the occult tradition. However, by the fifth century A.D., with the unity of Christian belief imposed by Augustine and by the breakup of the Roman Empire, these ideas seemed to disappear or go underground.

In late fifteenth-century Florence, however, Cosimo de' Medici began employing monks to scour Italy, Greece and the Near East for old manuscripts. This is how the work of Plato and many others was saved. Among these rescued manuscripts were the magical texts of the Neoplatonists, Plotinus and the books attributed to Hermes Trismegistus. These were given to Medici's translator, Ficino, a priest, doctor and aspiring white magician. Further *Hermetica* was being translated from the Arabic. We also find at this time a resurgence of interest in the Cabala, which occurred when Jewish scholars were expelled from the Spanish universities in 1492 and found their way to universities in Italy, France, Germany and England. There followed over 100 years of passionate study of the occult, alchemy and magic with such great thinkers as Ficino, Pico della Mirandola, Paracelus, Cornelius Agrippa and Giordano Bruno. At the center of this study was a belief in sympathetic magic. In her book *Giordano Bruno and the Hermetic Tradition*, Frances Yates writes:

> The methods of sympathetic magic presuppose that continual effluvia of influences are pouring down onto the earth from the stars. . . . It was believed that these effluvia and influences could be canalized and used by an operator with requisite knowledge. Every object in the material world was full of occult sympathies poured down upon it from the star on which it depended. The operator who wished to capture, let us say, the power of the planet Venus, must know what plants belonged to Venus, what stones and metals, what animals, and use only these when addressing Venus. He must know the images of Venus and know how to inscribe these on talismans made of the right Venus materials and at the right astrological moment. Such images were held to capture the spirit or power of the star and to hold or store it for use. Not only the planets had attached to each of them a complicated pseudo-science of occult sympathies and image-making, but the twelve signs of the

Zodiac each had their plants, animals, images and so on, and indeed so had all the constellations and stars of the heavens. For the All was One, united by an infinitely complex system of relationships.[14]

These ideas were carried toward the twentieth century by different occultist groups, including the Rosicrusians and Freemasons. Then, in the mid-nineteenth century, there occurred a French revival of occultism, led by Eliphas Levi, Stanislas de Guaita and Sar Peladan. Mixed with this revival existed the philosophy of Emanuel Swedenborg, the Swedish mystic and scientist who lived from 1688 to 1772. Blake, Balzac and Baudelaire all considered themselves Swedenborgians. In her biography of Baudelaire, Enid Starkie wrote:

Swedenborgians are convinced that material objects exist in this world only because they have their origin in the world of the spirit, and the hidden relation between things here below and in the invisible world they call "correspondences." We cannot see the objects in the world of the spirit except indirectly through their worldly "correspondences," through their symbols. Everything in this world is merely a symbol, and these symbols are the language of nature, a hieroglyphic language in which every material form expresses an idea, and this language existed long before the languages which human being now speak were evolved. The philosopher is the man who can see beyond the concrete images, beyond the mere shell, into the heart of things. The true thinker will be the man who can decipher the hidden writings of nature, and interpret the mysterious book of the universe.[15]

The ideas of Swedenborg were influenced by the Renaissance study of sympathetic magic, and they had a great effect on French Romantic and Symbolist literature. The French poet

Gerard de Nerval was involved in these groups, and his poem "Golden Verses," with its claim that all life was sentient, was an avowal of sympathetic magic. Baudelaire was influenced by Nerval and by the occult movement. His poem "Correspondences" quoted on page 236 espoused Swedenborgian beliefs and acknowledged his friend Eliphas Levi, the magician, occult historian and poet who had written a poem using the same title. "Correspondences" became the manifesto of the French Symbolists, who also studied the ideas of Swedenborg and the Hermetic tradition. These writers influenced W. B. Yeats and the Order of the Golden Dawn with which he was so closely tied. Historically, the poet was a magus and this was what Yeats aspired to, just as Baudelaire aspired to being a Swedenborgian philosopher. In his book *The Mystery Religion of W. B. Yeats*, Graham Hough wrote, "Almost every specific claim made by these modern occultist fraternities to ancient authority is dubious, or mistaken, or simply false. Yet the underlying claim to ancient lineage, to belong to a train of belief and practice that goes as far back as sober history can reach—that is true, and even demonstrably true."[16]

To say that Swedenborg or a belief in sympathetic magic lies behind many twentieth-century poets' work is clearly false, but the idea of the interconnectedness of all things became a major idea of the French Romantics and French Symbolists, and it was deeply influenced by Swedenborg and the mid-nineteenth century occult revival. In some poets, such as Yeats, there was a clear connection. With others we find only an influence and a new sense of metaphor, a new way to use symbol. For T. S. Eliot, ideas that have their root in sympathetic magic were developed into his theory of the objective correlative. By the first part of the twentieth century, these ideas were to be found in the poetry of Apollinaire, Alexandre Blok, Ruben Darío, Antonio Machado as well as Italian, German and Greek poets. Even when Symbolism was left behind, a belief in sympathetic affinities persisted. We also find it in poets such as Rilke, Cesar Pavese, Tomas Tranströmer, Ritsos, Pablo Neruda, even in American poets such as Mary Oliver—a belief in the interconnectedness of all things, a belief that the Greeks felt originated in Orpheus, that was also found among the Renaissance magi and in the writings of Swedenborg. For some poets, this interconnectedness is an indisputable fact; for others, it is a useful metaphor. One can also suggest that without Swedenborg and the Hermetic tradition, this poetry wouldn't exist.

But let's look at the practice of the Renaissance magus more closely. Frances Yates writes, "Between the soul of the world and its body there is a *spiritus mundi* which is infused throughout the universe and through which the stellar influences come down to man, who drinks them to his own spirit, and to the whole *corpus mundi*. . . . It is to attract the *spiritus* of a particular planet that animals, plants, food, scents, colors and so on associated with that planet are to be used. The *spiritus* is borne upon the air and upon the wind, and it is a kind of very fine air and also very fine heat. It is particularly through the rays of the Sun and of Jupiter that our spirit 'drinks' the spirit of the world."[17]

Frances Yates is paraphrasing Ficino, and certainly this is strange to us, although we may recognize the term *spiritus mundi* from Yeats's poem "The Second Coming." Ficino himself was using the texts attributed to Hermes Trismegistus, texts that he believed were contemporary with Moses but that were actually written in the second and third century A.D. Yates writes: ". . . The theory of magic . . . depends on a series of *intellectus, spiritus, materia;* the material of lower things being intimately related to the *spiritus* material of the stars. Magic consists in guiding or controlling the influx of *spiritus* into *materia*, and one of the most important ways of doing this is through talismans, for a talisman is a material object into which the *spiritus* of a star has been introduced and which stores the *spiritus*."[18]

We remember from Yeats's autobiographies his experiments with established talismans and images to influence the thoughts and emotions of others. In *Picatrix*, a text attributed to Hermes Trismegistus, were given a list of talismans. Here are several that are discussed by Frances Yates.

Two images of Saturn.

"The form of a man with a crow's face and foot, sitting on a throne, having in his right hand a spear and in his left a lance or an arrow."

"The form of a man standing on a dragon, clothed in black and holding in his right hand a sickle and in his left a spear."

Two images of Jupiter.

"The form of a man sitting on an eagle, clothed in a garment with eagles beneath his feet. . . "

"The form of a man with a lion's face and bird's feet, below them a dragon with seven heads, holding an arrow in his right hand. . ."

An image of Luna.

"The form of a woman with a beautiful face on a dragon, with horns on her head, with two snakes wound around her. . . A snake is wound around each of her arms, and above her head is a dragon, and another dragon beneath her feet, each of these dragons having seven heads.[19]

The use of these talismans gave power to the magus. Ficino took the talismans from *Picatrix* and applied them. "For a long and happy life, says Ficino, you may make on a white, clear stone an image of Jupiter as 'A crowned man on an eagle or dragon, clad in a yellow garment. . .' For the curing of illnesses, Ficino advises the use of this image, 'A king on a throne, in a yellow garment, and a crow and the form of the Sun. . . .' For happiness and strength of body, Ficino advises an image of a young Venus, holding apples and flowers, and dressed in white and yellow."[20]

But let's look at this process slightly differently. It presupposes a wisdom, a knowledge, a power, a *spiritus mundi* that exists beyond human life. By concentrating on the correct talisman, that is, a specific image or symbol, we draw that wisdom through ourselves to the material world. This is in fact the activity of the poet as described by the Greeks. We find this in Hesiod, Pindar and even Plato. For the Greeks, as Dodd says, "poetic creation contains an element that is not 'chosen' but 'given'; and to old Greek piety 'given' signifies 'divinely given.'"[21] But the poet received this inspiration only after arduous training and by establishing the proper conditions for the act of creating, which often meant concentrating on certain talismans that might be no more than the image of the muse. "Give me an oracle," Pindar asked of the Muse, "and I will be your spokesman." Further, as Jaeger writes, "Pindar takes the eagle as a symbol of his consciousness of his poetic mission. It is not a mere decorative image. He feels that he is describing a metaphysical quality of the spirit, when he says that its essence is to live in the unapproachable heights, and to move freely through the kingdoms of the air, far above the lower sphere where the chattering daws seek their food."[22]

This eagle functioned as a talisman for Pindar, and to evoke it was to evoke the conditions necessary for creation. This recipe for writing is a common one: to concentrate on an image until something else accrues to it, until a door is opened to something larger, something that seems to come from the outside. This is what Yeats believed, what Baudelaire and the Symbolists believed, but one also finds it, in a slightly different form, in Rainer Maria Rilke. Rilke wrote to his wife on March 8, 1907, "Gazing is such a wonderful thing . . . with it we are turned completely outward but just when we are most so, things seem to be going on within us that have waited longingly to be unobserved, and while they . . . achieve themselves in us *without our help*,—their meaning is growing up in the object outside, a name convincing, strong, the only one possible for them, in which we blissfully and reverently recognize the event within us."[23]

Concentration on the image opens the mind to a new body of information that seems to come from outside, or, alternatively, the information may come from the unconscious. The inspiration—which may be no more than the sudden apprehension of metaphor—brings about the poem. And the poem is begun because of these sympathetic affinities, this cosmic interconnectedness, these Swedenborgian correspondences. Or perhaps it is a trick of the unconscious or free association or a linking of symbols or the discovery of metaphor or Jung's collective unconsciousness. It hardly matters. It gets the job done, although if it weren't for Swedenborg and the Hermetic tradition, we would be writing much differently. For Ritsos, the concentration on the image brings about other images. Something is given and the poet sees himself as the receiver. Look at his poem "Point."

> Deep roaring whirled around every star.
> Some power, secret, grieving,
> made the trees dark.
>
> The only point of orientation in the dark:
> two minute circles of light,
> the knees of the silent woman.[24]

The silent woman could easily be a hermetic talisman out of *Picatrix;* the deep roaring could be the *spiritus mundi.* But we do not need to read it like that. Still, we are aware of certain affinities that are also found in sympathetic magic. Within the poem exists some power connecting the stars, the natural world and the silent woman. And we also know that Ritsos sees the poem as something received, which he passes on as a piece of testimony to the fleeting miracle that he himself may scarcely understand. I have no evidence that Ritsos was a Swedenborgian, but he was a passionate reader of Baudelaire and translated many of his poems. His sense of sympathetic affinities seems to derive equally from Baudelaire and from the Symbolists and from his sense of himself as an inheritor of the Greek tradition.

In pre–fifth-century Greece, according to Jaeger, "the poet was still the undisputed leader of his people. . . . The Greeks always felt that a poet was in the broadest and deepest sense the educator of his people."[25] Not because of who he was, but because he had access to this wisdom that lay outside of himself. For Ritsos, Greek history is living history: the gods of Greece remain with us. One of his occupations as a poet was the retelling of these stories, for even though the gods are not worshipped, they remain powerful.

FROM POSEIDON

The houses on the shore disintegrate daily,
eaten away by salt, sun, and wind. In the rooms
the shutters have gone to sleep long since face downward.
    Once in a while
at noon or sunset some fisherman or shepherd goes in there
to defecate. And suddenly there's a creaking sound
in the clothes closet. Before the fisherman manages to cross
    himself
the clothes closet opens by itself. At the back, leaning
    against the rotted wood
there is a shining three-pronged pitchfork all in gold. The
    fisherman
vaults out of there with his belt still unbuckled. All around
the sea shimmers boundlessly with its most radiant
    indifference.[26]

Ritsos had a deep sense of cultural purpose, and he felt that his work could keep alive in the present what was important in the past. His belief in sympathetic affinities has a tradition of which most writers are unaware even though they may imitate its characteristics. The ancient Greek poets were also magicians because poetry and magic use language and images to make something appear out of nothing. Both offer testimony to a world beyond our powers of explanation. Both use talismans to draw down a wisdom that appears new to the world. For Ritsos, the talisman may be a very simple image as in his poem "Association."

He said: "the anchor"—not in the sense of fastening down,
or in relationship to the sea-bed—nothing like this.
He carried the anchor to his room, hung it

from the ceiling like a chandelier. Now, lying down, at
    night,
he looked at this anchor in the middle of the ceiling
    knowing
that its chain continued vertically beyond the roof
holding over his head, high up, on a calm surface,
a big, dark, imposing boat, its lights out.
On the deck of this boat, a poor musician
took his violin out of its case and started playing,
while he, with an attentive smile, listened
to the melody filtered by the water and the moon.[27]

We may say that the talisman of the anchor gives the "he"
of the poem access to the *spiritus mundi* and allows him to hear the
melody of the poor musician filtered by the water and the moon.
Or we may call it all metaphor. But we cannot deny that something
magical is happening: a magic that begins with the articulation of
a word, which leads to the evocation of a real anchor, real enough
to be hung from the ceiling like a chandelier. What does the
anchor do for the "he" of the poem? It reminds him of the existence
of the unknown. He *knows* that the chain leads up into the mystery,
and this belief, this knowledge, allows him to hear the music that
proves the truth of his belief and awakes in him an attentive smile.
The poem does not "mean" in the sense that it contains something
that needs to be interpreted; it bears witness. The title itself gives
a sense of sympathetic affinities while also demonstrating how
language works: where there is a anchor, there must be a boat,
where there is a boat, there must be a passenger, where there is a
passenger, there must be an activity. This chain of association
allows the "he" of the poem to listen to the activity. Let's look at
one last poem, "Miniature."

The woman stood up in front of the table. Her sad hands
begin to cut thin slices of lemon for tea
like yellow wheels for a very small carriage

made for a child's fairy tale. The young officer sitting
    opposite
is buried in the old armchair. He doesn't look at her.
He lights up his cigarette. His hand holding the match
    trembles,
throwing light on his tender chin and the teacup's handle.
    The clock
holds its heartbeat for a moment. Something has been
    postponed.
The moment has gone. It's too late now. Let's drink our tea.
Is it possible, then, for death to come in that kind of
    carriage?
To pass by and go away? And only this carriage to remain,
with its little yellow wheels of lemon
parked for so many years on a side street with unlit lamps,
and then a small song, a little mist, and then nothing?[28]

We can impose a narrative here. We can either see the
woman with her sad hands as the mother and the young officer
with his trembling hands and tender chin as her son, or we can see
them as lovers. In any case, we can imagine that the man is about
to leave for battle and both have an anxiety, a fear that they want
to express but don't express. "Something has been postponed. /
The moment is gone." The young officer is afraid of what will
happen, and there is an associative connection with the slices of
lemon that leads him to the subject that he never articulates. This
would not be an implausible reading.

But in terms of talismans, the yellow slices of lemon
become an image that evokes the further image of death arriving
in a carriage. And then, by moving into the interrogative, the poem
itself slips away, taking us far from the young officer. The carriage
remains parked on a side street for many years—a small song, a
little mist, and then nothing. The poem gives us a picture: a
miniature of these events. We would be hard-pressed to explain
how it touches us or exactly what it means. The poem evokes a

melancholy, a sadness that seems addressed not to us but to our unconscious minds. We share in a metaphysical moment that resists explanation but that remains satisfying. The poem gives us a sense of a world far larger than we had previously imagined. For Ritsos, what is important is that a connection is made between human beings and that our lives have been increased. This is his business as a poet: to help us live by awakening us to something beyond the mundane, by trying to connect us to a mystery that his poems celebrate.

13 | Cemetery Nights

Sweet dreams, sweet memories, sweet taste of earth:
here's how the dead pretend they're still alive—
one drags up a chair, a lamp, unwraps
the newspaper from somebody's garbage,
then sits holding the paper up to his face.
No matter if the lamp is busted and his eyes
have fallen out. Or some of the others
group together in front of the TV, chuckling
and slapping what's left of their knees.
No matter if the screen is dark. Four more
sit at a table with glasses and plates,
lift forks to their mouths and chew. No matter
if their plates are empty and they chew only air.
Two of the dead roll on the ground,
banging and rubbing their bodies together
as if in love or frenzy. No matter if their skin
breaks off, that their genitals are just a memory.

The head cemetery rat calls in all the city rats
who pay him what rats find valuable—
the wing of a pigeon or ear of a dog.
The rats perch on tombstones and the cheap
statues of angels and, oh, they hold their bellies
and laugh, laugh until their guts half break;
while the stars give off the same cold light
that all these dead once planned their lives by,
and in someone's yard a dog barks and barks
just to see if some animal as dumb as he is
will wake from sleep and perhaps bark back.[1]

COMMUNICATION

SOMETIMES I THINK COMMUNICATION IS ALL WE HAVE—a voice like a silver wire extending through the dark or one chunk of flesh pressing against another chunk of flesh. Sometimes I don't even think that.

But when I believe in communication, I think this is the best way out of our self-absorption and isolation. By communication I mean not only a consciously intended verbal exchange of ideas and/or feelings but also an openness to the possibility of that exchange. Certainly there is a lot of nonintentional or unconscious communication, but that is not so much an exchange as a form of barking. The air is always full of barking; that's part of the trouble.

It seems to me that a work of art has the potential for being the highest form of communication. It can remove us from our essential isolation and join us in a community of shared human experience. It can show us that our most private feelings are in fact common feelings. Art is an antidote to madness. It allows us to define ourselves with greater or lesser accuracy in relation to our fellow human beings. Furthermore, great art, by showing us our common feeling, shows us our common responsibility. It shows us how to live.

Thinking that art has the potential for being the highest form of communication enables me to write poems. It forms an ideal that I strive for. When I stop believing in the possibility of that communication, then I don't write. Why bother? The construction of the poem purely for the sake of the poem gives me no pleasure. It turns the poem into a kind of decoration, something akin to wallpaper.

Mostly I think there is no communication. When I talk to someone, what I often seem to hear is "I want, I want more, I am lonely, I hurt, I am unhappy." Besides that, there may also be the need to compete, to dominate, or to diminish. And me, too, I think, I must be doing the same thing. Here I am under the impression that I'm talking about Art, Truth, or Beauty, and instead I am jockeying for position while making little barks of need.

These are the active interferences with communication. There may also be passive interferences: indifference or the inability to listen. There is that moment in Chekhov's "The Lady with the Dog" when Dimitry wants to tell someone about this woman he doesn't even yet know that he loves. So he says to a card-playing friend as they leave their club, "If you only knew what a charming woman I met in Yalta." And his friend, after getting into his sleigh, responds, "You were quite right, Dimitry—the sturgeon was just a little bit off."

So I have two opposing beliefs that exist side by side— one, that communication is possible; two, that it is impossible— and I swing back and forth, writing or not writing. But even while communication is difficult, art is a way of making it palatable. Instead of saying "If you only knew what a charming woman I met at Yalta," you work it into a short story or poem or sonata. And what I find is that while the poem may begin with my little concerns, it finally, if successful, transcends my concerns. This is very liberating. Even if not communicated, the concerns have been shed. And so this becomes one of the many reasons why I write.

This brings us to "Cemetery Nights," which I began in November 1982. It was the first new poem I had written in about ten months. Instead of writing new poems, I had been finishing my fourth book of poems, *Black Dog, Red Dog*, which meant doing a lot of rewriting. I was also working on several novels.

But I also felt somewhat disillusioned with poetry, my own and all the others'. In *Black Dog, Red Dog*, I had tried writing realistic narratives, mostly using a 12- to 14-syllable line while manipulating the line breaks to maintain tension. But by early 1982, I had come to an end of it. Furthermore, I had spent six months in Santiago, Chile, and was beginning to believe that realism was an inadequate way to deal with the world's excesses; or rather, a realistic approach came across as fantastic—what people who know nothing about surrealism call surrealistic. I also felt (partly because of Chile) that I had to try harder to write poems that engaged with the world. It seemed obvious that we were going to blow ourselves up, and I wanted whatever I wrote to be enmeshed with that sense of our future. Also, it embarrassed me that Europeans and Latin Americans had endless scorn for American poetry—poems where the writer does little more than say I have a little pain.

What I wanted was to begin a new book of poems, and I wanted it to be as different from *Black Dog, Red Dog* as that book was from *The Balthus Poems*. The model I had in mind, although I didn't go back to look at his work, was the drawings and watercolors of George Grosz in his *Ecce Homo*, since in the American solipsism of the 1980s, I imagined I saw resemblances with Berlin of the 1920s. Additionally, I liked the way Grosz distorted the realistic into the fantastic yet kept the impression of realism.

I had also been reading a lot of Baudelaire, his essays as well as his poems, and it seemed that one of the factors that allowed him to get away with the harshness of his subject matter was the extreme rigor of his form. I had experimented slightly with a tighter form in *Black Dog, Red Dog*, especially in the poem "Bleeder," which deals with the desire to make a hemophiliac bleed. There I had used a loose blank verse and liked how the increased tension accentuated yet helped to control the emotion. Consequently, in moving toward a new book, I decided to use a vague *vers libére*[2] instead of purely free verse—to move back and forth between an iambic and free verse ten-syllable line. Along with this, I wanted to use more traditionally formal devices but use them unpredictably so that the rhythmic and aural direction of the poem could not be correctly anticipated.

So these were my concerns. Yet I had no poem, had not written a new poem for ten months and was currently going through a period of thinking that communication was impossible. All I knew was what I wanted to do, while wanting to shake the feeling of futility.

The poem came from deciding to make that idea—the belief in the futility of communication—into the subject of a poem: a neat paradox. The actual poem evolved from joining together three sets of images. The image of the dead in the first stanza derives from Stanley Spencer's Judgement Day paintings, where the dead are seen crawling out of their coffins in an English village. The image of the rats came in part from a metaphor found in W. S. Merwin's *Asian Figures:* Talk about tomorrow and the rats will laugh. As for the dog, I think that image of the howling or barking dog is often with me, and I use it again and again. Here it came to signify that sense of the futility of communication that had kept me from writing. The barking dog in the third-to-last line is the poem itself. The poet, if he or she exists in the poem at all, is probably the "someone" who owns the yard. The dog doesn't want an answer. It wants acknowledgment of its existence. What's the point of saying "Me, me, me" unless someone can hear you?

These three images had been circling with others in my head. Along with them was the idea that no matter how ugly life can be, it is still sweet. Along with that was the desire to make a certain sound: to again and again begin a loose iambic rhythm, then break it. Simplistically, that is how I write a poem. I have a number of aural, emotional and intellectual concerns floating with a series of images like flies circling in the center of a room. I repeat the rhythms and sounds in my head, run through the images as if through a tray of slides, and lean against the concerns as one might lean against a closed door.

The poem comes when I am suddenly able to join these concerns together under the aegis of one idea or feeling. Here it was the futility of communication, and I suppose at its most basic level the poem is about my coping with writer's block. Once the elements are joined, the rough shape of the poem comes very quickly. Then I spend months straightening it out and trying to become entirely conscious of the meaning, while moving the poem away from my personal concerns (writer's block) to a more general concern (the need and desire for communication).

What is now the first line of the poem was actually the last to be written. The second line (originally the first) is an iambic pentameter line beginning with what is almost a spondee. The present third line is also iambic pentameter, although the first unstressed syllable has been dropped. Lines 4 and 5 move away from the iambic, while the "no matter" in line 6 entirely disrupts the iambic movement. This was to be the movement of the first stanza—a constant playing with iambic pentameter and breaking it four times with the repetition of "no matter," which itself becomes a rhythmic device.

A main error in my early version was to assume that the reason for the deads' actions was clear—that by mimicking the daily actions of their lives they were attempting to recover a bit of the sweetness. Fortunately, I showed the poem to a friend who said, "But why do the dead do that?" So I added the first line, which also enabled me to increase the rhythmic tension by making the line iambic pentameter. Three of those iambs, however, are near spondees, and their placement gave me the chance to emphasize a pattern of spondees or near spondees in the first stanza—16 occur in those original 16 lines. By building up a pattern of double stresses, I wanted to prepare for the series of triple stresses that closes the poem. Other patterns in the stanza include a move between high-frequency vowels (*ee*) and low-frequency vowels (*ou*), a move between hard consonants (*b, d, g, p, t*) and soft consonants (*ch, f, th*).

The rats don't really realize what is going on. I suppose they represent me at my most cynical—believing that communication is impossible, that the whole mess is pointless. They don't understand that the dead are only trying to catch a taste of sweetness. It's the act itself that is important, not what comes of it. The rats, after all, are predators and scavengers—they think only in terms of gain. They can't imagine staring at a blank TV screen just for the memory it elicits, of getting some sweetness from the illusion. As the poem says, it doesn't matter that the TV is dark.

The image of the stars in lines 7 and 8 of the second stanza was a fortuitous discovery, although stars are another image that I tend to overuse. In any case, I needed a bridge to get to the dog and I thought how the dead, when young, had planned their lives under the same starlight that now glimmers above their antics. But I saw that doesn't matter, that what is important is to have a life even if it's a dumb one. What enables one to live is the most rudimentary form of hope. The barking dog, for all its foolishness, is a symbol of such hope.

Rhythmically, the second stanza resembles the first, but its pattern of ten spondees is further heightened by six triple stresses. The most obvious triple stresses are those ending lines 6, 7, and 11, while that last line is further intensified by a strong iambic beat. The line length in this stanza generally decreases to nine syllables, and there are a higher number of hard consonants. All this was intended to make the stanza more compact, move faster, and seem more desperate, while the repeat of the triple stress at the end was meant to create a conclusion similar to a piece of music.

As a change from earlier work, what I liked best about the poem was its tone—dealing with the fantastic in a matter-of-fact manner, using flat assertion and perfectly plain description. I was also attempting to use this tone in my fiction, and although I was drawn to it in Apollinaire, I thought I saw it best used in the fiction of Gabriel García Márquez. Yet he had partly learned it from Faulkner, and in thinking about that tone I went back to Faulkner to try to re-create the slow-paced, highly detailed, matter-of-fact relating of fantastic events—say, a horse galloping through a house.

It seems that each successful poem must challenge and overcome the complacency of a reader. Before beginning this poem, I had a number of concerns that were further emphasized by my desire to change the direction of my work. I myself was becoming complacent with the methods and strategies I had used in Black Dog, Red Dog, and I felt it was time to stir up the pot. The desire to use a new tone, humor, elements of the fantastic, a tighter form, use less personal material, use direct speech, abrupt juxtapositions and surprise, to write a more aggressive poem—all these concerns I had defined to myself in a six-month period before writing the poem. Then all I could do was wait for that coming together of image, idea, emotion and language. It also took that shift in attitude—the belief that communication is possible. Still, people can barely talk together. The fact that we remain on the brink of nuclear holocaust seems the clearest evidence of this.

I think a poem has the ability to sensitize people toward themselves and the world around them. As Suzanne Langer says, a work of art is the objectification of subjective life. It gives form to inward experience and makes it conceivable. It helps a person to define himself or herself in relation to the world and even predict the course of that world. For me, this makes each poem a political act, and, even though I expect no results from these political acts, it keeps me writing. There is another Asian figure that I often quote to myself: "Sardine threatens, who knows it?" But writing poems is what I do best and so I keep doing it. It is also what I like to do best. Clearly, my definitions as to the function of poetry are connected to the series of definitions that allow me to tolerate myself, let me get up each morning and not put a bullet in my head. That finally is why I keep coming back to thinking that communication is possible. Not only does it allow me to write, it keeps me alive.

14 | The Maker's Manipulation of Time

OUR MEDIUM IS TIME; it is the abstraction through which we negotiate our passage. But we do not live in the present moment; all our attention is fixed on the moment after this one—when we will scratch, when we will speak, when we will hit a tennis ball. And our skill in living depends in part on how we imagine that next moment. If we ignore it, then we become the victim of events. If we place that next moment too far into the future, then we damage our present: the hours and days of our present life. We need to live mentally in the moment beyond the one in which we are living physically, but not too far. One day at a time, the 12-step programs say. Indeed, power may be defined as control over the next moment—the ability to direct or influence the consequences or effects of causes that are happening now or have happened in the past. Yet this power is only a partial power. Every day, leaving Belmont Park, are doleful losers whose infallible system of picking winning horses developed a glitch. Every day the obituary columns print the names of surprised men and women who had other plans.

We tend to take much of our engagement with the next moment for granted. We do this with any learned behavior. It happens without much conscious thought. When I reach for the cup at my elbow, I hardly take more than a brief glance. My eye/hand coordination is pretty good. I can shoot a basket or toss a crumpled-up piece of paper into a trashcan. I can drive my car at high speeds through heavy traffic and feel confident about doing it, already planning my evening at home, even though more than 40,000 people are killed in traffic accidents every year. Those people, too, had other plans.

Eye/hand coordination is learned behavior. The infant wriggling on its back does not want to wriggle. It wants to snatch and grab. It, too, is making plans. And bit by bit it gets things under control. Clearly the next moment will come no matter what we do, but people plan for it or engage with it to different degrees.

Since the beginning of history, philosophers have been trying to define or caution us about our relationship to the next moment. According to Plutarch, Heraclitus said, "One cannot step twice into the same river, nor can one grasp any mortal substance in a stable condition, but it scatters and again gathers; it forms and dissolves, and approaches and departs."[1] This is a warning about change and our difficulty in anticipating what will happen next. And for my book *Cemetery Nights* I used an epigraph from Marcus Aurelius: "Loss is change and change is Nature's delight. This has been true from the beginning and will be true till the end. Then how can you say it is wrong, forever wrong, that no power in heaven can fix it, and that the world lies condemned to a thralldom of ills unrelenting."[2]

The unexpected will occur no matter what we do—a tornado will take the roof off your house, the house itself will fall into the sea, or, conversely, you will win the lottery. Change is Nature's delight. How then can you say that it is unjust? Doesn't that come from confusing reason with desire?

Our concentration on the next moment is primarily affected by a number of physical, emotional and spiritual conditions. For instance, discomfort is a physical condition that seeks to cause certain corrections to bring about the return of comfort. The child is wet and begins to cry; a parent comes to change the diaper. The child learns that crying can bring about the return of comfort. Or the child is hungry, which is also a form of discomfort, and again begins to cry, and so on. After discomfort as an initiator of change may appear desire, and we all know how complicated that can be: ambition, greed, sexual desire, the desire to be celebrated, praised and have our vanity appeased. But in fact these desires are also a form of discomfort—they are itches that want to be scratched. What is hope but the desire to eliminate some present discomfort, the wish to improve upon something in the present? Indeed, one can argue that all our engagement with the future—physical, emotional, spiritual—is an attempt to achieve an idealized state of comfort. The sexual itch, the sadness itch, the god itch—all seek to be scratched.

But our engagement with the future can be much less than this. Even as you read, most of your attention is on the future, ranging from trying to anticipate the direction of my sentence, the nature of my argument, to matters completely separate from my words: how nice you would look in a certain pair of shoes, what you hope to eat for your next meal, sexual fantasies, and a vast body of material that concerns yourself and the world at large—for example, will it rain tomorrow?

Our ability to control events in the future is plainly limited, but any control we might have is based on experience and what we learned from that experience. For example, a preconception is a mistaken judgment about the future based on one or more experiences in the past. Experience is made up of both direct and secondhand experience. Gossip presents up with secondhand experiences, so does a newspaper, so does art. The act of reading fiction and poetry expands our experience of the world. Once that experience—any experience—is part of our memory, then it becomes something we look through when we try to determine what is going to happen next. It informs how we see the future. When we are caught up in the suspense of a novel and wonder how it will end, part of the information we rely on to inform our wondering is our entire reading experience. The hero always lives, we tell ourselves, or almost always. We read a novel through the window of all the novels we have ever read. And if, in life, we try to figure out why a person has acted in such and such a way and what that person might do next, then our reading experience, our experience with art, becomes part of the information we consider.

We are always in transition, moving from past to future, and no matter how much we consider the past, most of our attention is focused on the future. We do this for reasons that exist at different levels of importance but most simply we do it in order to avoid discomfort, to perceive what is coming and avoid as long as possible our approaching end. This concern occupies our entirety—it is instinctual and intellectual, psychological and spiritual. And it exists alongside all other concerns, so even when we read a novel one of our concerns is, What can I take from this that will help me meet or avoid my approaching end? Maybe we will learn a lot, maybe little, and whatever we learn will be affected by our emotional, psychological, intellectual and spiritual makeup, which affects our degree of subjectivity or objectivity, which may affect whether we are able to learn anything at all.

Because our concern is how to meet or avoid our approaching death, we surround ourselves with metaphoric reenactments for this process. Play is used to create such metaphors. Every sporting event is in part a metaphor for the unfolding of our personal fate. This says nothing about the importance or banality of a football game; the metaphor exists in addition to the football game. And it has been argued that in periods of social and cultural instability, far more emphasis is given to this sort of play, these enactments of our fate. Certainly the arts see greater change and development at such periods. The Renaissance was not called a rebirth until long after the fact. When it was occurring, it was seen only as upheaval and frantic change in directions that couldn't be imagined.

Art too is such an enactment. It sets what is known—our experience—against what is not known. It engages our expectations, our ability to anticipate. In a sporting event we watch two teams compete for victory and most commonly we have a favorite. We identify with one of the teams. In a work of art we have instead the viewer or reader or listener—the audience—and the maker. And just as two teams are engaged in a struggle, so are the audience and maker engaged. What the audience is attempting to achieve is more than plain understanding, it is some kind of reward—the sort of reward that art allows whether it is full-blown catharsis or a simple blip of pleasure. And for this to be effective, the audience must participate, must become a kind of competitor. A person's mind must be engaged, even minimally, and be wondering, even minimally, what is going to happen next. In most television viewing this is a fairly passive process.

In the various arts it becomes more elaborate. As I have written elsewhere, one understands a poem by aggressively asking questions of it. One anticipates; one has expectations. The other team—the maker—works against our anticipation, our expectations, by the manipulation of events. Things do not work out as we expect. They work out differently. But ideally we are surprised and satisfied, even if the end is horrific, like the end of *King Lear*.

"All poetry is born of play," wrote Johan Huizinga in *Homo Ludens*, "the sacred play of worship, the festive play of courtship, the martial play of the contest, the disputatious play of braggadocio, mockery and invective, the nimble play of wit and readiness."[3] And also, "What poetic language does with images is to play with them. It disposes them in style, it instills mystery into them so that every image contains the answer to an enigma."[4] To say poetry originates in play doesn't mean it isn't to be taken seriously. The opposite of play is not seriousness but earnestness. Play is very important indeed. "Frivolity and ecstasy," wrote Huizinga, "are the twin poles between which play moves."[5]

The field of play on which the audience and maker are engaged is time itself, that future we have been discussing. Literature and music are sequential, and sequential art demands the manipulation of future moments. We approach them one after another, and it is the maker who manipulates these moments to achieve specific ends. Even the plastic arts make use of sequence, of time. A three-dimensional sculpture cannot be perceived all at once, while any painter works to order his or her design so that one thing (whether it be shape, line, color, or texture or a combination of those elements) is seen first, one thing second and so on. Breughel often blocked the sides of the picture with a person or tree and then created a zigzag pattern to lead the eye of the viewer into the picture to create a sense of sequence. In his painting the *Fall of Icarus*, the legs of Icarus disappearing into the water are perhaps what we discover last, while what we see first is the oblivious farmer plowing his field.

A lyric, either in poetry or music, attempts to create a strong emotional experience in one moment of time, but because it has duration, we experience the lyric over a series of moments. A narrative, on the other hand, exists in two or more moments of time: this happened, that happened. Historically, this was seen as requiring progression, of being causal, but the surrealists put a stop to that. It is perfectly possible for modern narratives to have two or more completely unrelated events. They require only duration, until duration itself becomes part of the definition of narrative, and a lyric—which we think of as being the opposite of narrative—has duration.

All of this has been introduction. Our subject is the maker's manipulation of time, his or her manipulation of events within the sequence to create tension, suspense, anxiety, the fear that what we expect or anticipate is false or at least different and we don't, finally, know the outcome or have any control. Yet the outcome may be rewarding nonetheless. The maker manipulates events, in part, to keep the audience engaged with the work, to make the reader want to read. In this definition a word is an event, a sound is an event, a line break, a silence or pause is an event. And all of this is a form of play in which there is a relationship between the audience and maker that at times resembles the competition that exists between two teams engaged in a game: the audience has certain expectations and the maker deflects, avoids or frustrates those expectations while still not letting the piece fall apart; that is, the audience continues to have hope.

Among the characteristics of play, wrote Huizinga:

> we reckoned tension and uncertainty. There is always the question: "will it come off?" This condition is fulfilled even when we are playing patience, doing jig-saw puzzles, acrostics, crosswords, diabolo, etc. . . . The more "difficult" the game the greater the tension in the beholders. A game of chess may fascinate the onlookers though it remains unfruitful for culture and devoid of visible charm. But once a game is beautiful to look at its cultural value is obvious; nevertheless its aesthetic value is not indispensable to culture. Physical, intellectual, moral or spiritual values can equally well raise play to the cultural level. The more apt it is to raise the tone, the intensity of life in the individual

or the group the more readily it will become part of civilization itself.[6]

"There is something at stake,'" wrote Huizinga, "the essence of play is contained in that phrase. But this 'something' is not the material result of the play . . . but the ideal fact that the game is a success or has been successfully concluded."[7] One begins reading the poem or piece of fiction wondering whether or not it is going to come off, whether it will complete its little arc, whether it will give us that blip of pleasure or a full-blown catharsis. Ahead lies frustration or fulfillment—even indifference is a form of frustration in that comfort has not been achieved. The tension one feels comes from a balancing of hope and anxiety—the hope that it will come off and the fear that it won't. That tension is one of the artist's major tools.

Beginning writers tend to order their work chronologically. They start with the first event in terms of time and move step by step until they reach the concluding event, which is often a death, the most conclusive of all events. Chekhov's suggested revision for such stories was to cut them in half and start in the middle, by which he was urging the writer to start with action and not exposition. But it is more complicated than that. Many beginning writers think in terms of subject matter rather than in terms of the medium. They see the poem or story or novel as no more than a vehicle for their self-expression. The form of the poem, or the medium, becomes like the wrapper around a stick of candy: something to be discarded on the way to the good stuff. A painter at the commencement of creation may have a sense of how he or she wants the picture to be, but the painter doesn't necessarily think in terms of cows and trees and fields—of subject matter. He or she thinks in terms of color, line, shape, texture and light, all of which may be manipulated into representational forms or may be left abstract. In the same way, the poet or composer may have in mind a period of a certain duration filled with certain events: sounds, rhythms, tempo, changes of pitch, silences and so on. The subject matter may come later or may arise from the contemplation of these events and, in the case of a composer, it may not come at all—the feeling that gave rise to the musical composition may never be verbally articulated. In 40 years of teaching, I've known hundreds of intelligent men and women with a burning desire to write who have failed because they see the form as no more than the vehicle for what they wanted to say. They have a story to tell that takes precedence over the medium they are using to tell it. But poetry doesn't work like that.

In the same way that a painting—simplistically speaking— organizes space, so does a piece of writing or music organize time. Since a piece of writing uses words and words have specific meanings, then that meaning is also organized, but it is still governed by time, by sequence, by duration. And there are two durations: the duration of the event or narrative being recounted and the duration of the piece of writing. Tolstoy's *War and Peace* and Napoleon's invasion of Russia have entirely different durations. But one of Aristotle's rules for a tragedy, that of unity of time—which insisted that the action take place within a single revolution of the sun—was an attempt to unify the duration of the event and the duration of the form in order, among other things, to create verisimilitude.

Another requirement complicating the business is that a work of art must be affective; it must touch the emotions. Whatever the work—*War and Peace,* the ceiling of the Sistine Chapel, Beethoven's Ninth Symphony—it is first of all a metaphorical image of human consciousness, of felt life. Art must touch the emotions because it is a metaphor for human feeling, and it must communicate that feeling. The poem begins in an emotional experience, and, in the process of making and revising, that feeling determines every aspect of the poem—even the commas—till the whole poem, form and content intertwined, attempts to express that feeling. In fact, it tries to *be* that feeling, to re-create it in order to allow another human being to experience it. I simply want to touch on this and pass on, but it is the reason why the events of the poem must be affective, why the poem can't simply be the articulation of numbers or gratuitous words or even simple anecdote. It is not enough for the poem to try to engage us by its intellect, wit, even by its form—we also have to care about it. Otherwise it may be brilliant but it also will be trivial.

Another point I want to make and then leave behind is that the artist usually does not have the end in sight when he or she begins the work. The poet writes to discover why he or she is writing. As John Gardner wrote in *On Moral Fiction*, "What the writer understands, though the student or critic of literature need not, is that the writer discovers, works out, and tests his ideas in the process of writing. Thus at its best fiction is, as I've said, a way of thinking, a philosophical method."[8] And: "Moral fiction communicates meanings discovered by the process of the fiction's creation."[9]

Implicit in this is the conviction that the poem or piece of fiction is a made-thing. It is neither received from outside or erupts out of the artist's peculiar sensitivity and superiority. It is worked on, struggled over and the final product may be many things but it is also a form of play.

"The affinity between poetry and play is not external only," wrote Huizinga,

> it is also apparent in the structure of creative imagination itself. In the turning of a poetic phrase, the development of a motif, the expression of a mood, there is always a play-element at work. Whether in myth or the lyric, drama or epic, the legends of a remote past or a modern novel, the writer's aim, conscious or unconscious, is to create a tension that will "enchant" the reader and hold him spellbound. Underlying all creative writing is some human or emotional situation potent enough to convey this tension to others. But there are none too many of these situations—that is the point. Broadly speaking, such situations rise either from conflict, or love, or both together. ... The central theme of poetry and literature generally is strife.[10]

What I want to look at is the final poem, the completed manipulation of events within a specific period of time. One begins reading a poem with an increasing sense of tension arising from hope and anxiety, which also comes from an increasing sense of the stake. That tension derives equally from form and content, and form and content equally affect one another; that is, manipulation of form affects the tension surrounding the content and vice versa. The poem comes to the reader, instant by instant, out of future time, and the reader looks to that future by anticipating what will come next, by a series of expectations that are formed by his or her entire life and reading experience. If the reader has never read a poem or has experienced only bad or confusing poems, then the expectation is rather low and the tension almost nonexistent. But even curiosity is a form of tension.

The poet seeks to influence and control the reader's temporal experience by manipulating time—that is, with surprise and suspense. Surprise occurs when something happens you haven't anticipated and it can be extremely small. A rhyme can be a surprise. And the requirement is actually a paradox: that something be completely surprising and yet feel exactly right.

Suspense occurs when the writer creates in the reader a desire to know—the reader becomes emotionally and intellectually invested in the outcome. Each sentence and line has to have within it a reason to read the next sentence and line. And again, this is both a matter of form and content. I have written about this in the chapter "Pacing," and I don't wish to repeat myself, but, most simply, pacing is controlled variations in the forward momentum of the poem and is dependent on making the reader want to know, using the reader's ignorance as energy to propel him or her down the page, and increasingly there is the tension: will it work out or will it fall apart? Clearly, one reads the poem more than once and, ideally, new discoveries are made each time, while it is one of the characteristics of an image that it cannot be encompassed, that it continues to engage the mind by seeming to present us with more material, by seeming to contain the answer to an enigma.

We begin to anticipate the moment we pick up the book, open the page, see the shape and length of the poem, read the title, read the first line and consider the relation between them. These events occur one after another, and it is the character of this sequence that is either going to lead to fulfillment or make us turn away. Consider John Donne's poem "Woman's Constancy." The very title creates tension by engaging certain humorous expectations. We all have ideas or preconceptions about woman's constancy.

> Now thou hast loved me one whole day,
> Tomorrow, when thou leav'st, what wilt thou say?
> Wilt thou then antedate some new made vow?
>> Or say that now
> We are not just those persons, which we were?
> Or, that oaths made in reverential fear
> Of Love, and his wrath, any may forswear?
> Or, as true deaths, true marriages untie,
> So lovers' contracts, images of those,
> Bind but till sleep, death's image, them unloose?
>> Or, your own end to justify,
> For having purposed change, and falsehood, you
> Can have no way but falsehood to be true?
> Vain lunatic, against these 'scapes I could
>> Dispute, and conquer, if I would;
>> Which I abstain to do,
> For by tomorrow, I may think so too.[11]

The poem makes a complete shape with beginning, middle and end, which is the shape of its argument and its form. About its form I don't wish to say much, though the surprises found in a formal poem may be different from those in a free verse poem. Tension can be created and surprise can occur when a pattern is established and then is moved away from. Any rhyme or metrical scheme can be used in such a pattern. The strong iambic beat in the first line allows Donne small surprises later on when he employs substitutions. The first line is tetrameter, and surprise occurs when he changes to pentameter in the second. By surprise I mean that it hasn't been anticipated. The short lines become a surprise and at their third appearance he has two short lines. The AA, BB, CC rhyme pattern is overthrown in the seventh line when he gives us another C rhyme (even the off rhymes are surprises). Then he gives us D, E, E, D before returning to couplets. Many of the surprises in a formal poem come from tensions put against the form: metrical substitutions, off rhymes, unexpected pauses or caesuras, shifting line length, stanza length, assonance, alliteration, stress—and many occur also in a free verse poem. Huizinga points out that every culture in every period of history has developed poetry before any other art form and that in every case these same formal elements have been used. "The rhythmical or symmetrical arrangement of language," he wrote, "the hitting of the mark by rhyme or assonance, the deliberate disguising of the sense, the artificial and artful construction of phrases—all might be so many utterances of the play spirit."[12]

Contextually, Donne's poem begins with the speaker making a statement and then asking his lover a question based on that statement. The element of strife exists in the possibility that the lover may throw over the speaker despite her promises to be faithful. The speaker then offers five possible answers, each more complicated and surprising than the last, and reaches a false or penultimate conclusion by saying that he could defeat all of these arguments with arguments of his own. Then the poem makes a turn to its true ending, the final surprise: that I may not need to make any argument because by tomorrow I might feel the same way that you do.

The play element is obvious—any argument is a competition, and a bogus argument has the additional element of humor. And the speaker also seems to compete with himself as each of his answers becomes more complicated and paradoxical. In the last possibility we reach the most serious level of the poem: since you yourself proposed the falsehood, that is, adultery, why should I believe you would be faithful to me? Indeed, if falsehood is your nature, then only by falsehood can you be true. The woman is a vain lunatic—her value system is based entirely on her desires and not on any system of cause and effect. Consequently, woman's constancy is a sham, but the poem's final surprise is that it may be no different from man's constancy.

The poem has a duration of about 45 seconds—during that time the reader's various expectations are teased and frustrated as one element comes to us after another. Not only is the meaning sculpted, as it were, so is the sound through the poem's diction, rhythms and syntax. And both sound and meaning are inseparable. By going in directions that we have not anticipated, the poem increases our anxiety that it might all fall apart. It walks the tightrope of sense. But then Donne resolves the tension by reaching a conclusion that feels both surprising and exactly right.

Surely the most effective implement the writer has in manipulating the expectations of the reader is the English sentence itself. When we hear a noun, we anticipate a verb; when we hear a verb, we anticipate a direct object. The complexities of grammar and syntax are among the writer's strongest tools. The word "now" that begins Donne's first line leads us to a different sort of expectation than the word "tomorrow" that begins the second. The four "or's" that begin the alternative answers function as miniature heralds announcing new options. The finite patterns of the English sentence are signaled by specific grammatical elements. Hearing one, we engage in a particular kind of expectation. We don't know what will be said, but we have a good idea of the grammatical shape it will take, which provides us with shape for the meaning.

Look at a poem by Mary Oliver from her book *West Wind*.

The Dog Has Run Off Again

    and I should start shouting his name
    and clapping my hands
    but it has been raining all night
    and the narrow creek has risen
    is a tawny turbulence is rushing along
    over the mossy stones
    is surging forward
    with a sweet loopy music
    and therefore I don't want to entangle it
    with my own voice

calling summoning
my little dog to hurry back
look the sunlight and the shadows are chasing each other
listen how the wind swirls and leaps and dives up and down
who am I to summon his hard and happy body
his four white feet that love to wheel and pedal
through the dark leaves
to come and walk by my side, obedient.[13]

This is a free verse poem with many peculiarities. It appears to be one sentence yet within it are two exclamatory commands and an interrogative. Other than the period at the end of the poem, the only piece of punctuation is the comma that precedes the last word. The poem states a condition in the title, and the rest of the poem gives a series of reactions to that condition. And it is a common condition—it is hard to get through life without one time or another chasing after a runaway dog. The necessary strife would appear to be in the title—a dog has escaped. But that is not the case, and we are surprised to discover that the actual strife comes with the hidden question—"who am I to summon his hard and happy body." The syntax of that long sentence is signaled by the words that begin most of the lines—and, and, but, and, is, over, is, with, and therefore, with, look, listen, who am I.

The poem uses its syntax to imitate the creek that is "rushing along" in the fifth line. The poem, too, rushes along and simulates the breathlessness of the speaker who is chasing after the dog. And this continues for 12 lines until the speaker interrupts the movement with two commands aimed at herself, followed by a moment of reflection: who am I? The speaker concedes there are two worlds: the free and the constrained, the natural and the civilized. These are the worlds presented in the poem, and they are separated by the single comma—obedience on one side, all the rush on the other. What grand play this is. In reading the poem, we chase after it until we're stopped by the two commands—look, listen—which surprise us and chastise us. For isn't Oliver saying that we don't do enough of that in this world, that in our own personal rush we are ignorant of the world that surrounds us? Who are we all to impose our will on that of which we are ignorant? Then the rush of the poem grinds to a halt with the two ponderous iambs that begin the last line.

Oliver's poem also surprises us in its diction—tawny turbulence, sweet loopy music, hard and happy body, to wheel and pedal through the dark leaves—while the very breathlessness of its rush adds another kind of tension to the tension of the game—will the poem's momentum remain under her control? The suspense is very small— will she get her dog back?—and it is diminished even more with the line "my little dog to hurry back." We are not worried that a rabid Great Dane is on the loose. Oliver has organized the poem's duration to create a number of specific effects. The poem's sequence of moments changes speed, changes focus, redirects emphasis and becomes an emblem of what Oliver finds wonderful about the natural world—its energy and untamability. She does this by manipulating time, by crafting the sequence, and what drives this along, among other things, is a passion for play. The poem itself is a game of tag that the author wins—but that very winning tries to define a distinction between the natural and civilized worlds. More than 120 words exist on one side of the comma, only one on the other; and to such a degree, Oliver is saying, is the natural world more important than the civilized.

Here is a poem by Roger Fanning: "Shoelace" from his collection *Homesick*. [14]

> Her deceased husband's shoelace must be unknotted;
> the widow, plunging her face at the foot of the casket,
> set her teeth to work. Little changes: long ago
> some villages believed the soul would fret with such a knot
> and thus be kept from its journey, whereas others (spooked
> about sundown) used to drape fishnets over their dead
> to keep them from rising up and roving as vampires.
> As for the widow—whose folklore flickers, thoughts
>
> consisting of non sequiturs—she can barely focus
> on her fingernails loosening the knot; the rest of her

feels floaty, awobble as someone trying to stand up
in a rowboat. Now she knows: we live above a gulf
from which, fog-huge, rise nightmares (disease, car wrecks,
endlessly) that snuff the luminous flesh we love.
She ties his shoelace. Our dopey hope and deep deep
need for ceremony show in that neat black bow.

Fanning snatches our attention right away with the image of
a woman plunging her face into her husband's coffin to unknot his
shoelace with her teeth. He heightens this with a diction and syntax
that is itself knotty. The situation is bizarre to the extreme, and he
follows it with a joke: "Little changes," as if the widow's action were
ordinary. Fanning's use of stressed and unstressed syllables, alliteration, rhyme, assonance, line breaks, word choice and neologisms, all
the verbal paraphernalia of poetry, keep us off balance—that is, we
are unable to predict the direction of the poem. Our expectations are
frustrated and the tension increases. Notice how the full and partial
rhymes of unknotted, at, foot, casket, set, work, fret, knot, kept,
spooked, drape, net, keep, up, flick and thought form the scaffolding
of the first stanza. We cannot help but see this as play, and the play
surrounds a subject of deep seriousness—the woman is attempting to
deal with her tremendous grief and face the realization that nightmares
can "snuff the luminous flesh we love." That line would seem to
conclude the poem, but then there comes a second conclusion that
grief can be offset and to some degree softened by ceremony: the neat
black bow.

The play that occurs here is typical of poetry, and it should
be seen that the play of the form is completely interwoven with the
content to the degree that the content would be nonexistent or utterly
banal without that play. The paraphrase is only the shadow of the
whole. The unfolding of the poem is not a means to an end—some
epithanic moment—it is itself an end. One doesn't read a poem for its
kernel of truth or for its story interest but for the very experience of
reading a poem. The kernel of truth, as it were, the emotion that gives
rise to the poem's articulation, arrives out of the whole, is integrated

into the entire process. The manner of the telling communicates meaning. Fanning's meaning cannot be separated from the poem's temporal sequence. The widow in the poem deals with a small strife—the knotted shoelace—as a way of shielding herself from a larger strife—her grief. This is one of the functions of art itself—it is a small puzzle that distracts us from the large one. And just as the knot in Fanning's poem is an emblem of the widow's emotional condition, so is the poem an emblem of the human condition, while the play that is its mode of operation also becomes a way of dealing with the world.

"In archaic culture," wrote Huizinga,

> the language of poets is still the most effective means of expression, with a function much wider and more vital than the satisfaction of literary aspirations. It puts ritual into words, it is the arbiter of social relationships, the vehicle of wisdom, justice and morality. All this it does without prejudice to its play-character. . . . But as civilization increases in spiritual amplitude, the regions where the play-factor is weak or barely perceptible will develop at the cost of those where it has free play. Civilization as a whole becomes more serious—law and war, commerce, technics and science lose touch with play; and even ritual, once the field *par excellence* for its expression seems to share the process of disassociation. Finally only poetry remains as the stronghold of living and noble play.[15]

Play has the ability to distract us and instruct us about our fate, yet as civilization gets more serious, the distraction comes to take precedence over the instruction. The temporal sequence of events in the arts ceases to be emblematic of our condition. Suspense and surprise become valuable for their own sakes and are no longer integrated into the whole. Spectacle replaces thought. Sporting events, films and television function to divert our attention from our anxieties, rather than leading us to analyze them. The result, unfortunately, is increasing cultural blindness, and the importance given to poetry declines. It becomes one of the frills excoriated by politicians. It is not taken, as they say, seriously.

This is civilization's loss, but I ask what responsibility the poets themselves bear for bringing it about. The play aspects of poetry are dependent on communication and on the poet's need to think at every moment of the revision process where the reader is in relation to the work in order to "enchant the reader and hold him spellbound," as Huizinga wrote. In technical terms the poet achieves this by controlling the reader's temporal experience of the poem. In larger terms, however, the poet needs to define to himself or herself what is meant by communication and even the function of poetry within the culture. Indifference to such matters on the part of poet is perhaps a reason for an increasing indifference to poetry in the world at large.

15 | The Passerby in the Birdless Street

CONSIDER TWO SYSTEMS by which we take in knowledge about the world. The first is discursive and characterized by analytical reasoning. We see it most easily in a syllogism:

> All men are mortal
> Socrates is a man
> Socrates is mortal.

A syllogism consists of two premises and a conclusion, each premise having one term in common with the conclusion and one term in common with the other premise. The *Merriam-Webster Dictionary* defines it as "a deductive scheme of a formal argument consisting of a major and minor premise and a conclusion." And it defines deduction as "the deriving of a conclusion by reasoning, *specifically:* inference in which the conclusion about particulars follows from general or universal premises." It gives the following example: "Every virtue is laudable; kindness is a virtue; therefore kindness is laudable."

From such discursive thought, the sciences take their origin. The Zeroth Law of Thermodynamics states: "When each of two systems is in equilibrium with a third, the first two systems must be in equilibrium with each other." And in geometry we learn that if Angle A is equal to Angle C and Angle B is equal to Angle C, then Angle A and B are equal to each other.

Computer technology, courts of law, corporate trading—all depend on discursive thought that uses a mixture of empiricism, an appreciation of cause and effect and the ability to postulate what is not known from what is known according to rules of logic and analysis.

The second system by which we take in knowledge is nondiscursive. It is based on resemblance or analogy rather than the consecutive and incremental development of idea. Often is it dependent on an image that can be turned into a figure of speech. Here is a favorite of mine from W. S. Merwin's *Asian Figures*.

Life
Candle flame
Wind coming[1]

The figure begins as a simile that develops into an analogy: just as life resembles a candle flame, so does death resemble the wind. And just as the candle flame will be extinguished by the wind, so will life be extinguished by death. Now, this too is logical. It derives from our experience and how that experience has expanded our sense of cause and effect. A point of similarity is postulated and with that is the conclusion, not necessarily valid, that what is true of one will be true of the other.

However, while the discursive system may make many consecutive moves before a conclusion is reached, the nondiscursive system can make its point in a way that feels immediate. Our understanding seems spontaneous, and pages of explication will hardly give us a greater grasp of the figure than we have understood in that seemingly immediate flash of comprehension. But let us observe what happens. We are given three pieces of information and are asked to imagine a fourth. Two of those three pieces of information are presented as a simile: life is like a candle flame. Then a possible analogy is created by the third piece of information: a wind is approaching the candle flame. The question posed by the missing piece of information is that if life is like a candle flame, what is comparable to the wind? We only have to ask the questions how and why to know the answer. Indeed, that asking seems unconscious and automatic.

But in order to arrive at an answer, we have to supply a temporal dimension. The figure gives only one moment in time; to understand it, we must imagine a past and future. We have to supply a small narrative, to imagine consequence. This information is filtered through our experience: we know about the effect of wind upon candle flames. It can be tested empirically.

Let's return to the first system, our discursive system. The First Law of Thermodynamics states that when an object is brought into contact with a colder object, a process takes place that brings about an equalization of temperatures of the two objects. The law identifies heat as a form of energy that can be converted into mechanical work and stored, but it is not a material substance. Heat, measured in calories, and work and energy, measured in ergs, were shown by experiment to be equivalent. This law was derived from something first noticed in nature: for instance, rocks warmed by the sun. Then it was tested, the law was formulated and applied. Simplistically, it became possible for someone to imagine what would happen if a fire were placed under a tank of water and the force of the steam was manipulated. This led to the steam engine. That act of imagination was analogical: if this is to this, then that is to that. But the law, the fact that two objects put side by side will become equal in temperature (your feet, for instance, on a hot water bottle), was at the beginning. But that isn't quite right. It wasn't the fact that was the beginning—it was the formal articulation of the fact.

Let's go back to the other figure:

Life
Candle flame
Wind coming

This too is an analogy with the fourth element missing: Death. By asking how and why, we discover that fourth element. A figure such as this illustrates one of the major elements of a poem. It is a linguistic construct that brings together three disparate elements and leads us to infer a fourth in an image, which we may term a metaphor.

Here is a poem by Emily Dickinson:

A toad can die of light!
    Death is the common right
    Of toads and men,—
Of earl and midge
The privilege.
    Why swagger then?
The gnat's supremacy
Is large as thine.[2]

This poem also sets up a comparison: death is the common right of toads and men, earls and midges, you (or possibly the speaker) and a gnat. A fourth element is left out: as toads are to men, so is some unnamed abstraction to arrogance. When we ask the questions of how and why, we realize that Dickinson is writing about humility. Why should I swagger? Why should I feel that I deserve so much? What great reward is coming to me out of my future? Only death, and it comes to gnat, midge and toad as well. Consequently, why am I arrogant?

The process of the poem—three elements and a fourth to be inferred through analogy—is similar to the use of analogy found in the application of the First Law of Thermodynamics. This is not to give special emphasis to the First Law of Thermodynamics but to show that in both it and the poem there is a comparable working out of analogy. Most scientific application is the working out of such an analogy. And most poems use analogy, either in their entirety or by using a specific metaphor in part of the poem, or both.

The other action required when trying to understand a metaphor—imagining a narrative structure—is achieved by Dickinson in the line "Why swagger then?" which is itself a metaphor for "Why do you live the way you do?" That very question takes the poem out of the single moment and, ideally, leads the reader to imagine the entire arc of his or her life.

Look at a poem by the French poet Jean Follain called "The Women Who Sew Livery." The translation is by W. S. Merwin.

When night falls
the women who sew livery
stop and wait to be given the light they wish for.
The town is covered with snow,
it is then that they sing
and the passer-by hears in the birdless street
the warm clear voices rising
from those girls who make clothes for valets
and he goes off sad and alone
to phantom dinners.[3]

The situation is simple. A man walking at nightfall in the winter hears a group of girls begin to sing. In the original poem, the French word for these women is *les couseauses,* which does not mean seamstresses, but women who do the menial sewing work, the buttons and hems. These are the daughters of the very poor, girls of extreme humility. They do not do sewing for anyone important. They sew uniforms for valets who work either in hotels or the houses of the wealthy. And there is an implicit comparison: as the valet is so far beneath the people he serves, so are these girls far, far below the valet.

The man hears the girls' voices and it increases his sense of sadness and solitariness. Note, the poem doesn't say that he is going home; he is going "off." Most likely he will eat alone in a restaurant. In French, the last line of the poem is *à des tablées fantômes.* The word *tablées* means a group of people sitting around a table. For example, the *tablées* of Christ refers to the Last Supper. One cannot have a *tablées* by oneself, so the man has a *tablées fantômes.* Even the word "phantom" isn't an exact cognate. His dinner is a ghost meal, something of a fantasy. It will be joined by people who are invented, living elsewhere or dead.

This analogy bears some resemblance to the analogy in the Dickinson poem. The very humble is juxtaposed against the man— we have no real idea of his rank or station, but *tablées* can also suggest an intellectual gathering. The women sing; the man is silent and the street is birdless; that is, without song. The women's voices are warm; everything outside is cold. The women are the poorest of the poor and would seem to have no reason to sing. Yet they sing. In asking our questions of how and why, other details move to the surface. The first line—when night *comes* in French—we first read literally and then it takes on metaphorical meanings—solitude, death—which Merwin stresses with the choice of the word "falls." Then we have the odd syntax of the third line: stop and wait to be given the light they wish for. They are singing in darkness; they are singing because they are waiting. They have no doubt that the light will come. Both the women and the man on the street are in the same place: the dark. But the women believe in the imminence of the light; the man doesn't. He only has fantasies and imaginings.

Follain has other poems about the lot of the atheist: the man "who sees only a void in the depth of the heavens."[4] Possibly he is suggesting something similar here, a meaning that is pushed to greater distinctness by reference to the coming of night, the town being covered with snow as a coffin is covered with earth and the birdless street; while the girls' voices are warm, clear and rising. But what Follain wants most is the contrast: this is to this as that is to that. And he wants the irony of the contrast. The semi-impoverished girls have joy and hope. The man has sadness, aloneness and something else, which is the missing element of the analogy. He is without hope. The poem is about the man's hopelessness in the face of impending darkness. He does not believe in the coming light.

Now neither this poem nor any other poem is an intellectual code or a riddle. The point of the Follain poem is not to come up with a definite answer: a man is nearing the end of his life and he feels no hope. The answer is not the ends of the poem but part of the means of the poem.

It is one of the functions of a poem to make the reader a participant. By leaving out one of the elements of the analogy Follain removes his narrative from the level of anecdote and forces the reader to ask the questions of how and why. And, ideally, the reader imposes a temporal frame on the poem, taking the poem out of the static moment and imagining a past and future: where the man has come from and where he is going. The logic involved here is as logical as our use of the First Law of Thermodynamics to create a steam engine. The reader is no longer an onlooker, he or she becomes emotionally invested. If one reads the poem with care and reaches this point, one doesn't simply get the answer—as you get five times five is twenty-five—one suddenly grasps the state of mind of the man on the birdless street: I am going no place, no one is waiting for me, I am reaching the end of my life in a state of isolation and separation from the mass of humanity, and when I die, which will be soon, I believe I will stop, I will be no more than a scrap of darkness. At that moment, one experiences a sense of profound empathy. This isn't a matter of identification with the man because we know nothing about him. We identify with what he feels, not who he is. We identify with his existential predicament. We feel and feel intensely—though briefly, because fortunately we can step away—what this man experiences when, while walking down the snowy street in increasing darkness, he suddenly hears these girls sing—human beings so lowly that it is hard to imagine why they have any reason to sing.

"The town is covered with snow, / it is *then* that they sing." Notice how the word "then" creates a sense of cause and effect. It implies that their singing is in response to the cold and dark. It is because of the snow that they sing. It *makes* them sing. You think it is an accident that there is a suggestion of angelic voices? It isn't. Nor is it an accident that the French word *tablées* carries with it a hint of the Last Supper. It is simply how poetry can work in the hands of a master.

The deeper one goes into the poem, the clearer one understands that no word has any arbitrary element. Even the word "wish" in the third line takes on greater meaning. They are not simply expecting or wanting or demanding this light—they are wishing for it and as they wish they sing, although in their lives, it would seem they have nothing to be joyous about. What they are joyous about is what lies ahead: their belief in a future life after death. They have hope.

Follain poses a series of riddles in order to engage us. Once we become a participant in the poem, he leads us to a moment of empathy with the man's condition. What is his condition? When we attempt to name it, we see, in fact, there is no exact name for it.

Hopelessness? Loneliness? Isolation? Spiritual angst? Each of these terms is such a diminishment of the man's emotional condition that it is almost comic.

Here is another element. The man is walking in the dark and suddenly he hears singing. This is the present moment of the poem that Follain signals with the word "then," the moment that begins the narrative, when the man almost pauses and asks, What is that sound? In response, a sense of recognition floods in upon him and his own awareness of his situation becomes tremendously heightened. The process the reader goes through is exactly the process that the man goes through. As the man asks a question, so do we ask a question. As the man is suddenly struck, so are we struck. The man is given a flash of insight about his own predicament. He is taken out of the single moment where he is putting one foot after another on the slippery path, and he suddenly he grasps the entire curve of his life and the entire system of belief through which he sees his life. And we—don't we have a similar experience?

Here we were pursuing our lives in the given moment thinking of little more than our feet on the uncertain terrain, when suddenly we have this larger moment. Briefly we are confronted with our entire spiritual infrastructure, while the man exists a point of contrast. He believes this, we believe . . . what? But whatever we believe, we also understand what the man believes, and, very likely, we see that our own beliefs are not impossibly idiosyncratic, but link us to the human family. Just as the man is suddenly linked to the girls who are singing, so are we linked to the man. In the experience of the poem, everything works to contribute to this: the selection of words, how the words are ordered, the metaphors, the narrative element— all, which we take in sequentially, work to create something that occurs in one moment of time: the reader's abrupt moment of recognition, which is comparable to the man's abrupt moment of recognition.

Well, many things happen here. The unfolding and totality of the poem we experience as a work of art. We are made a participant in this process. In fact, the poem will not work unless we have been made a participant. Follain intends us to feel, not simply to recognize. But he doesn't want us necessarily to feel sympathy or compassion but empathy: to feel, however briefly, what the man in the poem feels. And to have that moment not only give us a sense of recognition about the man's life—a Frenchman in a small town in northern France around the turn of the century—but to experience a sense of awareness about our own lives. Everything in the poem contributes to this. Even the sound. So forget for a moment that this is a translation. Merwin was, at best, trying to find a comparable sound or, at least, attempting to find a sound that did not detract from other elements of the poem. We experience a pleasure from this. We also experience a sense of connection and recognition and knowledge. We are given a linguistic construct that defines a precise emotion for which there are no other words; defines an emotion that did not exist in our vocabulary—all we have are abstractions: sad, lonely, hopeless.

Every poem with an emotional center tries to make an emotional, intellectual, spiritual and physical link with the reader. Some do it simply, some in a more complex fashion. Nearly all do it by leaving out information that the reader discovers by working out the analogy—the puzzle—which leads the reader to experience the poem. The poem does not simply refer to an event, it enacts the event by providing answers to the reader's questions of how and why.

What is the consequence of this? It is easy to say that art has no moral role—that, basically, is a piece of instruction for the maker. But once the poem is made and has a public life, then it is impossible to deny that social and moral aspect. The poet is not attempting to teach, but, nonetheless, the poem teaches.

So we go back to that Zeroth Law of Thermodynamics: "When each of two systems is in equilibrium with a third, the first two systems must be in equilibrium with each other." First this was observed, then it was formulated. Once it was formulated, it became possible to apply its principles. A steam engine was built. The automobile evolved. We use the automobile, and so on.

In the poem "The Women Who Sew Livery" we are brought to the point of experiencing a powerful emotion that we have never before experienced or have never experienced in this particular way. Once we experience it in the poem, the emotion becomes part of us. We know it, we recognize it; the emotion becomes one of the many tools we use to understand the world. And this points to one of the functions of art—that a work of art leads us to experience one or more complicated emotions for which we do not have specific language or possibly very limited language. In such a way the arts educate our emotions—we become freed from the limitations of words like "sad," "happy," "lonely," "angry." In addition, by making this an empathetic experience, it takes us momentarily out of our existential isolation and links us with other human beings. And by wakening our sense of connection to the Other, it rouses our sense of responsibility. That other—it feels as I feel. My neighbor feels as I feel.

Babies are not born with this sense: for a baby there is only I. The first time your child hurts you, it is amazed you can be hurt. The child had thought, till then, that only it was capable of feeling pain. Once the child grasps there is a separation, it begins to develop language to call you back. The child learns language in an attempt to re-create the oneness that seemed to exist at birth and in those first few months. But of course as the child's language evolves, the separation increases. Language then is both the attempt to create connection and the admission of distance.

It is empathy that helps us to bridge this distance and allows us to live in a society that is more than a police force and exists for reasons more than self-preservation. And it is art that teaches us—by allowing us to experience—that other human beings have the same complicated emotional structure that we have, that they can be hurt as we can be hurt, happy as we can be happy. These discoveries begin in infancy with our families, but then begin to dissipate or remain undeveloped. How does one learn to live in a community and where does one learn it?

If someone claimed that the Laws of Thermodynamics shouldn't be taught in school, because they were a luxury, a frill, he would be thought crazy. Yet the arts have a pedagogical role as great as that filled by the sciences, mathematics, languages, history, and so on. I don't mean that seventh graders should be made to write poetry. That may be pleasurable, but it will do little to educate their emotions. Follain's poem moves step by step until an epithanic moment is created when the emotional life of the reader and the emotional life of the man in the poem—Follain's mechanism—become one. What is then given, among other things, is a piece of knowledge as significant and useful as any piece of knowledge that we take from the sciences: knowledge about a specific emotion that may affect our behavior and the behavior of people around us. I'm not stressing poetry over physics; I'm saying we need both equally. If either discipline is slighted, then we not only ensure ignorance, but we weaken a person's ability to live within a society. We ensure that people will remain emotionally stunted. Do we refrain from robbing and murdering because we fear the law, or because of our sense of responsibility, which develops out of our empathy, lets us understand how our victim would feel, how he or she would suffer? Art does many things, but one of its most important functions is that it educates our emotions. It teaches us to live within a society.

Some might say it doesn't matter what you take from a poem (or any work of art). If the artist was writing a poem about zebras and someone thinks it is a poem about cows, then that is acceptable. But people who make that argument are discounting 10,000 years of artistic production. This was never how art worked. Once we argue that art doesn't need to communicate, that it isn't, among other things, an exchange of information, then we turn the work into a piece of decoration. It functions as distraction and creates not shared experience—with each reader drawing a similar experience from the poem—but private and idiosyncratic experience. It becomes onanistic. It diverts the mind from the human predicament for no purpose other than for the diversion itself. Likewise, if we say that art doesn't need to be affective, that it doesn't need an emotional center, then we are again opting for the decorative: something that may amuse, distract, even instruct, but lacks that emotional linking we see possible in the best of art. The purely decorative is to art what masturbation is to love—something vital has been left out.

Let's look at another Follain poem, "October Thoughts." The translation is Merwin's.

> How one loves
> this great wine
> that one drinks all alone
> when the evening illumines its coppered hills
> not a hunter now
> stalks the lowland game
> the sisters of our friends
> seem more beautiful
> at the same time there is a threat of war
> an insect pauses
> then goes on.[5]

We learn to read a poet. After spending time with Follain, we come to see a word like "October" or a line like "when the evening illumines its coppered hills" as also suggesting the autumn or evening of one's life. The first nine lines of the poem define an emotion of autumnal contentment. There is even a touch of humor when the speaker mildly pokes fun at himself: "the sisters of our friends seem more beautiful." But what makes the affective nature of the poem convincing is its emphasis on transience. The emotion is fleeting, and it is made so partly by the intrusion of the outside world: "at the same time there is the threat of war." That awareness brings an end to the feeling. It also suggests our own smallness—after all, war is so vast—and sets up the last image, which is an analogy: "an insect pauses / then goes on." The speaker is the insect. I am the insect. You are the insect. This contentment is experienced by something unspeakably puny. Even if the person is powerful, he or she is still acted upon by forces far more powerful. We experience the contentment and then, with the last two lines, an almost whimsical sense of the contentment. We step outside of ourselves, as it were, and become conscious of what we were feeling: "an insect pauses / then goes on." There is no judgment. The poem, among other things, works to define a complicated emotion that takes its value in part from its fleetingness and in part because that feeling of well-being is experienced by a creature so tiny, so vulnerable, so short-lived, that even this moment of well-being is nothing short of miraculous.

Perhaps we have felt something like this or can imagine it or will feel it soon. Just as the speaker, with his reference to the threat of war, is taken out of the moment, so does the poem take us out of the moment to see the arc of our life. The poem lets us enjoy a moment of ephemeral pleasure that is located in the taste of this great wine sipped as the sun is reddening the wooded hills, a moment between fading light and darkness: the hour between dog and wolf, as Follain writes in another poem.[6] That perception of fleeting tranquility is exemplified in the taste of the wine on the tongue at a certain time of day and within a certain season. But for the poem to let us experience a sense of the ephemeral, the moment has to go by: "an insect pauses / then goes on." We ask ourselves: "What's that insect doing there?" Then we realize that *we* are the insect. Even the poem's presence suggests the ephemeral: eleven short lines.

Art can't be separated from its ability to teach: we experience something that we haven't experienced before. As a result, our world is expanded. Many times a poem will give us an experience we are unable to paraphrase, that exists as an image that we think about and draw wisdom from but are unable to name. Or maybe it's not wisdom, maybe it's just of the sound of the brain's gears grinding as they attempt to engage with the question.

Here is a poem by Yannis Ritsos called "The Crazy," which Ritsos wrote at the age of seventy-eight. The translation is by Martin McKinsey.

> What lies we come up with to keep
> our little place in the world. At night
> the traffic cops go home, shops close,
> the stars grow bolder to the west. Later,
> out in the muddy street, you hear
> the neighborhood crazy with the red cap

singing something to himself, sadly—
a children's song infested with wrinkles.[7]

Ritsos gives us four elements, just like an exercise in logic. We have a topic sentence, followed by pieces of evidence and then a conclusion that doesn't seem to be a conclusion. As with the other poems, we are presented with parallel structures with the cops and shop owners set against the crazy man. And the lie we come up with to keep our place in the world, what is that set up against? Doesn't it become the thing we ask about? It has to be set against the "children's song infested with wrinkles." So we ask ourselves, Why is the crazy man crazy? Perhaps it is because he hasn't moved past the child's world or wears a red cap or wanders around the muddy street after everyone has gone home. And who calls him crazy? Presumably the traffic cops and shop owners. And notice that the traffic cops are given muddy streets. As educated readers we have grown accustomed to the metaphorical value accorded to streets.

The fact that the stars are put on the same footing as the crazy man—they grow bolder after the others have gone—indicates Ritsos's sympathy with the man. But the man's song, which he sings sadly to himself, seemingly doesn't present us with a paraphrasable conclusion. The wrinkles, presumably, belong to the crazy man: he has aged in his body while keeping a child's mind. What we have in the end is a juxtaposition: the first sentence—"What lies we come up with to keep our little place in the world."—and the crazy man's action—singing a children's song infested with wrinkles. The question for us is why do we value what we value, why do we pretend what we pretend? And there is Ritsos's suggestion: are we any better than this crazy man? Our complicated systems of cause and effect, which we build up to establish who we are and what we deserve, are they any better than that children's song infested with wrinkles? And those lies, don't they derive from the ego? And that ego, isn't that the child within us? And so, through this contemplation of the image, we see that there is no difference: the traffic cop and crazy man are one, except that the latter at least has sincerity on his side. While the song—the children's song infested with wrinkles—becomes an emblem of art and how it is often received. In fact, this very poem—written by the 78-year-old Ritsos—is a children's song infested with wrinkles, while the lie in the first line may be no more than the denial of art—that it is supposedly irrelevant to the world of traffic cops and shopkeepers.

Two systems. The discursive and analytical—

All men are mortal
Socrates is a man
Socrates is mortal.

And the nondiscursive and nonanalytical—

Life
Candle flame
Wind coming

The first is a model, the second an image. Suzanne Langer wrote, "An image is different than a model, and serves a different purpose. Briefly stated, an image shows how something appears; a model shows how something works. The art symbol, therefore, sets forth in symbolic projection how vital and emotional and intellectual tensions appear, i.e., how they feel."[8]

Our enemy is ignorance. Discursive and nondiscursive thought are ways of decreasing it. Ignore one or the other and we have decreased our ability to reduce ignorance by half. It astonishes me that there are people who continue to label art as a frill that has no place in education. It astonishes me that critics with major reputations see only the puzzles available in art and ignore its affective nature, its gift to develop our sense of empathy, to expand our ability to intuit (itself a type of thought), its role in helping us learn how to live. And I'm astonished by those poets who go by many names—language poets, postmodernists, neo-surrealists—who choose to replace the affective nature of poetry with something else—sound, wit, form, whatever—thereby reducing poetry to the level of decoration.

Finally, there is the joy of the poem. What else does one call it? That moment when its parts click together and we at last see what the poet is doing, when we are able to experience the emotion that the poet is attempting to encapsulate. When, briefly, we are taken out of our own world and inhabit the world of the poem. This is the experience of art, whether it be in a poem, a novel, a Beethoven quartet or a Cézanne painting. We exit the other side feeling in some way expanded. What we have taken from the experience remains with us. It becomes part of the filter through which we see the world.

It's almost a paradox: the experience is our relief from the world, and it forms one of the tools with which we deal with the world. Both systems—the one of the model and one of the image—work to cultivate our sense of cause and effect in order to refine our notion of what is going to happen next; that is, what will be the consequence of one or more actions that have occurred, are occurring, will soon occur or may be imagined. Our experience, what we have learned, what we have encountered in the arts as well as the sciences, becomes the glass through which we analyze what will be the outcome of the events that fill our days. The ability of human beings to forecast future consequences from present actions is one of our primary survival tools, as well as being a tool for growth. The character in the Follain poem, making his way down the snowy street as darkness falls—suddenly he hears girls voices raised in song and he asks, What is that? And immediately he has a perception of the confusion and shadow that stretches ahead in his own life. What he felt in that instant, you can feel it now.

16 | The Problem of Beauty and the Requirements of Art

BEAUTY AS A VALUE IN ART HAS FALLEN INTO DISFAVOR. This seems especially true for the literary arts. A work can be interesting, passionate, brilliant, but "beauty" as a word of praise has been turned over to fashion designers, home decorators. Yet it isn't enough to want to write a story or novel or poem; the writer must also want to make something beautiful—even though that might mean making it ugly. Think of it this way: it is a requirement of art that a work add up to more than the sum of its parts. This isn't true, for instance, of journalism. So we have the sum plus X. That X may have a number of different components, but one of its components must be beauty.

Here are three quotations: the first from Rainer Maria Rilke for whom beauty and the difficulties of its expression was a primary subject. Rilke believed his 10 "Duino Elegies" to be his masterwork, and this is how the first begins. The translation is by Edward Snow.

> Who, if I cried out, would hear me among the angelic
> orders? Even if one of them pressed me
> suddenly to his heart, I'd be consumed
> in his stronger existence. For beauty is nothing
> but the beginning of terror, which we can just barely endure,
> and we stand in awe of it as it coolly disdains
> to destroy us.[1]

Here beauty is process—like orgasm, our experience of it rises to the almost unbearable moment. We perceive the beautiful object, catch our breath and fall back in fear and wonder—or the feeling increases and it destroys us. Yet it remains indifferent to our existence.

The second quotation is from Simone Weil's essay "Human Personality" written in 1942-43, shortly before her death.

> Beauty is the supreme mystery of this world. It is a gleam which attracts the attention and yet does nothing to sustain it. Beauty always promises, but never gives anything; it stimulates hunger but has no nourishment for the part of the soul which looks in this world for sustenance. It feeds only the part of the soul that gazes. While exciting desire, it makes clear that there is nothing in it to be desired, because the one thing we want is that it should not change. If one does not seek to evade the exquisite anguish it inflicts, then desire is gradually transformed into love; and one begins to acquire the faculty of pure and disinterested attention. . . . Beauty can be perceived, though very dimly and mixed with many false substitutes, within the cell where all human thought is at first imprisoned. And upon her rest all the hopes of truth and justice, with tongue cut out. She, too, has no language; she does not speak; she says nothing. But she has a voice to cry out. She cries out and points to truth and justice who are dumb, like a dog who barks to bring people to his master lying unconscious in the snow.[2]

For Weil, beauty is a perfect quality that has the ability, through the "exquisite anguish" it inflicts and then through love, to help us create in ourselves a "faculty of pure and disinterested attention." This ability is the voice that cries out, the dog that barks, which leads us onward to an awareness, perhaps even the discovery, of truth and justice, other perfect qualities, while also suggesting to us our responsibility to them. Weil's sense of beauty is governed by her deeply held religious beliefs. Beauty, truth and justice, she writes at the end of the essay, "are the image in our world of [the] impersonal and divine order of the universe."[3]

The third quotation is from Dostoevsky. The translation is by Constance Garnett.

> Beauty is a terrible and awful thing! It is terrible because it has not been fathomed and never can be fathomed, for God sets us nothing but riddles. Here the boundaries meet and all contradictions exist side by side.... Beauty! I can't endure that thought that a man of lofty mind and heart begins with the ideal of the Madonna and ends with the ideal of Sodom. What's still more awful is that a man with the ideal of Sodom in his soul does not renounce the ideal of the Madonna.... Is there beauty in Sodom? Believe me, for the immense mass of mankind beauty is found in Sodom.... The awful thing is that beauty is mysterious as well as terrible. God and the devil are fighting there and the battlefield is the heart of man. I loved vice, I loved the ignominy of vice. I loved cruelty; am I not a bug, a noxious insect? In fact a Karamazov![4]

In Dostoevsky, we have the beauty of Weil plus something else—the beauty of the abyss, beauty become terror, even the beauty found in ugliness.

In Greek, the words "beauty" and "truth" are nearly synonymous, while the word "pretty" is a synonym for "graceful." In his *Poetics*, Aristotle wrote, "To be beautiful, a living creature, and every whole made up of parts, must not only present a certain order in its arrangement of parts, but also be of a certain definite magnitude. Beauty is a matter of size and order."[5] By "a certain ... magnitude," he means that the beautiful thing must be something of significance; and by an "order[ly] ... arrangement of [its] parts," he is pointing to harmony, the balanced relationship of elements to one another.

It is a requirement of the arts that they represent beauty. The arts, Aristotle wrote, are modes of imitation, and in the literary arts what is imitated are men in action.

It is clear that the general origin of poetry was due to two causes, each of them part of human nature. Imitation is natural to man from childhood, one of his advantages over the lower animals being this, that he is the most imitative creature in the world, and learns at first by imitation. And it is also natural for all to delight in works of imitation. . . . Imitation, then being natural to us—as also the sense of harmony and rhythm, the metres being obviously species of rhythm—it was through their original aptitude, and by a series of improvements for the most part gradual on their first efforts, that they created poetry out of their improvisations.[6]

Aristotle called Plot the first principle or soul of the tragedy; next is Character, "which reveals the moral purpose of the agents, i.e., the sort of thing they seek or avoid."[7] Third is Thought, which is shown in everything said by the characters "when proving or disproving some particular point."[8] The fourth and fifth principles are Diction and Song.

By being an imitation of nature, the writing of a tragedy or the creation of a work of art is, to Aristotle, a fairly objective process. There is no place for the personality of the writer. Then, by requiring subject matter of a certain magnitude governed by the principle of harmonia, the writer cannot simply copy nature. The writer selects, and the writer's ability is determined by how well he or she selects between the important and unimportant and then orders and presents the material. Furthermore, the work has a moral purpose within the society, the city-state. When an Athenian paid his taxes, he could indicate whether he wanted his money spent on a trireme to add to the fleet, to the writing of a tragedy or to some other civic purpose.

Human beings, wrote Aristotle, have an instinct for mimesis, which we may call imitation, and harmonia, that is, structure, balance, harmony. By appealing to this instinct, by causing the audience to sympathize with the condition of the tragic hero and by having the hero act according to the laws of probability and necessity, the writer can bring about a moment of recognition and reversal of intention on the part of the hero—Oedipus realizes he has killed his father, married his mother and he stabs out his eyes, itself an act of hubris for which he is punished. These elements of recognition and reversal of intention should "arise out of the structure of the plot itself, so as to be the consequence, necessary or probable, of the antecedents."[9] A consequence of this recognition and reversal "will arouse either pity or fear—actions of that nature being what Tragedy is assumed to represent; and it will also serve to bring about the happy or unhappy ending."[10] For pity in a tragedy "is occasioned by undeserved misfortune, and fear by that of one like ourselves; . . . and the cause of it must not lie in any depravity, but in some great error on his part."[11]

Aristotle called this experience of pity or fear catharsis, which is purification, a purifying of the emotions. By purging us of pity and fear, tragedy rids us—if only for a short time—of our subjective element and forces us to look outward. The critic Walter Jackson Bate wrote:

> For beneath the theory of catharsis lies the general Greek premise that art, in presenting a heightened and harmonious "imitation" of reality; that is, enlarging, exercising, and refining one's feelings, and in leading them outward, art possesses a unique power to form the "total man," in whom emotion has been reconciled to intelligence and harmoniously reconciled with it.[12]

Clearly many differences exist between Aristotle and Simone Weil, but we also find similarities. In both beauty, truth and justice are perfect qualities—harmony being almost synonymous with justice. Harmonia is the daughter of the goddess of love, Aphrodite, and the god of war, Ares. She is the reconciliation of opposites, of all things being in their proper places and in just relation to one another. Disorder or injustice is cacophony, a word that has its root—*kakos*—in bad or evil. Beauty in Weil and Aristotle has the ability to draw our attention to truth and justice—the dog that barks. And in both we also see that beauty has a moral purpose. For Weil art leads to the divine, while for the Greeks it goes back to the idea of the examined life—what Werner Jaeger in his *Paideia* described as the "intellectual search for and interest in the true nature of man."[13] For the Greeks, he wrote, "The vital factor is the Beautiful as the determinant ideal." The function of a cultural education is to fulfill "an ideal of man as he ought to be,"[14] which means, to go back to Bate, "to complete himself: to carry out, to the fullest extent, what is best and most distinctive in him."[15] This too is harmonia: love and war reconciled, all of one's parts in a balance. Great art, by being "an imitation of what is essential in nature, [that is] concerned with persisting objective forms,"[16] presents an example of harmonia, which is the true and beautiful: the human ideal. At the same time, art may be also other things—entertainment and whatnot—but those elements exist under the charge of mimesis and harmonia.

The Greek ideals and definitions of beauty have remained major influences on art for over 2,000 years—the biggest modifications beginning in the late eighteenth century with Romanticism, which increasingly emphasized the subjective and then came to doubt that the objective was even possible. From the Romantics arose the idea of organic form—that the work determines its own shape, instead of shape being imposed on the work from without—and they also introduced changes in types of subject matter. Yet these ideas didn't so much alter as perhaps emend the Greek ideals, and it wasn't till Marx and Freud that the Greek ideals were seriously challenged. Still, aesthetic theory remained through most of the twentieth century as the science of the beautiful in art.

Since the late 1970s, however, the term "beauty" has become a pejorative in criticism. Elaine Scarry discussed "the banishing of beauty from the humanities" in her book *On Beauty and Being Just*.

> The political critique of beauty is composed of two distinct arguments. The first urges that beauty, by pre-occupying our attention, distracts attention from wrong social arrangements. It makes us inattentive, and there-

fore socially indifferent, to the project of bringing about social arrangements that are just. The second argument holds that when we stare at something beautiful, make it an object of sustained regard, our act is destructive to the object. This argument is most often prompted when the gaze is directed toward a human face or form, but the case presumably applies equally [to any] beautiful thing. . . . The complaint has given rise to a generalized discrediting of the act of "looking," which is charged with "reifying" the very object that appears to be the subject of admiration.[17]

Scarry contends that the arguments contradict each other. The first states that intense regard—gazing—should be focused not on beautiful objects, but, for instance, on "an injustice in need or repair." The second "assumes that generous attention is inconceivable, and that any object receiving sustained attention will somehow suffer from the act of human regard."[18] In both, the value placed on beauty is seen as morally wrong. In the first, our attention to beauty may distract us from a necessary attention on injustice and falsehood. In the second, to project our idea of beauty on to, for instance, another human being, is to change that human being into a thing, to violate it. In addition, Scarry discusses "the problem of lateral disregard"; that is, when you focus on the so-called beautiful thing, you are not paying attention to something else, which extends the fault.[19] Then, of course, to say something is beautiful is, by implication, to say something else is ugly—another fault.

I raise these issues because what a political argument demands is that the work have a moral purpose. This is not a new idea. Plato puts it forward in *The Republic* and then comes to the conclusion that the poet should be excluded from the Republic altogether. And it was why some critics accused Chekhov of writing pornography—his stories didn't provide exemplary models of middle-class life. But plainly another element is missing. In Scarry's first political argument, beauty has been separated from truth and justice. Harmonia and mimesis are no longer credible theories. Weil's dog, if it barks at all, barks for its own amusement.

Two points, however, may be made about moral art. First, it has never produced a work of any magnitude. I am not referring to works like *Oedipus Rex*, or even a novel like *David Copperfield*, where we see a man travel a complex path and either fall victim to or triumph over adversity. Although those works may have a moral purpose, that purpose is secondary to something else. The difference may be seen in a statement Chekhov makes in a letter to his editor: "You are right to demand that an author take conscious stock of what he is doing, but you are confusing two concepts: answering the questions and formulating them correctly. Only the latter is required of an author."[20] Moral art attempts to answers the questions. By manipulating characters to make certain those questions get answered, the writer guarantees that his or her characters will be forced to violate the laws of probability and necessity. In addition, to write with a sense of political correctness is to produce a version of moral art.

There is also a statement of Baudelaire's that I like. After having argued that a poem can have "no other air than itself," he writes.

> Let there be no misunderstanding: I do not mean to say that
> poetry does not ennoble manners—that its final result is not
> to raise man above the level of squalid interests; that would
> be clearly absurd. What I am saying is that, if the poet has
> pursued a moral aim, he will have diminished his poetic
> power; nor will it be incautious to bet that his work is bad.[21]

We should see that the first part of Baudelaire's statement bears a resemblance to Bate's definition of the Greek ideal of self-completion, "to carry out, to the fullest extent, what is best and most distinctive" in man, although Baudelaire, the consummate outsider, would reject how the ideal of self-completion meant being a participant within the polis.

The second point about moral art is that it will never achieve the beautiful, though it may be decorative, pretty, graceful—just as wallpaper may be all those things. Rilke defines sentimentality as the artist presenting something as if he were saying "I love this" instead of "here it is."[22] Moral art uses beauty similarly (if it tries to use beauty at all). The writer says, "This is how it should be." Beauty is given a function; it is being used as a tool.

But the main fault with political or moral art is that it's created out of one's improved self, one's censored self. For art to be successful and beauty to be approached, it has to be created out of one's totality—the light and dark parts, with nothing held back. That doesn't mean that the darkness has to appear in every sonnet and story, but it has to be made available. Rilke argued this point, and as an example he discussed Baudelaire's poem "The Carrion." I have written about this before in my chapter on Rilke, so let's look at another Baudelaire poem, "For Her Who Is Too Gay." The translation is by William H. Crosby.

> Your head, your gesture, and your air
> Are beautiful as sunlit space;
> Laughter plays across your face
> Like winds that blow the heavens clear.
>
> A downcast fellow passing by
> Is dazzled by the healthy gleam
> That like a beacon pours a stream
> Of brightness from your breast and eye.
>
> The clear cacophony of colors
> With which you accent every dress
> Awakens in my consciousness
> A dream, a ballet of the flowers.
>
> The mad designs of stuffs that clothe you
> Are emblems of your motley mood,
> You madcap who have made me mad.
> I hate you even as I love you.

When to a garden's loveliest
Of beds I drag my apathy,
I feel—it seems an irony—
The sun is tearing at my breast;

And there the springtime and its verdure
So humiliate my heart,
I want to rip a flower apart
To punish the insolence of Nature.

And so one night when you're asleep,
Sharp on the hour of ecstasy,
Close to your body's treasury,
A silent coward I will creep

To chasten your vivacious flesh,
Murder those breasts, which I forgive,
And in your startled flank I'll drive
A stab wound deep and generous;

My sister, what sweet vertigo!
Between those lips so newly spread,
Most beautifully bejeweled,
To pour my venom into you![23]

When the poem appeared in *Les Fleurs du Mal* in 1857, Baudelaire was taken to court on charges of publishing obscene writing. In the subsequent decision, this poem and six others were banned. They weren't published in France until the late 1940s.

The second political critique of beauty described by Scarry— that "noticing beauty brings harm to the thing noticed"[24]—is clearly demonstrated in Baudelaire's poem. No doubt about it the narrator— whom we will call Baudelaire—is turning the woman into a thing and he doesn't mean her any good. She could be a shop girl on her lunch break or a young working woman strolling on a Sunday afternoon—

the garishness of her costume suggests her class—but her actuality is erased under the gaze of the poet and the nature of that transformation has been determined by the poet's psychological state.

But nothing is left to accident. Whatever the poem's beginnings, years of revision have brought every nuance under Baudelaire's control. In his second essay on Edgar Allen Poe, Baudelaire praised Poe for subjecting "inspiration to the strictest method and analysis,"[25] and as Baudelaire wrote in his essay "The Painter of Modern Life," "Everything beautiful and noble is the result of reason and calculation."[26]

That said, we see that, while the narrator is drawn to the girl's beauty in the first stanza, the similes in the poem link her beauty to natural beauty—sunlit space and the "winds that blow the heavens clear." She is not singular; she is plural. Baudelaire is the downcast fellow passing by, and he is suddenly assaulted by this vision that awakens others—"a dream, a ballet of flowers." His response is anger—"I hate you even as I love you"—and he gives two stanzas as his reasons: that the beauty of a garden makes his own experience of misery and failure even worse; that it mocks, humiliates and reminds him of his condition, which leads him to anger. "I want to rip a flower apart / To punish the insolence of Nature." And so he imagines punishing the girl—he will creep into her room at night. It seems that he will stab her, but there are double meanings. The "wound deep and generous" and "those lips so newly spread" are also her vagina, while his venom (Baudelaire was syphilitic) is his sperm. Thus he punishes her beauty for reminding him of his ugliness; he renders her ugly as well. Well, this was too much for the French judges. They felt it showed a nasty nature.

But to return to Rilke—in a letter to his wife in 1907 he wrote that Baudelaire's poem "A Carrion" (other Baudelaire poems would have done as well) was a milestone in poetry, because it meant that after its appearance a poet was unable to turn his or her back on any subject.

Artistic perception had to overcome itself to the point of
realizing that even something horrible, something that

seems no more than disgusting, *truly exists,* and shares the truth of its being with everything else that exists. Just as the creative artist is not allowed to choose, neither is he permitted to turn his back on anything: a single refusal, and he is cast out of the state of grace and becomes sinful all the way through.[27]

This is a powerful statement and I repeat it often—not to bully others but to remind myself. What makes "For Her Who Is Too Gay" a great poem is the very reification that many critics find objectionable.

But let's look at another poem in *La Fleur du Mal,* the one that begins the book and sets the tone for the whole. I only want to quote parts of it. The translation is by Stanley Kunitz. Here are the first two stanzas.

> Ignorance, error, cupidity, and sin
> Possess our souls and exercise our flesh:
> Habitually we cultivate remorse
> As beggars entertain and nurse their lice.
>
> Our sins are stubborn. Cowards when contrite
> We overpay confession with our pains,
> And when we're back again in human mire
> Vile tears, we think, will wash away our stains.

And the fifth stanza:

> Like an exhausted rake who mouths and chews
> The martyrized breast of an old withered whore
> We steal, in passing, whatever joys we can,
> Squeezing the driest orange all the more.

Then he comes to the worst of all the crimes and we have a difficulty. The word "ennui" is used in the original and the same word is used in the translation. But "ennui" in English is not an exact cognate. In French, the word has a deeper and more complicated meaning, being a sort of existential indifference and despair, with perhaps a touch of malice. Here are the last two stanzas.

> There's one supremely hideous and impure!
> Soft-spoken, not the type to cause a scene,
> He'd willingly make rubble of the earth
> And swallow up creation in a yawn.

> I mean Ennui who in his hookah-dreams
> Produces hangmen and real tears together.
> How well you know this fastidious monster, reader,
> —Hypocrite reader, you—my double! my brother![28]

Here Baudelaire addresses the dark and the light, the hangman and real tears together, the denial mixed with the strength to confess. Moreover, what is paramount is Baudelaire's claim to being the reader's representative—"my double! my brother!" These are not his private sins, they belong to all of us. He claims a universality, which though Romantic and subjective, also embraces a perverse form of mimesis and harmonia. At this same time Walt Whitman was publishing *Leaves of Grass*, one year separates the two books. Although the poets are different in a hundred ways, they are the first to make this declaration of being the readers' representative their primary posture. For Wordsworth the poet is a man speaking to men. For Baudelaire the poet and the reader are one.

In "For Her Who Is Too Gay," even though the girl is victimized, the speaker is also a victim. He has fallen victim to his anger and his passion. In the last stanza, he calls the girl "my sister," which returns us to the closing line of the poem that begins the book— "my double! my brother!" We see that in stabbing/raping the girl, he is also stabbing/raping himself. The real girl, in fact, is not harmed at all. By being turned into a symbol, she has been spared.

We find several sources of beauty in the poem. Although a translation is at best a shadow of the original, Crosby tries to maintain the rhyme, meter, alliteration, and so on, and clearly the beauty of the form exists in stark contrast to the violence of the content. We see a person expressing the totality of his nature, and in that totality we recognize his tragedy; for while in his imagination he destroys the girl, the very act of imagining contributes to his own destruction. He is as much a victim as Dante (an example cited by Scarry), whose life is changed utterly by looking upon Beatrice. Baudelaire's experience of this beauty strips it of any prettiness. He extracts from beauty the abyss, the obsession and desperation, the frenzy and self-destruction—all of which we also see in the work of Dostoevsky. In addition, Baudelaire creates a metaphor for the complexity of beauty, and how the act of gazing and the desire to possess and destroy beauty makes a victim of the gazer. And he says this is you and the creature you wish to destroy, your sister, is you as well. And Rilke says that for the writer to turn away from these feelings, to censure the writing, will destroy the work and destroy the writer.

The confrontational nature of Baudelaire's poem makes it hard for us to maintain our complacency. Our most common entry into a poem is to ask ourselves what led the poet to write the poem, what is the poet trying to do and how is the poet doing it. Of this the poem's so-called meaning forms only part of the answer. If we don't reject the poem out of hand, it will force us to deliberate and perhaps further along we come to deliberate on the subject of beauty. This is one of Baudelaire's intentions: to expand our definition of beauty. If he is successful, something else happens, which is that the poem has fulfilled a social purpose, because we will take this expanded sense of beauty and apply to the things outside the poem. Indeed, it will expand our sense of the world. However, if Baudelaire's poem was our only example of beauty, then our idea of beauty would be rather skewed. Instead, we add it to the mix and, if we think of the Greek idea of harmonia and Simone Weil's barking dog, this increased understanding of beauty may also expand our sense of truth and justice, simply because of their interconnectedness.

As for the issue of beauty and reification, all gazing is to some degree a creative act. Baudelaire in looking at the girl in the poem makes her into an emblem of his desires and disappointment, his wish for self-forgetting and self-destruction, while the girl herself all but disappears. Is this a violation of the girl? Desire transforms the object of desire. To perceive something as beautiful changes the object under regard, while the gazer's perception of beauty is affected by his or her physical, psychological and spiritual condition, as well as other unconscious and external forces, which robs the perception—perhaps all perceptions—of any possibility of objectivity.

Actually this is an idea that occurs in Baudelaire and that he formulated through reading the work of Edgar Allen Poe and the schizophrenic poet Gerard de Nerval. Simply, it argues that what the writer says about what he or she sees gives information about the writer—either a little or a lot, depending on whom you read. One is always writing through one's psychology and so on. Now, after Freud, this seems so obvious as to be hardly worth mentioning, but in literature it is something that is first consciously (it is the conscious part that is important) employed by Baudelaire. And it is one of the reasons he is pointed to as the first modern poet.

What has this to do with beauty? If everything reflects back to the self, it makes of the self a prison. By seeing the world through the filter of your psychology, your past, your cultural conditioning, you do not see the world but many versions of the self—or rather, you never truly know to what degree the perceived object is the reflected self or "the real thing." This is a subject upon which the existentialists were so gloomily and convincingly eloquent.

Baudelaire called beauty "the greatest and noblest aim of the poem,"[29] and in searching for beauty he was trying to transcend his existential self. When I stand in the middle of a room surrounded by four walls of Monet's giant paintings of water lilies, I am lifted out of myself. Chaliapin singing *Boris Godunov*, certain Beethoven quartets, Chekhov's "In the Ravine," certain poems of Yeats—I seek out the moments such works provide, and in pursuing my experience of art, I try to make that experience as wide as possible, which is why I demand that the artist give me his or her human totality. What we see in the beautiful—as opposed to the pretty or decorative—is something larger than the self. And the amazing paradox about the beautiful in art—at least I find it amazing—is that this thing that so much larger than a single human being—the encaged creature—was actually made by a human being. Mussorgsky was a terrible drunk-in-the-gutter alcoholic who died of his disease at 41 and never finished any of his operas, yet *Boris Godunov* is one of the greatest operas in the repertoire. Beauty is many things, and what is beautiful to one person may not be beautiful to another, but we recognize beauty in part by the awe it inspires. Scarry mentions this, as does Weil, and we see it in the idea of catharsis. Even the lilac is capable of inspiring awe.

So here is another social function in art—its ability to lift a person out of himself or herself, even if ever so briefly. Because in that time one's subjectivity diminishes, one's personal concerns slide away, one's empathy increases and, ideally, one takes a look at the world. And what is seen becomes part of one's metaphysical infrastructure. We observe the world through our experience, and that includes the books we have read.

Scarry claims that one's response to beauty is to want to "replicate" it—a larger word than "copy" and a somewhat different word from "imitate" or "mimesis." As a writer, I'm not in total agreement; or rather, replication is only one of my concerns. I have a number of definitions of beauty—some I would call permanent, some fluctuating. These occupy a mental warehouse that I draw upon when I begin to write.

I also have a variety of intellectual, psychological, emotional and spiritual concerns. Some have been with me always, some grew over the years, some are more recent. These too occupy a warehouse. Then I have the elements of my craft developed over 40 years of writing, which include a certain attentiveness, a patient waiting, a motionless tension, as a Zen master called it—my third warehouse. Then I have my present experience of the world as well as my imagination, fantasies, sense of play.

I constantly sort through these elements, trying to put balls in motion. For instance, I might begin with the idea of a powerful man who decides to divide his property among his three daughters, but first he decides to ask which one loves him best. What happens next? Most writing occurs like this—banging the balls together to see what happens. But those balls can be just words, images, sounds. At the beginning, one writes to find out why one is writing. It is related to play, yet the direction it takes is determined by one's most urgent concerns. As it takes shape, one turns to the various warehouses. Scarry quotes Wittgenstein who said that when the eye sees something beautiful, the hand wants to draw it. Even gazing, she writes, is the attempt to impress or copy the beautiful object into the mind.[30] But the artist doesn't simply make a copy. How could you make a pure copy if you are unable to keep from seeing it through the filter of your mood, emotions, psychology, and the like? And how could you present anything of which there has been no human experience exactly like your own?

Scarry discusses a number of other elements to be found in beauty. The first three she calls key features: "beauty is sacred . . . beauty is unprecedented,"[31] and beauty is life-saving. She exemplifies this in the moment when Odysseus, recently crawled up out of the sea, watches Nausicca playing ball with some other girls and is amazed by her beauty and believes that she has no precedent. Then Odysseus begins to remember comparable precedents, but in that first moment of surprise there appeared to be none.

Baudelaire made a similar statement about beauty being unprecedented, although with his own idiosyncratic twist, in his essay "The Exposition Universelle, 1855."

> *The Beautiful is always strange.* I do not mean that it is coldly, deliberately strange, for in that case in would be a monstrosity that had jumped the rails of life. I mean that it always contains a touch of strangeness, of simple, unpremeditated and unconscious strangeness, and that it is this touch of strangeness that gives it its particular quality as Beauty. It is its endorsement, so to speak—its mathematical characteristic. Reverse the proposition, and try to imagine a *commonplace Beauty!*[32]

In describing beauty's life-saving qualities, Scarry wrote, "Homer is not alone in seeing beauty is life-saving. Augustine described it as 'a plank amid the waves of the sea.' . . . Beauty quickens. It adrenalizes. It makes the heart beat faster. It makes life more vivid, animated, living worth living."[33] And beauty is also a greeting. Scarry wrote, "At the moment one comes into the presence of something beautiful, it greets you. It lifts away from the neutral background as though come forward to welcome you—as though the object were designed to 'fit' your perception."[34]

And beauty, she argues, has a fourth feature: "it incites deliberation."[35] I discussed something similar when describing how beauty can jar us from our complacency and force us to relate it to the world. We see something surprising or strange, and we engage in an act of deliberation as we search for precedents. That deliberation leads us from the thing to the world.

Scarry eventually turns to beauty within art as having a moral purpose, and some of her points seem influenced by Weil. She argues that beauty's "single most enduringly recognized attribute"[36] is justice, which is described in part as "a symmetry of everyone's relation to one another,"[37] which is also harmonia. Then she writes, "Beauty is pacific: its reciprocal salute to continued existence, its pact, is indistinguishable from the word for peace. And justice stands opposed to injury: 'injustice' and 'injury' are the same word."[38] A few pages later she quotes Weil, that beauty requires us "to give up our imaginary position as the center. . . . A transformation then takes place at the very roots of our sensibility, in our immediate reception of sense impressions and psychological impressions."[39] This is also the effect of awe, and it is why Baudelaire makes beauty the end of poetry: it lifts oneself out of oneself and leads one to look at the world.

But in stressing the implications of harmonia, Scarry moves away from the need of a writer to be willing to express his or her totality, the good and the bad. If beauty is pacific and "indistinguishable from the word for peace," where do we put "For Her Who Is Too Gay" or "The Carrion" or many other Baudelaire poems? Where do we put the novels of Genet or Celine or the paintings of Francis

Bacon? Someone once asked Bartok, "Why is your music so ugly?" He replied, "Because the world is ugly." Scarry presents a classical view of art, but where are the thunderstorms, typhoons, broken towers and mountain crags that appealed to Romantic painters? Where are the inner demons that Rilke said must not be turned away from? Where is the sense of beauty found in the earlier quote from Dostoevsky.

In *Feeling and Form* the aesthetician Suzanne Langer described another sort of beauty.

> Every good work of art is beautiful; as soon as we find it so, we have grasped its expressiveness, and until we do we have not seen it as good art, though we may have ample intellectual reason to believe that it is so. Beautiful works may contain elements that, taken in isolation, are hideous; the obscenities that Ezra Pound piles one upon the other in Cantos XIV and XV are revolting, but their function in the poem is that of a violent dissonance. . . . Such elements are the strength of the work, which must be great to contain and transfigure them. The emergent form, the whole, is alive and therefore beautiful, as awful things may be—as gargoyles, and fearful African masks, and the Greek tragedies of incest and murder are beautiful. Beauty is not identical with the normal, and certainly not with charm and sense appeal, though all such properties may go into the making of it. Beauty is expressive form. . . . What [art] does to us is to formulate our conceptions of feeling and our conceptions of visual, factual, and audible reality together. It gives us forms of imagination and forms of feeling together, inseparably; that is to say, it clarifies and organizes intuition itself.[40]

In Langer's final and major work, *Mind: An Essay in Human Feeling,* she discussed George Santayana's theory of beauty as "pleasure objectified": that instead of locating beauty in a specific person or object, the beholder projects his or her own subjective responses onto the work so that "the projected feeling is one which the beholder of the beautiful object is undergoing as he sees or envisages the object."[41] Consequently, each person's interpretation of the work will most likely be different, which doesn't make it any less valid.

Langer disagreed, arguing against "the 'error' of taking something subjective, that occurs in [one's] own mind, for a property of the object."[42] This reduces one's sense of beauty to an expanded form of taste—a subjective projection formed by the viewer's emotional, physical, psychological, spiritual, as well as current cultural values. In fact, according to such a theory, one thing is no more beautiful than another; it is only the viewer's objectified pleasure that makes it seem more beautiful. In the past 25 years certain areas of critical thinking have returned to very similar ideas— that one form of entertainment (a boxing match) is no better or more beautiful than another (Shakespeare's *Hamlet*), and it is only our own subjectivity that makes it seem so.

It is impossible not to project one's own subjective response onto a work, but that doesn't mean that the work lacks properties of its own. Look again at Baudelaire. In his 1859 essay, *A Painter of Modern Life*, a study of the illustrator Constantine Guy, he wrote:

> Beauty is always and inevitably of a double composition, although the impression that it produces is single. . . . Beauty is made up of an eternal, invariable element, whose quality it is excessively difficult to determine, and of a relative, circumstantial element, which will be, if you like, whether severally or all at once, the age, its fashions, its morals, its emotions. Without this second element, which might be described as the amusing, enticing, appetizing icing on the divine cake, the first element would be beyond our powers of digestion or appreciation. I defy anyone to point to a single scrap of beauty which does not contain these two elements. . . . The duality of art is a fatal consequence of the duality of man. Consider, if you will,

the eternally subsisting portion as the soul of art, and the variable element as its body.[43]

He then quoted Stendhal, who had said that "Beauty is nothing more than the promise of happiness,"[44] which Baudelaire wrote was only partially correct, referring in some measure to beauty's relative, circumstantial element, what he elsewhere calls "modernity." It should be seen that Stendhal's definition is akin to Santayana's definition of beauty as "objectified pleasure," while what Baudelaire called the "relative, circumstantial element" resembles Langer's subjective projection.

It is this "relative, circumstantial element," this modernity, that makes contemporary expressions of beauty in art accessible to us, while in this eternal, invariable element we can perhaps see—to greater or lesser degrees—harmonia, mimesis and other of the elements that Scarry identifies. The difficulty with the political arguments cited by Scarry is they block or ignore the eternal, invariable element. In addition, the effect of political arguments on the writer is they can put the writer under a psychological constraint. They hinder the unconditional commitment that must exist when one begins to write, and they introduce consciousness and critical attention too soon in the writing process. They lead the writer to ask from the very beginning how his or her work will be received by the reader. They assure that beauty will either exist as a tool or be deliberately excluded. And you recall the words of Rilke about the artist who steps away from what he thinks is politically incorrect: "he is cast out of the state of grace and becomes sinful all the way through."

Instead, a writer needs to redefine beauty every time he or she begins to write, bearing in mind that beauty can be violent and ugly. Our milieu, the contemporary, the time in which we breathe, is our entry into our work—the door we open to reach the beauty that is the work's purpose, the dog that barks. We can't let the contemporary become a locked door by being controlled by a dominating fashion that, if listened to, will trivialize the work.

NOTES

Preface

1. William Wordsworth, Preface to the *Lyrical Ballads* in Walter Jackson Bate, ed., *Criticism: The Major Texts* (New York, 1952), p. 340.

Chapter 1

1. Frank O'Connor, *The Lonely Voice* (Cleveland, 1962).

Chapter 2

1. Samuel Johnson, "Life of Gray" in Walter Jackson Bate, ed., *Criticism: The Major Texts* (New York, 1952), p. 240.
2. W. B. Yeats, "The Symbolism of Poetry," in *Essays and Introductions* (New York, 1961), p. 156.
3. Graham Hough, "Reflections on a Literary Revolution" in *Image and Experience: Studies in a Literary Revolution* (Lincoln, 1960), p. 44.
4. Tomas Tranströmer, *Selected Poems: 1954-1986*, ed. Robert Hass various translators (New York, 1987), p. 48.
5. W. S. Merwin, *The Lice* (New York, 1967), p. 62.
6. Jean Follain, *The Transparence Of The World,* translated by W. S. Merwin, (New York, 1968), p. 111.
7. Heather McHugh, *Hinge & Sign* (Wesleyan, CT, 1994), p. 163.
8. Thomas Lux, *The Drowned River* (Boston, 1990), p. 48.
9. James Wright, *Above the River: The Complete Poems* (New York, 1990), p. 158.

Chapter 3

1. Anton Chekhov, *Anton Chekhov's Life And Thought: Selected Letters and Commentary*, ed. Simon Karlinsky, trans. Michael Heim (Berkeley, 1975), p. 104.

2. Aristotle, *Poetics* in Walter Jackson Bate, ed., *Criticism: The Major Texts* (New York, 1952), p. 23.

3. W. S. Merwin, *Asian Figures* (New York, 1973).

4. Charles Baudelaire, "Further Notes on Edgar Poe," in *Selected Writings on Art and Artists*, trans. P. E. Charvet (Cambridge, 1972), p. 206.

5. Charles Baudelaire, "The Painter of Modern Life" in ibid., p. 425.

6. Baudelaire, "Further Notes on Edgar Poe," p. 200.

7. Ibid., p. 206.

8. Ibid., p. 202.

9. Merwin, *Asian Figures*.

10. Philip Larkin, *Collected Poems* (New York, 1989), p. 175.

11. Frank O'Connor, *The Lonely Voice* (Cleveland, 1962), p. 26.

12. Aristotle, *Poetics*, p. 23.

13. William Flint Thrall and Addison Hibbard, *The Handbook of Literature* (New York, 1936), p. 356.

14. Lon Otto, *A Nest of Hooks* (Iowa City, IA, 1978), p. 77.

15. William Trevor, "The Art of Fiction CVIII," *The Paris Review*, 110 (New York, 1989), p. 135.

Chapter 4

1. Alex Preminger, ed., *Princeton Encyclopedia of Poetry and Poetics* (Princeton, NJ, 1974), p. 669. (Hereafter cited as *Princeton Encyclopedia*.)

2. I. A. Richards, "Rhythm and Meter," in Harvey Gross, ed. *The Structure of Verse* (New York, 1979), p. 69.

3. Ibid., p. 71.

4. Ezra Pound, "Treatise on Meter," in ibid., p. 235.

5. Charles O. Hartman, *Free Verse: An Essay on Prosody* (Princeton, NJ, 1980), p. 14.

6. *Princeton Encyclopedia*, p. 670.

7. Ibid.

8. Richards, "Rhythm and Meter," p. 72.

9. Robert Hass, "Listening and Making," in *Twentieth Century Pleasures* (New York, 1984), p. 112.

10. Alexander Pope, "An Essay on Criticism," in William K. Winsatt, Jr., ed. *Selected Poetry and Prose* (New York, 1961), p. 73, lines 362-373.

11. Robert Creeley, *The Collected Poems of* (Berkeley, CA 1982), p. 132.

12. *The Collected Poems of William Carlos Williams*, A. Walton Litz and Christopher MacGowan, eds., (New York, 1986), pp. 217-219.

13. Hass, "Listening and Making," p. 123.

14. Paul Fussell, *Poetic Meter and Poetic Form* (New York, 1979), p. 10.

15. Rafael Alberti, *The Lost Grove*, trans. Gabriel Berns (Berkeley, CA, 1976), p. 231.

16. Guillaume Apollinaire, "The New Spirit and the Poets," in *Selected Writings*, trans. Roger Shattuck (New York, 1971), p. 235.

17. Ibid., p. 233.

18. Osip Mandelstam, *Mandelstam: The Complete Critical Prose and Letters*, ed. Jane Gary Harris, trans. Jane Gary Harris and Constance Link (Ann Arbor, MI, 1979), p. 64.

19. Ibid., p. 70.

20. Ibid., p. 77.

21. Pound, "Treatise on Meter," p. 4.

22. Ibid., p. 7.

23. Ibid., p. 52.

24. T. S. Eliot, "Reflections on *Vers Libre*," in Harvey Gross, ed., *The Structure of Verse* (New York, 1979), p. 233.

25. Robert Graves, "Harp, Anvil, Oar," in ibid. (New York, 1979), pp. 24-25.

26. Ibid., p. 24.

27. Ibid., p. 24.

28. George Saintsbury, *A History of English Prosody* (New York, 1968) vol. 1, 79.

29. Fussell, *Poetic Meter*, p. 70.

30. Ibid.

31. Ibid., p. 71.

32. William Wordsworth, "Preface to the Lyrical Ballads (1800)," in Carlos Baker, ed., *The Prelude, Selected Poems and Sonnets*, (New York, 1961), pp. 3-4.

33. Ibid., p. 21.

34. John Keats, *Selected Poems and Letters*, ed. Douglas Bush (Boston, 1959), p. 267.

35. Samuel Taylor Coleridge, "Shakespeare's Judgement Equal to His Genius," in Walter Jackson Bate, ed., *Criticism: the Major Texts* (New York, 1952), p. 392.

36. Ralph Waldo Emerson, "The Poet," in Carl Bode and Malcolm Cowley, eds., *The Portable Emerson* (New York, 1981), p. 244.

37. Nadezhda Mandelstam, *Hope Against Hope*, trans. Max Hayward (New York, 1970), p. 187.

38. Pound, "Treatise on Meter," p. 54.

39. Emerson, "The Poet," p. 256.

40. Ibid., p. 242.

41. Ibid., p. 245.

42. Ibid., p. 254.

43. Ibid., p. 262.

44. Justin Kaplan, *Walt Whitman: A Life* (New York, 1982), p. 101.

45. John Townsand Trowbridge, *My Own Story: With Recollections of Noted Persons* (Boston, 1903), p. 367.

46. Walt Whitman, *Leaves of Grass*, ed. Sculley Bradley and Harold W. Blodgett, (New York, 1973), pp. 715-716.

47. Ibid., p. 716.

48. Gay Allen Wilson, *American Prosody* (New York, 1935), pp. 217-218.

49. Kaplan, *Walt Whitman*, p. 69.

50. *Princeton Encyclopedia*, pp. 890-891.
51. Ibid., p. 890.
52. Pound, "Treatise on Meter," p. 3.
53. P. Mansell Jones, *The Background of Modern French Poetry* (Cambridge, 1951), p. 81.
54. Ibid., p. 80.
55. Kaplan, *Walt Whitman*, p. 325.
56. *Princeton Encyclopedia*, p. 11.
57. Charles Baudelaire, "Further Notes on Edgar Poe" in *Selected Writings on Art and Artists*, p. 204.
58. Alex de Jonge, *Baudelaire: Prince of Clouds* (New York, 1976), p. 118.
59. Baudelaire, "Further Notes on Edgar Poe," p. 185.
60. Ibid., p. 200.
61. Ibid., p. 204.
62. Ibid., p. 199.
63. Ibid., pp. 201-202.
64. Ibid., p. 203.
65. Ibid., p. 205.
66. Graham Hough, "Edgar Allan Poe," in *Selected Essays* (Cambridge, 1980), p. 142.
67. Ibid., p. 139.
68. Whitman, *Leaves of Grass*, p. 569.
69. Charles Baudelaire, *Les Fleurs du Mal* (New York 1989), p. xix.
70. Charles Baudelaire, "The Painter of Modern Life" in *Selected Writings on Art and Artists*, p. 392.
71. Ibid., p. 403.
72. Ibid., p. 405.
73. Ibid., p. 402.
74. Ibid., p. 400.
75. Ibid.
76. Charles Baudelaire, *Le Spleen de Paris. Petits Poemes en prose*, trans. Edward K. Kaplan (Athens, GA, 1989), p. 129.
77. Ibid., p. 129.
78. Ibid., p. 1.
79. Arthur Rimbaud, *Complete Works, Selected Letters*, trans. Wallace Fowlie (Chicago, 1966), p. 311.
80. Cited in Jones, *Background of Modern French Poetry*, p. 107.
81. Ibid.
82. Anna Balakian, *The Symbolist Movement: A Critical Appraisal* (New York, 1977), p. 67.
83. Arthur Symons, *The Symbolist Movement in Literature*, intro. Richard Ellmann (New York, 1958), p. 44.
84. P. Mansell Jones, *The Background of Modern French Poetry* (Cambridge, 1951), p. 112.
85. Balakian, *Symbolist Movement*, p. 95.
86. *Princeton Encyclopedia*, p. 126.
87. Jones, *Background of Modern French Poetry*, p. 101.

88. Balakian, *Symbolist Movement*, p. 70.
89. Ibid., p. 82.
90. Jones, *Background of Modern French Poetry*, p. 118.
91. Ibid., p. 71.
92. Symons, *Symbolist Movement*, p. 61.
93. Ezra Pound, *Literary Essays*, (New York, 1968) p. xiv.
94. Ibid., p. 418.
95. Jones, *Background of Modern French Poetry*, p. 123
96. Jean Pierrot, *The Decadent Imagination*, trans. Derek Coltman (Chicago, 1981), p. 121.
97. Ibid., p. 121.
98. Ibid., p. 56.
99. Ibid., p. 56.
100. Ibid., p. 57.
101. Ibid., p. 121.
102. Symons, *Symbolist Movement*, p. 57
103. Angel Flores, ed., *An Anthology of French Poetry from Nerval to Valery in English Translation* (New York, 1958), p. 224.
104. Kaplan, *Walt Whitman*, p. 30.
105. Jones, *Background of Modern French Poetry*, p. 117.
106. Balakian, *Symbolist Movement*, p. 72.
107. Ibid., pp. 70-71.
108. Jones, *Background of Modern French Poetry*, p. 121.
109. Balakian, *Symbolist Movement*, p. 90.
110. Ibid., 91.
111. Jones, *Background of Modern French Poetry*, p. 127.
112. Ibid., p. 128.
113. Balakian, *Symbolist Movement*, p. 94.
114. Whitman, *Leaves of Grass*, p. 529
115. Jones, *Background of Modern French Poetry*, p. 79.
116. Ibid., p. 149.
117. Flores, *Nineteenth Century French Poetry*, p. 171.
118. Stephane Mallarmé, *The Poems* (New York, 1977), p. 225.
119. Ibid., p. 227
120. Graham Hough, *Image and Experience: Studies on a Literary Revolution* (Lincoln, NB, 1960), p. 52.
121. Ibid., p. 53.
122. Balakian, *Symbolist Movement*, p. 96.
123. Ibid., p. 97.
124. Ibid., p. 98.
125. William Butler Yeats, *Essays* (London, 1924), p. 201.
126. Jones, *Background of Modern French Poetry*, p. 135.
127. Symons, *Symbolist Movement*, p. 5.
128. Hough, *Image and Experience*, p. 89.

129. Ibid.
130. Ibid.
131. Harvey Gross, ed., *The Structure of Verse* (New York, 1979), p. 104.
132. Ibid.
133. Ibid., p. 107.
134. Ezra Pound, "A Retrospect," in *Literary Essays of*, p. 3.
135. Ibid.
136. Ibid.
137. Pound, "A Retrospect," p. 4.
138. Ezra Pound, *Personae: Collected Shorter Poems of* (London, 1961), p. 119.
139. Hough, *Image and Experience*, p. 9.
140. Pound, *Personae*, p. 5.
141. Osip Mandelstam, *Mandelstam: The Complete Critical Prose and Letters*, ed. Jane Gray Harris, trans. Jane Gray Harris and Constance Link (Ann Arbor, 1979), pp. 128-30.
142. Pound, *Personae*, p. 9.
143. Baudelaire, "Further Notes on Edgar Poe," p. 206.
144. Pound, "A Retrospect," p. 6.
145. Ibid.
146. Ibid., p. 9.
147. Ibid.
148. Pound, "The Serious Artist," in *Literary Essays*, p. 51.
149. Ibid., p. 12.
150. Gertrude Stein, *Selected Writings of*, intro. and notes Carl Van Vechten (New York, 1990), p. 142.
151. William Carlos Williams, *Autobiography* (New York, 1967), p. 151.
152. Ibid., p. 138.
153. Hartman, *Free Verse*, p. 24.
154. Baudelaire, "Further Notes on Edgar Poe," p. 200.
155. Hough, *Image and Experience*, p. 91.
156. Ibid., p. 94.
157. Ibid., p. 94.
158. Ibid., p. 94.
159. Robert Hass, "Listening and Making," in *Twentieth Century Pleasures* (New York, 1984), p. 112.
160. Hough, *Image and Experience*, p. 104.
161. Ibid.
162. *Princeton Encyclopedia*, p. 687.
163. Hartman, *Free Verse*, p 92.
164. James Wright, *Above The River: The Complete Poems* (New York), p. 331.
165. Hartman, *Free Verse*, p. 104.
166. Philip Larkin, *Collected Poems* (New York, 1989), p. 208.
167. Ibid., p. 29.
168. Ibid., p. 81.

169. Ibid., p. 165.
170. Robert Hass, "Heroic Simile" from Praise (New York, 1979) pp. 2-3.
171. *Princeton Encyclopedia*, p. 95
172. Ibid., p. 289.
173. Ibid.
174. Larkin, *Collected Poems*, p. 175.
175. Samuel Taylor Coleridge, "Shakespeare's Judgement Equal to His Genius," in Bate, ed., *Criticism: The Major Texts*, p. 392.
176. Hough, Graham, *An Essay on Criticism* (New York, 1966), p. 19.
177. Larkin, *Collected Poems*, p. 33.
178. Michael Ryan, *In Winter* (New York, 1981), p. 25.
179. Otto Jespersen, "Notes on Metre," in Harvey Gross, ed., *The Structure of Verse* (New York, 1979), p. 112.
180. Donald Justice, *Selected Poems* (New York, 1979), p. 102.
181. *Princeton Encyclopedia*, p. 289.
182. Hartman, *Free Verse*, p. 13.
183. Richards, "Rhythm and Meter," p. 72.
184. Robert Graves, "Harp, Anvil, Oar," in Gross, ed., *The Structure of Verse*, p. 36
185. Samuel Taylor Coleridge, from *Biographia Literaria*, in *Criticism: The Major Texts*, (New York, 1952), p. 378.

Chapter 5

1. Philip Larkin, "The Pleasure Principle," in *Required Writing* (London, 1983), p. 80.
2. Zbigniew Herbert, interview in *Antaeus*.
3. Suzanne Langer, "Expressiveness," in *Problems of Art* (New York, 1957), p. 23.
4. Graham Hough, *An Essay on Criticism* (New York, 1966), p. 19.
5. Philip Larkin, *Collected Poems* (New York, 1989), p. 106.
6. Louise Glück, *The Triumph of Achilles* (New York, 1985), p. 52.
7. David Bottoms, "On the Willow Branch" from *Under the Vulture Tree* (New York, 1987), p. 42.
8. James Wright, *Above the River: The Complete Poems* (New York, 1990) p. 357.
9. Charles Baudelaire, "Further Notes on Edgar Poe," in *Selected Writings on Art and Artists*, trans. P. E. Charvet (Cambridge, 1972), p. 206.

Chapter 6

1. Rilke Letters, p. 286.
2. Philip Larkin, "The Pleasure Principle," in *Required Writing* (London, 1983), p. 80.

3. *Princeton Encyclopedia of Poetry and Poetics*, Alex Preminger and T. V. F. Brogan, eds., (Princeton, NJ, 1993), p. 1293.

4. Suzanne Langer, "Imitation and Transformation in the Arts," in *Problems of Art* (New York, 1957), p. 91.

5. *Princeton Encyclopedia*, p. 1293.

6. Ibid.

7. Ibid.

8. *Anton Chekhov's Short Stories*, selected and ed. Ralph Matlaw (New York, 1979), p. 273.

9. Ibid., p. 273.

10. Raymond Chandler, "Red Wind," in *The Simple Art of Murder* (New York, 1968), p. 333.

11. P. G. Wodehouse, *Uncle Fred in the Springtime* (London, 1939), p. 5.

12. Franz Kafka, "The Metamorphosis" in *The Complete Stories*, ed. Nahum N. Glatzer (New York, 1983), p. 89.

13. Charles Simic, *Selected Poems, 1963-1983*, rev. and expanded (New York, 1990), p. 229.

14. William Stafford, "B.C.," in *Traveling through the Dark* (New York, 1962), p. 11.

15. Rainer Maria Rilka, "From a Childhood," in *The Book of Images*, tran. Edward Snow (San Francisco, 1991), p. 45.

16. W. B. Yeats, "Leda and the Swan," in *The Collected Poems of W. B. Yeats* (London, 1963), p. 241.

17. Roger Fanning, "Flirt," in *The Island Itself* (New York, 1991), p. 23.

18. Suzanne Langer, "Deceptive Analogies," in *Problems of Art*, p. 80.

19. Suzanne Langer, "Artistic Perception and 'Natural Light,'" in *Problems of Art*, p. 73.

20. Langer, "Imitation and Transformation in the Arts," pp. 92-3.

Chapter 7

1. Anton Chekhov, *Anton Chekhov's Life and Thought: Selected Letters and Commentary*, ed. Simon Karlinsky, trans. Michael Heim (Berkeley, 1975), p. 104.

2. Rainer Maria Rilke, *Letters of Rainer Maria Rilke*, trans. Jane Bannard Greene and M. D. Herter Norton (New York, 1945), p. 124.

3. Charles Baudelaire, "Further Notes on Edgar Poe" in *Selected Writings on Art and Artists*, trans. P. E. Charvet (Cambridge, 1972), p. 200.

4. Chekhov, *Chekhov's Life*, p. 104.

5. Rainer Maria Rilke, *Letters on Cézanne*, ed. Clara Rilke, trans. Joel Agee (New York, 1885), p. 75.

6. Chekhov, *Chekhov's Life*, p. 62.

7. Rilke, *Letters on Cézanne*, p. 67.

8. Bill Knott, *Poems 1963-1988*, (Pittsburgh, PA, 1989).

9. Rilke, *Letters on Cézanne*, p. 73.

10. Ibid., p. 74.

Chapter 8

1. William Butler Yeats, "Crazy Jane Talks with the Bishop," in *The Collected Works of W. B. Yeats,* ed. by Richard J. Finneran, vol. 1 (New York, 1989), pp. 259-60.
2. Suzanne K. Langer, *Problems of Art,* (New York, 1957), p. 7.
3. Ibid., p. 9.
4. John Shawcross, ed., *Shelley's Literary and Philosophical Criticism,*(London, 1909), p. 155.
5. See Vasko Popa, *The Golden Apple,* trans. Andrew Harvey and Anne Pennington (London, 1980).
6. Suzanne Langer, "Deceptive Analogies" in *Problems of Art* (New York, 1957), p. 80.
7. Popa, op.cit.
8. Langer, *Problems of Art,* p. 6.
9. Ibid., pp. 92-92.
10. Ibid., p. 71.
11. Ibid., p. 23.
12. Ibid., pp. 104-105.
13. Ibid., pp. 23-24.
14. Ibid., p. 151.
15. Philip Larkin, "The Pleasure Principle," *Required Writing,* (New York, 1984), p. 80.
16. Langer, *Problems of Art,* p. 69.
17. William Wordsworth, "Preface to the Lyrical Ballads," in Carlos Baker, ed., *The Prelude, Selected Poems and Sonnets,* (New York, 1961), p. 58.
18. C. Day Lewis, "The Nature of the Image," in *The Poetic Image* (New York, 1947), p. 36.
19. Samuel Taylor Coleridge, *Biographia Literaria* (London, 1975), p. 177.
20. Alex Preminger, ed., *Princeton Encyclopedia of Poetry and Poetics* (Princeton, NJ, 1965), p. 140.
21. Larkin, "The Pleasure Principle," p. 80.
22. Lewis, "The Nature of the Image," p. 34.
23. Langer, *Problems of Art,* p. 91.
24. Larkin, "The Pleasure Principle," p. 82.
25. Langer, *Problems of Art,* p. 26.

Chapter 9

1. Rainer Maria Rilke, *Letters of Rainer Maria Rilke,* trans. Jane Bannard Greene and M. D. Herter Norton (New York, 1945), pp. 98-99.
2. Ibid., p. 99.
3. Donald Prater, *A Ringing Glass: The Life of Rainer Maria Rilke* (Oxford, 1986), p. 8.
4. Rilke, *Letters,* p. 25.
5. Prater, *Ringing Glass,* p. 19.
6. Ibid.

7. Ibid., p. 26.

8. Rilke, *Letters*, pp. 27-28.

9. Prater, *Ringing Glass*, p. 37.

10. Ibid.

11. Lou Andreas-Salomé, *Looking Back: Memoirs*, ed. E. Pfeiffer, trans. B. Mitchell (New York, 1991), p. 70.

12. Ibid., p. 88.

13. Ibid., p. 85.

14. Ibid., p. 68-69.

15. Ibid., pp. 85-86.

16. Ibid., p. 70.

17. Prater, *Ringing Glass*, p. 47.

18. Ibid., pp. 46-47.

19. Rilke, *Letters*, p. 32.

20. Prater, *Ringing Glass*, p. 68.

21. Rilke, *Letters*, p. 57.

22. Rainer Maria Rilke, *The Notebooks of Malte Laurids Brigge*, trans. Stephen Mitchell (New York, 1982), p. 251.

23. Ibid., p. 250.

24. Rilke, *Letters*, p. 310.

25. Ibid., p. 76.

26. Ibid., p. 88.

27. Ibid., p. 123.

28. Rainer Maria Rilke, *New Poems [1908]: The Other Part*, trans. Edward Snow (San Francisco, 1987), p. 3.

29. Rilke, *Letters*, p. 191.

30. Ibid., p. 84.

31. Ibid., p. 84.

32. Ibid., p. 85.

33. Ibid., p. 86.

34. Ibid., p. 88.

35. Ibid., p. 93.

36. Ibid., p. 90.

37. Rainer Maria Rilke, *New Poems [1907]*, trans. Edward Snow (San Francisco, 1984), p. 73.

38. Rilke, *Letters*, p. 107.

39. Rainer Maria Rilke, *Letters to a Young Poet*, trans. Stephen Mitchell (New York, 1987), pp. 23-25.

40. Rilke, *Letters*, p. 108.

41. Ibid., p. 120.

42. Ibid., p. 122.

43. Ibid., p. 124.

44. Ibid., p. 145.

45. Ibid., p. 161.
46. Ibid., p. 181.
47. Rilke, *New Poems [1908], The Other Part*, p. 149.
48. Rilke, *Letters*, p. 107.
49. Ibid., p. 266.
50. Ibid., p. 286.
51. Rainer Maria Rilke, *Letters on Cézanne*, ed. Clara Rilke, trans. Joel Agee (New York, 1885), p. 34.
52. Ibid., p. 42.
53. Ibid., p. 36.
54. Ibid., p. 40.
55. Ibid., p. 50.
56. Ibid., p. 51.
57. Ibid., p. 65.
58. Ibid., p. 73.
59. Ibid., p. 74.
60. Ibid., p. 75.
61. Ibid., p. 76.
62. Ibid., p. 67.
63. Rilke, *Letters*, p. 85.
64. Rilke, *Letters on Cézanne*, p. 23
65. Ibid., p. 24.

Chapter 10

1. Nikolai Gumilev, "The Life of Verse" in *On Russian Poetry*, ed. and trans. David Lapeza (Ann Arbor, MI, 1977), p. 12.
2. Charles Baudelaire, "The Painter of Modern Life" in *Selected Writings On Art And Artists*, trans. P. E. Charvet,(Cambridge, 1972), p. 425.
3. Charles Baudelaire, "Further Notes on Edgar Poe" in ibid.
4. Ibid.
5. Ibid., p. 204.
6. Charles Baudelaire, *Selected Letters of Charles Baudelaire: The Conquest of Solitude*, trans. and ed. Rosemary Lloyd (Chicago, 1986), p. 198.
7. Letter to Henri Cazalis, July 1866 in *Mallarmé: Selected Prose Poems, Essays & Letters*, trans. Bradford Cook (Baltimore, 1956), p. 89.
8. Letter to Henri Cazalis, May 14, 1867, in ibid., p. 94.
9. Stéphane Mallarmé, "The Book: A Spiritual Instrument," in ibid., p. 24.
10. Ibid.,
11. Ibid., p. 50.
12. Anna Balakian, *The Symbolist Movement: A Critical Appraisal* (New York, 1977), p. 87.

13. Graham Hough, "Reflections on a Literary Revolution," in *Image and Experience: Studies in a Literary Revolution* (Lincoln, NB, 1960), p. 10.

14. Osip Mandelstam, *Stone*, trans. and intro. by Robert Tracy (Princeton, NJ, 1981), p. 16.

15. Ibid.

16. Osip Mandelstam, *Mandelstam: The Complete Critical Prose and Letters*, ed. Jane Gray Harris, trans. Jane Gray Harris and Constance Link (Ann Arbor, MI, 1979), p. 608.

17. Ibid.

18. Mandelstam, *Stone*, p. 16.

19. Nadezhda Mandelstam, *Hope Abandoned*, trans. Max Hayward (New York, 1981), p. 645.

20. Ibid., p. 43.

21. Ibid., p. 44.

22. Ibid., p. 49.

23. Ibid., p. 42.

24. Nikolai Gumilev, "The Life of Verse" in *On Russian Poetry*, p. 15.

25. Ibid., p. 20.

26. Ibid., p. 11.

27. Ibid., p. 11.

28. Nikolai Gumilev, "Acmeism and the Legacy of Symbolism" in *On Russian Poetry*, pp. 21-22.

29. Ibid., p. 23.

30. Ibid., p. 24.

31. Nikolai Gumilev, "The Reader" in *On Russian Poetry*, p. 29.

32. Nadezhda Mandelstam, *Hope Against Hope*, trans. Max Hayward (New York, 1970), p. 262.

33. Ibid., p. 170.

34. Ibid., p. 196.

35. Osip Mandelstam, Letter No. 3. to V. I. Ivanov [August 13/26, 1909] in Mandelstam, *Mandelstam*, p. 477.

36. Ibid.

37. Osip Mandelstam, "Morning of Acmeism" in ibid., p. 61.

38. Ibid.

39. Ibid.

40. Ibid., pp. 61-62.

41. Ibid., p. 62.

42. Ibid.

43. Ibid., p. 63.

44. Ibid.

45. Osip Mandelstam, "François Villon" in Mandelstam, *Mandelstam*, p. 59.

46. Mandelstam, "Morning of Acmeism," p. 64.

47. Osip Mandelstam, "Notre Dame," in Mandelstam, *Stone*, p. 121.

48. Ibid., p. 29.

49. *Mandelstam: The Complete Critical Prose and Letters*, ed. Jane Gray Harris, trans. Jane Gray Harris and Constance Link (Ann Arbor, MI, 1979), p. 606.

50. Ibid., p. 113.

51. Ibid., p. 77.

52. Ibid.

53. Ibid., p. 588.

54. N. Mandelstam, *Hope Against Hope*, p. 177.

55. Mandelstam, *Mandelstam*, p. 90.

56. N. Mandelstam, *Hope Against Hope*, p. 157.

57. N. Mandelstam, *Hope Abandoned*, p. 17.

58. Osip Mandelstam, "On the Addressee," in Mandelstam, *Mandelstam*, p. 70.

59. Ibid., p. 72.

60. Ibid., p. 64.

61. Ibid.

62. Ibid., p. 69.

63. N. Mandelstam, *Hope Against Hope*, p. 188.

64. *Mandelstam: The Complete Critical Prose and Letters*, edited by Jane Gray Harris, translated by Jane Gray Harris and Constance Link (Ann Arbor, 1979), , p. 71.

65. Ibid., p. 71.

66. Ibid., p. 73.

67. Mandelstam, *Mandelstam*, p. 119.

68. Ibid., p. 616.

69. Ibid., pp. 131-32.

70. N. Mandelstam, *Hope Against Hope*, p. 266.

71. Mandelstam, *Hope Abandoned*, p. 42.

72. Mandelstam, *Mandelstam*, p. 539.

73. Mandesltam, *Hope Abandoned*, p. 47.

74. Ibid., p. 25.

75. Ibid., p. 31.

76. Osip Mandelstam, *Selected Poems*, trans. Clarence Brown and W. S. Merwin (New York, 1983), pp. 69-70.

77. N. Mandelstam, *Hope Against Hope*, p. 165.

78. Ibid., p. 363.

Chapter 11

1. *Anton Chekhov's Life and Thought: Selected Letters and Commentary*, trans. Michael Henry Heim in collaboration with Simon Karlinsky, selection, introduction and commentary by Simon Karlinsky (Berkeley, CA, 1975), p. 85.

2. Ibid., p. 109.

3. Anton Chekhov, *Three Years*, in *Seven Short Novels*, trans. Barbara Makanowitzky (New York, 1971), p. 228.

382 | Best Words, Best Order

4. Chekhov's Life and Thought, pp. 217-18.
5. Ibid., p. 129.
6. Ibid.
7. Ibid., p. 36.
8. Ibid., p. 127.
9. Vladimir Nabokov, [A Definition of *Poshlost'*] in *Anton Chekhov's Plays*, trans. and ed. Eugene K. Bristow (New York, 1970), p. 322.
10. *Chekhov's Life and Thought*, p. 50.
11. Ibid., pp. 50-51.
12. Ibid., p. 87.
13. *Anton Chekhov's Short Stories*, selected and ed. Ralph E. Matlaw (New York, 1979), p. 269.
14. *Chekhov's Life and Thought*, pp. 58-59.
15. Ibid., p. 367.
16. Ibid., p. 374.
17. Ibid., p. 146.
18. Ibid., p. 341.
19. Ibid., pp. 165-166.
20. Ibid., p. 163.
21. Ibid., pp. 323-332.
22. Ibid., p. 338.
23. Ibid., p. 362.
24. Ibid., p. 409.
25. Ibid., p. 206.
26. Ibid., p. 269.
27. Ibid., p. 61.
28. Ibid., p. 52.
29. Ibid., p. 112.
30. Ibid., p. 104.
31. Ibid., p. 117.
32. Ibid., p. 317.
33. Ibid., p. 414.

Chapter 12

1. Yannis Ritsos, "Triplet," from *Parentheses, 1950-61* in *Repetitions, Testimonies, Parentheses*, trans. Edmund Keeley, (Princeton, NJ, 1991), p. 177.
2. "Marking," in ibid., p. 166.
3. Yannis Ritsos, "The Day of a Sick Man," from *Testimonies B (1966)*, in *Yannis Ritsos: Selected Poems*, trans. Nikos Stangos, (London, 1974), p. 62.

4. Yannis Ritsos, "Midnight Stroll," from *Scripture of the Blind* (1972), trans. Kimon Friar and Kostos Myrsiades (Columbus, OH, 1979).

5. Yannis Ritsos, "Approximately," from *Testimonies B (1966)*, in *Yannis Ritsos: Selected Poems*, trans. Nikos Stangos (London, 1974), p. 78.

6. Yannis Ritsos, "The Meaning of Simplicity," from *Parentheses, 1946-47* in *Repetitions, Testimonies, Parentheses*, trans. Edmund Keeley, (Princeton, 1991), p. 125.

7. "Maybe, Someday," in ibid., p. 129.

8. Yannis Ritsos, "Necessary Explanation," from *Exercises (1950-1960)*, trans. Kimon Friar in *Yannis Ritsos: Selected Poems 1938-1988*, ed. and trans. by Kimon Friar and Kostas Myrsiades, (Brockport, NY,) p. 88.

9. Yannis Ritsos, "The More Sufficient," from *The Distant, 1975* in *Repetitions, Testimonies, Parentheses*, trans. Edmund Keeley, (Princeton, NJ, 1991), p. 208.

10. Yannis Ritsos, "Motionless Swaying," in *Gestures and other poems 1968-70*, trans. Nikos Stangos (London, 1971).

11. Georg Luck, *Arcana Mundi* (Baltimore, MD 1985), pp. 3-4.

12. E. R. Dodds, *The Greeks and the Irrational* Berkeley, CA, 1951), p. 140.

13. Werner Jaeger, *Paideia; The Ideal of Greek Culture*, trans. Gilbert Highet, vol. 1, (Oxford, 1939), p. 162.

14. Frances Yates, *Giordano Bruno and the Hermetic Tradition* (Chicago, 1964), p. 45.

15. Enid Starkie, *Baudelaire* (New York, 1958), p. 228.

16. Graham Hough, *The Mystery Religion of W. B. Yeats* (Brighton, Sussex, 1984), p. 28.

17. Yates, *Gioradano Bruno*, pp. 68-69.

18. Ibid., p. 69.

19. Ibid., pp. 52-53.

20. Ibid., pp. 70-71.

21. Dodd, *Greeks and the Irrational*, p. 80.

22. Jaeger, *Paideia*, p. 221.

23. Rainer Maria Rilke, *Letters of Rainer Maria Rilke*, trans. Jane Bannard Greene and M. D. Herter Norton (New York, 1945), p. 266.

24. Yannis Ritsos, "Point," from *Parentheses, 1950-61* in *Repetitions, Testimonies, Parentheses*, trans. Edmund Keeley, (Princeton, NJ, 1991), p. 158.

25. Jaeger, *Paideia*, p. 35.

26. Yannis Ritsos, "From Poseidon," from *Repetitions, 1963-65* in *Repetitions, Testimonies, Parentheses*, trans. Edmund Keeley, (Princeton, NJ, 1991), p. 5.

27. Yannis Ritsos, "Association," from *Testimonies A (1963)*, in *Yannis Ritsos: Selected Poems*, trans. Nikos Stangos, (London, 1974), p. 54.

28. Yannis Ritsos, "Miniature," from *Parentheses, 1946-47* in *Repetitions, Testimonies, Parentheses*, trans. Edmund Keeley, (Princeton, NJ, 1991), p. 137.

Chapter 13

1. Stephen Dobyns, "Cemetery Nights" from *Cemetery Nights* in *Velocities, New and Selected Poems, 1966-1992* (New York, 1994), p. 81.
2. French prosody distinguishes between *vers libre* and *vers libére*, that is, between verse that is completely free and verse that is partly free yet still contains an element of meter. Vers libére is what T. S. Eliot was advocating when he said that "the ghost of simple metre should lurk behind the auras in even the 'freest' verse; to advance menacingly as we doze, and withdraw as we rouse. Or, freedom is only true freedom when it appears against the background of artificial limitation." (From T. S. Eliot, "Reflections on Vers Libres" in *Selected Prose of T. S. Eliot*, intro. Frank Kermode [New York, 1975], pp. 34-35.)

Chapter 14

1. Heraclitus, *The Art and Thought of Heraclitus*, ed. and trans. Charles H. Kahn (Cambridge, 1979), p. 53.
2. Stephen Dobyns, *Cemetery Nights* (New York, 1987), p. vii.
3. Johan Huizinga, *Homo Ludens: a Study of the Play Element in Culture* (Boston, 1955), p. 129.
4. Ibid., p. 134.
5. Ibid., p. 21.
6. Ibid., pp. 47-48.
7. Ibid., p. 49.
8. John Gardner, *On Moral Fiction* (New York, 2000), p. 107.
9. Ibid., p. 108.
10. Huizinga, *Homo Ludens*, pp. 132-133.
11. John Donne, *The Complete Poetry and Selected Prose of John Donne and the Complete Poetry of William Blake* (New York, 1941), pp. 4-5.
12. Huizinga, *Homo Ludens*, p. 132.
13. Mary Oliver, *West Wind* (New York, 1997), p. 6.
14. Roger Fanning, *Homesick* (New York, 2002), p. 8.
15. Huizinga, *Homo Ludens*, p. 134.

Chapter 15

1. W. S. Merwin, *The Asian Figures* (New York, 1973), p. 87.
2. Emily Dickinson, *Selected Poems & Letters of Emily Dickinson*, ed. Robert N. Linscott (New York, 1959), p. 88.
3. Jean Follain, *Transparence of the World*, trans. W. S. Merwin (New York, 1969), p. 15.
4. Ibid., p. 27.

5. Ibid., p. 65.
6. Ibid., p. 27.
7. Yannis Ritsos, *Late into the Night: The Last Poems of Yannis Ritsos*, trans. Martin McKinsey, FIELD Translation Series 21 (Oberlin, 1991), p. 29.
8. Suzanne K. Langer, *Mind: An Essay on Human Feeling*, Volume I (Baltimore, 1967), p. xix.

Chapter 16

1. Rainer Maria Rilke, *The Duino Elegies*, trans. Edward Snow (New York, 2001), p. 5
2. Simone Weil, "Human Personality" in *Simone Weil, An Anthology*, ed. Sian Miles (New York, 2000), pp. 72-73.
3. Ibid., p. 78.
4. Fyodor Dostoyevsky, *The Brothers Karamazov*, trans. Constance Garnett (New York, 1929), pp. 130-131.
5. Aristotle, "De Poetica," trans. Ingram Bywater, in *The Basic Works of Aristotle*, ed. Richard McKeon (New York, 1941), p. 1462.
6. Ibid., pp. 1457-1458.
7. Ibid., p. 1462.
8. Ibid.
9. Ibid., p. 1465.
10. Ibid., p. 1467.
11. Ibid.
12. Walter Jackson Bate, ed., *Criticism: The Major Texts* (New York, 1952), p. 19.
13. Werner Jaeger, *Paideia: The Ideals of Greek Culture*, trans. Gilbert Highet (Oxford, 1965), p. 280.
14. Ibid., p. 30.
15. Bate, *Criticism*, p. 6.
16. Ibid., p. 7.
17. Elaine Scarry, *On Beauty and Being Just* (Princeton, NJ, 1999), p. 58.
18. Ibid., p. 59.
19. Ibid., p. 65-66.
20. *Anton Chekhov's Life and Thought: Selected Letters and Commentary*, trans. Michael Henry Heim in collaboration with Simon Karlinsky, (Berkeley, CA, 1975), p. 117.
21. Charles Baudelaire, "Further Notes on Edgar Poe," in *Selected Writing on Art and Artists*, trans. P. E. Chavert (Cambridge, 1972), p. 204.
22. Rainer Maria Rilke, *Letters on Cézanne*, ed. Clara Rilke, trans. Joel Agee (New York, 1985), p 51.
23. Charles Baudelaire, *The Flowers of Evil & Paris Spleen*, trans. William H. Crosby (Brockport, NY, 1991), p. 279.
24. Scarry, *On Beauty and Being Just*, p. 64.
25. Baudelaire, "Further Notes on Edgar Poe," p.202.
26. Charles Baudelaire, "The Painter in Modern Life" in *Selected Writing on Art and Artists*, p. 425.
27. Rilke, *Letters on Cézanne*, p. 67.
28. Bauldelaire, "To the Reader," in *The Flowers of Evil*, trans. Stanley Kunitz, ed. Marthiel and Jackson Mathews (New York: New Directions, 1989), pp. 3-4.

29. Baudelaire, "Further Notes on Edgar Poe," p. 200.
30. Scarry, *On Beauty and Being Just*, p. 3.
31. Ibid., p. 23.
32. Charles Baudelaire, "The Exposition Universelle, 1855," in *The Mirror of Art, Critical Studies of Charles Baudelaire*, ed. and trans. Johnathan Mayne (New York, 1956), pp. 196-197.
33. Scarry, *On Beauty and Being Just*, pp. 24-25.
34. Ibid., pp. 25-26.
35. Ibid., p. 28.
36. Ibid., p. 96.
37. Ibid., p. 97
38. Ibid., p. 107.
39. Ibid., p. 111.
40. Suzanne Langer, *Feeling and Form* (New York, 1953) pp. 396-397.
41. Suzanne Langer, *Mind: An Essay in Human Feeling*, (Baltimore, 1967), p. 108.
42. Ibid., p. 110.
43. Baudelaire, "The Painter of Modern Life" in *Charles Baudelaire, the Painter of Modern Life and Other Essays*, ed. and trans. Johnathan Mayne (New York, 1964), p.3.
44. Ibid.

INDEX